leonard cohen
prophet of the heart

© 1990 Omnibus Press
(A Division of Book Sales Limited)

Edited by Chris Charlesworth
Book designed by Monica Chrysostomou
Art direction by Lisa Pettibone
Picture research by Paul Giblin,
Clive Rawlins and Loranne Dorman
Typesetting co-ordinated by Caroline Watson

ISBN 0.7119.1821.X
Order No. OP 45426

Every effort has been made to trace the copyright holders of the photographs in this book but one or two were unreachable. We would be grateful if the photographers concerned would contact us.

Exclusive distributors:

Book Sales Limited,
8/9 Frith Street,
London W1V 5TZ, UK.

Music Sales Corporation
225 Park Avenue South
New York, NY 10003, USA.

Music Sales Pty Ltd.,
120 Rothschild Avenue,
Rosebery, NSW 2018, Australia.

To the Music Trade only:
Music Sales Limited,
8/9 Frith Street,
London W1V 5TZ, UK.

Typeset by Saxon Printing Ltd, Derby, England.

Printed by Courier International, Tiptree, Colchester, Essex.

leonard cohen
prophet of the heart

LORANNE S. DORMAN AND CLIVE L. RAWLINS

OMNIBUS PRESS
LONDON · NEW YORK · SYDNEY

In Honour of Fatherhood
and three in particular:

NATHAN B. COHEN (1887-1943)

JOSEPH C. DORMAN (1922-1985)

LEONARD W. RAWLINS (1906-1986)

'Though the world be Histrionical, and most men live Ironically, yet be thou what thou singly art, and personate only thy self. Swim smoothly in the stream of thy Nature, and live but one man.'

SIR THOMAS BROWNE

'This is a serious affair, this existence of ours. It's important that the real feelings in society, and the life of the heart, be affirmed.'

LEONARD COHEN

part one: the making of a wordsmith

part two: word as discovery

part three: word as meaning

part four: word as song

part five: word as life

part six: rediscovering the word

part seven: word as healing

I t w a s S i g m u n d F r e u d ' s opinion that the intending biographer 'pledges himself to tell lies, to hush things up, to be hypocritical, to paint things in glowing colours, even to conceal his ability to understand; because biographical truth is unattainable, and were one to attain it, one could not make use of it.' The great psychoanalyst probably would not have altered his views for a collaborative effort such as ours; but we have not felt any need to pull punches, still less tell lies or be hypocritical – which may well have more to do with Freud's psychoanalysis than biography!

We have simply sought to understand and portray the background to Leonard Cohen's life, the social, familial and religious traditions which nurtured him, his childhood and youth, his young manhood, and how his life in art – and in the round – developed. We have tried to do so not by writing a chronicle (with most of his personal papers embargoed for 60 years that would in any case be impossible, even if desirable) but by essaying a tapestry. As he once wrote in a poem, 'I will not be held like a drunkard, under the cold tap of facts.' Biography signifies the writing of life, not the listing of events. We have simply sought to weave together the most important threads of his life, their connections and their contributions to its pattern, as well as depict the salient episodes and their own connections in this man of changes.

And change is as characteristic of his life as the age through which he has lived; a sign of his restless growth, and an indication of his inner strengths. The first seven years of his life certainly forged the essential traits of his character, but he is today a different man from the one who burst on the scene of Canadian letters in 1956 to great acclaim with his first book of poetry; and different again from the one who became a cult-figure of the seething sixties with such trend-setting novels as *Beautiful Losers* and a new style of popular song, which some of the most gifted and successful singers (not to mention that talent-spotting genius, the late John Hammond) could not resist. He changed again in the mid-seventies, in the process becoming an older and wiser man, now the father of two, but in reality the 'street father' of many who have been only too glad to follow where he led. One, moreover, proud of – and committed to – the awesome Tradition from which he came, of which he learned much, to give much. He changed yet again in the mid-eighties, now more peaceful of heart, and charged with a style and sensibility of music – he calls it Jewish Blues – which has stilled the hearts and nourished the souls of many who seriously seek to live.

But 'change' is not perhaps the *mot juste*; 'developed' is more appropriate. There is an unmistakable aspect to Leonard which has resisted substantial change, and that of the mind more than the life. Several key concepts which framed and formed his thinking (e.g. the ideas of 'equilibrium', 'grace', a particular 'sainthood', the energies of love) all appear in his earliest writings and continue to reappear over and over again; sometimes in different guises, but genuine constants in a highly fluid age. Towering above these is a high regard for art itself, as a serious expression of the life-force of humanity, indeed the cosmos itself; most powerfully in word and music.

We have not sought to emulate Freud's cynical description of biography writing, simply because we do not believe that biography is about someone's aberrations and defeats – pimples in youth and petulance in old age (neither of which characterises Leonard Cohen, incidentally, though he is far from reaching the latter point yet!). Biography is about the essence of a life; and most of all, its goal or direction. 'Everyman,' said the rabbis, 'has his own *meshugas* (craziness).' That is so, be he a Churchill, a Whitman, a Johnson, a Paul, or even a Moses. Character, like literary criticism itself, is best understood within Alexander Pope's wise formula:

> '*In ev'ry Work regard the Writer's End,*
> *Since none can compass more than they intend;*
> *And if the Means be just, the Conduct true,*
> *Applause, in spite of trivial faults, is due.*'

We did not set out to praise, still less to bury, Leonard Cohen. But we did seek to understand him, his poetry and prose, his words and his music. We sought to understand what he has given, in 10 volumes of written work and as many albums of music – what he described as "20 monstrous altars" of himself – and an abundance of clippings, reviews and profiles in several languages; not least in the 60 or so hours of interview time he generously gave us. We sought to paint what we saw: a manscape of highly variable scenery, texture and colour; now tender and charming, now tough, now defensive, now mystical, high in religious tone, now agnostic, even scornful. But ever searching, whatever the mood or the projection of time or place. We found him on a firm, if meandering path; an upward path, which signalled deep desire and lofty aspiration. It could not be otherwise with a man whose tradition is usually expressed under the term 'law' – a way of life. (The word *halacha* – law – is derived from the root meaning 'to journey'.)

We found Leonard's own way more unified than we had expected; more unidirectional than we had believed possible. True, it twisted and turned from time to time, traversing some very rough ground, but it was always the same path, always moving in the same direction. It was never the shortest route between two points, never a particularly comfortable path; but it was always his and no other's, impressed with his own stamp – and all the more impressive for that. It was always driving on, fired by his own deepest stirrings, his own restless imagination, his own inner constraints to his true self: a path of persistence and courage; an adventure. It is a truism of Jungian psychology that the only real adventure left to 20th century man is the exploration of his unconscious psyche. This is particularly so of Leonard Cohen, an indefatigable traveller, "a connoisseur of islands" as he once described himself; a man who followed the very old tradition of making his life, his experiences, his subconscious inputs, the groundwork of his art; as we shall see.

"Ambiguity is the key to this man's soul," commented one of Leonard's closest observers of more than 30 years. It is certainly there, this ambiguity; in almost schizoid intensity at times. He commented, in that piercingly honest book, *Death Of A Lady's Man*: 'I need . . . to keep my different lives apart. Otherwise I will be crushed when they join, and I will end my life in art, which a terror will not let me do.' Therein resides a major source of the clash within him, the inner constraints to work at his life-in-art, which he had earlier stated he 'pledged (his) deepest health' to work out. The clash comes in a sense of destiny, of drivenness, to offer and explore his life-in-art; driven by 'a terror' no less (of failure, of betrayal), on the success of which his 'deepest health' – his equilibrium, the maintaining of that all important 'state of grace' – depended. He knew the risks he was taking; he felt deeply the mockery of those who failed to comprehend or, in comprehending only too clearly, scorned the endeavour. Not unexpectedly, he titled the piece in question, 'The Price Of This Book'. There is always a price; it is the *sine qua non* of true art: the scars of the word made flesh.

And through it the man was always identifiable, his vectors constant, his trajectory visible. Wobble he did; prevaricate, at times; even stray from time to time. But he always picked himself up and got back on with it; in so doing deftly adding another metre, another mile, to his measured striding through life: simple, if painful, steps for him – bridges of rescue for tens of thousands around the world who sought to hear and understand. 'Cohen' means 'priest', and its Latin equivalent – *pontifex* – appropriately means 'a bridge'. He makes explicit the point in his third book of poetry, *Flowers For Hitler*, when he draws attention, somewhat audaciously, to the difference between him and the beat-poets and reciters of the sixties:

'In my journey I know I am
somewhere beyond the travelling pack of poets
I am a man of tradition
I will remain here until
I am sure what I am leaving'

He never 'left', but went on – searching and finding, becoming ever more sure of what he knew.

His journeyings have been from complexity to simplicity; from which the essence has been distilled from a labyrinthine opulence to a lifestyle not unworthy of Gandhi himself, though his patterns were very much older, and even more influential. Commented the *New York Times*, he is 'a wandering, saintly minstrel, a jet-set Mahatma,' and *Billboard* referred to his 'mystical edge of revolutionary consciousness.'

It was, of course, a sixties trait to glorify simplicity; to advance the cause of unity against complexity; wholeness against the increasing fragmentation of life; integrity against crude power – whether the power of the politician, the soldier, the boss, the parent, the priest, the guru, or whatever. Its message has still to be heard. Few have sought to further its cause over so many years (now in its fourth decade, no less) than Leonard Cohen; not by overt campaigning, still less politicised activities – he eschewed all that! – not by moralising, but by describing the interior landscape *seriously*, the terrain of the heart, whose prophet he became – in poetry, novels, song, film, video, drama, and commentary. 'Every man is a world in miniature,' the rabbis said, and Leonard – in seeking to understand and reflect the world-within-a-world – has indicated a meaning in which many have found an answer for their own needs.

It was not an easy thing to describe. Earlier, he had refused even to comment on it himself: "I write the poetry, you do the commentary," he told an exasperated Pierre Berton of Canadian television, who had been trying to force self-explanation from him. But he has since moved on from that austere position. He has aligned himself more with the Indian tradition, that the message of a book is incomplete without a commentary, be it 'holy' or otherwise; though his own commentating remained political, even elliptical. His first novel, *The Favourite Game*, about to be made into a film, describes one of its subjects' favourite pastimes – the game itself: It was to be thrown by one's friends into a snowdrift, in so doing to try to make as interesting a landing-pattern as possible. Then to step carefully away leaving the flower-like imprint, the landing pattern, behind. A children's game perhaps, but one of significance for the author, even more than for the book. Ironically, his American publisher was so obtuse that the paperback cover read, *The Courageous New World Of Love In Which Sex Is The Favourite Game*, thereby missing the point altogether. As many have since continued to do.

Life has flung Leonard Cohen into many such drifts, some of great and icy depth. But he has always walked away from them with dignity, always produced something positive, even beautiful, from the landing. His life has been, from a very early point (perhaps even antedating the death of his father, which had an enormous effect on him), charged with this search for meaning; an attempt to understand the shape into which his life has been cast; a defiant (sometimes pliant) gesture to make of that fall a pattern of his own, as he walked – not always steadily – away from it. The pursuit of truth ('accuracy' is more often his word for it), the juxtaposing of connections, is his real game; a relentless search, with his roots deeply embedded in history. He has often commented on it lately, quietly soldiering on when others have taken his words, his style, his life and his relationships, and twisted them – simplistically, mindlessly or malignly. It is no better today than 12 years ago, when Professor Stephen Scobie drew attention to the way critics and reviewers had been obsessed with the man to the detriment of his work. Scobie reversed the process, and all but ignored the man! Hence there has scarcely been a more myopic opinion than his, 'Cohen's public career and the facts of his biography are largely irrelevant to an understanding of his writing.' To draw the distinction between 'the private person' and 'the public persona' (as he does for *Beautiful Losers*) is misleading, as we shall see when we encounter Leonard's ethic of 'accuracy' in his work. Whatever others made of it, he ventured on, pondering, speaking, making his own shapes and connections.

We have merely sought to listen, with intense concern, to what he has been saying, even when the language was raw and the mood black. We were driven to listen because we felt that what he had to say (as opposed, sometimes, to the way in which he said it) was immensely important. We think that we have discovered the overall shape, the design and direction to which he points. Like him, we have sought to tell its truth; to paint its reality in the colours in which we found them; to find – and write of – the essence of this very complex man.

And that is what we found, a man; one somewhat pained at our enterprise, our impertinence; but a large measure of a man, a sympathetic and helpful man; one with insight and the ability to speak of it; a prophet of the heart. The heart, which Leonard truly described as 'a rage of directions,' and a prophet, whose work Richard Howard correctly defined as, 'not . . . prediction, but truth-telling,' forth-telling, if you like; not foretelling. 'There are many hearts,' Leonard once wrote (enumerating several *en passant*), and 'there is my own, the heart of a translator who has tried to render into common usage the high commands of pure energy, who has not declined his own inclination to obey.' It is that of which we have endeavoured to write. Such 'biographical truth' as we found, we have transcribed, hoping that what became our favourite game may become yours: the unveiling of a warm and genuine man, with something important to say.

LORANNE S. DORMAN

CLIVE L. RAWLINS

KAIKAS, ASKELI,

POROS, TRIZINAS, GREECE. (SEPTEMBER 21, 1989)

O u r   p r i m a r y   d e b t is to express our thanks to the subject of this book, Leonard Cohen. Not merely for his great helpfulness in answering our endless questions, offering numerous suggestions and leads, loaning books and manuscripts, and making introductions for us, but for the many years of increasing enjoyment in his art – both literary and musical.

In this latter regard we offer our thanks to his music publishers, Music Sales Ltd., of London and New York, and his music company, Stranger Music Inc., and to CBS Inc., for quite different scales of interest. (Said Leonard of the latter, on being presented with their Crystal Globe Award for special services overseas, "I have always been touched by the modesty of its efforts on my behalf." To which we add our own morsel of gratitude to its publicity department for sending us on a wild goose chase from New York to Los Angeles, unaware apparently that Leonard's own office was but a stone's throw from their building!) Happily, we found Sharon Weisz, Leonard's promotional agent in Los Angeles, who put us in touch with the ever-helpful Kelley Lynch, Leonard's Girl-Friday – if not his Sabbath Eve. In New York he also introduced us to Robert Bower, his unofficial archivist, whose enthusiasm laid a good foundation on which we were able to build our own modest effort.

Yet further afield, Michael Lohse and Gerhardt Schinzel (in Munchen and Frankfurt respectively) supplied very helpful information from the 'Leonard Cohen Information Centre', not least their extremely useful *Recordings Of Leonard Cohen: 1957-1986* (second edition, 1988); and Schinzel's *A Concordance Of The Songs Of Leonard Cohen As Released On Record* (second edition, 1988). Jim Devlin, who runs a similar service in Sheffield, was an important link in this.

Our long stay in the Aegean would not have been bearable without the professional services of Nikos Kaikas and his wife Maria, whose travel agency and apartment bureau safeguarded our day-to-day requirements on Poros, the neighbouring island to Leonard's Hydra. Similarly, Mesdames Maria Kohler and Jacqueline Lemonnier provided us with a home-from-home at their beautiful Hotel de Paris in Montreal, aided by the charms and wholesome food of El Gaucho Empanadas Restaurant and Ben's Delicatessen. In New York Mr Bard Jnr, manager of The Chelsea Hotel, proved to be a most informative guide to that veritable art-and-folk institution over several decades, which perhaps reached its zenith in Leonard's time there under Mr Stanley Bard Snr.

Professors Louis Dudek and Irving Layton consented to long interviews in the warm hospitality of their homes, to whom we offer (along with their wives) our thanks for their careful – and candid – recollections of their pupil and friend. Leonard's *Alma Mater*, McGill

University in Montreal, also placed at our disposal its very fine facilities, thanks to the helpfulness of the Dean of Arts, Professor Richard F. Salisbury, and the Registrar, Jean-Paul Schuller. We also wish to thank the tireless staff of the MacLennan Library for their ever-helpful attention to our needs, especially in its Reference and Rare Books' Departments.

Gratitude must be expressed to the National Film Board of Canada and to Mr Bernard Lutz for their splendid archives, and willingness to show privately old material, at point-blank notice. We are also grateful for the museum facilities of the Chapelle Notre-Dame de Bon Secours and La Bibliotheque municipale de Montreal. And the staff of Columbia Law School in New York. Two institutions in particular facilitated our work in the Big Apple: The New York Public Library on 42nd Street, and the Lincoln Arts Centre for the Performing Arts on 65th Street, (not least its De Witt Wallace Periodical Room which offers an abundance of material in 24 languages). The provision for research at Lincoln is second to none, in creature-comforts and in their range of data; and their staff are a lesson in unwearied helpfulness – even five minutes before closing!

We encountered a like helpfulness at the Country Music Hall of Fame and Museum in Nashville, whose brilliant evocations of past musical – and not so musical! – times will live for ever in our memories. Its historian, John W. Rumble, allowed us complete access to its archives, for which we thank him. The Public Library of Nashville were very helpful as were the staff of libraries in such diverse places as Athens, Edinburgh, London, Cambridge, Birmingham, Los Angeles, Oklahoma City, Albuquerque, Taos, Rawlins City (!), Chicago and Philadelphia. (Curiously, the only place of non-co-operation was at International House, New York, whose 'welcome in any language' had somehow expired by the time we got there!)

On a more personal level we wish to thank the following for their support, and their sacrifices in various ways: Senora Susana Suarez Dorman; Mrs Mary Rawlins, Veronica Rawlins, and especially Alex McKendrick. Also Chris and Mary Dorman; Philip Rawlins; Pat and Ken Jones, Dr Daniel Araoz; Archie Anderson; Liz Douglas; Premtosh and Chintamani; and Leola, for her bright and beautiful self. Also to Susan Birmingham in Wall Street, New York. To Zander Wedderburn for his computer expertise, whose constant readiness to help in any way and whose hospitality (along with his wife Bridget and daughter Joanna), has been second to none, we express our heartfelt thanks. Also to Gerard and Barbara Dorman, Gillian and Stephen Rawlins, Archie Anderson, Cy Pirrie, Tom Arah, Jane Sillars, Elizabeth Douglas, Robert Ansell and particularly to our super supermarket people without whose provisioning we could not have gone on: Nikky, Heleni and

Giorgos Stayrianakis. We encountered admirers of Leonard's music and writing everywhere, and thank Suzi and Jurgas Lucas, Sigmund Petersen and Anita Staikou, Andreas Bozarellos and Giannis Speis particularly.

We record our thanks for the permission to use copyrighted material from Leonard's written works, as noted *ad locum* in our text:

Contact Press, Toronto, for *Let Us Compare Mythologies* Jonathan Cape Ltd., London, for *Spice-Box Of Earth*; *Flowers For Hitler*; *The Energy Of Slaves*.

Panther Books, Granada Publishing Ltd., St Albans, for *The Favourite Game*; *Beautiful Losers*.

Penguin Books Ltd., Harmondsworth, for *Selected Poems 1956-1968*.

Andre Deutsch Ltd., London, for *Death Of A Lady's Man*.

Douglas McIntyre Ltd., Vancouver, for *Leonard Cohen* by Stephen Scobie.

The Macmillan Company of Canada, Ltd., Toronto, for *Poetry Of Our Time* by Louis Dudek.

Editions Albin Michel, Paris, for *Leonard Cohen* by Jacques Vassal. Edicomunicacion, S.A., Barcelona, for *Leonard Cohen: Canciones y Nuevos Poemas, Volumes One and Two*, by Alberto Manzano.

We also record our thanks for permission to use copyrighted material from Leonard's songs, in both their written and variously recorded forms as separately identified *in situ*:

Stranger Music, New York.

Music Sales Ltd., New York and London.

Columbia Records Inc., (CBS), New York.

Folkways Records Inc.

The Canadian Broadcasting Co. Ltd., Toronto.

Warner Bros. Inc., Los Angeles.

Passport Records Inc.

Similarly we offer the many journalists and interviewers our thanks for their endeavours their insights – and their myopia! Also the photographers and their respective journals. Should we, inadvertently, have omitted any acknowledgment, we apologise in advance, offering our assurance that the matter will be righted in the next edition of our book. Lastly, our editor, Chris Charlesworth, and his colleagues, deserve a special note of thanks for their interest and encouragement, not least in the occasionally disconnective life that we were bound to lead on both sides of the Atlantic – and sometimes in the middle of it!

CLIVE RAWLINS AND LORANNE DORMAN,

OCTOBER 1989.

the making of
a wordsmith

'Children show scars like medals. Lovers use them as secrets to reveal. A scar is what happens when the word is made flesh.'

LEONARD COHEN

'If I do not utter a word, I am its master; once I utter it, I am its slave.'

IAN GABIROL

'All my work is the evidence of a life, and not the life itself.'

LEONARD COHEN

the man
in question

Some people impress by what they do, others by what they say, yet others by what they are. The last is always the more interesting type; not infrequently he or she is an impressive doer, sometimes an eloquent speaker; some, very few, are both. Leonard Cohen is one, but in his own inimitable way.

We first met him at an elegant hotel in the 'uptown' district of Manhattan, New York, overlooking Central Park, a watering place well known to artists (Joe Cocker also happened to be in residence at the time). We had travelled over 12,000 miles to see him – from Greece to New York via Edinburgh, thence to Los Angeles via Nashville and back to New York via Salt Lake City and Chicago. It was worth every mile, and somehow the travelling was particularly appropriate, for he is himself a travelling man, at home everywhere and nowhere.

He is one of nature's gentlemen. Aware of the distances we had covered, aware too of the reason for our travels – this book and our interest in his deeper self – though far from eager, indeed, 'alarmed' by it, he nevertheless agreed to meet – a moment of dual appraisal. Several cups of coffee later, and many cigarettes (not to speak of his midday *repast*, a small bowl of Rice Crispies – a suitable delicacy, given his previous late night explorative jazz session with Sonny Rollins and the group Was Not Was) later, he kindly consented to our task: the victim was ours.

He left town the next morning, for Montreal where he feels most at home. Our plan was to meet there in a few days' time, once our researches in New York were concluded. These were now more eagerly undertaken, and soon completed; thanks not least to the good offices of his very able assistant, Kelley Lynch, and his unofficial archivist, Robert Bower.

A few days later, after we had established ourselves in Montreal, we called him. "Mr Cohen?" we asked in response to the "Hello" at the other end of the telephone. "Yes" came the unmistakable, deep-voiced reply. We reintroduced ourselves. As before, he was concerned to hear that we had enjoyed a good flight to his native city, had found a good hotel and that we were managing to survive the bitter cold, the snow and the ice of a Canadian winter. One could never have guessed from his enquiries that the matter was somewhat uncongenial to him.

It was an ambition come true. We were now face to face with this man of diverse talent – poet, novelist, song-writer, performer – after following his career for nearly two decades, reading his books, playing his records, watching him sing, reading of him through the eyes of his critics – no easy feat when one is not inhibited by astigmatism! There is no 'side' to him. He who had performed for royalty, dined with national presidents, rubbed shoulders with the greatest names in the world of art and theatre, film and music, became a delightful companion and – it was never absent – a solicitous host. The 60 or so hours he put at our disposal fled by. Our questions ranged far and wide and his courtesy and patience turned them into an intriguing trail of discovery which was endlessly fascinating and richly rewarding, for he is also a natural raconteur. When he commits himself to an assignment – be it a poem, a book, a song, or merely aiding a fellow-scribbler's itch, he does it with gusto – *con brio*, as he might annotate one of his scores. Our second meeting, once the regulative *café au lait* had been taken and a strenuous five hours' of talk had been put behind us, was concluded by a guided tour of his beloved Montreal, whose night-time allurements were enthusiastically described in a car hired for the occasion, and concluded by a celebratory meal at one of his favourite Indian restaurants, toasting each other's health and futures in an excellent Chablis.

Leonard Cohen is a man of medium height, five-feet, eight-inches (173 cm); lean, with a rugged, world-weary face. He looks like a man who should be heavier than he is, and one soon realises that an iron discipline keeps it that way. He enjoys his food and wine, but disallows its enjoyment to distort the image which is important chiefly to himself, and then to his public. He is frequently described as 'having the stoop of an ageing crop-picker and the face of a curious little boy' – which may have been true 30 years ago, but now belongs to the discard-tray with other caricatures: caricatures, as Oscar Wilde observed, are compliments that mediocrity pays to genius. Greying a little at the temples, Leonard unconsciously confirms why he is labelled one of Canada's sexiest men, a handsome and elegant man with dark eyes (they are said to be green, but that never showed in the light of Montreal, nor in its wintry sunshine). His skin is somewhat winter-pallid, thickening a little, but nevertheless disguising his 54 years. His hands are slim and well manicured, as becomes an artist-musician, somehow they seem especially sensitive – strong and caring hands!

He is always well-dressed, usually in smart suits and casual shirts, though in deference to the Jewish tradition which he discreetly adorns, he rarely wears a tie. Occasionally he appeared in a bomber jacket and he frequently wore a hat – when we were there it was an engaging and stylish grey and white cap, though sometimes an American baseball hat in honour of Stevie Ray Vaughan. What was entirely missing was any sense of flamboyance, in clothing or lifestyle. His clothing was always dark, usually black, with few concessions to colours of the brighter hue. As was his general demeanour. He speaks softly and very reflectively, with few flights of passion. He is content for everyone else to have their say first, though his everyday associates and friends respect his views too much to let him get away with that too often. They wait and are seldom disappointed. A word, an insight, a *jeu d'esprit*, is offered. The conversation moves on, all the better for the comment, not infrequently the gayer for it. His is not a dour presence, still less a melancholic one. His humour constantly breaks through in asides and anecdotes, as does a delightful and mastering smile that transforms his face like Aegean sunlight on a frowning sea.

The first impression is of a quiet, reflective, determined man of the world, of affairs. But the eyes give him away: sometimes they are all-seeing, giving the impression that he is quietly dissecting one's soul. Sometimes they are especially tired, as if sleeping had been difficult. (We almost always met in the late mornings at his favourite café, always starting the day with a reviving bowl of *café au lait*, followed by another – and not infrequently another!) Sometimes they were misty and abstract, especially when one talked intimately of the past, of subjects he had long forgotten – or wanted to forget – awakening memories – nightmares? – from deep within. Sometimes they were a little lifeless, not with lethargy or simple weariness (they could be that, but then his whole body-language 'drooped' accordingly), but with a specific withdrawn quality which, when taken with a certain passivity of the face, can be hard and unyielding: betokening a concern – even a resentment – in being examined in that particular way. It is this which some journalists, using a phrase made popular by A.M. Klein, have referred to as his 'stony, Semitic stare.' It can be very disconcerting. But he never succumbs to what Max Scheler termed *ressentiment* – that mixture of resentment and anger and injured pride that destroys so many, even if it were present in earlier years. If one trespasses beyond the limits, he quietly corrects the fault in a plea, never a paroxysm.

His general attitude is one of an untiring and immense courtesy and helpfulness. He knows the routine, he appreciates the need, if without relishing it, he is too much the practised professional to show more than the briefest irritation. And he is a man of enormous good humour, with a highly developed sense of fun and laughter which many second-hand commentators have failed to understand, or preferred to ignore. When he laughs, it is different from the smile spoken of above. His face is transformed into one of rapturous pleasure over which suffuses a boyish sense of fun. It is a contagious thing that laugh, and healing too. The Talmud says, 'Happy is he who knows his place and stands in his own place,' and Leonard Cohen is such a man today. 'Seriousness', a key word in his vocabulary, and perhaps the most important trait of his character, is ever ready to break down into self-mockery, ever willing to enjoy the *jeux d'esprit* with which his work and art are replete. He is a man of balance and careful equilibrium, a man with something to say by his life as well as by his words. Indeed, a man whose life is his word: a word made flesh.

His house, into which he welcomes his visitors with open hospitality, is a charming, three-storeyed Victorian building attached to a smaller unit which acts as the *atelier* for his lifelong friend, the sculptor Morton Rosengarten, and his charming painter-wife, Violet. It backs on to another property owned by a professional photographer-friend, Hazel. It overlooks a pretty communal park which, though much smaller, reminds one of Gordon Square, London: base of the famous Bloomsbury Group. The artistic emphasis of the locality (there are other writers and musicians nearby, all in close contact with Leonard) is symbolic of his life. He now lives alone, but his entourage is extremely friendly if wary of interlopers and proud of their friend, their mentor and sometime benefactor.

His house is sparsely, rather than modestly, furnished. There is just enough décor and furniture to prevent it from looking empty, but space and simplicity are the most powerful impressions made on the visitor – what Leonard called in a different context 'the voluptuousness of austerity.' The environment suggests a particular character. In an unselfconscious way, it makes a profound statement about him and his place in the world. It is kept very warm – a real relief from the biting cold outside – and suffuses a strong feeling of tranquillity. There are no easy chairs, save for a single wooden rocking chair; no cushions, save for three ornamental ones in a corner. The essential projection is of simple wooden furniture, plain walls, some carpeting on the polished floorboards. For a man given to painting there is a surprising lack of colour, of *objets d'art*. Everywhere is white. A single figurine sits in the kitchen, significantly representing Catherine Tekakwitha, and a sculpted head of his friend, the poet Irving Layton, adorns his study. An old twenties or earlier photograph of Jewish emigrants to Palestine adorns the top of a bookcase. Everything is very clean, neat and tidy, dusted and polished – but plain, like the man himself. He is reluctant to preach, but if his lifestyle conveys anything, it is an emphatic witness to the importance of the things of the spirit; a disclaimer of the acquisitive society.

While provision for his guests is more than adequate, his bedroom consists of a single bed with a small television at its foot, remotely controlled. One suspects that it is his concession to a profound loneliness, a loneliness which he dare breach only at great cost to his true self, his equilibrium as thinker/artist. To that extent it is a harsh existence, quite unlike that of the artists, musicians and writers with whom he normally mixes. Seymour Siegal wrote 'In everyone's heart stirs a great homesickness,' Leonard Cohen's home is itself a symbol of such homesickness; not a gesture, but an emblem of man's existential isolation and alienation, which he represents discreetly, without ever advertising it. ('Lonely' or 'loneliness' occurs a dozen times in his songs. 'Solitude' and its cognates – a much more positive expression of the reality – but seven times, a not insignificant indication to which we must return.)

We should note, however, that loneliness is itself a feature of many Canadian writers, fruit of that belittling vastness of country in which they are placed. As Professor Desmond Pacey emphasises in his brilliant survey, *Creative Writing In Canada*, in the words of Duncan Campbell Scott:

> 'So lone is the land that in this lonely room
> Never before has breached a human being . . .'

Pacey also argues that terror is another of its features:

> '*Terror of the wilderness, of storm and flood, of savages and of the intense extremes of cold and heat.*'

Significantly he adds:

> '*But there is also exultation, the fascination as well as the fear of great strength.*'

In such comments we find ourselves in the precise atmosphere of Rudolf Otto's 'numinous', the '*mysterium tremendum et fascinans*' – the mystery that creates wonderment as well as terror – which surely accounts at least in part for the high level of religious feeling in Canadian folklore and literature; not least in Leonard's expression of it. It also accounts for poetry being a more natural instrument of its literary expression than fiction or drama.

His frugality extends to his two work-places. The plural is required for this multi-talented worker: his ground-floor music-room included a chair, a not over-expensive hi-fi unit with a modest collection of cassette tapes and a synthesiser; in the corner stands one of his guitars. His writing-room on the first floor contains an unprepossessing table and a sideboard, on which sit his word-processor and printer. A small chair and bookcase completes the picture.

The books – almost as much a symbol of Jewishness as the *Mogen David* itself – are by and large well thumbed, though fewer than one would expect. They offer a microcosm of his mental world in their range: Zen Buddhism, poetry, English and French literature, mysticism and spirituality (not least that of Simone Weil), music, a few general books. He speaks of them with enthusiasm, and he lends them with abandon. In another room adjacent to one of his two bathrooms lies some weight-lifting equipment: the needs of the mind are counter-balanced by those of the body. But the spirit is never forgotten. In an age mesmerised by quantitative values – 'big is beautiful', 'small is beautiful' – he projects another, and immensely more important aspect: kind is beautiful. It is his principle ethic. Here then is a man, a large measure of a man: your man!

a prestigious
family

Leonard Norman Cohen was born on September 21, 1934, to Nathan B. Cohen and his wife Masha, citizens of Montreal, Quebec. The times, to say the least, were not propitious. The New York stock-market had collapsed but five years previously, ushering in a period of need and anguish not only across America and Canada (New York is but 400 miles from Montreal), but throughout Europe, too.

In Canada it came to be known as 'The 10 Lost Years', which were devastating for those on the prairies and very difficult for those in the cities. To the scourge of this Depression dark voices were being added, and the shadows of armed conflict were beginning to impinge – a most unwelcome, even unbelievable thought to those who had, within the last 20 years, already risked their lives for King and country in 'The War To End All Wars.'

Nathan Cohen was one of them, and he had just cause to fear the upturn of the events, as did his younger brother, Horace. (A third brother, Lawrence, was too young to enlist). They had both served in the armed forces, and Nathan had been disabled as a result. They knew what was threatening. Masha Cohen also knew of such things, not in the same way, but from her own very different experiences as a young girl whose family had been harassed and hounded in the anti-semitic agitations that rent Poland. She had seen her country overrun by both the German and the Russian armies; she knew at first-hand the madness of war and the fear it transmits to the civilian population. Her memories and her character had been indelibly scarred by the suffering engraved in mind and flesh. If Nathan Cohen – some years older than his wife – had known the dangers of battle as a young lieutenant in the army, then Masha Cohen had known its civilian equivalent, what it was like to have been humiliated, to have lost everything, and to have been forced to flee from one's country and kindred.

Masha had, in fact, learned the terrible lesson as the despicable pogroms developed into a policy of national hatred and persecution, later to be transformed into actual genocide and thence into the horrors of the Holocaust. If Nathan conveyed confidence and buoyancy to his progeny, Masha brought distrust and fear and the recollection of terrible suffering. But with it all, an indomitable hope of the finest calibre.

Nathan Cohen himself was the eldest son of Lyon Cohen, one of the really influential men of early Canadian consolidation over five decades, not least among his own Jewish people. His father, Lazarus Cohen (known as Reb Leizer), was formerly a *bochur* (teacher) in the rabbinical college of Wolozhin, near Wilkovislak in Lithuania. Born in 1844 to a family noted for its piety and scholarship, Lazarus had decided to emigrate to Canada in 1869, having heard reports of the young country's potential: its federation was then but two years' old.

The writing was already on the wall for those willing to read it in his own country. Within two years he had so firmly established himself that he was able to bring to Canada his wife and young son, Lyon, where they settled happily, first at Maberly, Ontario, then in Montreal, a home with more than a touch of aristocratic manners and style. (Lazarus's brother, Hirsch, was a man of similar energy and stature, who became the Chief Rabbi of Canada. He was of a more literary bent, and wrote a biography of King Louis, as well as a book on ethics and business titled *Put Money In My Purse*). Lazarus's business ambitions soon elevated him from storeman to lumber merchant, thence to a partnership in the coal industry which bec *me his sole business – L. Cohen and Son – after a few years, and thence to a high-profile dredging company which could boast that it had kept every one of the lifelines of the young nation – the St. Lawrence tributaries between Lake Ontario and Quebec – open.

Lyon soon emulated his father's zestful example. By the time he was 16, *The Montreal Herald* was reporting the great success of his four-act play *Esther*, which he had written and produced (and played a leading part in) – shades here of his precocious grandson! This so impressed the then president of the Canadian branch of the Anglo-Jewish Association that he invited the young man, scarcely more than a boy, to be its secretary; the start of a highly successful and very wide range of business and charitable interests.

Quite apart from his business acumen (by the end of his commercial life he was the head of the largest clothing manufacturers – which his father had acquired earlier, originally named Freedmans – in the British dominions, as well as chairman or president of the most important trade bodies related to that industry) he held very senior positions in such organisations as the Baron de Hirsch Institute, the Montreal Reform Club, the Montefiore Club, the Montreal Insurance Co, the Jewish Public Library, the Hebrew Educational Institute, the Canadian Jewish Committee for the Relief of War Sufferers in Europe, the Executive of the Canadian Jewish Congress, the Canadian Colonisation Committee, the Zion Athletic Club, the Zionist Organisation of Canada, and many, many more. From 16 to 70 he worked assiduously and well, justifying the proverb that 'Work is easy – for those who like to work.' The rewards, financial and social, were commensurate with this, to the great benefit of family and community alike.

In all this he found time to address meetings for these and many other bodies, hold weekly classes for teaching the youth of his synagogue post-biblical history and related subjects, write articles for the Jewish press (he founded an Anglo-Jewish Journal called *The Jewish Times* later to be absorbed into the *Canadian Jewish Chronicle*). By the age of 35 he had become the youngest president of the largest and most prominent synagogue in Canada; brilliantly engineered the merging of all the philanthropic societies of Montreal ("With a view to obtaining the greatest efficiency with the least possible expense and labour," – surely his own life-principle next to his religious and familial devotions); and placed himself in the forefront of the social and economic battles of the period. This paved the way for leadership in an even greater battle – world war. He led the war-effort locally by encouraging volunteers to enlist, saying, "I would not consider my son fit for recognition in civil society if he would not fight for his land, his flag, and his king." Not only one but both his elder sons did so, and thereby became the first Jewish officers to be commissioned.

In time he was to meet and correspond with the most prominent political leaders of his nation, and become a trusted adviser to them. Indeed, on September 12, 1924, he journeyed to Italy to meet the Pope on behalf of his people; which some commentators viewed as 'historic'. His home was ever open, a centre of wisdom and influence for decades; admired even by cabinet ministers from Britain. Among many high-level tasks, he drafted an Appeal to the League of Nations on minority rights, and made many approaches to various government authorities through a wide range of memoranda, petitions and similar appeals. He was asked to stand for parliament, but declined, having no particular relish for party-politics; he was too large-hearted a man for that.

For all his organisational and business efficiency, he was a man of immense personal charm and dignity: 'Well-dressed, aristocratic, calm, and with a ready and reassuring smile,' it was said. Moreover he was a man of great devotion, who upheld the high ideals of the synagogue's pulpit, the beauty of its services, as well as the splendour of the building itself. He was elected President of the Congregation in 1934, the year of Leonard's birth, which helped to cement even further that deep family loyalty to the institution. He once said that his ambition was to make of it "the Cathedral Synagogue of Canada," and that is exactly what happened. Years later, in a moment of youthful self-disclosure, his grandson commented through one of his fictional characters, 'It didn't matter to him how he faced the congregation: his grandfather had built the synagogue.' One of Lyon's responsibilities was to ensure that the cantor, who led the singing on behalf of the congregation, was fit for the job. He could not abide those who went in for exhibitionism, considering such to be irreligious. On engaging a new cantor he would say (in Yiddish), "You must be able to sing; but don't you dare!" A view which undoubtedly reached down through his family, as we shall see.

For all his communal effort, he was a strong family man, head of a 'truly aristocratic home,' according to Albert Cohen, no relation, but the Hebrew teacher who privately taught Lyon's children on Rosemount Avenue. He loved to speak Yiddish, and every Sabbath would find family and guests, rabbis and friends, some of them world-famous, discussing the sermon, the latest books (of which he had a very fine collection), Jewish history and literature – in Yiddish, Hebrew and English. Curiously, he had a pronounced Scottish accent, in an area whose street names reflected the provenance of the early settlers at Westmount: Douglas, Montrose, Ramsay, Aberdeen, Argyll and so on.

His son, Nathaniel Bernard (shortened to Nathan, as was the custom), Leonard's father, exited from his war service disabled. Whether it was through actual injury or through falling foul of one of the debilitating illnesses (such as trench fever), we do not know. But he was to spend the next dozen or so years of his life as a partial invalid. To be sure, he still upheld the standards of his father; he played a full role in the family business on the manufacturing side, but the crown went to his younger brother, Horace, who had not only secured field-promotion to Captain, but went on to bring the family business – and his industry – to new heights, for which he was awarded the OBE several years later. (Lawrence managed the brass-works.) It was through such ascendancy that 'the power of the uncles,' from which Leonard appears to have suffered somewhat in adolescence, obtruded itself on the maturing boy. They were a close family, who gathered at Lyon's and his wife Rachel's home each week, cementing the family solidarity by such meetings sabbath by sabbath.

Because of his father's incapacity, Leonard grew up with all the advantages of family prestige, and few of its responsibilities. His home, a very well disposed, if modest, semi-detached residence in the affluent part of Montreal known as Westmount, backed on to a park overlooking the city and the mighty St. Lawrence River and port. Despite the Depression, the family were well provided for, and spared the rigours that many others endured. Mrs Cohen was 'queen' of her domain and, aided by a maid (suitably attired), a nurse for the children (Leonard had an elder sister, Esther), and a chauffeur-gardener (a coloured man named Kerry), they were particularly fortunate. When Mr Cohen was well, they lived the life of any well-to-do family of the time, in the Edwardian style of the period. Indeed, Leonard's main recollection of his father lies in that style, rather than more personal attributes or memories, and he is wont to describe him with his top hat and gloves, his cane and spats, and miniature service medals. Breavman, the main character of his autobiographical novel *The Favourite Game* recollected his father singing the old soldiers' song 'K-K-K-Katy . . .'!

When ill, which was often, Mrs Cohen acted as his nurse, and thus their children were largely left free to do as they liked, or at least as much as their 'nanny' allowed them. Curiously, she was of Irish descent, a Roman Catholic, and so they grew up influenced by her form of Christianity, which is the dominant religious influence in Montreal. It is this which partially explains Leonard's openness to, and understanding of, Catholicism which we find in his poems, books and songs. From the earliest years he was enveloped in a clash of 'mythologies', to use his word, and grew up aware of their contributive, as well as their competitive, differences.

Nathan Cohen was necessarily a quiet and reflective man, 19 years older than his wife. He had inherited his family's respect for learning, and though not a *savant* himself, he nevertheless brought his children up with a healthy respect for books and the independence they instil. One of Leonard's great joys in his teenage years was a full set of the English poets, bound in leather, which had been given to his father for his *Bar Mitzvah*. Already drawn to poetic vision and utterance, Leonard discovered this world for himself, cutting the virgin edges of the books which his father had left uncut for 40-plus years. It was true self-education, and accounts for the enjoyment he still shares in the works of poets now regarded as *passé*. But there were many other joys for the family, and they led a privileged and enjoyable lifestyle, despite Nathan's indispositions.

The day-to-day running of the house was in Mrs Cohen's hands. She was herself the daughter of a rabbi, whose father and grandfather before him had upheld the light of Jewish learning in their part of Poland. Her own father, Solomon Klinitsky-Klein (sometimes Kline, who was born at Vilkaviki; the other side of the family come from Vilna), was hugely influential there; through his books, notably his *Lexicon Of Hebrew Homonyms* which received excellent reviews in North America, Great Britain and Israel when published, became very well

known in his adopted land. Another of his famous works was the *Otsar Taamei Chazel*, or *The Treasury Of Rabbinic Interpretations*, a thesaurus of views and definitions which was hailed as brilliant, indeed, unique in the sacred literature of his people.

Rabbi Klinitsky-Klein and his family had escaped to Canada through the good offices of a Jewish agency in 1923 – the sort movingly described by Norman Glimotsky in his *My Life, My Destiny*. Up to that time their lives had been appallingly difficult, given the savage treatment their fellow-Poles meted out to them. Insecurity, hunger, constant vilification and injustice were their lot, and it was as exhausted escapees that they made their way from Europe via Liverpool to Halifax (then the most important port on the Atlantic coast), before finally settling in Montreal. 'A stab in the heart leaves a hole,' says the proverb of a people Leonard refers to as 'professionals' when it comes to suffering and loss; this trauma was one in which Leonard and his sister grew up. Not that Masha was unable to enjoy herself – she had a fine sense of humour and loved to sing, which she could do well, serenading the songs of her homeland – lullabies and airs which still resonate in her son's head to this day.

As do the stories she told him. But she would never forget the very different lifestyle of her early years – she was 20 when they emigrated; the veneration of her father and her father's father, the gross insecurity under which they lived; the ever-present threat of injury and loss, and the belittling malice; experiences which moulded and coloured her whole existence, as did her knowledge of Polish, Russian and Yiddish.

It was natural for such a leading Talmudic authority as her father to earn the respect and friendship of one such as Lyon Cohen, the prestigious future president of the synagogue and nephew of the Chief Rabbi; he had corresponded with Lyon prior to settling in Montreal. It was natural, too, for his unattached son to be smitten by the courage and buoyancy of Masha Klinitsky-Klein – whose name in Yiddish, appropriately, means 'brave'. Self-pity was absent from her make-up; she had that indomitable strength of acceptance and total commitment. Following her arrival, she obtained a temporary job as a nurse in the Hospital of Hope, and this situation was destined to be of great use, not least to her future husband. It was not long before the two families were joined with ties other than zeal for their faith and a deep devotion to its outworking. Thus came together two very divergent streams of highly talented, family tradition, representing very different experiences: the one blessed with order, security, great success and prestige; the other reflecting a similar piety which had been tested and purged in the fires of persecution and suffering.

# of birth
and bereavement

The Montreal into which Leonard was born was deeply segmented, as is Canada itself in its famous 'two solitudes', the legacy of its Franco-British history; a difficult dimension for those outside its rivalries to understand. It is not merely a question of its vastness (it is the second largest country in the world, measuring 9.2 million square kilometres), but its breathtaking *grandeur*: God's own country, as the Canadians delight to call it.

There is, indeed, a divine magnitude to this demi-continent of nearly four million square miles, almost half of which constitutes the backbone of the country – the famous Canadian Shield, a range of ancient rocklands (the world's oldest) which arcs from Labrador in the east, through Quebec far into southern Ontario, thence piercing north for 2000 miles into the Arctic itself. This natural phenomenon has forced human occupation, by all races since Canada was first inhabited, not just her French colonisation in the 16th century, into its disparate parts and localities, a situation further exacerbated by the Appalachians to the east and the Cordilleras to the west.

In the smallest yet most intensely populated of the two main lowland regions, the St. Lawrence, lies the city of Montreal, an island in the St. Lawrence River itself. By no means the first place to be discovered, it soon established itself as a maritime port of central importance to Canada's growing economy; though it commenced as a Jesuit mission-place, which explains its ethereal qualities. At one time a fifth of the town was occupied by religious houses or mission centres. That 'colonisation' has now gone. In its place is a charming, modern city, bursting with French culture and sensibilities and gaiety.

The city is divided geographically from mainland Canada. But the geographical differences pale when they are compared to the deep threefold divisions which rend the city itself: of *language* (four-fifths of the population speak French, only one fifth English and the smaller languages); of *culture* (the French-speaking part naturally looks to France and French literature for its mores, while the English-speaking part relies on the attachment to the Commonwealth and its close neighbour, the United States of America); and of *religion* (for the gulfs here are wider than the Atlantic as the former Protestant cross-sectioning of Episcopalianism/Presbyterianism meets the Roman Catholicism of the French, and both meet the surging secularism and agnosticism of our day). To all this is added (and it must be emphasised that Catholicism has always been in the ascendancy), a healthy input from the Jewish fraternity whose civic and educational emphasis greatly increases the town's well-being, albeit from a proportionately tiny community. (Professor Dudek has demonstrated that from a base of only 1.7 per cent of the population, the input in terms of literature and art amounts to a staggering 25 per cent.)

Montreal is an unusual city, made up of 50 villages which have grown and merged together over the years to form the modern conurbation: about 100 square kilometres in size (60 square miles), encircled by the St. Lawrence River. The various groups keep a fairly sharp difference between them, centering their activities, not least through the exigencies of the two languages, in their own areas: essentially in the East (French) and West (English – which includes the large Scottish and 'other' cultural elements).

So it was that the Cohens' life was very largely circumscribed by the Montreal riding, which had as its most prestigious centre West-mount, where they lived. Here this very affluent neighbourhood spreads out southwards and westwards from the Mont Royale, after which the city is named. The Cohens were situated a little below the halfway mark, just below the grand boulevard that cuts through the neighbourhood. By the late twenties, they were no longer a single-family unit centered on Rosemount Avenue, where Lyon's prestigious and influential residence (bedecked with a Star of David, in bold honour of the family's commitments) was situated. All three brothers had settled themselves in the area, Nathan's being a pleasant semi-detached residence of three storeys. It was ample for a small family of four of modest intent, yet large enough for a maid and a nurse to be employed. (The maid was called Mary; the nurse simply 'Nursie'. She stayed with the Cohens for the first seven or eight years of Leonard's life.) There was never any sense of deprivation, but 'frugality' (Leonard's word) was definitely part of the family's style.

Years later he said in 'The Telephone':

'Did we ever use those battered pots, I wondered once while rummaging in the basement. We must have been poor or deliberately austere, but I was not told . . .'

Leonard's main recollection was one of orderliness, not extravagance. "My father ran a pretty tidy ship," he recalled, in wistful recollection. While its gardens were small, it had the inestimable good fortune to back on to a park with splendid views across the city and one arm of the river. For a family with particular needs for quiet it was ideal, and when Mr Cohen was well a short walk took them into this repose of diverting potential. Moreover, it was but a few minutes' walk from the Junior School (Roslyn), and only a little further from the senior school (Westmount High) to which Esther and Leonard were duly sent.

Of particular importance to the family was the proximity of the synagogue itself, a mere few minutes' walk through the park. The Shaare Hashomayim Synagogue, 'the cathedral synagogue in all Canada,' stands in sovereign splendour at the heart of the community. It was their synagogue not only by religious right, as members of the local community, but because the Cohen family had, very largely, been the driving force behind its foundation and continued expansions through the years. There were other families whose contributions were also very important, but the leadership qualities of the Cohens – Lyon's in particular – had been unmatched. These were acknowledged publicly by no less a figure than a former Prime Minister, W.L. MacKenzie King, at the communal celebrations of Lyon's 60th birthday and his 35th anniversary of engagement in social interests, as well as those of his friend of many years (to whom Lyon Cohen had diverted the honour of being invited to be the Member of Parliament several years before), Sir Samuel W. Jacobs, KC: "Our friend finds himself today," commented Jacobs, "the acknowledged leader of Jewry in Canada, a position acquired by years of self-denying effort . . . respected by his own, and also by the larger community in which we dwell." Just words indeed, and of more general application than that of Canadian Jewry only. For his abilities and interests had been felt throughout the land, and had touched Palestine itself; the day would not be far distant when a woodland would be dedicated to him, the Lyon Cohen Memorial Grove, at Kadesh Naftali, south of Jerusalem.

What we know of the family shows that it enjoyed its privileges to the full, and shared a positive and happy lifestyle, without hardship, yet without vaunted excess – a balanced lifestyle, despite his indispositions. Their life was founded on love and mutual respect: father for mother, and parents for children, to which other members of the family were regularly invited. Nathan's illness apart, theirs was a home

life of high-minded living, fun and goodness; one which rang with
Masha's high spirits, an acceptable foil for her husband's Edwardian
style and manner, a real *baleboste*. One of Leonard's few memories of
his father (in addition to his monocle, his spats and his hair smelling of
Vitalis) is that of his reading, both privately and aloud, to him and his
sister – precious moments that fired the young boy's imagination and set
him, although no one realised it at the time, in the direction of his life's
work. (One of his father's particular delights was found in the *Reader's
Digest*, perhaps an indication of his limited energies.) Leonard's
overriding impression was of a stout man, reticent and somewhat
withdrawn, at least introspective, who enjoyed a good laugh; a proud
member of the Royal Canadian Legion and its military traditions. From
time to time other members would appear – the grandparents, the
uncles, the cousins, business contacts and friends, a community within
the community, and one of great internal strength.

We know very little of these early years, beyond that it was a
family of privilege, untouched by the economic scourge that surrounded it, though Nathan Cohen must frequently have feared it might
touch them, too – not least when he was blessed with a much hoped-for
son, whom he named Leonard Norman. The first name was aimed at
keeping the initial 'L' in line with family tradition; the second was much
more significant, relating to the family's Jewish ethos and hopes, as we
shall see. 'Norman' is the anglicised form of Nehemiah, who stands in
the history of his people as the master-builder, rebuilder more
accurately, prior to the People's return from Babylonian captivity. The
name actually means 'God is comfort', or 'comfort of God' – a word
which will be found to have high and particular meaning for Leonard,
and for those touched by his perceptions. In the 17th century one
Nehemiah Cohen made himself particularly famous by opposing 'the
false prophet of Smyrna,' Sabbatai Zevi, who sought to lead his people
back into the Holy Land. We have no knowledge of this being in his
parents' minds, but it is interesting to note that this Cohen was a
Cabalist, in which tradition Leonard was deeply immersed.

We should not minimise this naming, nor its effect on Leonard's
early life. Coming as it did from such a family – not only from Lazarus'
and Lyon's own strenuous devotions to their faith, in which names are
of the greatest significance, but also from that of Solomon Klinitsky-
Klein, his maternal grandfather and his very similar tradition. His
names projected an above-average sensitivity and commitment, which
was to haunt Leonard throughout his life. Names, like words, in
Hebrew are *things*; they are not merely descriptive labellings, but possess
a dynamic of their own which can be communicated to those touched
by them. It is as if, with the name, an extra dimension of personality is

added – not merely as a pious recollection of the great, but as a stimulus (at times a goad) to the one so named.

The naming of a child is a rite of the greatest importance in Judaism. In addition to the secular names, there is an additional one by which the person is known in the synagogue, by which he is 'called to the Torah'. That is given to the child at the all-important ceremony of circumcision, which re-enacts the covenant between God and Abraham 'the father' of the Jewish people, and admits the child into the family of Israel. So Leonard was given his secular names (Leonard Norman) at the Sabbath on which his mother first attended synagogue, and his Hebrew name, Elieser ('God is my help') at the circumcision-ceremony itself. And what more propitious names for the devout and hopeful parents than those of the chief servant of the Father of the People and the great rebuilder of Jerusalem! But what more daunting burden for a young man, in addition to the prestigious and ancient name of Cohen itself? We can be very sure that the story-telling with which Leonard grew up – from grandparents, parents and Hebrew teachers – never failed to emphasise this aspect of his heritage; never failed to add to his sense of duty and destiny.

Leonard's circumcision took place, in accordance with Jewish law, on the morning of the eighth day after his birth; several prayers of blessings being recited before the actual ceremony, at which Nathan his father offered the solemn prayer:

'Blessed art Thou, O Lord our God, King of the Universe, who hast sanctified us with Thy commandments, and hast commanded us to make our sons enter into the covenant of Abraham our Father.'

In deference to custom, there was a party in the child's honour, central to which was a dish of peas, which symbolises the lessening of grief to those who have been in sorrow – never far from the Jewish consciousness, and of particular relevance to this family; a copy of the scriptures was placed in the child's hands, along with a pen – how especially appropriate for this child! – which will have been followed by the usual Talmudic discussions in which, no doubt, Lyon and Solomon will have capped each other's comments. Whether the parents planted a cedar tree in honour of the occasion, as another custom dictated (girls only got a pine tree!) we do not know, but we can rest assured that the salutation-prayer was made with particular relish for this first son of a first son: 'A boy is born into the world; a blessing has come into the world.'

There was another aspect of all this which will have heightened his sense of duty and commitment: in Judaism there is a law of redemption which must be applied to the first-born of any family. It goes back to, and celebrates, the deliverance of the Israelites from Egypt's bondage under Moses. Originally, all first-born sons were dedicated to God, but monetary gifts later took their place, which were given to the priests. But in the case of the Kohanim this was waived. It was not necessary for the priests to fulfil the tradition, for their sons were automatically dedicated to the service of God and their fellows. No redemption-money was needed, the child itself was the actual embodiment of the prayer-gift. With the disappearance of temple-worship as such, this fell into misuse, but a new significance took its place, which would have had particular significance for Leonard's parents and grandparents. At this time the father dedicates his son to the study of the Torah or to the rabbinate. There can be no doubt that something of this sort took place at this time in Montreal, and that it forms one of the subconscious inputs in the growing boy's development, along with the high family traditions and the significance of his names.

Moreover, the covenant with Israel signified by circumcision was offered to make of the nation 'A kingdom of priests and a holy nation.' The whole people were theoretically 'a kingdom of priests' by virtue of their privileged relationship with God. But it was from the first emphasised that a priesthood of succession should be established through Aaron, Moses' brother. Thus the priests were known in Hebrew as the Kohanim – the Cohens – and it is this name (which Leonard later signified in his poetry by references to his 'blood'), which exerted most influence on Leonard, primarily in his formative years, but throughout his career – consciously and otherwise. There was imposed upon him, which he reaffirmed at his *Bar Mitzvah* at 12 years of age, a double mark: not only the circumcision by which all Jewish males are placed under the covenantal blessings and duties, but also the onus of priesthood. From that time he was dedicated, a marked man.

We need to take good note of this, for it is an aspect of Leonard's life, little stressed to be sure, at times perhaps deliberately down-played, that is of immense significance to him. And to us if we are to understand him in anything more than a superficial way. The priest in Israel was not merely a temple functionary, a master and manipulator of sacred ritual by which the people's offerings and worship were duly performed. He was also a spokesman for God, even as Aaron was Moses' spokesman. (Moses, the great founder and lawgiver of the nation, had a speech impediment which necessitated this. Aaron the priest was thus the spokesman, even though the authority was that of Moses.)

The temple ritual turned out to be of passing significance to Judaism. In the history of the nation, the temple – and its associated ritualism – rose and fell, as oppression and persecution (not to speak of the Israelites' hot-and-cold religious attitudes) promoted or denied its expression. By AD 70, that fateful year of Roman conquest and banishment, the temple had fallen for good, and the classic priestly ritual was no more. Never again, except in the nostalgic hopefulness of a few – would the ceremonies be performed; gone were the offerings, the blood-shedding, the fire and incense, the gorgeous (and the plain) robes, and the rest of the sacred imagery which 'fenced-off' God's otherness from the people – and brought them close to him in awe and penitence. But the priestly role was not finished, and their equally sacred duty of reading and explaining the law remained. No person is more important in the history of the people since Moses, than 'Ezra the priest'. Ezra ha-kohen not only played *the* leading role in reordering the nation's religious establishment (re-establishment), but was almost certainly responsible for a great deal of the safeguarding and consolidation by which the scriptures have come down to us today. Accordingly, in all the synagogues since the destruction of the temple, the Kohanim (the word Kohen in Hebrew actually means 'one who officiates') have pride of place. They are the ones first called to read the scriptures, and offer the priestly blessings whereby the people are blessed of God – another key aspect of their office and work. So, despite the loss of the temple, and its intricate system of worship and sacrifice, the hereditary priesthood had a role – a role which expanded, in fact, as the People themselves were thrust out into the world.

Enter into the world, therefore, the newest member of this exalted family: Leonard 'the priest', whose early years were shadowed – albeit not too solemnly – with a high sense of Tradition, and of the divine plan and ordering, even divine mission. There is a fascinating folk-tale about a child's pre-birth experience which adds weight to this, though it is not reserved to the Kohanim. It is said that prior to birth the angels instruct the child in full knowledge of life and the universe. At the time of birth, however, an angel strikes its upper lip, so causing it to forget everything that it has seen and learned. The physical mark of this is to be seen in the indentation between the upper lip and the nose. (In Leonard's case this is well marked, sign no doubt of superior knowledge!)

Another superstition relates to the day on which a person is born. Those born on a Friday are said to be marked out for special piety, which does not mean that they will be pious necessarily; only that their natures are imbued with that proclivity. According to Jewish calculation, the year of Leonard's birth was 5694, in the month of Tishri (the biblical name is Ethanim), which is the first month of the religious year with several of the most important religious festivals in it: New Year's Day itself; the 10 Days of Penitence prior to *Yom Kippur* (the Day of Atonement); and the pilgrimage festival known as Succoth, also known as the Feast of Booths (or Tabernacles or Ingathering) which is a harvest festival, an especially colourful and joyous one traditionally, in which the priestly activities in the Temple climaxed. Leonard was thus especially welcome, especially privileged, and especially burdened: on that Friday, September 21, 1934.

So the family settled down in its definitive shape: father, mother, daughter and son. It was overshadowed by two problems: one personal; the other national, indeed, international. To Nathan's persistent ill-health, always attentively managed by Masha, was added the growing concern about their fellow-Jews in Europe. Their own family experience had spelled out the horrors of bigotry and racial hatred; to these general and now somewhat distant things came the chilling reality of Adolf Hitler's seizure of power in Germany. By 1935 the infamous Nuremberg laws which deprived Jews of their citizenship had been effected; with them went the boycotting of their businesses, their harassment in public places (such as education and law), and the first signs of ultimate horror – the moves to be rid of them completely. A daunting background for the growing boy even though his parents wisely sought to cushion him from the realities. Nevertheless, he was touched by it, as references to his people, his blood, military words, rank and weapons all show in his earlier poetry.

Jewish education is understood in three phases: primarily in the home, which is regarded as a sort of mini-temple, so strongly are the emphases and traditions posited there; at school, in the normal way, as with all growing children; and at Hebrew school, which is attached to the synagogue under the rabbi or the teachers appointed by him. Leonard's ears, from his earliest moments, were conditioned to hear not only his mother talking but also singing in her lovely, deep alto voice the Yiddish lullabies she had known since her own childhood. By this time she had been away from her native Russia scarcely a dozen years. Little wonder that they were so fresh in her mind; creating a very powerful effect on his mind and unconscious, musically and rhythmically, that would remain with him for life. Later the legends and stories with which she had grown up would be added to them – stories of astonishing miracles and heroic adventures, by which she and her father, Solomon Klinitsky-Klein – whose influence on Leonard should not be overlooked – fired his imagination and stimulated his ideas. (Heroes are an important motif in his work.)

It was a childhood rich in the family traditions of Judaism, one that was made to feel all the more in need of protection, thanks to the brutality against them and their people in Europe. Additionally, his father's side of the family were very enthusiastic adherents of the British Empire and in addition to their being (as Leonard preferred to call them) "gentlemen of Hebrew persuasion," they were perhaps more British in some respects than the British themselves, recalling what Hugh MacLennan said in his superb novel of the period, *The Two*

Solitudes: 'The French are Frencher than France and the English are more British than England ever dared to be.'

As soon as Leonard learned to talk he was taught to recite the first words of the *Shema*, the 'creed' of Judaism which originated on Sinai with Moses and is recited daily:

'Hear, O Israel, the Lord our God is One . . .'

To this, as he matured, more was added, until the whole declaration of faith was perfectly grasped, part of his deepest consciousness:

'And thou shalt love the Lord thy God with all thy heart, and with all thy soul, and with all thy might. And these words, that I command thee this day, shall be upon thy heart; and thou shalt teach them diligently unto thy children, and shalt talk of them when thou sittest in thy house, and when thou walkest by the way, and when thou liest down, and when thou riseth up. And thou shalt bind them for a sign upon thy hand, and shalt be for frontlets between thine eyes. And thou shalt write them upon the door-posts of thy house, and upon thy gates . . .'

In so doing, from his earliest possible moments, Leonard Cohen became a witness in testifying to the unity of God (his 'oneness') and his creation. His deeper and more influential education was thereby commenced, based on the key concept of 'oneness', which would be intensified by the traditional recitations and questionings the eldest son asks of his father at Passover and the other festivals, and by his presence from an early age in the synagogue. (The Cohens' place was very prominent there, in deference to their priestly status and local influence.) Here he was allowed to take part in the processions, kiss the mantle girding the Torah scrolls; and sip the wine of sanctification (the *Kiddish*) on Friday evenings. These recitations are of crucial importance, not only religiously (whereby the reciter 'reactivates' the stories, the traditions, the revelation) but socially, in integrating the participants into a unity with them – as their stories and traditions, from which strength and morale were drawn. The practice is at the back of all Leonard's writing, poetry and especially his songs, as we shall see. Not merely in form, but in the old rhythms and modulations – the 'sounds' built deeply into his subconscious.

Nathan Cohen was, even in those spartan days, an enthusiastic if amateur cameraman. Thanks to his hobby some splendid pictures of his son and daughter's early life were preserved – on their tricycles, walking through the local park, playing with their cousins, skating and skiing, and some more imposing ones of them with the grown-ups – getting into the car while Kerry the chauffeur holds the door open; looking very serious with the uncles and aunts, their mother appearing to be taken up with the idea of not being photographed with them!

Nevertheless, a close relationship was sustained, each Sunday evening saw the three brothers and their wives and children gathering together at Rachel Cohen's home in highly convivial mood, Leonard's grandmother being especially delighted in her firstborn's firstborn.

Nothing exemplifies the spirit of the family more than *musar*: instruction (as moral training) which is given to Jewish children. It is best expressed in the admonition 'To act nobly, to speak purely, and to think charitably,' and nothing exemplifies Leonard's deepest nature than this triune pattern, then and now. Leonard's recollections of his early childhood are very indistinct. He does remember, puckishly, an incident when he was about three years of age. The doctor, a family friend, had called to see his father, after which Leonard was invited to sit on the good man's lap. Alas! his only response to the friendly gesture was to urinate accidentally on him, which was of consummate embarrassment to his mother, and not quite in the spirit of *musar*!

His introduction to day-school went more or less unnoticed. Esther had already whetted his appetite, and it was close enough to his parents' home for him to return there for lunch each day. Their parents had a sensible approach to the matter. The children were expected to do well, carefully encouraged, but never laid under strain to do or be the best. In Hebrew School it was a little different; he was a Cohen, after all. There he was expected to be in one of the top three places – and first is better than third! In keeping with this traditional matter went another, equally traditional: 'Spare the rod and spoil the child,' though in Leonard's case it was not 'the rod' but the dog-lead that reminded him of his responsibilities, accurately wielded by his mother. Necessary, he confessed, in his case, as his independence and 'bohemianism' showed itself early . . .

Roslyn Junior School is a large, square building less than five minutes' walk away from his home. It is one of which the neighbourhood, for all its prestige, is proud, with an excellent academic record as well as a vigorous 'Home and School Association' – the forerunner of Parent-Teacher Associations. At this level there was normally little more than 'The Three R's': reading, writing and arithmetic. But this was no ordinary school. Thanks to its vigorous and far-seeing headmaster, it also found time for physical recreation, handiwork classes and art. Once it was mooted that there should be a study-period after school, but this was vetoed by the parents' meeting which protested that it would interfere with after-school sports. They were so enthusiastic for these that its pupils regularly walked off with all the trophies on sports' days. And they paid extra for one Mr Simonds to coach in football and hockey.

But they were also difficult days, finances being severely restricted by the government. (Leonard's recollection is different. He has no memory of any such difficulties, only of how stable society was then. He does, however, remember the yardstick or strap which was then used to facilitate good conduct and discipline by the teachers.) Dr Jessie Scriver made a speech stating that the economies were affecting the health of the mothers, though not that of the children as yet. To offset the problem, the teachers agreed to salary cuts! Nevertheless, they were able to continue the art classes (to Leonard's chagrin, a Saturday morning event) alongside needlework and other crafts, which were exhibited locally from time to time.

Jewish tradition said this about the education of the child: 'Scripture at five; *Mishnah* (that is, the explanation of the scriptures; *mishnah* means 'repetition') at 10; *Bar Mitzvah* at 13.' And so Leonard, from an early age, at home and at Hebrew school, was brought to the source of his faith. Academically, he was a bright pupil, though it would appear he had difficulties in concentrating on the day-to-day routines – perhaps through boredom, often an indication of the brighter child. One recollection of Leonard's concerns his reciting a prayer at Synagogue, which he got wrong. Instead of the authorised prayer, he recited one for the dead. Nathan was not too troubled by the error: "He'll have to learn about it soon," he commented, perhaps even then aware of the grimmer realities behind his words for his family. In an interview with Mark Paytress in 1988 Leonard stated that by the age of six he was already acquainted with rudimentary Judaism and recalled being deeply touched by the stirring language and imagery of the Bible – in English and Hebrew. Each day after school he would wend his way to the synagogue for instruction in the sacred scriptures, the stories and history of his people, which reached its climax in 1946, when Leonard was made 'A son of the law'.

'All hell rules over the man who is angry,' says the Talmud, and by September 1939, when Leonard was beginning to come to terms with the thresholds of life's reality, hell was ruling the world, or at least appeared to be. War had been declared, and the fate of Czechoslovakia, Austria and Poland was sealed, as it would be for several other countries. It would be six years before that anger would begin to subside, six years of unspeakable anguish for those of 'Hebrew persuasion', when unbelievable monstrosities would be inflicted on them, by the end of which half of the world's Jewry had been murdered.

This was carefully shielded from the growing boy, though horror of a personal, more penetrating sort was to obtrude itself soon enough on him. The genteel and pleasant routine of life which he understood, despite the lengthening shadow of his father's illness, was convulsed in 1943, when Nathan Cohen died, and the family was plunged into loss and grief. Masha Cohen had always felt an outsider, vis-à-vis her more Westernised sisters-in-law. She did not have the New England style of the others, and was made to feel it strongly. This was now cruelly exacerbated; for she became even more dependent on them, not least financially. As the old Jewish proverb has it, 'From happiness to suffering is a step; from suffering to happiness seems an eternity.' She had taken that step; and now she, at only 36 years of age, had to bring up her children alone, and help them in their turn to make that large and difficult step. The loss was irreplaceable, and the pain was never forgotten, even if stoically shouldered. Leonard was but nine when his father died, and Esther 13. Both were old enough to feel keenly the savage blow, one from which Leonard suffered in particular, albeit outwardly in guarded silence: 'The deeper the sorrow, the less tongue it has,' said the rabbis.

His mother sought to protect him from the usual customs such as summoning the relatives to his father's bedside, but the trauma was nevertheless very deeply felt. Leonard recently referred to the memory of his father as "a dark mass or mountain," of which, clearly, the details were too painful for the young boy to register or the adult to express. (The image actually appeared in a somewhat different way in *The Favourite Game*: 'Concerning the bodies Breavman lost . . . a man on the mountain,' a reference to the cemetery on Mont Royale probably.) Loss, the most alienating of all experiences; the most unbelievable, and therefore the most easily forgotten (or repressible) thing. There can be no doubt that he was devoted to his father – his first book, published 13 years later, was dedicated 'To the memory of my father: Nathan B. Cohen' and there are a number of references to him in Leonard's work. There was deception and anger, too. As he said in one of his early poems, 'Rites' (*Let Us Compare Mythologies*, p227):

> '*My uncles prophesied wildly,*
> *promising life like frantic oracles; and they only stopped in the*
> *morning, promised*
> *after he had died*
> *and I had begun to shout.*'

In his autobiographical novel, *The Favourite Game*, he tells how Breavman 'tried to fight his anger with a softer emotion,' and how 'he tore the books as his father weakened.' He was being cheated. It was all too premature. He had things to ask, things to learn of his father, things to tell him. In a moment of youthful inspiration, the day after the funeral, he took one of his father's bow ties, one reserved for special occasions, and opened up its seams, into which he infiltrated a message – his first poetic utterance, as he told his Spanish biographer, Alberto Manzano – long since forgotten (or too painful to remember?). He buried it in the back garden, near the fence, overlooking the park that overlooks the city of which his father was so proud. It was winter, and something of its icy strains entered the young boy's soul, never to be forgotten.

The funeral itself he remembers only for his mother's withdrawn, uncommunicative state; and for the solemnity with which his uncles – always sober and grave – conducted themselves on the day. Jewish mourning, as with every other aspect of life, is strictly regimented. By law no attempts may be made to hasten death or prolong the life of the sufferer. By law no preparations are to be made in anticipation of death, apart from allowing the loved ones due access, and the positioning of candles – symbolic of the flickering life and to chase away the forces of darkness. The funeral arrangements are a sacred duty, a *mitzvah*, and intense mourning (weeping and wailing) is encouraged. We need have no reservation that such memories, not least the sounds, entered deeply into the young boy's consciousness, as his mother gave vent to her distress in English and her native Yiddish, as well as symbolically rending her clothes and chanting the dirges. Head coverings were normal, as was the removal of one's shoes; (in some quarters the placing of dust or earth on one's head, even flesh-cutting and head-shaving, were tolerated). It is also traditional to burn spices for the deceased; to cover the mirrors (or soap them); and to remove from the house any photographs of the deceased. All in all, apart from the loss itself, a deeply traumatic experience heightened by the rituals.

And the day of the funeral, recalled in a quasi-fictionalised form 18 years later, was no less memorable or searing: Breavman's mother had stayed alone in her room leaving 'Nursie' to get the children ready. (Leonard confirmed to us that "the details in *The Favourite Game* were true"): Breavman sat stiffly on his bed. Whispers from the people downstairs floated up to him.

He remembered the descent down the stairs, the wintry sun reflecting off his mother's stockings, the lines of cars outside the house. He recalled his uncles, 'tall and solemn,' standing behind them, patting him on the shoulder affectionately; neighbours and friends behind them, and the factory workers taking their own, lowlier places. He remembered seeing his father's face for the last time; the coffin being lowered into its final resting place – and the hateful wake which followed. Most of all the cheerfulness of it; his uncles' jokes, the traditional fare of eggs and bagels; the pervading sense of loneliness after they had all gone home – his uncles last of all. And his anger, as well as his mother's night-long laments. An experience that no boy should have; that no boy can forget. As he admitted, "In real life (as opposed to his novel) there was repression . . . I did not discover my feelings until my late thirties . . . The psychologists would say something had been repressed . . . There was a traumatic effect, blocked feelings . . . It is beyond alienation . . . I had to *adopt* the aspect of receptivity. I was very receptive to the Bible, authority. I *wasn't* interested in argument, philosophy . . . I took the simple biblical past . . . Having no father I tried to capitalise (on his absence), resolve the Oedipal struggle, (create) good feelings." Whether there can be a true 'Oedipal struggle' with a very sick, and then absent, father is a mute point. Its centre normally lies in the conflict between father and son (of which Leonard never speaks) and the ensuing guilt (which, likewise, has no explicit reference), though the anger may have eclipsed that.

son of the law
– and son of lorca

By the time the first sharp feelings of his loss had begun to wear off – it would be very many years before all of it did so, and arguable that it ever did – other voices were beckoning. As he said in *The Favourite Game*: 'Seven to 11 is a huge chunk of life, full of dulling and forgetting,' though perhaps some of the 'forgetting' was deliberate. It is clear that a certain possessiveness took over in his mother, always deeply caring and attentive, from which Leonard had to struggle to free himself. The tumult of war had undoubtedly touched Leonard, though his immediate family were spared its direct horrors. Indeed, he seems to have been more influenced by the adventure of war: '*Que la guerre est jolie!*' Apollinaire (who coined the word 'surrealism', to which we must return) had commented.

In pensive vein he had published 'an early warning' in *The Favourite Game* against those who would follow 'our future leaders, the war babies'; for the simple reason that while the world convulsed in its madness and death-throes, 'we grew up with toy whips,' 'games' played by old and young alike. And as he moved from boyhood to early youth, tales of heroism and daring-do accumulated, luring him by their unreal charms. Military language and imagery entered his consciousness more forcefully at this time too. Though soon to be exposed to Nazi atrocities as returning soldiers and the world's press became free to speak, he enjoyed the feeling of being on the winning side, of seeing his country's troops and their allies making strong progress across Europe.

By this time, he was in the second phase of his Jewish formation – that of the *Mishnah*, and attending his Yeshiva with some diligence, if not zest. The Talmud Torah ('Study of Torah'), the official name for Hebrew school, was very close to the family's heart, his forebears having put much energy into its foundation and extension. And

Solomon Klinitsky-Klein's rekindled reputation, albeit now based in New York, increased that determination. (Leonard called him, "a wise man; a world-study teacher," adding "I received a great deal from my grandfather.") His daughter Masha was careful to deposit in the synagogue's library copies of his works as they appeared, to the great appreciation of those who minded such things.

But there is cause to suspect that even by this time, a certain boyish scepticism had erupted in Leonard's mind. The anger over losing his father had barely diminished, and the older he grew, despite his uncles' attentiveness to many of his needs (as they saw them), the more the loss was felt. As he said in his first novel, answering one of his early girlfriend's naïve questions, 'What was it like to have no father?' he laconically answered, 'It made you more grown-up. You carved the chicken. You sat where he sat.' And that sitting, for a Jew, was particularly meaningful: it was where the head of the household sat; responsibility was encroaching upon him, even then.

All this made his instruction in the scriptures and the explanation attached to them more dramatic; not least his studies in the sacred language which he was expected to acquire. Leonard has admitted to a certain indifference to these studies, particularly his grasp of Hebrew with its strange characters and back-to-front writing (with which he grew up). But it should not be taken too literally. When needed, he displays a fine and intimate grasp of the Hebrew scriptures, and its rhythms and images (not least its parallelism – a form of free verse – the *versets* of the Bible) suffuses his work. *Ressentiment* is a more precise word; he may well have been blaming God in these developing years for the loss he felt – for the anguish it gave not only to himself but also that witnessed by him in his mother and sister.

His early need of solitude may also suggest this; more so the story of daring to curse God in his novel, and his refusal to kiss his prayer-book when it was accidentally dropped. Memories of the synagogue are also few, and its uplifting worship ceremonial almost completely absent. The buildings and the scripture-readings he loved, especially its evocative music; but he was never conscious of 'surrendering my heart to worship,' only conscious that therein was 'the tree of life, for all who follow the path.' Nevertheless, advance he did, and so the time came for his *Bar Mitzvah*, at 13 years of age, by which every Jewish boy technically becomes adult (i.e. morally responsible for his actions), a 'son of the law'.

Next to the circumcision ceremony, this is the most important event in a young Jewish boy's life, and invests him with a measure of maturity as well as a commensurate sense of responsibility. It is 'a non-obligatory' ceremony, an unreal description to one of Leonard Cohen's background. Specifically, it obliges the young person to wear the *tefillin* (the symbolic 'boxes' of the law worn by the orthodox) when engaged in weekday prayers; to participate in the synagogue services by being 'called to the law' (a particular privilege and responsibility for a Cohen); to be counted as an adult in the community for the purpose of establishing a quorum by which no service (or synagogue, indeed) could be instituted. So his Hebrew schooling thereby climaxed; his public participation galvanising him to accelerated study.

But for Leonard and his family there was special sadness at this point, for the traditional 'prayer of release' (from responsibility for his son) by the father was necessarily absent, a pang he could recall 40 years after the occasion. So Leonard was called by name from among the congregation, arose and ascended the steps, stepped on to the special box placed for short candidates like himself, and recited in Hebrew the traditional blessing before the reading of the Torah:

'Praise ye the Lord to whom all praise is due. Praised be the Lord who is to be praised for ever and ever. Praised art Thou, O Lord our God, King of the universe, who hast chosen us from among all peoples, and hast given us Thy Torah . . . Blessed art Thou, O Lord, who givest us the Torah.'

The lesson itself was then read by the rabbi or cantor; Leonard taking up the concluding part – the *maftir*. Following this, he recited the blessing set to follow the reading:

'Blessed art Thou, O Lord our God, King of the universe, who hast given us the Law of truth, and hast planted everlasting life in our midst. Blessed art Thou, O Lord, who givest the Law.'

The family celebration, at his grandmother's house where they frequently met, was enjoyable – to a point, but the loss of his father could only be exacerbated at such a time.

His secular school-work proceeded as well as that in Hebrew school; particularly well in English literature where Leonard had an excellent and sympathetic teacher by the name of Waring, "A fond, kindly man," in Leonard's phrase. Here he was able to indulge a growing passion for literature, but not poetry, he recollects. That seems to have been inspired by his father's excellent library, as well as the spiritual contact with him that such studying brought. Prized most of all was the collection of classical poetry – from John Donne to Robert Browning – which enhanced the Hebraic and Yiddish verse that had been with him from the first. Already a boy given to solitariness and a certain economy of words, he found in poetic diction (thanks, not least to Wordsworth) the most congenial vehicle for comprehension and self-expression.

'In the multitude of words there wants no transgression; therefore let thy words be few,' is but one admonition regularly repeated in scripture and the sayings of the Fathers. In poetry it found its perfect fulfilment; already, his vocation was being felt. As he said to us 42 years later, "I was interested in some kind of sense, that I descended from Aaron, that I was some kind of high priest. I was creating my own mythology." He re-emphasised it on another occasion: "I identify with this notion . . . Sometimes my psychic life was touched by this inspiration . . . The super-ego was very strong."

And, indeed, he was already beginning to write some poetry. (His mother was not a great reader. Indeed, Leonard can only recall a volume of the Russian writer Gogol on her shelf, by which she presumably kept in touch with her own more distant – if painful – affiliations, though influencing Leonard, perhaps, unconsciously, with Gogol's sense of fantasy and comic genius – as well as his need to travel.) Ironically, it was at this time that Ezra Pound, who had been arrested and imprisoned for treason, was examined by four prominent psychologists and judged to be insane. It had a marked effect on those who read his poetry, and a few years' later Leonard was to find himself tutored by one of Pound's most sympathetic admirers and directed to the understanding of the American's verse, somewhat to Leonard's concern, as we shall see.

We should not, however, think that these years were those of some frustrated novice-monk (not that Judaism has such in any case!) of solitary and sober reading from dawn till nightfall. Leonard was full-blooded, physically and temperamentally, and these teenage years saw him active in a wide range of sporting interests: cycling (one of his favourite pastimes then), skiing, swimming, canoeing, sailing and ice-hockey (in which he made the school team), boxing and wrestling, though he was very little involved in the last two. He did not attend any professional fights nor, unlike his later friend Irving Layton, did he get much involved in fisticuffs.

There was, of course, the all-important interest in the opposite sex. Indeed, he has commented that the only sensation that he recalls from his youth (which did not evaporate on his coming of age) was one of persistent desire. This underlines perhaps the damage done to him by his father's death, which appears to have robbed him of the memory of many of the normal sensations. In this regard it is interesting to hear him comment in *The Favourite Game* that 'deprivation is the mother of poetry.' The sexual feelings were there, and were overwhelming, as they are to many teenagers. They encroached upon him very early, leading to imaginative experiences very like those wild and rumbustious scenes he describes in his first novel. He, like many others, was to learn the truth of the Talmud that, 'our passions are like travellers: at first they make a brief stay; then they are like guests, who visit often; and then they turn into tyrants, who hold us in their power.'

But this should not obscure from us the fact that Judaism resisted stoutly the prudery that stultified sexuality throughout the West, and always retained a high and honoured place for bodily functioning and its pleasures – as becomes indeed, a gift from God: 'Man and woman are one body and one soul' (oneness reasserted, as ever), and it is this powerful union which it projects and enhances. The *Zohar* states that 'The pleasure of cohabitation is a religious one, giving joy to the divine presence.' And Martin Buber (in that same tradition as Leonard's) stated that, 'A husband is united with his wife in holiness, and the *Shekhina* rests over them,' – male and female and the glory of God combining at copulation! Andrew Greeley encapsulates it well in his phrase 'the sacramentality of human sexuality,' to which is allied a concept we shall repeatedly discover in Leonard, of women as the 'sacraments *par excellence* of God's attractive love,' to use another of Greeley's telling insights.

At a graduation ceremony from the school, on Tuesday, May 31, 1949, Leonard was chosen to offer, in Hebrew, the opening prayer (the fate of his being a Cohen!) and take part in a short presentation entitled, 'What Is Torah?' which went down extremely well. The president was his own uncle, Horace Cohen OBE. Another connection with his family's involvement was the presentation of the Lyon Cohen Memorial Medal (to Mark Bercuvitz), and the Lazarus and Fanny Cohen Memorial Medal (to Lewis Batshaw). Leonard, one of seven graduates that year, was merely awarded the graduation certificate; a sign, he says of his half-hearted application.

For several years Leonard had attended various camps held for youngsters whose parents were able to afford to send them. (He met Morton Rosengarten at the Hiawatha Camp.) This year was notable in that Leonard was assessed, among other things, for his leadership potential. The following is the counsellor's report on him, and demonstrates the 14-year-old's all-round interests and abilities:

CAMP WABI-KON: CAMPERS' REPORT

NAME: Leonard Cohen. Age: 14. Cabin: 22. Unit: 3. Counsellor: Marcy Goldstein.

This report about your son's adjustment to group life in camp has been compiled by the members of our staff who have been working with Leonard.

We hope it will be of interest as well as help to you. It is not meant as a criticism but as a frank report of how we think your child gets along at camp as an individual and as part of a group.

HEALTH: Lenny's health has been excellent all summer.

PERSONAL AND HYGIENE HABITS: He is neat and clean. He is careful about his clothes and always appears well dressed.

PERSONALITY: Leonard is cheerful, intelligent, and pleasant to everyone. He has a fine sense of humour, and he shows strong leadership qualities.

REACTION TO CAMP ROUTINE AND RESPONSIBILITIES: Lenny can be trusted to carry to completion any task given to him. He follows the camp routines well, but at times he becomes disinterested and a little slow in carrying them out.

RELATIONSHIP TO OTHER CAMPERS: Lenny is the leader of the cabin and is looked up to by all members of the cabin. He is the most popular boy in the unit and is friendly with everyone.

RELATIONSHIP TO CAMP STAFF: He is well liked by the entire staff and they enjoy his company just as he does theirs.

INTERESTS AND ABILITIES: Leonard is particularly interested in sailing and is one of of the best skippers in the unit. He participates enthusiastically in all the activities and is good in all of them.

GENERAL BEHAVIOUR: He is an excellent camper. Lenny responds quickly to requests made of him both by campers and counsellors alike.

REMARKS AND RECOMMENDATIONS: Lenny has had an excellent summer. He has had ample opportunity to exercise leadership, which he almost invariably directs along positive channels, and has improved in the various skills.

(August 26, 1949)

In addition to his leadership potential, it is interesting to note the particular emphasis on character and deportment: excellent self-imaging (in cleanliness and clothing); good social awareness (cheerful and pleasant, friendly to everyone); marked intelligence; a fine sense of humour; tendency to boredom ('disinterest'); sportive, especially in sailing and skippering, but a good all-rounder; biddable.

Such objective reporting offsets his own recollections that he "never was a teenager," and recalling only sexual feelings. (Later, he returned to one such camp to work as a counsellor himself. 'Sunshine Camp' was a community camp for disturbed children. It may not have been the origin of his interest in such people but clearly played a formative part in his development. It finds fuller expression in The Favourite Game in which he describes 'the divine idiot' – though not to his satisfaction, as we shall see.) Leonard was fortunate in the leaders and counsellors running the camps. At one of them Irving Morton, an early folk-singer and left-wing agitator taught Leonard a number of songs, using The People's Song Book. Alongside him was Alfie Melderman, an official in the union/labour movement. They may not have enthused him for their particular brand of political idealism, but they certainly sowed seeds of great potential musically.

For some time Leonard had been listening to the music of the day, which he shared with his mother and sister. He also recalls his father's love of Sir Harry Lauder's songs and those of Gilbert and Sullivan – important aspects of an otherwise sombre man. Their Jewish inheritance apart (and no serious understanding of his music interests can afford not to give this a very high place, as we shall see), was formed by such artists as Eddie Fisher, Gordon Jenkins, Vaughan Monroe, Patti Page, Dinah Shore, Frank Sinatra, Tony Bennett and Johnny Ray, who followed in the wake of the big bands. 'Teenage music' had not yet arrived, and what there was was essentially for adults, in the form of country and western and rhythm and blues; jazz was popular, of course, in some circles, but for the rest it was this or classical music, which Leonard also enjoyed, and waltzes. For the opening years of the sixth decade 'R&B was King' – thanks, not least, to the popularity it had enjoyed among the troops. This soon gave rise to such names as Hank Ballard And The Midnighters, Georgie Gibbs, The Clovers, Ruth Brown, Joe Hill and, not least, Leonard's idol of many years, Ray Charles.

Leonard himself was enthused to make his own music, an inspiration which developed from being induced to learn the piano as a young boy with Miss McDougall, in which he said that neither he nor his sister made any headway. He had, however, a natural ability with a penny-whistle, of which he had a great number, one of which he always carried in his pocket. Much as poetry was becoming a part of him, his most natural form of self-expression, and the one that reached him first, was music; side-by-side they were to advance with him throughout his developing days and early professional life.

One of his particular enjoyments at camp was the log-fire singing, whose ebullience and rhythms remain with him even today, many of them drawn from *The People's Song Book*.

By this time the guitar had made its popular impact, and in just five years' time it would be considered virtually *the* instrument of musical expression. On one of his walks through Murray Park (now King George VI Park) he encountered a young Hispanic who was playing the guitar to himself. Leonard talked him into giving him a lesson. It went well, as did the second and the third lessons. Leonard quickly and enthusiastically learned the rudiments of the instrument, those first chords basic to its mastery. On the appointed time for his fourth, however, his young instructor failed to turn up. More concerned that this reflected on his own abilities than his tutor's zest, Leonard telephoned his residence at Bowdy House, in the poorer district of Montreal. To his horror he found that the young boy had hanged himself in a moment of despair. For the second time in his life the icy fingers of death pierced his innermost self. Life was teaching him its grim realities – the hard and close way.

Yet there were bright moments, and the overall feelings in his life were those of contentment and growing confidence. One of these showed itself in his prowess as a teenage hypnotist. "I could get anyone under the spell," he says, adding that he had hypnotised their maid (as Breavman had in *The Favourite Game*) and feared that he had driven her insane by it! Another was that he had been elected to the Students' Council at his school, Westmount High, and to its Board of Publishers. His literary prowess was now enforcing itself upon him with the urgency of a destiny, as with all true writers, 'born, not made'.

It had been given particular poetic stimulation a few months earlier when, at 15, and musing in a second-hand bookshop in the city, he had come across a book of poetry by the Spanish poet, Federico Garçía Lorca, a book he has carried with him ever since, as Manzano records. Leonard was to say later, "Lorca ruined my life!" The part which caught his eye so dramatically that day was in the Spaniard's great work 'Divan del Tamarit' (1936, quoted from *The Selected Poems Of Federico Garçía Lorca*, Ed. Francisco Garcia Lorca, New Directions Publishing Corporation, pp 169):

> *'Through the arch of Elvira (the wife of Don Juan)*
> *I'm going to see you pass,*
> *to feel your thighs*
> *and begin weeping.'*

Brought up, as Leonard was, to admire the Romantics and their charming, reliable, amiable world-view, their delight in nature, not least man's own nature which had an organic relationship with the world by which sensibility and feeling – frequently emphasised as a pleasure-principle, paved the way for his being catapulted into the 'surreal' world of the Spanish writer. Not that we should over-emphasise Lorca's surrealism. He was as Romantic as any man of his time, and more so than most; one ideally suited to Leonard's own deeply Romantic (and romantic) strains – imagists both, rather than surrealists.

If the hallmark of the Romantics was 'imagination', that of the Imagists was 'verbal concentration generating energy'; they shared both, and were to demonstrate both tirelessly. Lorca's attempts at surrealism issued in response to his friend Salvador Dali's savage criticisms of his lack of modernity in his *Gypsy Ballads* ("Bound hand and feet to the old poetry," as Dali commented). They never quite came off. They merited John Ash's epithet 'old-fashioned modernism,' and most of all Jaim Manrique's judgement, that the secret of Lorca's appeal is *nostalgia*: "His art does not deepen as we grow older!" he said, another trait the Canadian shared with the Spaniard.

His brother, Francisco Garçía Lorca, has very finely defined the *canciones*, one of the most notable poetic forms used by Lorca, as a lyric in which: the poet checks his first flights in order to achieve greater purification . . . The atmosphere of transcendental romantic sensibility gives way to fleeting states of mind, momentary sensations, or a disinterested humour, often imbued with a note of elegiac melancholy. Moreover, Lorca influenced Leonard's world-view too; his 'transcendental and far-reaching' ideas about life touched him: "Lorca changed my way of being and thinking radically," he told a Spanish journalist. "His books taught me that poetry can be pure and profound, and at the same time popular."

This emphasis on people – the populace – has the ring of truth about it. It was part of 'the patrician Jew's' mental furniture (without compromising his special status, to be sure). It has an immensely old lineage, not merely in Alcuin's famous *vox populi, vox dei* ('the voice of the people is the voice of God'), but in Jewish societal awareness going back beyond Moses to Hammurabi. It touched Lorca to the point that he reduced his poetry to a secondary status, concentrating on theatrical communication as a better means of getting his message over. (He even ran a government-sponsored travelling company, serving mainly the peasants in outlying areas.)

We shall see Leonard likewise being 'diverted' from pure poetic concentration in order to achieve maximum hearing. Another aspect may well be Lorca's rejection of industrialisation – a Romantic hangover, no doubt! – which appears in Leonard's oscillation in his late teens between commerce and art. Yet another is Lorca's love of the city, a curious contradiction of his anti-industrialism, which only comes out explicitly in Leonard's devotion to Montreal, though he soon became snared by New York, London, Paris, Athens and Los Angeles, to name but a few of his favourite cities.

All this is of great significance for exploring Leonard's characteristics, for what was natural to Leonard's incipient viewpoint and versification now found stimulating and corroborative encouragement. The fact that Leonard was influenced so deeply by *Divan del Tamarit* is very suggestive, for it is one of the types of poems known as *gacela* (the other is *casida*), a short-rhymed fixed verse-form in Arabic poetry. It naturally shares much with its literary cousin, Hebrew poetry, on which Leonard had been raised from his earliest days. Another aspect, quite apart from this shared verse-form and linguistic usage, is the natural hyperbole endemic to it, which is but a step away from the 'surrealist' usage of language that Lorca essayed. Further, his Catholicism also deeply influenced, if subconsciously, Leonard's own awareness of it in

Catholic Montreal. As he said of it much later, "We who belong to the city have never left The Church. The Jews are in The Church as they are in the snow . . . Every style in Montreal is the style of The Church."

Further, Lorca, a gifted painter and pianist, had little time for the academic *qua academe*. Although educated at the universities of Granada and Madrid, he distrusted purely intellectual emphases, and poured scorn on the idea of the Muses – albeit the most lovable and influential of creatures! Lorca stood for something else – for life and the day-to-day dynamic of men and women. He had returned from a sojourn in New York to aid his oppressed people in the Spanish civil war, in which he lost his life just over one year after Leonard was born. (Others have said that his death was due to his homosexuality. Interestingly, Lorca was much more influenced by Walt Whitman, also a homosexual, than T.S. Eliot, though he knew *The Waste Land* well.)

In seeking to grasp this dynamic, and portray it, he had become enthused with the *duende*, the spirit unleashed by the *flamenco* – music and dance – which he believed to be the dynamic of true art and artistic expression: "Repel the angel, kick out the muse," he was wont to exclaim; arguing that artists must work "from the gut," with the conviction and intensity that the expression exudes; allowing the life-force it releases to flow – torrentially, vividly, dramatically; as in the *flamenco* itself.

It was precisely this spirit – this agitation against the staid and the genteel – which Leonard had perceived in the guitar-playing of his late youthful instructor, whose demise had the intensity of surreal life. It was to hound and hasten Leonard's waking thoughts, eliminate any residual interest he may have possessed in mere intellectual commit-ment, and open to him the stark reality of life downtown. From now on he was an enthusiastic convert; a propagandist, indeed.

word as discovery

Poetry is images wrapped up in rhythm.

SIR STEPHEN SPENDER

The poem is the place where occasions are exhausted,
where opportunities are used up.

RICHARD HOWARD

'I didn't kill myself
when things went wrong
I didn't turn
to drugs or teaching
I tried to sleep
but when I couldn't sleep
I learned to write
I learned to write
what might be read
on nights like this
by one like me.'

LEONARD COHEN

the emergence
of a poet

September 21, 1951 was a propitious day in Leonard's life. It was his 17th birthday, when family affection towards him was especially warm and confident and feelings of young manhood were rife. It was also registration day at McGill University, which marked a particular and new phase in his early life – in one sense, a new independence. So it was that a bold, if boyish, hand completed the form; but not over carefully! He omitted, as he was wont to do, his middle name, Norman; he put the present year down for his date of birth, not 1934; and instead of entering 'Canadian' for his parents' and his own nationality, he entered 'Jewish'. (This was done by those Jews who wished to make a Zionistic point, but it was not so shared by Leonard or his family.)

Other aspects of his answers are equally interesting: he admits to not having won any prizes or scholarships, having apparently settled for doing what was required – that, and no more! He mentions his presidency of the Student Council, and his chairmanship of 'Student Productions'; as well as an interest in debating 'current events'. He declined to add anything in the column for 'Other Personal Information'. He also gave his mother's new name, as she had recently remarried. (To both Leonard's and his mother's regret, sadly; another of those alienating-reconciling events which seem to have been characteristic of this family.) As named relatives or friends, he listed his ever-caring grandmother, Mrs Lyon Cohen, resident at the prestigious Haddon Hall, on Sherbrooke Street, and his uncles Norman Friedman and Horace Cohen. Thus completed, he signed the form 'accepting and submitting himself to the statutes, rules, regulations and ordinances of McGill University and of the Faculty or Faculties in which I am registered, and to any amendments thereto which may be made while I am a student of the university and I promise to observe the same.'

It was a momentous step for him in the awesome institution, which had received its Royal Charter from George IV exactly 130 years previously, thus antedating the Federation. The land, formerly the Burnside Place estate, and a monetary gift of £10,000, had been bequeathed to the city by one James McGill, a fur-trader and noted merchant. It took a further eight years before classes got under way, and then only in medicine, and it was not till well into the 1850s that it became really established. It prospered and expanded under the principalship of Sir William Dawson; by the time he had completed 38 years as Principal (1855-1893) the student body had risen from 100 to over 1000, and Dawson had had the satisfaction of seeing great strides made in both the building programme and the various curricula – not least in his own scientific fields.

As well as academic achievements, McGill was noted for originating two major sports: ice hockey, in 1875, largely from the rules written by J.G.A. Creighton; and a species of rugby which was played by the citizens and soldiers (for Montreal had remained a garrison town) as well as the students. A McGill team introduced it to Harvard University in 1874, which marked the formal birth of 'football'. Montrealers are not inclined to overlook their influence on Harvard! To this broadly-based academic institute – arts and science; intellectual and physical prowess – Leonard now set his hand.

His entrance examination, three months earlier, had shown a student of above-average ability, whose overall marks averaged 74.1 per cent, tantamount to a Second Class Honours, called Distinction at McGill. Curiously, his lowest mark was in English Literature (a mere 57 per cent), though in Composition he achieved 69 per cent. His performance was better in French, where he obtained 71 per cent and 75 per cent in the grammatical and oral examinations respectively. Physics realised 67 per cent; History a promising 77 per cent; and Mathematics was strongest of all, with an average of 77 per cent over three subjects: algebra I and II at 72 per cent and 80 per cent, geometry at 86 per cent and trigonometry at 70 per cent; (he admitted to us that he had opted for the latter at school, because it enabled him to evade Latin!). In Chemistry he obtained a splendid 84 per cent. Had vocation advisors been around they would doubtless have recommended a commercial future on the scientific side.

Certainly he came under such guidance from within his family which clashed with his own predilections, for his varsity life seems to have been plagued by vocational uncertainty and more than a touch of its weakening indifference. At any rate, they are the best marks that were to appear on his performance schedule over the next four years, when his average ran at 56.4 per cent. In his own beloved English, it was always higher, averaging 71.3 per cent in the three years he offered the subject; French, which was only offered in his first year produced a convincing 75 per cent; and Economics, offered in two years, 62 per cent. Philosophy, at 70 per cent, was significant; but he barely squeezed by in Latin, taking a refusal at his second attempt and attaining a mere 'pass' at the repeat stage (thanks, no doubt, to his past opting out, which necessitated his taking Latin from scratch at university). Zoology, the joker in his pack, offered in his final year, also achieved 62 per cent. Perhaps the choice was his way of declaring his consuming interest in *life*, not learning, which was becoming an obsession. Readers of *The Favourite Game* will remember Breavman dissecting a frog, which arose out of such early experiences; they will also remember his tearing up an economics textbook outside a bank on Sherbrooke Street – another reaction to the struggles and disinterest he later recalled.

The choices he made, and the way his achievements oscillated, show a decided lack of conviction, or perhaps of direction, in his thinking. That the ability was there is beyond question. And his third year First Class results (known at McGill as 'Great Distinction') in English demonstrate where his heart truly lay, as did his obtaining the coveted Chester Macnaughton Prize for 'Creative Writing' in 1955; as well as the Peterson Memorial Prize in literature. He recalled that Ian Duthie, a graduate of Edinburgh University, was one of his tutors in 'English 101' (a compulsory subject), who provided interesting connections with his father's accent and the general Scottishness of West-mount. Behind the indecision lay a youth torn in one direction by the family business, not least perhaps his father's shadow hanging over him; and the preferences of his mind and ever prolific imagination in the other. Accordingly, he read arts in his first year; commerce (which included accounting, commercial law, political science and a couple of doses of mathematics) in his second; arts (though strangely retaining political science) for his third and fourth years, to which was added zoology.

The choices are both a reflection of his inner confusion, and a statement of his determination to let his curiosity run wherever it would – and that long before 'mixed' courses were popular. The results confirm that he could have done very much better, but his mind was partly elsewhere, ever active, ever engaged, ever busy. But not in his set books! Still less at lectures which, Rosengarten recalled they avoided on a regular basis. He was not single-minded in the manner preferred by *academe*; scholarship *per se* was not going to be his métier. In fact, if truth be told, he despised the breed. His attitude reminds one of Southey's dictum, 'Your true lover of literature is never fastidious.'

There is a point here of immense importance for the understand-ing of Leonard which he shares with Layton (who preferred to be regarded as a poet-prophet in the Hebrew tradition). It lay along the lines of Layton's understanding of the poetic *function* "which exists somewhere between fact and imagination," as Eli Mandel said of him. Not pure fact, not meretricious research, which observes and 'tames' the insightful-prophetic thrust; not 'mere' imagination or mental excitement – but the fruitful intercourse between the two, in an artistic equilibrium. Leonard could be fastidious to the nth degree in completing his own work – he has always said that he works "one word at a time," and can spend months, even years, in adding finesse to it; he is nevertheless dismissive of anything approaching scholarly exactitude, still more so pedantry. It is not clear where this comes from. There is certainly an element which highly values the proprieties of artistic freedom: a work of art must be a work of free spirit, untrammelled by rules and regulations, wherein absolute consistency – or conformity of any sort – is out of place.

But there also seems to be a more personal element, too. In *The Favourite Game* he turns on those who produce such work in a wholly negative way. Of Breavman (his alter ego) he states, 'He didn't know why he hated the careful diagrams and coloured plates. We do. It was to scorn the world of detail, information, precision, all the false knowledge which cannot intrude on decay.' Whether this is the result of oppressive criticism by his school-teachers or family, or whether it comes from a reaction to the finer-than-fine scholarship visible in some branches of Judaism (which counts letters and finds significance in the smallest linguistic minutiae), is not certain. But it is there, and grew with the passage of time. (The 'on decay' aspect is significant, encapsulating a cynical view of life, not least in the shattered security resulting from his father's death.)

Nevertheless, he did not go to university unwillingly. He was keen for success and learning on his own terms, and to that he now set his face. Two names in the English department stood out especially: Professors Hugh MacLennan and Louis Dudek. The former was known, albeit chiefly in Canada, as a novelist of distinction, whose *The Two Solitudes* won for its author fame and comment throughout the land. It is a brilliant, evocative and inspiring story of the clash of the two founding cultures of modern Canada – the two solitudes – and was to have a telling significance educationally and politically. (When Leonard came to write his second novel, he paid MacLennan the finest compliment of all – and the riskiest – by imitating his theme, as we shall see.) Professor Dudek's name was familiar to Leonard beyond the academic sphere, in the (to him) much more important and fascinating area of poetry, in which Leonard was now inextricably enmeshed.

Determined to follow his own star, he was drawn to his classes in Canadian Literature (which Dudek did hand-in-hand with MacLennan); and the Great Writers of Europe (from 1850 till the present); as well as

Poetry of the 20th Century (in particular that of W.B. Yeats, T.S. Eliot, Robert Frost, Ezra Pound, W.H. Auden and Dylan Thomas). He also took courses in Continental, European and American Drama (from Ibsen to the present day); and English Prose from Francis Bacon to the Present (which included both fiction and non-fiction). He brought these to a fitting conclusion by doing the Advanced Course in Creative Writing, which was open only to students selected on merit. Significantly, Leonard did not enter for the 'Art Of Poetry' course, a study of its forms and techniques under Professor Dudek. That for a practising poet, as Leonard had now become, was unnecessary!

The period between 1939 to 1949 has been called the most productive and significant period in Canadian letters to date, which matches the '10 Lost Years' of the post-Depression period exactly. Leonard was fortunate to come to it when he did, for he was able to enter into the fruits and the confidence born of it, as well as classical English literature. If, under Hugh MacLennan, he was able to form his judgment and turn his phrases under the eye of a skilful novelist, in Louis Dudek's adroit hands he was able to fashion and test his poetic acumen to the full; both were to be of absorbing interest to him. Moreover, Dudek's scholarship was of a more penetrating kind than anything under which Leonard had yet sat, or was to sit, as became that of a Doctor of Letters from Columbia University. He was a highly reputable and incisive critic of art and culture as well as literature; a bilinguist of note, and – more important than all those! – a poet of rare accomplishment; a poet's poet.

He was also a disciple of Ezra Pound, more (one suspects) because Pound was 'the most controversial, dynamic and stimulating figure in modern literature,' than for personal *rapport* between the two men. Pound was a bohemian figure, despite his Quaker origins, who espoused an anti-credit economic philosophy which thrust him into anti-Semitism. Leonard found this hard to stomach, and frequently expressed himself vehemently against his professor's defences of the founder of Imagism (which advocated free rhythm as well as concreteness of expression in poetry); and against his disdainful, if teasing, comments of those who came from Westmount. Nevertheless, Leonard was to learn much from the Pennsylvanian, who helped to inspire his interest in Eastern thought, not least through his translations of the Chinese poet Li Po. "I love Pound," Leonard said to us late one afternoon. "There are still lines that resound in my mind. You cannot overlook his craft. But he is hard to understand!"

The reading-list to which Leonard's mind was directed was broad and enticing. It is worth looking at, for from it sprang his fund of knowledge along with the all-important Jewish scriptures and his family's experiences with them in eastern Europe. The formidable recommended reading-list adds a proviso: 'There is no list of minimum readings. You are responsible for a field. This list and its two supplements, far from setting limits, offers suggestions.' Here is that list printed as given. Scant consideration was given to getting the authors' names or initials, or even their book titles, correct!):

AESCHYLUS, *Oresteia*; ANDERSON, S. *Poor White, Winnesburg, Ohio*; ARISTOTLE, *Poetics*; ARNOLD, M. *Culture And Anarchy*; AUDEN, W.H. poems; BAUDELAIRE, C. essays, *Les Fleurs Du Mal*; BENNETT, E. *Old Wives' Tale*; BLAKE, W. lyric poems; BOWEN, E.D.C. *The Death Of The Heart*; BRIDGES, R. poems; BUTLER, S. *The Way Of All Flesh*; CAMUS, A. *The Stranger*; CATHER, W.S. *O Pioneers, The Professor's House, A Lost Lady, Death Comes From The Archbishop*; CHEKHOV, A.P. *The Cherry Orchard*, and stories; CLEMENS, S.L. (sic) *Huckleberry Finn*; COCTEAU, *The Infernal Machine*; COLERIDGE, S.T. *Biographia Literaria*; CONRAD, J. *Lord Jim, Nostromo, Heart Of Darkness*; CRANE, H. poems; DANTE; DICKINSON, E. poems; DIDEROT, D. *Rameau's Nephew*; DONNE, J. poems; DOS PASSOS, J.R. *U.S.A*; DOSTOEVSKY, F. *The Brothers Karamazov, Notes From The Underground, Crime And Punishment*; DOUGLAS, G. *South Wind*; DREISER, T.H.A. *Sister Carrie, An American Tragedy, Jennie Gerhardt*; ELIOT, T.S. *Murder In The Cathedral, Notes Toward A Definition Of Culture*, essays and poems; EMERSON, R.W. *Nature, The Poet*; EMPSON, Sir W. *Seven Types Of Ambiguity*; FARRELL, J.T. *Studs Lonigan*; FAULKNER, W. *Absalom Absalom!, As I Lay Dying, The Bear, The Sound And The Fury, Light In August*; FITZGERALD, S. *The Great Gatsby*; FLAUBERT, G. *Madame Bovary*; FORSTER, E.M. *Howard's End, A Passage To India*; FROST, R. poems; GALSWORTHY, J. *The Man Of Property, Strife*; GIDE, A. *The Counterfeiters*; GONCOURT, E.J. DE *Germinie, Lacerteux*; GREEN, *Loving*; HARDY, T. *The Dynasty, Far From The Madding Crowd*, poems, *Tess Of The D'Urbervilles*; HEMINGWAY, E.M. *For Whom The Bells Toll, A Farewell To Arms, The Sun Also Rises*, short stories; HOMER; HOPKINS, G.M. poems; HOUSMAN, A.E. *A Shropshire Lad*; HOWELLS, *A Hazard Of New Fortunes, The Rise Of Silas Lapham, Indian Summer, A Foregone Conclusion*; HULME, T.E. *Speculations*; HUXLEY, A.L. *Antic Hay, After Many A Summer, Point Counterpoint*; HUYSMANSZ, J.K. *Against The Grain*; IBSEN, *A Doll's House, The Wild Duck*; JAMES, H. *The Portrait Of A Lady, The Princess Casamassima, The Bostonians*, stories, *The Ambassadors*; JOYCE, J. *A Portrait Of The Artist, Finnegan's Wake* (ch 1), *The Dead, Ulysses*; KAFKA, F. *Metamorphosis*; KIPLING, R. *Kim*; LAFORGUE, J. poems; LAGERKVIST, *Barabas*; LAWRENCE, D.H. *The Plumed Serpent, Sons And Lovers, Women In Love, Birds Beasts And Flowers*; LEWIS, *Main Street, Arrowsmith*; LINDSAY, poems; LORCA, F. G.; MALRAUX, A.

Man's Fate; MANN, T. *The Magic Mountain, Tonio Kreaer, Death In Venice*; MANSFIELD, K. *The Garden Party*; MASTERS, E.L. *Spoon River Anthology*; MAUPASSANT, Guy de: *Une Vie*; MELVILLE, H. *Moby Dick, The Confidence Man*; MEREDITH, *The Egoist*; MILTON; MOORE, G.A. *A Mummer's Wife, Confessions Of A Young Man*; O'CASEY, S. *Juno And The Paycock*; O'NEILL, E. *Mourning Becomes Electra*; OWEN, W. poems; PATER, W.H. *The Renaissance*; PLATO *Phaedrus, Symposium*; POUND, E. poems, *Hugh Selwyn Mauberly, Cantos*; PROUST, M. *Swann's Way, The Past Recaptured*; RILKE, R.M. poems (Norton Trans); RIMBAUD, A. *Alchemy Of The Word, Illuminations, Le Bateau Ivre*; ROBINSON, E.A. poems; OUSSEAU, *Confessions*; SANDBURG, C.A. poems; SARTRE, J.P. *Nausea*; SHAKESPEARE; SHAW, G.B. *Mrs Warren's Profession, Heartbreak House, Candida, Man And Superman*; STEINBECK, J. *Grapes Of Wrath, In Dubious Battle*; STERN, L.L. *Tristram, Shandy*; STEVENS, W. *Harmonium*; SWIFT, J. *Gulliver's Travels*; SYMONS, A.W. *The Symbolist Movement*; SYNGE, J.M. *Riders To The Sea, The Playboy Of The Western World*; THOMAS, J.M. poems; TOLSTOI: *War And Peace*; TURGENEV, I. *Fathers And Sons*; VALRY, P. *Le Cimetière Marin*; VERLAINE, P. poems; WELLS, H.G. *Tono-Bungay*; WHITMAN, W. *Leaves Of Grass, Democratic Vistas*; WILDE, O. *The Importance Of Being Earnest, Intentions, The Picture Of Dorian Gray*; WILLIAMS *Paterson*; WOLFE, T.C. *Look Homeward, Angel*; WOOLF, V. *Mrs Dalloway, Jacob's Room, To The Lighthouse*; WORDSWORTH, W. *Preface To Lyrical Ballads*; YEATS, W.B. *The Education Of Henry Adams*; BAB-BITT, I. *Rousseau And Romanticism*; BENDA, *Belpheger*; BERGSON, H. *Introduction To Metaphysics, Matter And Memory, Creative Evolution*; BODKIN, *Archetypal Types In Poetry*; BROOKS, *The Well Wrought Urn*; CASSIRER, *An Essay On Man*; CAUDWELL, M.C. *Illusion And Reality*; COLUM, P. *From These Roots*; FERGUSON, A. *The Idea Of A Theater*; FLETCHER, G. *Literature Of The Italian Renaissance*; FRAZER, Sir J. *Adonis, Attis, Osiris*; FREUD, S. *The Interpretation Of Dreams, A General Introduction To Psychoanalysis*; GREGORY and ZATURENSKA *A History Of American Poetry*; GILSON *Heloise And Abelard*; HIGHET, *The Classical Tradition*; KAZIN, *On Native Grounds*; KRUTCH *The Modern Temper*; LANGER, *Philosophy In A New Key*; LEAVIS, *New Bearings In Modern Poetry*; LOVEJOY, *The Great Chain Of Being*; MARX and ENGELS *Communist Manifesto*; NICOLSON, *The Breaking Of The Circle*; NEITZSCHE, F.W. *Beyond Good And Evil*; NORDAU, *Degeneration*; RAYMOND, *From Baudelaire To Surrealism*; READ, *Surrealism*; SPENGLER, *The Decline Of The West*; TAUPIN, *The Influence Of French Symbolists On American Poetry*; TILLYARD, E.M. *The Elizabethan World Picture*; TINDALL, *Forces In Modern British Literature, The Literary Symbol*; TRILLING, *The Liberal Imagination*;

WHITEHEAD, A.N. *Science And The Modern World*; WILSON, E. *Axel's Castle*; WINTERS, A. *Maule's Curse*.

This is a formidable range, containing no less than 143 titled works; the poems, stories, prefaces and essays of 29 authors; and 41 works of criticism or related literature. Moreover, in his third year, in which he read modern, European and American drama, there were a further 44 works from 20 authors not included in the above list; some in French! Omitting his radical change of direction (i.e. of subject) in his second year, it represents a demand of surrealist proportions, especially when one considers that alongside these he was reading French, Latin, Mathematics, Philosophy and History. His task, one of unending and heady excitement, was now well and truly under way! Little wonder that he sometimes gave the impression of inattentiveness in class; he was inebriated in a world of letters, engulfed by an avalanche of ideas and images, forms and metres, essays and critiques: a fast-changing, provocative kaleidoscope which took his already well-stocked and fertile mind to fresh heights.

Paradise it was not; but at least it resembled something like its antechamber. He plunged himself into all this and more, avidly reading everything that came his way; especially poetry, and not least Spanish, Chinese and Japanese poets in translation, but chiefly that of Federico García Lorca and W.B. Yeats, of whom he mused, "I loved Yeats; his connections (such an important code-word with Leonard!) his rhythms."

A single prose piece, written early in his course, has survived the fates of time. It represents one of his assignations. More importantly, it reflects his laconic style, and what was going on under the surface:

'X died last Sunday. The event had absolutely no emotional or intellectual effect on me. In fact I don't give a damn. Neither do you. Neither do the 30 odd thousand people who read the Gazette on March 11. His family probably cares (no one to support them) but very few others. Here was a fellow human, Canadian, and Montrealer who went to the same movies and read the same papers as you or I. 1.) He rode beside you in the streetcar and complained about the traffic and the weather with you. The eyes of his beloved wife, are tear-reddened (sic) and she has come to the awful realisation of a gap in her waning life which will never be filled. She had always sworn to herself that she would never impose on her daughter's marriage 2.) but she knows now that she cannot possibly decline an invitation to spend the rest of her days at her son-in-law's house. It sounds like a soap opera but so does any tradgedy (!) that happens to real people. Death is a tradgedy (!) and whether it strikes at an eight-year-old*

youngster 3.) or a senile old man, a scar is always left on one 4.)
of the survivors – a scar that does not heal quickly.

'*We still don't give a damn that X died last Sunday. I*
listen to the World Federalists and the Communists talk about
One World and The Brotherhood of Man and how much they are
doing to bring them about. They uphold the feasibility (!) of two
billion people, diverse in language, colour, nationality and
religion, living together in harmony. And yet, none of them, who
have so much in common with X, who have so much regard for
their fellow man, was at the funeral this afternoon. Neither
was I.'

It is curious that he should select such a subject for his essay,
drawn from a newspaper announcement of a man's death. We also have
the comments of his tutor, Ian Duthie, on the piece, which shows that
he found it curious, too. Across the top he has written, 'This verges on
being in poor taste, but makes a twist and escapes.' He drew attention to
the three spelling mistakes Leonard manages to include in so short a
piece, marked by (!), and at the points we enumerate offers the
following marginal comments:

1.) 'Be concrete'. 2.) No 'comment' here actually. Merely a
questioning underline, presumably to emphasise the looseness of the
phrase. 3.) 'Boy' is suggested in place of 'youngster'. 4.) 'Why
necessarily one?'

Why this preoccupation with death (if such a word is allowable
on the evidence of but one piece)? There must have been several dozen
possible suggestions for an essay from that paper – political, industrial,
military (the Korean war was still ongoing), in sport or arts, etc. etc. He
chooses death and bereavement! On which he makes two statements:
first, that we are unmoved by it; second, that it is a tragedy, especially to
the *eight-year-old* son. (Where did he get that information from?) But
the second is surely contradicted by the first; especially if one adds to it
the sympathetic view he evinces of the widow's plight.

It is difficult to avoid the feeling that this, one of his first
university essays, is purely subjective. He *is* that eight-year-old boy. He
knows how it feels to lose a father at a tender age. Moreover, 'a scar is
always left on *one* of the survivors.' The others, to his way of thinking,
got away more lightly.

He suffers still, even if the widow's life is said to be 'waning',
her eyes 'tear-reddened', her freedom blighted – along with her
happiness. The daughter, apparently, had no feelings; she did not come
into the picture, as elder sisters frequently do not. The real situation was
between the widow and the youngster who was effectively older than a
boy, in feeling and reaction at least. It was 'a scar that does not heal

quickly.' He knows; his own – now of eight or nine years, was still fresh, still hurting. The piece is essentially about that. It proclaims that he does care. Moreover, he is angry that the rest of us – including the so-called caring brotherhood of World Federalists and Communists – do not. He was not there, at X's funeral. But could he have been? Would it not have been too painful, not least having to watch another youngster take his first steps into the fatherless state? X died in March, but it was close enough for the connection that Eliot wrote of in *The Waste Land*:

> '*April is the cruelest month, breeding*
> *Lilacs out of the dead land, mixing*
> *Memory and desire, stirring*
> *Dull roots with spring rain.*'

Things were stirring, all right, at his roots not least. Stirring at these roots in a different way was his friend of eight or nine years, Morton Rosengarten. One year older than Leonard, he went through the varying experiences of adolescence with him, sharing not least Leonard's musical interest (Morton played both the banjo and the trombone), as well as a variety of pastimes and a healthy interest in the fairer sex. Unlike Leonard, he had very little interest in the synagogue and broke from its traditions much more decisively, finding Leonard's continuance somewhat irritating. ('Krantz' is modelled on Rosengarten in *The Favourite Game*, though highly fictionalised.)

He was always impressed with Leonard's room, which he found to resemble more a study than a youth's bedroom – already the style was evident. In particular he remembers the very smart set of poetry classics, and noted his friend's compulsive reading of them. Indifferent student Leonard might have been formally, he was nevertheless already showing those precocious marks of the *littérateur*, "always an ideas man," as Rosengarten commented. Leonard also had a little room in the basement in which a piano was kept, where they spent much time together. But he had become 'addicted' to the guitar, which drove Morton 'crazy' – for it went everywhere with them, and was played incessantly.

Neither of them had pure academic interests. At school they shared truancy escapades, which developed a more interesting potential once they had matriculated. Rosengarten's *forte* lay in the fine arts, painting and sculpture in particular, to which he committed himself at McGill ahead of Leonard. Part of his spare time was taken up with the marching band of the university, but much of it was given to boisterous evenings drinking and singing with his companion – always with a view to winning the girls' eyes and hearts.

Some of these escapades upset Mrs Cohen, who was given to "flying off the handle," in Rosengarten's phrase. And she would stay off it for days on end. Young as he was, he could see the conflict she evidenced as an 'off-the-boat Russian' with the rest of Leonard's 'classy' family. Their adventures made life no easier for her. But Leonard himself was smitten, he says, by his family's past, by its name and meaning. He used to drive his cousins 'crazy' with its 'mythology'. Like his mother, Leonard was even then subject to alternating highs and lows, which added spice to their friendship. Morton saw that Leonard and Mrs Cohen were very close, and nothing emphasised this more than her willingness to take them and their friends out for meals, especially to a favourite Greek restaurant where she would be the life of the party, not least in singing, and encouraged by good wine which the restaurateur would ply them with in order to get the mood of the evening going. At other times she would refuse to let Rosengarten in the house, especially if Leonard had had a late night out. And woe betide both of them if Leonard failed to phone her if he decided to stay out and thereby wasted the food!

These were the high days of 'square-dancing'. Chief of the musicians in that genre were Burl Ives and The Weavers. In 'Goodnight Irene', the latter had an outstanding hit, a key point in the development from traditional folk to modern in 1950. The musicians' ability to involve their listeners – they worked mainly in sub-concert settings (campuses, churches, libraries and union halls) matched their left-wing accents, a major aspect of the peoples' song movement. (Their *Peoples' Song Books* were released in two volumes. They even published pamphlets of a political nature.)

Many of the songs, perforce, had to deal with injustice and exploitation, and it was their effective and social melancholia that inspired Rosengarten and Leonard. They still have good memories of The Weavers playing together in concert – before Pete Seeger quit in the wake of Decca's dropping them for their politicking – a symptom of McCarthyism, then gathering pace. Happily, they were contracted by Folkways Records, with which Leonard himself became involved later.

But perhaps the biggest thing in popular music took place in 1948 when the LP was introduced; an innovation of immense importance for the industry and public alike, and not least for Leonard who set about acquiring an enviable collection.

Rosengarten was at McGill for Leonard's first two years or so, and they ran the Fraternity together. There is an 'élitist thread' in such places, and joining was by oligarchic selection and specific invitation, followed by a suitably off-beat initiation. Their natural rebelliousness achieved its heights now, not least in their violation of the traditional rules, their attempts to undermine the institution by radical policies, their attempts to breach the system. They invited people whose backgrounds were very different to join this 'high class Jewish fraternity,' and tried to run it as a continuous party. They even instituted a rule of drinking in front of the Fraternity House, for which Leonard was impeached! And he conducted its meetings to the sound of his guitar, singing to his fellow-students suitable – and unsuitable! – songs and ditties. (One of them was 'Sunshine 1950 Will Be Nifty'; another was 'Racing With The Moon'.) Once a girl was smuggled into the proceedings in her boyfriend's overcoat. Removing the coat revealed her to be completely naked, which finally put the cat among the pigeons: they were banished!

All this coincided with the start of the coffee-shop movement, and many opened in Montreal. The *Café André* was one such place, near to the Students' Union building. They called it The Shrine – even then secular sanctity was in vogue! It was situated in an old house, a three-storey building which the students and others had the run of, more or less. One of its rooms was given over to chess-playing, a pastime enjoyed by Rosengarten and Leonard.

After the second or third week of starting his course, Leonard asked to speak to Professor Dudek, and showed him some of his own poetry. He was aware that the professor was deeply involved in the burgeoning poetry movement of Canada, chiefly in the form of 'the little books and magazines' which were in the van of the movement. Dudek was surprised at the request; it was not a course designed to deal with such matters. He consented to talk and to look at Leonard's work. It moved him not at all. It was merely interesting, somewhat pedestrian; not a promising start. Two weeks later the same thing happened. Dudek flicked over the pages, found them to be a little better, but still somewhat hum-drum. Then his eye chanced on a sheet headed 'The Sparrows'. The first lines gripped him; as did the next verse; and then the whole poem. This was the real thing! This was *poetry*! A discovery had been made. By this time they had left the classroom and were walking down one of the long, high-ceilinged corridors of the Faculty building.

"Kneel down," commanded the professor. Startled, his young student did so. Using his rolled-up manuscript, Dudek dubbed Leonard. "Arise," he commanded. "You are a poet. I have knighted you. Now you are one of us." There was no turning-back after such an experience. The poet was commissioned.

Here is what Leonard wrote, which set the shape of his life (later published in *Let Us Compare Mythologies*, pp26):

The Sparrows

'Catching winter in their carved nostrils the traitor birds have deserted us, leaving only the dullest brown sparrows for spring negotiations.

'I told you we were fools
to have them in our games,
but you replied:
They are only wind-up birds
who strut on scarlet feet
so hopelessly far
from our curled fingers.

'I had moved to warn you,
but you only adjusted your hair
and ventured:
Their wings are made of glass and gold and we are fortunate
not to hear them splintering
against the sun.

'Now the hollow nests
sit like tumors or petrified blossoms between the wire branches
and you, an innocent scientist,
question me on these brown sparrows:
whether we should plant our yards with breadcrumbs
or mark them with the black, persistent crows
whom we hate and stone.

'But what shall I tell you of migrations?
When in this empty sky
the precise ghosts of departed summer birds
still trace old signs;
or of desperate flights?
when the dimmest flutter of a coloured wing
excites all our favourite streets
to delight the imaginary spring.'

Another influence – arguably of even greater influence – burst upon him at this time, in the form of Irving Layton, the *enfant terrible* of Canadian poetry then a local school-teacher, who was invited to participate in a poetry workshop on the campus, and did so with great élan. In those early days Layton had much in common with Dudek, not least their ability to poke fun at the richer districts of Montreal Jewry – including Westmount, which greatly irritated Leonard. Ironically, they both live there now; and Leonard does not, having opted for their former 'downtown' districts! Leonard was aware of Layton before this, of course. He had published his first book of poetry, *Here And Now*, in 1946; his second, *Now Is The Place*, in 1948 – shortly before Leonard chanced on Lorca's poetry. Leonard had even met him briefly in 1949, but this meeting at McGill was the one which quickly developed into a strong and mutual respect, a lifelong friendship.

Irving Layton is not one to be lost in a crowd. Though short, he stands head and shoulders above most. He is one of those characters whose personality is somehow several sizes too large. He comes across in large, energetic, engulfing, captivating waves, at once friendly and disturbing.

Poetry in motion. And what poetry! It is larger than life, more real than truth, dramatic and daring, perceptive and flowing, and, significantly, full of paradox and ambiguity. Above all – like the *duende* itself – he works 'from the gut' and to the gut. Perhaps more than any other man in Canada, he has put poetry on the map – at the centre, indeed; and fought and argued and worked demoniacally to preserve it there. His poetry – there are now 50 books of it, no less – comes in all shapes and sizes, all colours and sounds, except the muted. Leonard later wrote of him:

> '. . . you finally came in,
> more furious than any Canadian poet . . .'

He has been so occupied since before his first book was published; in season and out of season, through thick and thin, and always with the certitude that his views, his perceptions, would prevail: a catalyst and an agitator of the first order. Born in Romania (and thus sharing part of Leonard's eastern European background), transferred by his parents to Canada in the harsh years of the early century, he represents, perhaps more than any other, not the genteel 'English' background common to many of his fellow-workers, but a rough, raw Canadian view that is intensely patriotic, proletarian, passionate and pure. If some (such as F.R. Scott, A.M. Klein or P.K. Page) represent the priestly caste, Layton represents the prophetic – in language and manner, in word and symbol.

And as with all true prophets, he respects no man, nor spares any. One of Layton's traits, as Leonard was at pains to emphasise, was to distinguish between priest and prophet; and Layton is not slow to emphasise the historic conflict between both offices. In poetry, as in life, Layton is held captive to his own Muse, no subject being too sacred nor too delicate especially the previously 'taboo' ones of violence, cruelty, politics and sex. All have been exposed to his scarifying eye and his audacious judgments; he has projected on all his volatile wit and a searching wisdom. He is totally dedicated to his calling, his art, and spares no expense to fulfil it. He is merciless to other poets whom he considers to have sold the pass:

> 'Since Auden set the fashion
> Our poets grow tame;
> They are quite without passion,
> They live without blame.'

Indeed, he is at his most virulent when attacking his fellow-poets, so caught up is he in the seriousness of the poetic task. If Soren Kierkegaard vitiated the easy-going philosophical idealism of his day with his heavily personalised challenges to it; if von Rochau brought in the concept of *Realpolitik* to Bismarck's Germany; and if Karl Barth ushered in 'Crisis Theology' in Switzerland; it is at least arguable that Irving Layton fathered 'Crisis Poetry' in Canada': poetry that demanded a decision, a response; that cut through the emollient patter and posed a rough demand on the reader or hearer. In order to get that response he was prepared to dispense with the niceties of convention and the formulae of polite language: 'from the gut, to the gut.'

It was exactly what Leonard expected of a poet, and he and Layton have remained firm friends ever since. (Moreover, he was, like Lorca, another 'L' – and that could not be merely coincidental!) Indeed, the relationship has been more than mere friendship, but one of familial depth. Leonard has described his youth as being "free from adult figures," but Layton overturned that. Here was not an authority-figure, of school or university or civic discipline; still less a relation who could 'pull rank' by virtue of family influence or purse string manipulation. He was a man, a friend, a fellow-rebel, a *poet*, with whom one could simply be oneself; and write knowing that it was understood, respected. A father-figure in the deepest sense of the word. Significantly, when Esther, Leonard's sister, introduced Jennifer Warnes to him, she commented that Layton had been "like a father to Leonard." There was much truth in it, despite their respect for each other's freedom and independence. There are major differences of personality and style, as well as background, but these complement each other rather than antagonise. Layton appreciates in Leonard the patrician-Jew aspects that he finds so ridiculous in others; Leonard, the anti-establishment (and anti-everything else!) that he finds in the older man.

Layton described the four things which stand out in Leonard, which give him the confidence to work as he does, and promote his work: The strong tradition of learning; the business entrepreneurship of his family; the broad philanthropy/charity which hall-marked it; and, lastly, the self-awareness that comes from being a Cohen – not understood as class-distinction, but from the high symbolism of 'the priest and his role.' This latter is particularly interesting. It was raised by Dudek in somewhat different form when he said that Leonard "always had an image of himself as a rabbi." We are talking of two very perceptive men – whose métier is perception; and their recollection of Leonard at this young age, his late teenage years. Layton put it somewhat differently when he added that "the two great qualities a young writer has are his arrogance and inexperience," and on another occasion he picked out the twin characteristics of "precocity and independence.'' Leonard was never arrogant, but he was – as Pierre Berton once remarked on Canadian television, ''a very confident young man.''

By the time they met, Leonard was indeed pushing hard at the doors of his own individuality – in one sense he had been doing that for years. But university life, not least his ability to rent a flat with Morton Rosengarten in Lower Stanley Street (for some time unbeknown to his mother), now allowed him to do this actually. (When she was told, she was surprisingly sympathetic, and tolerant of this need for independence. ''Just follow your little heart,'' she commented; as she ever did in matters of important self-expression.) Irving Layton was exactly the sort of man to further that: enthusiastic and bold, erudite and observant, worldly and street-wise, compassionate and cavalier; he could throw all caution to the wind and sing and drink and dance the night away. Not merely poetry in motion, but surrealist poetry! As with the Hebrew prophets, there were no greys, no subtle shades. Though he is meticulous in his choice of words and turns of phrase; his attitude, his demands, are for black and white: take it or leave it; but at least recognise that you have been offered it.

selfhood,
poetry and music

In the year in which they met, 1954, Layton had two books of poetry published – he does nothing by halves! – and Leonard was clearly dazzled by the man's prolific genius. When it mattered, Leonard was a learner; he could sit at a man's feet and absorb completely. In Layton he saw the splendour, and the viability, of the poetic destiny. A life in art began to make real sense. Unlike his rabbinic forebears who were not allowed 'to use the Torah as an axe,' to earn their keep from its knowledge and application, this was a métier which both claimed him and offered a fulfilling vocation. His questions flared fast and furious. As Layton emphasised, theirs was the Jewish tradition of the *Lehrer*: the teacher/learner relationship. In amiable mood one day Leonard remarked of his friend, "I taught him how to dress; he taught me how to live forever." And so began this friendship of 35 years, between the older and the younger man (Layton is 20 years senior to Leonard); between the master and the apprentice.

Whenever Layton had a promotional tour or appearance, a poetry reading or a workshop (poetry-reading in Canada predated Ginsberg's sensation with *Howl* that set in motion the 'beat-poetry' style, despite Scobie arguing it as an influence on Leonard's background), he would take Leonard along, acquaint him with the nuts and bolts of the business and get him to read some of his own poetry. And they had such fun together! On one occasion they were so preoccupied with their discussion, driving from Montreal to Toronto, that they failed to notice how low in petrol they had become. Too late! They ran out of petrol some miles from their destination, fortunately near to some houses whose occupants came to their rescue. Two years later, incredibly, the very same thing happened, at the very same spot. Only the discussion had changed!

Nothing captures this profound relationship like Leonard's poem, 'Last Dance At The Four Penny' (*The Spice-Box Of Earth*, pp73), which perfectly catches the way they could cock a snook at the establishment, scholarly and religious:

> *'Layton, when we dance our Freilach*
> *Under the ghostly handkerchief,*
> *the miracle rabbis of Prague and Vilna*
> *resume their sawdust thrones,*
> *and angels and men, asleep so long*
> *in the cold palaces of disbelief,*
> *gather in sausage-hung kitchens*
> *to quarrel deliciously and debate*
> *the sounds of the Ineffable Name.*
>
> *'Layton, my friend Lazarovitch,*
> *no Jew was ever lost*
> *while we two dance joyously*
> *in this French province . . .*
>
> *'Reb Israel Lazarovitch,*
> *you no-good Romanian, you're right*
> *Who cares whether or not*
> *the Messiah is a Litvak?*
>
> *'Let them step with us or not*
> *in their logical shrouds.*
> *We've raised a bright, white flag . . .'*

In this poem we see their shared Jewishness, and the 'irreverence' (as some would see it) they each had for the Tradition – at least for that view of it which some espoused; we also see a shared disdain for rabbinic (and priestly) logic, to them both a form of mental death. As Leonard commented in *Police Gazette*, "I'd rather sleep with ashes than with priestly wisdom," which has even more point when we understand that the ashes referred to are those of the victims of the Holocaust. Professor Pacey referred to Layton as 'a poet of revolutionary individualism,' and there can be no doubt that that individualism was a common tie, and not merely religiously but in every way. Not least in the sexual, for both projected a red-blooded response to their manhood which goes beyond the merely sexual or corporeal, claiming – demanding! – the full world of nature and manhood as their proper spheres: nothing was to be too sacred, for all is sacred – a Blakeian conception which predates Blake in its patent Jewishness by millennia, not centuries.

Said Leonard to us over a bottle of Sabbath wine, "I did not have a scholar's bent; at that time I spent many evenings with Layton and we would 'crack' poetry together – discover the poet's meaning. (That is) training at its best: serious, dedicated . . . (Ours was) an *ad hoc* group. We lived for it, in between homes and restaurants." Significantly, he adduced the work of the American poet Wallace Stevens at this point, a man torn between the profession of law and the poetic muse, whose view of lost faith and a 'disconnected' tradition imbued his poetry with a wistfulness and a challenge that was taken very seriously by Leonard and Layton; or, perhaps, viewed by them as a satisfactory replacement. As Layton asked in his poem 'To The Roaring Wind' (or was it to the Spirit-behind-the wind?):

> *'What syllable are you seeking,*
> *Vocalissimus,*
> *In the distances of sleep?*
> *Speak it.'*

This was the year in which Leonard was elected President of McGill's Debating Society. He was, as we have seen, already President of his fraternity. The following is his acceptance speech as President and, while betraying a certain youthfulness, it demonstrates the cast – the humour and the audacity – of his mind at that time:

> *"Mr Chairman, Ladies and Gentlemen. The foreigners in Ottawa constitute an ominous threat to the integrity and autonomy of our province. The Communists in the CBC have tried to poison our minds with bolshevism and the capitalists of Ontario have tried to poison our bodies with margarine. Twice in the last half century they have plunged us into British wars and twice have they taken our finest youth from under our beds and from behind our barns. We are incompatible with them because they cannot understand us or comprehend our heritage. In our Church they see bigotry; in our homespun cloth they see provincialism; in our wooden ploughs they see something primitive; in our fallen bridges they see corruption. And, ladies and gentlemen, how long before they interfere with the very guardians of our existence and prevent the provincial police from shooting down vicious unarmed textile strikers? These are the things we believe in – the things they are trying to take away.*
>
> *"There is open to us only one course of action: we must quit the Confederation, consolidate and centralise our own power. But who is qualified to lead us on this Crusade? The answer is as obvious as the sign on a streetcar – it is a business man. In this day governments handle astronomical sums and a multitude of people. In effect, a government today is big business. Who then more logical to head our new government but a business*

man? There is nothing so admirable as a man who applies his knowledge with forceful direction and from his efficiency reaps a profit. To be a good business man is the epitome of development and these learned people secretly aspire to that goal. For what are their professions and avocations per se without the business sense? The lawyer is a deceptive sophist half smothered in ipso factos. The artsman is an antique fossil and at best will make a fine filing clerk. And would we trust the doctor to rule? I am reminded of a short verse written in Roman times when even then they knew the nature of doctors. It goes:

*'But when the wit began to wheeze
And wine had warmed the politician
Cured yesterday of my disease,
I died last night of my physician.'*

"And the engineer – or scientist – an automaton, his imagination chained to a drawing board by a formula and a slide rule. Will he be our new leader? Quebec was the last province to give the vote to women. Under the new régime we would be the first province to disenfranchise them. For as Ambrose Bierce said, 'Here's to woman. Would that we could fall into her arms without falling into her hands.' And frankly, ladies and gentlemen, what is a theological student but a sebastomaniac?

"But don't despair, my friends. Even for the engineer there is still hope. Charles E. Wilson, the newly appointed Secretary of Defence, graduated as an engineer but soon realised there were better things in life and he took a course in commerce and went into business and is now engaged in the most complicated of businesses – that of running a country. But perhaps I should not encourage you. The business man can use you all in the new régime. But you must all acknowledge his obvious superiority.

"To close, I should like to quote from a source that especially some of us find more authoritative than a business man. It is the Holy Bible and if you will turn to Proverbs 22:29 the following quotation will be found: 'Seest thou a man diligent in his business? He shall stand before kings'."

A keen and powerful debater, he was not amused at the dreariness of the Executive's meetings, the small talk and the administration (never his strong point). So he refused to call the Executive at all! It led to a major fracas, in which some tried to get him 'unelected', but failed. The rebel was sharpening his teeth!

Such behaviour did not recommended itself to another, more discreet, influence on Leonard during those undergraduate years: Professor F.R. Scott, later Dean of the Faculty of Law, presently, while Leonard swithered and swayed as to whether he should commit himself to the arts or commerce, his lecturer in law. (An influence on Leonard equal to that of A.M. Klein, also a lawyer, but more importantly a poet-novelist of considerable skill, whose familiarity with literature equalled his Jewish erudition and commitment unlike Leonard he was a 'ghetto' Jew of Montreal). Leonard dedicated a poem to him 'Song For Abraham Klein', in which poetry and song find their first and significant expression. Steinberg, introducing Klein's brilliant novel *The Second Scroll*, draws attention to, 'The obsessive theme of the discovered poetry (of New Israel) is the miraculous, and the key image necessary to explain the remarkable vitality, the rebirth evidenced in every aspect of life, is the miracle.' A theme and an image which will be apparent – and crucial for Leonard's own novel *Beautiful Losers*.) It is doubtful if Leonard learned much law from Scott. Even when in lectures, which was not often, his mind was elsewhere. But there was a degree of comprehension, if not agreement, from the professor.

Scott was in fact a poet of considerable skill himself; a founding father, no less, of Canada's emerging poetry movement, and the *doyen* of poetry in Montreal, which has produced so many excellent poets. An odd diversion, perhaps, from one of the country's leading constitutional lawyers, but he was seized of the gift, and so the poetry became assertive. His presence had a telling, if quieter, effect on Leonard than that of Dudek or Layton, but it was nevertheless very important. Scott made no secret of Leonard's ambiguities regarding law, and he sought to ease him into a position nearer to his own, of both lawyer and poet. But Leonard is not of that cloth; his nature is obsessive; what he does, he must do with abandon; he has to work in total conviction, and dedication. As he said himself of this time, "I yearned to live a semi-bohemian lifestyle, an unstructured life; but a *consecrated* one; some kind of calling." It was this that fostered an even more radical bid for his independence. Being adequately provided for, he was able to book himself into a downtown hotel which cost him three dollars per night, though he often failed to make it back to the hotel, finding the cosmopolitan and nocturnal life of the town there entirely to his liking: consecration dismantled!

Leonard was fortunate in being welcomed – virtually as an equal – into the regular company of such as these older poets. Not merely welcomed among them, but escorted around the country by them to various literary and poetry events, and often presented to their confrères as their protégé.

It was during this time that he was invited to the discussions of the CIV/n group, a gathering of poets of the more serious sort – and to some extent inspired by Ezra Pound's revitalising energies, even as its name was culled from his writings – who had just launched a new poetry magazine of that name.

It included such as Wanda Staniszewska, Jackie Gallagher, Buddy Rozynski (cousin of Louis Dudek) and Aileen Collins (later to be Mrs L. Dudek), Robert A. Currie, Yaffa Lerner, Anna Azzulo, Betty Sutherland (later Mrs Sutherland Layton), and Dudek himself. Between April 1953 and March 1954 they produced the first five issues, meeting in Layton's home, occasionally at Rosengarten's, to discuss The Things That Matter – their latest poetry and material offered by others, not infrequently being led in song by Leonard on his ever-present guitar. Despite the fun and gaiety, it was a very serious concern – the concern of poetry itself. It was also revolutionary, an emphasis that attracted Leonard particularly. Commented Aileen Collins retrospectively, ". . . our study of literature in no way reflected what we knew was happening in the world . . . (we aspired) to let in new voices, and essentially to jolt Canadians from their lethargy and narrow-mindedness. We were set against (the Canadian Authors' Association) poetry and maple syrup!"

The magazine was set to be 'a new force in writing and criticism in Canada'; based on Pound's comment: "CIV/n (civilisation) – not a one-man job." And not always ironical, either, as Layton commented: "The discussion would be lively, boisterous, and prolonged; no fistfights, but plenty of abuse and insult . . . What really stands out in my mind was the homage that was instantly paid to a good poem and the individual who had written it." Some years later he and Dudek parted company; the former being too much the evangelist-propagandist for the 'pure' scholar.

As Pacey said of Dudek – he could never say it of Layton! – "(his strength) lies in his serious attempt to give as purely as possible the experience which is pure and isolated in his own mind," a view which is offended by the notion of 'popular culture' and the torch-carrying it requires.

Into that group came Leonard. He grew mentally and spiritually, and his art increased accordingly, in depth and dexterity. As became poetry of a new civilisation, it was socially conscious as well as spiritual, incisive as well as whimsical; as the following demonstrates (*Let Us Compare Mythologies*, pp69):

Les Vieux
'North-eastern Lunch
with rotting noses and tweed caps,
huddling in thick coats

and mumbling confidential songs
to ancient friends –
the public men of Montreal:

'and in parks
with strange children
who listen to sad lies
in exchange for whistles
carved from wet maple branches;

'in Phillips Square,
on newspaper covered benches,
unaware of Ste Catherine Street
or grey or green pigeons
inquiring between their boots –
public men,
spitting blood in crumpled handkerchiefs,
twisting fingers against brittle years.'

But rising as his star was, there was one aspect to Leonard's poetry which was encouraged by Layton and discouraged by Dudek. What the former valued as a proper earthiness and sensuality, the latter condemned as mere vulgarity. To Leonard, who long had felt the masterful power of passion – when the guests become tyrants – Layton's honesty was as refreshing as his candour was liberating. Dudek, no prude, had already delivered his concern at this, finding the 'adolescent sexuality' an offence against the higher standards of art. In Layton's company Leonard could be himself, recognise his own nature, and celebrate its pleasing to the full. No Talmudic saying was nearer to him than that at the end of the *Kiddushin*: 'When a man faces his Maker, he will have to account for those (God-given) pleasures of life which he failed to enjoy,' and the Mezeritzer Rabbi commented, albeit a little more warily, 'You may reach a compromise between evil and good by enjoying legitimate bodily pleasure and serving God at the same time.' The 'Dionysiac' qualities of life were an essential part of Layton's view; they were so in Leonard's, too. So these beginning years focused on reality – the underbelly of creation as well as its brightness – which was of immense importance to the making of the man and his mind. In them opposing forces sought to violate his commitment: the physical versus the spiritual; the free versus the regimented; the religious versus the secular; and so on. He repeatedly found himself asking the question Who? – and What? – was he? Believer or agnostic? Saint or Sinner? Writer or Businessman? Musician or Poet? His emotions, the Tradition, pulled one way; art and the imaginative impulse, another.

The earlier call of music, now happily developing into 'teenage' forms and addressing their concerns for freedom and individuality, as

well as evoking a certain resentment at the growing post-war materialism, was sweeping many along in its wake. And Leonard's interests in it
were moving from the amateur to the professional. He was to be
frequently found at various 'gigs' with his Buckskin Boys – a square-
dance group of three, of which he was the leader. They played mainly
country tunes, at high-school and church-based venues most weekends.
Terry played bucket-base, Mike played the harmonica, and Leonard
played the rhythm-guitar.

Two of the numbers they played were 'Red River Valley' and
'Turkey In The Straw' (the former finding expression in 1989, when it
was included in the video *Songs From The Life Of Leonard Cohen!*) His
guitar was his companion, its music his soul-mate, not only at such
'professional' expressions as these but everywhere. Rosengarten recalls
an afternoon when Leonard, sitting on the Faculty steps with his guitar,
started to sing. Other students joined in and before long, quite
spontaneously, a crowd of some 200 or so was found to be singing
lustily, with Leonard as the ecstatic, unselfconscious conductor. The
music by which he frequently composed his poetry (a natural continuance of a centuries-old tradition) was asserting itself as an independent expression.

But recent reality had also taken its toll: his father's lamented
death, his guitar teacher's suicide, and that of a cousin; the presence of
his grandfather Klinitsky-Klein, now reduced unhappily to senility in
his mother's house (at which he would surprise Leonard by encounter-
ing him suddenly, in odd moments of clarity, saying, "Oh, yes, you're
the writer, aren't you?") created other pressures. And then his
grandfather died, and Leonard was faced with other traumas: his
mother's remarriage and its unhappy dissolution. Another related to his
canine companion, Tovaritch. (Leonard also kept white rats and mice –
even as late as his thirties, when on the Greek island of Hydra.) The dog,
named before the pact between Stalin and Hitler, as Leonard was wont
to emphasise in certain quarters, was a Scottish terrier of above-average
sentiment and intelligence. It fell ill, unknown to the family, and as it
was mid-winter it crawled under a neighbour's balcony to escape from
the cold, where it expired. Leonard spent hours walking and cycling
around the neighbourhood looking for it. When it was eventually
found it was almost summer, and another sharp lesson on the
ephemerality of life and relationships had been learned. Twenty years
later he could still recall the event: 'I can think about my loyal dog buried
in the snow,' (*Death Of A Lady's Man*).

No one brought up in the Jewish faith with his sort of European
connections could fail to be unaware, or convulsed, by the nightmare
we call the Holocaust. Nightmares and night-time anxiety, are a regular
feature of Leonard's work, though he did remark to us, "I don't think

that I was scarred by anything." For someone whose life has been lived in search of the word, who perceived that 'a scar is what happens when the word is made flesh,' who owned that his education began on hearing of the Holocaust, it is not a convincing comment. It may well be that his nocturnal anxieties began on hearing the nightly ministrations by which his father was nursed – to a young boy, eerie and mysterious, doubtless at times frenetic; no doubt they were exacerbated after his death, as sorrow and loss impinged.

'Night' itself occurs several times in his early books of poetry, as it was bound to do, and its references are of an intimidating sort: 'the night never ending' (in 'Letter'), and 'the clinic of your thighs against the night' (in *Let Us Compare Mythologies*; the latter intimating that other experience of the night which such high thinkers as Bertrand Russell found laden with sexual feelings). In *The Spice-Box Of Earth* he has a particularly pointed reference to it: 'Night, my old night . . . The black, the loss of sun; it will always frighten me . . . always leave me to experiment.'

His songs have an even greater preoccupation with it, no fewer than 52 references to date, in fact. Dreams similarly occupy him, the first occurring in 'Letter' which was quoted above: 'your dreams of crumbling cities and galloping horses . . .' In 'It Swings, Jocko' he says, 'I want my dreams to be of deprivation . . .' (which is, after all, the mother of poetry). He wrote candidly of Breavman in *The Favourite Game* being 'an insomniac with visions of vastness,' by which a more positive element is projected. But by the time *Parasites Of Heaven* was written an intensely negative aspect is unveiled: 'The nightmares do not suddenly develop happy endings, I merely step out of them.'

Whatever we may make of this, it is interesting to observe that Professor Hartman of New York has established a link between those who suffer from this nocturnal disposition and a high level of creativity. (Hartman has shown that the average person has one or less nightmares a year; and only one person in 500 has them on a weekly basis.) Moreover, he assesses such people (in his book *The Nightmare*, 1985) as being 'markedly open and defenceless, not having developed the psychological protection most people have . . . they have thin boundaries (between conscious and unconscious states) and let things through.'

Professor Andrew Greeley extended this by drawing attention to the special sensitivity of the sufferers, by which they are easily hurt, which he found often resulted from an unhappy childhood. For, in addition to any 'genetic inheritance', he noted that such individuals frequently suffered from an interlude in which motherly care was unavailable. It is always dangerous to draw individual implications from social and psychological survey-work such as this, but it does fit:

Leonard's admission of insomnia, of disturbing dreams and night-mares, his high sensitivity, his creative abilities; not least his father's demise and his mother's need to attend to him during his frequent bouts of sickness before it.

The horrors of the Holocaust started to burst around Leonard's ears when he was 11. He actually called it elsewhere 'a central psychic event' in his life. The word itself is derived from two Greek words: *holos* and *kaustos*; the former, 'wholeness', has a tragically ironic edge to it in the light of Leonard's concerns for 'oneness'. Whatever we may make of its influences, Leonard is clear that he 'never recovered' from its *dénouements*; its 'illumination of human behaviour'; its horror (which he termed 'metaphorical'). But he was honest enough to say that he was 'fascinated' by it too; as he was by all forms of physical violence. It raised immense questions of fundamental reality; as was translated (badly!) of Joseph in his experience of suffering: 'the iron entered his soul.' Leonard was not so much brutalised by the experience, as anaesthetised: hence the recollection of only desire throughout his youth.

His poetry tells a different story: there was wide and profound sentience – of man and nature, of beauty and the beast, of times and seasons, of perception and tactility, of hearing and tasting, and smelling; at the bottom of which remains an unresolved questing, a whole gamut of unanswered questions which drove at the very heart of what he most wished to believe. His own faith did not have the answers to this, any more than it had the power to prevent the catastrophe, which exacerbated Leonard's growing disaffection from it, or, should we say, his endless self-questioning of it. He said, "There was a lack of teachers in my own tradition. There were great rabbis in the cities, but I was not part of that. No preparation was given (me) for the religious vision. That was not the emphasis; rather, it was a preparation for Canadian citizenship . . . My grandfather was dividing himself . . ." (The latter, of Lyon Cohen, a signal appraisement which finds similar expression in his uncle's behaviour, as we shall presently see.) Looking around at the suffocating power of the Roman Catholic Church and the less humane churches of Protestantism, he found that he had nowhere else to go; they had no answers for this situation either. He wondered sometimes if they even understood the questions.

Little wonder, then, that Professor Dudek viewed him as "always a troubled young man." He took himself, his name and his calling seriously. But did anyone else? What was it all about, and where did he fit in? There is a passage of great beauty and relevance to this in *The Favourite Game* (pp116), in which Breavman reflects on his family, its prominent position, and its meaning:

'He thought that his tall uncles in the dark clothes were princes of an élite brotherhood. He had thought that the synagogue was their house of purification. He had thought that their businesses were realms of feudal benevolence. But he had grown to understand that none of them could even pretend to these things. They were proud of their financial and communal success. They liked to be first, to be respected, to sit close to the altar, to be called up to lift the scrolls. They weren't pledged to any other idea. They did not believe their blood was consecrated.'

There is an authentic ring about such passages. They reflect the sense of disquietude, of alienation even, that broke into his consciousness, wrenching him from contentment and popularity and success into a feeling of grave unrest; as they have continued to do, exacerbated by his own failures and guilt. Hence the prominence of such words as 'comfort' in his writings; not of their plush armchairs or velvet drapes, but the comfort of a quiet mind and a balanced equilibrium in life. We see the struggle asserting itself in the preface to his poem 'The Glass Dog' (*Flowers For Hitler*):

> '*Let me renew myself*
> *in the midst of all the things of the world*
> *which cannot be connected.*'

He, like his uncles, was a Cohen, with a rank and a calling. But, for all their excellence, he did not like, he could not agree with, what he saw. His self-image and his idealism were being threatened at the anvil of reality. He continued:

'No, his uncles were not grave enough. They were strict, not grave. They did not seem to realise how fragile the ceremony was. They participated in it blindly, as if it would last for ever. They did not seem to realise how important they were; not self-important, but important to the *incantation*, the altar, the ritual. They were ignorant of the craft of devotion. They were merely devoted. They never thought how close the ceremony was to chaos. Their nobility was insecure because it rested on inheritance and not moment-to-moment creation in the face of annihilation. (Our italics, see below.)

He found them wanting. The annihilation had all but occurred in far-off Europe, but that with which he wrestled was of even deeper concern – the cessation of the faith from within. So he continued:

'. . . Breavman knew the whole procedure could revert in a second to desolation. The cantor, the rabbi, the chosen laymen stood before the open Ark, cradling the Torah scrolls, which looked like stiff-necked royal children, and returned them one by one to their golden stall. The beautiful *melody* which soared proclaimed that the Law was a tree of life and a path of peace. Couldn't they see how it had to be nourished? All these men who bowed, who performed the customary motions, they were unaware that other men had written *the sacred tune*, other men had developed the seemingly eternal gestures out of clumsy confusion. *They took for granted what was dying in their hands.*' (Our italics.)

The observer had become a diagnostician; he was fast becoming a prophet. And, true to the tradition of prophets, he rebelled:

'But why should he care? He wasn't Isaiah, and the people claimed nothing. He didn't even like the people or the god of their cult. He had no rights in the matter . . . He didn't want to blame anyone. Why should he feel that they had *bred him* to disappointment? He was *bitter* because he couldn't inherit the glory they unwittingly advertised. He couldn't be part of their brotherhood but he wanted to be among them. *A nostalgia for solidarity. Why was his father's pain involved?*' (Our italics.)

Rebellion was one thing; severance or denial was something else. The responsibility was going to haunt him for years to come. The die had been cast. He had perceived. But to the 'rebellion' (which may have given rise to something far deeper, as we shall see) we must add two further emphases which we have italicised. One, the unforgettable 'incantation', the 'melody' and 'tune' of the services – things which were deeply rooted in his soul, and would reappear with striking force through his music and songs; and two, his distancing himself from its strictly religious aspects. Moreover his stark question, 'Why was his father's pain involved?' raises a very different note. In what ways did he feel it, his father's pain? How did he allow himself to feel it? And how often? 'The mills of God grind exceedingly small . . .' – even if 'the god of their cult' was disliked.

As with so much in Leonard's writing, the passages may be read at different levels. Unquestionably, the loss of his father was felt as a grievous blow for many years after the event. Ironically, Judaism's splendid emphasis on the father-son relationship, the most sacred there is next to that between the Creator and the created, exacerbates this loss; hence Judaism's very humane laws to do with 'the fatherless' – far ahead of its and any other time. So the consideration of his uncles' place in both the community and the synagogue calls to mind the fact that his father, as the first born son, should have had that pre-eminence. Leonard has been doubly cheated: of his father's presence and his rightful position. Hence his 'disappointment', and even his 'bitterness'. (It reached its zenith in *Beautiful Losers* when he referred to 'my factory', his metaphor for Judaism as, 'a pile of rags and labels, a distraction, an insult to my spirit.') For all this he has ever been grateful for his uncles' careful considerations – as his father's executors – of his family, and especially of their kindness towards him personally. Lawrence, in particular, was extremely concerned, and sought to influence his nephew's development advantageously. (It was Lawrence who "blew my cover," he said, on finding that Leonard was failing to attend Law School lectures, which was all the more concerning as he had no scholarship to go there, only his family's financial backing.)

It is this which suggests the secondary level. Was the pain, in fact, actually his father's as well as his own? In other words, was there not a feeling that, first through illness and then through his premature demise, he had been *supplanted* in his rights (through 'natural' causation, we emphasise), much as Jacob supplanted Esau's rights so many centuries ago (through devious schemes). Was Leonard aware, even at such a tender age, of the sense of grief his father had, not only in his life being shortened but with it his usefulness? Or if not then perhaps later as his mother – always self-conscious as to the difference between herself and her more Westernised sisters-in-law gave vent to the feelings of inadequacy they unconsciously inspired? (But we should understand that 'complaint' is part of the Tradition, and should not be interpreted as merely personal affront: it is a valid and recommended part of Jewish expression.) Such evidence that we have suggests that his father was more introspective than his brothers. If that is the case, then it is possible that he also thought that the synagogue ritual, as well as the direction of their commercial life and benefactions should have been handled differently.

Nathan Cohen would have been 'pledged' to another idea; his 'blood' would have been consecrated; he would have been 'grave' – though perhaps not 'strict'; he would better have protected the fragile ceremony; owning the importance of his proper role in it. It would, perforce, have been a 'devoted' service therein rendered; and adequately 'nourished'. Leonard has admitted to a general feeling in the family that Horace was somewhat 'arrogant', this son that now wore the mantle: "My father was the eldest but his health and nature (an interesting, significant addition) prevented him taking over." It was this 'nature' that caused Nathan to act as the factory supervisor – 'a good guy' so far as the workers were concerned; and allowed Horace the seniority, as 'a front-office man.'

But this throws into high relief Leonard's (or at least Breavman's!) denial of spiritual responsibility: if the onus had passed to his uncles, and thereby to his cousins, why should he care? If no one was now 'claiming' anything from him; if he had been marginalised, then 'he had no rights in the matter' any longer. Supplanted, perhaps; cheated (by fate) probably; but now self-absolved from its responsibility, though to bear for ever in his mind the trauma of a calling from which he had somehow been disinherited. It would indeed hound him for ever, and inspire the many references in dialogue to his father which we shall encounter, and his ambiguous sense of direction and self-fulfillment. When the priest cannot function as a priest, is he bound to become a prophet?

his mythological
phase

It is not possible, in a family such as Leonard's, to refuse the subtle (and the not-so-subtle) constraints. The business was in need of new blood, he had a widowed mother to consider, and his lineage through Nathan, Lyon and Lazarus claimed priestly – not to say professional – satisfaction.

Leonard, sensitive to such pressures, was in deep doubt. Such time as he had spent on commercial subjects (in vacations, etc) had produced a profound dislike for them. This was not life! He could not see himself chained to these realities for the next 40 or 50 years. The time spent at his summer jobs – perhaps not least that spent in his uncle Lawrence's brass foundry reinforced this view. Nevertheless, he felt bound to accept the challenge of post-graduate work at Columbia University in New York, albeit with deepening reservations. More-over, Dudek had taken his doctorate at Columbia, and Federico García Lorca had studied there a few years before Leonard was born.

Almost immediately on arrival, surrounded by the cosmopolitan excitement of New York, its immense anonymity, the total lack of personal interest shown towards him after having been the centre of warmth and appreciation in Montreal, he knew that it was not for him. Columbia University's Law School had no charms, no personal comfort (like the surrounding high-rise buildings); there must be another way. Paul Robeson – himself a belatedly famed son of the Law School – might embody law and song, and F.R. Scott might embody law and poetry, but even he recognised the more profound call of the muse: "poetry first," he had said "and the poetic element all the way through," which in the hurly-burly of the clothing industry, was even less possible. And, in any case such dual commitment Leonard could not share, commitment for him had to be the expression of what *drove* him; he was obsessive about his poetry and his life in art.

Having registered, he set about ordering his life as he saw it developing, by giving himself over to the muse, by associating with those whose lives found proper space for literary reflection and endeavour, by getting close to that bohemian existence which he loved and from which all modern art seemed to spring. Most of all, by writing poetry and seeking to enhance his skills at it. The 'Quiet Revolution' which was beginning to take place in Canada was now seizing Leonard himself; he would be a poet-writer, and he would find a place for his music alongside it. And there was much encouragement around him to do so. Layton's ebullience was on a par with Ezra Pound's 'showmanship', and Leonard now found himself not so very far from where the great revolutionary poet (of Imagism, Vortism etc.) was actually incarcerated.

What he was now unable to do, the 'Beat' poets fulfilled, in their own bohemian street-style in New York. Ginsberg's *Howl* actually came out while Leonard was there, doing for the fifties and sixties generation what Eliot's *The Waste Land* did for the twenties and thirties, and not least Ginsberg's 'A Supermarket In California', in which he questioned Lorca's lonely habits; as did Lawrence Ferlinghetti's *Picture Of The Gone World*. Others of a similar ilk were Gregory Corso, Gary Snyder and William Burroughs. Their whole emphasis was against conventionalism – in every form, not least the sexual, the religious and the artistic. It is almost certain that Leonard's interest in Zen Buddhism was sown at this time, and his 'anti-intellectualism' confirmed. It was the start of a serious counter-culture which achieved its *apogee* in the poetry and antics of Bob Dylan, The Beatles, The Rolling Stones *et al*.

Not so quiet was a parallel revolution that was reshaping the music scene, with which Leonard had an ongoing affair. Like any form of art, music has an intrinsic ability to revitalise itself; but when this is stimulated by 'external' factors, for example, those that become operative in the wake of the industrial revolution, the Darwinian ferment and the resurgence of nationalism in the 19th century, not least a species of war-mongering, then wholly new genres may emerge.

Such had happened in Scotland and Ireland in its employment of folk-themes for late 19th century 'classical music'. And in England – in the shape of Cecil Sharp and company – it too began to assert its own folk-music (over Continental, largely Teutonic forms) in the opening decades of the present century. Many of these had found their way across America and Canada with the early settlers, along with psalm versions and hymnody. The wave of interest in the rediscovery of Celtic music is particularly important, and not merely because of the Celtic-Scottish influence on Leonard's family (an aspect that the

Montreal Gazette highlighted regarding Lyon Cohen's Gaelic accent recently) and American eclecticism – often little more than a slavish following of European forms – which found itself in the development of 'pop' music, notably of ragtime around 1900 and jazz around 1918. The ignoramuses who deplored pop music in the fifties failed to understand how these new forms, far from being 'a return to the jungle,' were actually heightening genuine musical development by incorporating their rhythmic vitality and percussive effects into them, as Stravinsky had done. Gershwin and Gruenberg, in *Rhapsody In Blue* and *Daniel Jazz*, were to extend the process still further.

The First World War had caused massive sociological repercussions. In one sense civilisation as we know it had become unhinged. *Angst* took over from utopian ideas of man's upward march, quickly followed by despair on the one hand and pure silliness on the other. The 'twittering twenties' was one of its results, a concentrated version of the 'naughty nineties' papering over the fissures, which were undermining society at its heart – and mind. The influence of its music was greatly enhanced by the technological advances which then took place: first in gramophones; then in public broadcasting systems. The ballad-type songs of the day sung by such as Tony Bennett, Rosemary Clooney, Doris Day, Debbie Reynolds and Frank Sinatra, plus the great classical music she had heard from her youth, facilitated Masha Cohen's overcoming of her personal nightmares, and had become – along with the very important Yiddish music – the natural background to Leonard's life, too.

(Apart from these Yiddish songs, Judaism did not really have any modern music of its own, its practitioners – Mendelssohn, Meyerbeer, Rubinstein, Schonberg, for example – all incorporated the best as they saw it from the past. It was not until Ernest Bloch launched himself on the scene, with *Three Jewish Poems* in 1913 that 'Jewish music' *per se* arrived; even then it was only half-oriental, half-western in style and colouration. But even he, in his rhapsody *America*, in 1926, was not fully committed to its exclusive individuality. It did, however, have the 'incantations' referred to above, which were immensely old, very musical *in their own way*, and a powerful social force – cohesively, and as an instrument of struggle – as the *intifada* have found in modern Israel in our own day.)

During the forties and early fifties these, plus the romantic songs evoked by wartime partings, loss and refindings, found a worthy competitor in the more recent folk-songs of America, which were borne out of economic collapse (on the white hand), and subservience and racialism (on the black). What had hitherto been regional versions of folk and country music now joined with the former 'racist' music of the coloured population, creating through cross-fertilisation modern, i.e. 'pop', music. (An interesting confluence also took place between the development of classical music, which by now had moved away from tonality by vastly enlarging its range, and the coloured musicians' microtonality.)

This livelier music, at hitherto unimagined cheapness, combined with the postwar boom and the natural assertiveness of youth. Indeed, it depended on its buying-power for sustenance, for by 1949 the life of a 'hit' record was about three months, with a market profile of a third under 21-years-old and a further 45 per cent between 21 and 35; leaving only one-fifth of purchasers over 35 (many of whom bought for the younger generation in any case).

Leonard was a very close observer, and collector, of this scene; always keeping his hand in with his guitar, writing much of his early poetry to the sound of its music: the emerging Nashville sound, Muddy Waters, Chuck Berry, Big Joe Turner, The Drifters, The Clovers, Guitar Slim and, most of all, Ray Charles, whose first hit, 'Baby Let Me Hold Your Hand' in 1951, marked the onset of an astonishing career.

These, and many more, were easily accessible, thanks to the jukebox revolution. Even if the observation was not consciously made, Leonard recognised the great similarities which were taking place between music and poetry (and in art and sculpture, too), which went under the name of neo-classicism in the former and modernism in the latter. In them there is an avoidance of subjective emotion, an abhorrence of rhetoric, an emphasis on simplicity, with terseness and economy of expression (the first – subjectivism – not shared by Leonard, of course). And so the months passed quickly, filled with the sights, sounds, smells and tastes – all of them clamorous and variegated and, not least, the girls with which he filled his mind and his hours.

Even as Breavman's lectures in *The Favourite Game* 'didn't count', so the academic exercises dwindled – and faded away. His distaste for such work may be seen from the fact that Breavman refers to the (infrequently visited) lecture rooms of Columbia by saying to Krantz: 'Nothing smells more like a slaughterhouse than a graduate seminar. People sitting around tables in small classrooms, their hands bloody with commas . . .' Leonard stayed like Breavman at the International Student's House, from whose lofty heights he could see across New York 'relieved that it wasn't his city,' in the day wandering all over New York 'to stare and taste at will.' All of it grist to the mill of this young poet-in-the-making.

Said his friend-cum-mentor, Irving Layton, in looking back over the period, "I had a very sharp feeling in the early fifties that poetry in Canada had come in from the cold and was starting to gain momentum." Professor Pacey had epitomised the forties as one of 'vacillation and disillusionment,' but the tide had indeed commenced to turn, a new era was opening up. What was true on the wider front was also true at a personal level: Layton was about to go into his most prolific period of writing, and the whole literary scene was being galvanised into a productivity never before realised in Canada. In the century which Canadians believed belonged to them, poetry had come of age.

Leonard, too, was coming of age – precociously so. Between 1949 and 1954 much of his spare time had been given to poetic scribbling; and he was also giving voice to a measure of vacillation and disillusionment, which we shall encounter in his poetry from time to time. Dudek's 'knighting' him, and Layton and Scott's friendship, had set the seal on his gift; his two prizes (the Macnaughton and the Peterson) had confirmed it. For the former award he had offered his work under the title 'The Sparrows: Thoughts Of A Landsman', which was divided into four parts:

1. A Statement: 'For W(ilf) and his house'
2. A Criticism: 'Ste Catherine Street'
3. A Criticism: 'Lord On Peel Street'
4. An Alternative: 'The Song Of The Hellenist'

Plus 'The Sparrows' that we encountered earlier. He was also publishing some poetry in the 'little magazines', such as 'Had We Nothing To Prove', 'The Fly', 'To Be Mentioned At Funerals', and 'Just The Worst Time'.

Professor Dudek, as we saw, had been in the van of promoting the post-war interests of poetry in a variety of forms and outlets. *Contact*, which he edited with Souster, now closed. So he conceived the excellent idea of producing a new series designed to catch the emerging poets at their earliest publishable point, to be called the 'McGill Poetry Series'. The university authorities liked it, and readily consented to the use of its name. Leonard was a natural choice for the first of the new series, both in bearing and background he represented, not merely McGill, but Canada itself; he was accordingly approached. A man-uscript of poems was assembled by him for the Professor to view; the intention being (and Dudek was very well experienced in this sort of work) for him to take the matter over and see it through to publication. But Leonard had different ideas. He had seen beyond the excitement of being approached for his first book; he already visualised it on the bookshelves!

Following the professor's agreement to the material, Leonard now set his own hand to the matter entirely, learning at 21 the art of negotiation with typesetters, printers, binders and designers. (There had been no plan to illustrate the book, but Leonard talked his friend and fellow-student Freda Guttman into it, and so the book appeared with five designs from her hand). Professor Dudek had envisaged the series coming out in paper covers (the format that was just becoming *the* way to the mass market); Leonard ensured that it went into hard; Dudek had not meant the books to be prestigious in format but vehicles of introduction; Leonard saw to it that his book could stand alongside the best that there were from both sides of the Atlantic. And he himself covered the entire costs (of $300), and did most of the distribution and selling (on the campus, in the local cafés, in bookstores and so on, aided by a mini-advertising campaign in the McGill paper). In fact, within a month it had sold out – a unique feat for such a volume. He had clearly learned a thing or two from his family's entrepreneurship, and was not willing to be confined to any form of anonymity such as overtook some would-be poets.

The book appeared in the Spring of 1956, and was significantly dedicated to the memory of his father: the memory of whose dying he could not assuage:

> *'Bearing gifts of flowers and sweet nuts*
> *the family came to watch the eldest son,*
> *my father; and stood about his bed*
> *while he lay on a blood-sopped pillow,*
> *his heart half-rotted*
> *and his throat dry with regret.*
> *And it seemed so obvious, the smell so present,*
> *quiet so necessary,*
> *but my uncles prophesied wildly,*
> *promising life like frantic oracles;*
> *and they only stopped in the morning,*
> *after he had died*
> *and I had begun to shout.'*

('Rites', *Let Us Compare Mythologies*, pp22)

He could scarcely help himself in choosing this physical format. The dedication was a gesture of pained sorrow at his father's death as much as an act of filial piety, and the natural way to do it was to reproduce the style and character of his essentially Edwardian father. The first copy he inscribed 'To my dearest grandmother, with love and gratitude.' It was not merely a debt repaid, but a duty fulfilled. He had done it with consummate aplomb.

Let Us Compare Mythologies, the title of the book, placed Leonard at the forefront of the young poets of Canada. As well as launching the series, he had launched himself; he had moved from the ranks of a contributor to the little poetry magazines into the mainstream; his apprenticeship days were over.

The title is indicative of a movement generally in Canada away from the 'social environment towards the more permanent world of archetypal forms and myths,' (as Desmond Pacey reviewed it); but it represented much more the interests uppermost in Leonard's own mind: the juxtaposing and conflicting 'mythologies' of his youth in cosmopolitan Montreal. Not that he found them conflicting, still less was he offering a comparative mythology. The word is used by him in a somewhat extenuated sense; not the classical definition of a sacred narrative-cum-worldview of Levi-Strauss and the anthropologists, but the more ordinary sense of metaphor, image or symbol, 'rites' even, and especially 'mythologies within mythology' as Milton Wilson perceived. ('Platonic myth' might be more accurate, if we detach from that phrase the implied narrative element, though some of Leonard's poetry does 'narrate' in a Joycean sense.) This enabled him to bring together the Judaism of his upbringing and the Roman Catholicism and Anglo-Saxon Protestantism in which it was set in Montreal; the former dominating of course.

It also allowed him to include a wide range of 'non-sacred' ideas and images which colour our lives from the cradle to the grave, not least those of loving and sexuality. Understood thus it avoids the questions (and therefore the problems), which Leonard nowhere addresses: such as the historicity, canonicity and the like of the world-faiths – to his mind a species of academic involvement with which he was not interested and of which he was even disdainful.

It is for this reason that Professor Desmond Pacey correctly posits Leonard in his second category of Canadian poets, the socialist-realist group, of which Layton is 'the chief prophet'; not the first, the mythopoetic group of Frye, Reaney and Macpherson. In this sense Leonard's critic, Stephen Scobie, could not be more wrong. Indeed, his treatment of this first book (and we shall see that it is not very dissimilar from the others) is a blatant piece of *eisogesis* – reading into (as opposed to *exegesis*, 'out of') the text what he wishes to see, or rather plant. Taking the word 'mythologies' in its usual 'technical' sense, Scobie comments:

'The opening poem, 'Elegy' (13), announces the main themes with a firmness of tone and richness of texture that reverberate through to the culmination of *Beautiful Losers*. It takes either great pretentiousness or great brilliance (or an outrageous combination of the two) for a young poet to proclaim himself as Orpheus in the first poem of his first book.'

We have no quarrel with his perception of the poem's tone or texture, which is correct, but no such 'proclamation' was made, or intended. Leonard may have acted audaciously in determining his book's format and presentation (as he became wont to do with his later works), but his response to Professor Dudek's invitation was level-headed, indeed humbly – if enthusiastically! – grateful.

No such claim as Scobie posits was made, and grounds for it do not exist empirically. A better case can be made out for its subject being *Salmo salar*: the Atlantic salmon, than for Orpheus! In any case, even within technical, i.e. classical mythology, Orpheus was a singer, not a fish. In one form of the myth he was killed and dismembered, but then his head *floated*. The image, as with the subject itself, is far more ethereal, and meaningful.

(One of America's leading Jungian psychologists, Dr Joseph L. Henderson, in *Man And His Symbols*, edited by Carl Jung, has made the connection – without reference to Leonard's work, to be sure. But while he argues for general connections between the rites, incidentally ignoring the many repudiations of Gnosticism that were made of it by early Christian leaders, his viewpoint is much more balanced than Scobie's.)

Scobie appears to borrow the connection from an article by Sandra Djwa – 'Leonard Cohen: Black Romantic' which first appeared in 1967, where it is more skilfully and roundly argued: 'Cohen's dominant theme (is),' she says, 'the relationship between experience and art, and more specifically the suggestion that the value of experience is to be found in the art of 'beauty' distilled from it . . .' The central point of the book is a reflection of a non-technical 'wider ecumenism', 'a juxtapositioning of mental shapes or ideas through which the poet had learned to look at life, his own and that reflected by others.' Pacey grasps the matter more perceptively when he says, categorically, 'he does not take refuge in the ambiguity of myths, but expresses with engaging candour and simplicity his own personal response to experience.' But Djwa rightly perceives that 'reading through Cohen's work we become aware of an unsatisfied search for an absolute.' The indefinite article may be suggested by the broad 'mythological' framework; he still disliked 'the god of their cult'! It is not justified by viewing his work comprehensively, even to 1967; still less so to 1978 when Scobie wrote. (Another eisogetic blatancy occurs in Scobie's reading into the poem 'Exodus' a reference to the Suez war. *Let Us Compare Mythologies* was published in May 1956; the war took place later that summer!)

Djwa is precise in saying that his 'dominant theme' is 'the relationship between experience and art,' though it avoids the nature of the experience – 'art for art's sake' or art for truth's sake: the reality behind the mythology – whatever it is. The book is prefaced by a quotation from William Faulkner's *The Bear*, in which McCaslin says (in response to uncertainty as to what the poem they were discussing meant), "He had to talk about something." Leonard likewise. He was impelled to say something: it was in his blood, his whole being drove him on. But what? The only thing that 'rang bells' for him was his own consciousness – Djwa's 'experience' – and most of all the inner experiences which had always dominated his vision – his 'inner landscape'. (From which point we must not fail to understand the high importance of crypto-amnesiac inputs, as we shall see).

He commented specifically on this and his use of the Faulkner quotation by saying, "When the writer has some urgency to speak, the subject matter becomes almost irrelevant." Somehow his feelings became detached from the critical procedures (not that he does not handle and assess his own work critically, which he does). He feels something; is inspired by it; his mind takes off; his periods flow – and afterwards he has difficulty in recalling their point of origination, even their exact meaning (like Browning, see below). His experience is transmuted into art.

Understanding 'mythologies' thus, we might paraphrase his title: 'Symbols Of Life', which has the additional benefit of thrusting forward his debt to the 'surrealist' poet Lorca, a natural child of the symbolist movement, whose 'super-realisms' had infatuated Leonard from his teenage years. (The symbolists' position was best declared by Mallarm who, in a famous phrase, said, '*Peindre, non pas la chose, mais l'effet qu'elle produit.*' 'Painting is not what matters, but the effect it produces.' It is this which produces Leonard's startling use of juxtaposition, which goes on to become a disavowal technique.)

Whilst owing his debt to Lorca, it has to be said that this volume is markedly conservative. The language apart, Leonard also seems to have been drawn towards the scandal-provoking propensities of the social catalysts as well as their revolutionary emphases; drawn towards them, at times suggesting some involvement with them, but always as an outsider to their cause; never a fully committed revolutionary himself. It is another pointer to that ambiguity which is so much a characteristic of his life and work, in which the essential orderliness and formal morality of his upbringing clash with his more libertarian – and sometimes libertine – impulses and imagination. He could – and would – visit a revolution, be it political and national, or merely student; he would reflect on it, but he would never get 'involved' in it, be it Cuban, Ethiopian, Greek or Polish. (Priestly élitism undermining the prophetic?)

The book highlights such subjects as animism, Jewish, Christian and Hellenistic 'mythologies'; the realities of health, sickness and death; of nature – its seasons (notably Spring and Winter) and its glories, as well as its decadence (we find no evidence for Djwa's contention that 'the book moves through cycles of winter death followed by spring re-birth,' any more than for her 'structural myth' or 'controlling Orpheus myth' which form the foundation for her critique of the book); of

rationality and madness; loneliness and intimacy; of truth and treachery, prayer and protest; of prophet and priest, doctors and teachers,
angels and devils; freedom and slavery, sainthood and sinning, wonder
and despair, war and peace, love and loss, beauty and brutality; regret
and humour; sensuality and discipline, joy and sadness; of the greatness
of God and his creation, and the pitiful smallness and incompetency of
man; the city and the breadth of nature itself: sea and air, rivers and
countryside; savagery and urbanity; loss and its disappointing pangs.

In a word he offers a cornucopia of man's hopes and experiences,
his successes and his frustrations, set in Canada, but energised by a
trans-historical and global outlook of classical mythology and biblical
settings. (Memphis is the only city which gets a mention outside this
range; appropriately, considering its high profile in the mythology of
music!) It fits perfectly the charm and naïvety of the early to mid-fifties;
it has little to do with the self conscious posturings of the later period
that Scobie wishes to impute to it; most of all that of the 'Beat
generation', for most of the book had been written before *Howl*
howled and *Junkie* commenced the near-universal junketings.

It was this work, along with the subsequent brilliance of his
public performances, that created his reputation as 'Canada's leading
young poet': 'His virtues are his own, and they are considerable . . . at
his best he expresses himself, sometimes whimsically, sometimes
passionately, in speech which is beyond the capacity of mere formula to
produce,' commented Allan Donaldson at the time. 'Mr Cohen knows
how to turn a phrase, his poems at their best have a clean, uncluttered
line, and he writes *about something*,' said Milton Wilson. 'Easily the most
promising,' judged Pacey, in 1961; and George Woodcock added that
Leonard was one 'who could write lines which are no longer good
imitation Yeats; they are lines which only Yeats could have imitated.' 'A
fresh and exciting talent . . . a brilliant beginning,' commented the
anonymous reviewer in the *Queen's Quarterly*.

All of this he offered in a variety of poetic forms, from the
traditional quatrain to the more controversial prose-poem 'Friends'.
Stephen Scobie has called attention to the sheer *excess* with which
Leonard adorns his pages. It is natural that the surrealist should deal in
super-abundance, quite apart from it being a reflection of his youth.
Leonard was but 21 when it was first published, though the poems were
culled from his output from 15 to 20 years of age, according to an
interview he gave to Andrew Tyler of *Disc* in 1972.

It was not, however, the luxuriance of his style or language
which his former mentor, Louis Dudek, focused on in 1958, but 'the
total negation,' 'the high condition.' Professor Dudek, who had begun
to express criticism rather than encouragement for the young poet,
went on to speak of 'an intellectual disorder (not only in politics, but in

morality and religion) which leads to a primitive mythological effort to organise chaos . . . (it) proceeds from a state of mind fundamentally disturbed, and bordering on the deeply neurotic or worse.' Mythological or not, it has to be emphasised that he was speaking here of a group of poets – Ellenborgen, Hine, Mandel, Purdy, Macpherson, Layton and Cohen – not just Leonard himself. But he clearly places Leonard within this group which, he held, 'grasps at a confusion of symbolic images, often a ragbag of classical mythology, in the effort to organise a chaos too large for them to deal with in the light of reason,' which in turn causes them to express 'a sardonic bitterness in their social criticism, a realism without any utopian idealism to support it.' Not only sardonic bitterness, we must add but delicate irony, too. Leonard's mind was such that he always had several ironies in his fire at any one time, even when he was seeking to demythologise some of them!

This, so far as it concerns Leonard, simply goes too far. He was not trying to organise anything! He was speaking from a mind full of ideas and images, which all offered insight in varying ways, which he sought to reflect on over several years. It is placing an artificial, not to say architectonic, view on the whole work so to argue; it is to take his 'mythology' too seriously, too literally; to fail to see that the 'excess' was part of the message. It is unfortunate that the influential Dudek could only illustrate Leonard's work by quoting from the admittedly despondent poem 'Rededication', without a reference to the many other elements of positive delight that the book – and Leonard's work elsewhere at that time – demonstrates.

Regrettably, he makes the same point in his brilliant collection of causeries *In Defence Of Art*, gathered together by his wife Aileen, in 1988, when he links Susan Musgrave's 'inner nightmares' to Leonard's 'early poetry'. It is a pity; for it was commentators of his stature, followed by journalists of no stature, who promoted an excessive negative emphasis on Leonard which was out of balance with his work as a whole. And who, moreover, failed to differentiate between the artist and his art. This is not to say that such comment is wholly wrong; merely to say that it lacks precision, finesse. Leonard could be depressive along with many other poets (the psycho-endocrinological critique of poetry has yet to be written!); he could also be uplifting and assertive; he could, indeed, write 'about something' to use Faulkner's phrase from *The Bear*, and did so to the advantage of large numbers of people who gladly read, and asked for more.

We must remember that this collection was put together in late 1955, when most Jewish thinkers' minds were somewhere between the atrocities of the Holocaust and the fearfully questionable use of the Bomb. Further, Israel was now a reality – 'next year in Jerusalem' for millions had been fulfilled; but the reaction of the Arab world was very hostile – Suez was but months away, and glimmerings of its possibility (and worse) were evident. Moreover, the Cold War was not thawing; Eisenhower was firm, if complacent; Khruschev was, well, Khrushchevian; stamping round the world belligerently, rattling his bombs and adding reality to the nascent CND warnings. Young people were afraid, wondering if they would have time to have their children, and became agitated at the racheting-up of international tensions in East and West. They were not sure that they would see 30; millions had not, scarcely a decade ago.

Little wonder there was 'intellectual disorder' – if that is the correct word for daily thought stymied by explicit threats of destruction; 'a state of mind fundamentally disturbed' – if they are the *mots justes* for those who doubt whether they will be able to put their professional training into practice; 'bordering on the neurotic' – if that is an accurate description for lives lived under the fear of total extinction in the mushroom cloud. Many did so think, and fear; and saw nothing in the religious experience – or that to which it pointed – of the last decade and a half to cause them to think otherwise. The days were truly apocalyptic; sadly, many of the commentators and reviewers, the would-be art leaders, were merely apoplectic; not least in fastening on to his overt sexuality, their criticisms of him shielding their own neuroses.

The rabbis had a saying: 'Where there is too much, there is something missing.' The excess to which some have pointed may well disclose the absence of something crucial, but for that we must defer judgment. In the meantime we may note that, right or wrong, balanced or not, Leonard spoke from the heart – as did the prophets of old; the sell-out qualities of the book demonstrated the need, as well as his astuteness in compiling his selection. He was proving himself to be not only an accurate witness to the times, but a respected one, too.

There was one particular aspect to which all commentators drew their readers' attention: his sensuality, referred to above. For those raised in the prudery of puritanism or the celibacy-conscious preoccupations of Catholicism this ran against the grain. They could not see how one so patently spiritual in his emphases, so biblical in his references (to both 'Old' and 'New' Testaments), could be so frank about his appreciation of female beauty and his corporeal appetites. But this is part of the witness he bears; *celebrating* love and sex and intimacy. He speaks characteristically of his 'greed' as well as his need; of his 'longing' as well as his belonging (the latter more often by default – itself a mechanism of his alienation); of passion as well as affection; of fleshly appetites as well as the spiritual.

He was only too well aware of the Talmudic dictum that a handful does not satisfy a lion, but he was neither apologetic nor guilty over it. He prized too highly the Judaic emphasis of the wholeness of man's nature – oneness – his enjoyment of the gift of sexuality; and he criticised – at least *e silencio* – the false views that dichotomised and castrated man. We should not forget that it was not that long since Samuel Butler had published (in 1878) his famous poem 'A Psalm Of Montreal' which was evoked by finding that Canadian 'philistinism' had removed a Greek statue of Discobolus to a side-room in the Natural History Museum, presently used by a taxidermist, because of its 'vulgarity'. On being asked what constituted such vulgarity, it was explained that it was because it had 'neither vest nor pants to cover his lower limbs!' Lazarus Cohen would have laughed at that; Butler simply vented his spleen 'psalmically', whose chorus was, starkly, 'O God! O Montreal!' What the young Queen Victoria had to say about this, from her youthful posture on Sherbrooke Street, we shall never know. Such prudery was simply offensive foolishness; an attack on God's gifts and creation, against which Leonard set himself solidly. He was to be, as he called himself later, 'the poet of the two great intimacies': together, in balance, and genuinely.

'poet of the two
great intimacies'

The success of *Let Us Compare Mythologies* confirmed Leonard in his decision to be a poet-writer, even if it did not relieve Masha of her concern for his future well being. *Six Montreal Poets*, a short film made by CBC – which gained considerable American exposure through Folkways Records – re-emphasised that decision. (The other participants were A.J. Smith, L. Dudek, I. Layton, F.R. Scott and A.M. Klein, whose ages ranged from 40 to 60; Leonard was just 23.) In this film Leonard recorded eight poems from his recent book ('For Wilf And His House', 'Beside The Shepherd', 'Poem', 'Lovers', 'The Sparrows', 'Warning', 'Les Vieux' and 'Elegy'); the sleeve was careful to emphasise that he also wrote songs for a local group called The Stormy Clovers, by no means his first such work. And he was now frequently called to other public performances; his first 'professional' poetry recital was at Dunn's Jazz Parlour in Montreal, where he recited 'Gift' to piano accompaniment, in honour of the ancient traditions of poetry.

Another event took place at Birdland, a jazz-club in the centre of Montreal, where Leonard gave poetry readings after midnight, frequently to the accompaniment of his own guitar on which he improvised appropriate backings, though often in company with more experienced jazz musicians. His early involvement in this so-called jazz-poetry – which achieved such popularity in the sixties – shows that Leonard, not for the first time, and certainly not the last, was 'where it was all happening' before it actually happened. Similarly, he performed at various locations in the States, reading his poetry to the accompaniment of Maury Kay, a well known jazz musician of the time.

But poetry and music were not the only things that he wrote at this time. His prose-poetry had tumbled into full prose, and he was now engaged on his first novel, under the title of *Beauty At Close Quarters*.

Sadly, for it was a lively, largely autobiographical piece, it would never see the light of day. It went through several mutations, but he failed to convince his publisher of its commercial viability. He was also keeping notebooks Coleridge-like and in the time-honoured fashion these fed his later work, notably his novels and *Death Of A Lady's Man* in particular. Poetry still continued to claim much of his time, and several pieces were penned or started such as 'Snow Is Falling', written to the music of Ray Charles, Edith Piaf and Nina Simone, among others.

His domestic arrangements were somewhat bitter-sweet. He needed solitude to write, as well as a place of his own for entertaining his girlfriends, which he found on Mountain Street. But his mother was concerned, and lonely. Concerned as to whether he was adequately looking after himself, but especially concerned as to his future as a writer. She was only too well aware of the fragility of the undertaking, and had little confidence in his making it. She exhorted him to 'follow your little heart'; it was much more difficult for her to do so, and it showed.

He still saw Irving Layton, and they decided to put their hands to playwriting; which reinforced his mother's concern! (It will be remembered that he had studied drama at McGill, and the plays of Britain's 'angry young men' had made waves in Canada.) They settled on a series of four or five plays which are notable for anticipating subjects destined to become central issues in the sixties: student revolt, the hippie movement, violence and so on. A recollection of their work was given by Layton in an interview for the *Canadian Theatre Revue* in 1977, in the wake of *A Man Was Killed*, the first play to be written by them, but tardily presented.

Layton used to go to Leonard's flat each morning where they would work for three hours or so, though sometimes letting the work run on through the afternoons. They spurred each other on, allowing the action and the words to flow naturally. As Layton said, "He'd get off some line, and then I would take the part of a character and so on. We found ourselves working very beautifully together, and we finished this play . . . We had a good deal of fun doing it." Leonard recalled his own practice of that time, an 'instinctive' use of 'primitive meditation': "I sat with my hands on my lap, like a cataleptic . . . like Ezekiel! My head was bowed down. I was just a kid looking for the 'juice'."

Their optimism was confounded by CBC's impervious disinterest. And they got the usual terse rejection-slip to that effect. It has to be said that the plays are somewhat thin in material, and the characterisation weak, but they were both offended by the offhand refusal and the Corporation's unwillingness to offer even the slightest guidance for the betterment of the projects. It was not all going to be wine and roses;

and Leonard again felt the sharp problem of the Canadian writer at that time – having a small home market, not wishing to become artistically part of the '53rd State' of America, and yet having nowhere else to go. As Layton said, "I still regret that we got no encouragement from the CBC, because I think that we would have gone on to write plays."

So it was that they went on to do other things, but separately; a 'beautiful' working relationship was thereby broken up, and two highly creative thinkers had their play-writing ambitions stillborn. (This was not, in fact, the end of Leonard's ambitions in that regard. In *Flowers For Hitler*, pp 110ff, he published his 'The New Step': a ballet-drama in one act; and an involvement in film-making would help to sublimate it, as we shall see.)

Leonard did, however, manage to get a grant from the Canadian Arts Council. Having found both America and Canada limiting – for different reasons – he took the only other course open to him, he went east: to Europe which then meant London. Now London in the late fifties was very different from that of the 'seething sixties'. Harold MacMillan, Prime Minister, might still be saying to the electorate that they had never had it so good – which was true in terms of the change-round from post-war reconstruction, wartime destruction, and the days of depression; but to someone of Leonard's background, from Canada, the place was a bore. The scenery was grim, the food was unappetising, fashion was all but non-existent (he did buy a Burberry raincoat – his 'famous blue raincoat' – which he adorned till someone relieved him of it in New York 20 years later), the arts were struggling, almost moribund, despite the explosive qualities of Kingsley Amis, John Osborne, Colin Wilson, and Alan Sillitoe; and the weather was atrocious.

His friend Morton, who had recently been studying art and sculpture in London, mentioned his parents' old friends, the Pullmans, who had a place in Hampstead. To this Leonard went, and there he stayed for several months, playing his part in the Pullman household under the terse agreement: 'If you stay, you'll pull your weight, like the rest of us'; ensconced in a lively family atmosphere for the first time in years. Apart from organising his domestic life, Stella Pullman was a disciplinarian in the old British landlady tradition (her husband was a former RAF pilot who now flew for BOAC). She organised his professional life: she demanded to know his daily quota of work (three pages a day) and ensured he kept to it – on pain of leaving should he fail! That sort of failure does not belong to Leonard Cohen, he is by nature an industrious and self-conscious worker, if restless; and so he stayed. He got plenty of work done there; he made friends; he felt liberated and enjoyed himself. He even found English girls desirable, a girl called Elizabeth in particular. But he could not come to terms with the climate.

It lacked 'comfort' and that spiritual stimulation he needed for his work.

On one of his afternoon strolls (mornings were for work, once he had completed his domestic chores laid down by Stella), he chanced on Bank Street, in the East End. His attention was caught by the National Bank of Greece – not an inappropriate interest for one who had composed 'The Song Of The Hellenist', and was drawn to Judaism's most persistent 'enemy' through it. He went in to speak to one of the tellers. Struck by the young man's suntan, he asked where he had acquired it, and when. It settled his mind. To Greece he must go! And without more ado he booked his one-way ticket. A new and dramatic phase was opening up. Another factor was undoubtedly Layton's own involvement with Greece, which went back to 1951, about which he had written many poems. By 1974 he was able to publish his *75 Greek Poems: 1951-1974*.

It was the capital of Greece, Athens, that first captivated his mind; a very different place from the Decapolis of which he had written in 'The Song Of The Hellenist', and light years away from the London from which he had fled. Here was the Acropolis, which had dominated the city since the second millennium BC, and older than Judaic Jerusalem (King David's city) by 500 years; the Agora, the civic centre, formerly situated between the Acropolis and the main gate to the city; both being crowned by the remains of the Parthenon, that geometric and architectural treasure widely copied – from Birmingham, England, to Nashville, Tennessee.

Here the streets were alive with the chatter of tongues from all over Europe and the Middle East – the central meeting place of cultures, philosophies and religions, in which many found their roots. This was a city to get lost in, to come alive in, a city of immense contrasts, warmth and vitality. 'Athens, my chiefest joy,' he had written several years before he got there in vivid anticipation; now he experienced its individual dynamic. There was very little of his own faith to be seen in the city, even if he had wished to become involved. By this time the Jewish community in Greece had dwindled to something like 6,000 (from the 11,000 which remained after the Nazi occupation; 75,000 having been liquidated). His mind was elsewhere, exploring, recording, storing up scenes and experiences that would serve his work, even as the travel served his restless needs.

But it was the Greek islands on which his attention was finally fastened, notably Hydra (Ydra) in the Saronic Gulf, which had had an artistic community on it for some years. (Missolonghi, on the mainland opposite, had been Lord Byron's *pied-à-terre*, where he died in 1824, with whom Leonard shared much, romantically and in the fuller Romantic sense.) Here, on a small island of some 2,000 or so souls, pocketed by the encircling hills around its charming port, was the ideal place for him to gather his thoughts and address himself more seriously than he had been able to do in busy Montreal, grim London or frenetic New York.

It was a place of solitude, of plodding donkeys (even today no cars are allowed on the island; nor would they get very far if they were); cold water and kerosene lamps. In such primitive surroundings, amid the stunning beauties of the island and the glories of the Aegean, where fishermen still wrested a living from the sea and farmers scrabbled one from the land, Leonard found his peace; his "sitting-down time," as he called it, where he could – as all poets must – recollect in tranquillity. Here he could live in virtually complete seclusion, at a fraction of the cost it would take in northern Europe or Canada; where the people were unconcerned as to who you were or what you did; and where breathtaking vistas opened up for the seeing – both external and internal.

Here Leonard discovered the Greek way of life – its alternating rhythms of work and leisure, both on the seasonal and the daily basis, which are so conducive to creative thought and achievement. Here he was able to stand back from the onrush of western man and ask himself the real questions of life and meaning; get his young life, full and successful as it had been, into perspective. Here he began to crystallise the wisdom of some of his best poetry, writing and songs; for it was here that he was reborn, where he truly began to find himself; where, not least, the music of Greece entered his soul, evoking earlier memories and melodies, combining with them to suggest a new style, a new mystique. ("Filled with wonder at the sound of the bazouki," as Jacques Vassal commented; also emphasising Leonard's appreciation of Theodorakis's then emerging art.) Perhaps the words of his 'Old Dialogue' (*Flowers For Hitler*, p128) come from this time, over-shadowed as they are with other meanings and claims:

> '*Has this new life deepened your perceptions?*
> *I suppose so.*
> *Then you are being trained correctly.*
> *For what?*
> *If you knew we could not train you.*'

And it was here that he met Marianne, a young woman of great beauty, high intelligence, deep sympathy, and fun. The gods had drawn them together, and together for 10 years or so they would make music, exploring the world and themselves, unharried by outside pressures, responding only to the more meaningful pressures of life and love. Leonard had tried to get Elizabeth, his London girlfriend, to take the bold step of departure to Greece, but she had refused. (She had not liked his 'famous blue raincoat' either!) On arriving he missed that female intimacy which had been so important a part of his life for many years. He knew that 'it was not good for man to dwell alone'; and he sharply felt his loneliness. He admired, and we may guess coveted, the warmth of relationships he saw around him.

One in particular caught his attention: a blonde couple by the name of Jensen, Norwegians, who had sailed to the island on their 16-foot boat along with their young son, Axel. Like Leonard, they were given to the literary life. Leonard was actually looking in a shop window when he first saw them, noticing Marianne – naturally – first! She took his breath away, as she did most men's. He never realised, on that eventful day, that she would "come into my arms" (as he put it) and stay there for so many years, adding in no small degree to the legends of love which keep the world sane and hopeful.

There was serious work, however, at hand for Leonard. His writing, prose and poetry demanded rigorous attention, and received it with the same daily routine that he had established earlier: three pages a day, writing and rewriting, creative and self-critical. Moreover, he had added to his possessions a piece of luggage of inestimable value for now – and for the next 30 or so years: his Olivetti 22 portable typewriter, which he had bought in London for £40, no small investment for those days. There were also the calls from home with which, throughout this period and always, he was to keep in close contact.

He had built, or at least started to build, a public (in the Kierkegaardian sense: 'a gigantic something, an abstract and deserted void which is everything and nothing') and he was determined to stay true to it; recognising that publicity is the lifeblood of an author. As ever, his world was split into two contradictory rhythms: solitude and company, his own tough self-criticism and the adulation of those around him: ambiguities converging, and testing.

In November 1959 he found himself back in Montreal, 'to renew his neurotic affiliations' as he was to repeat endlessly to journalists; meeting his friends and family, sometimes bumping into his uncles who would take him for expensive meals at top restaurants – such as the Ritz – and hotels; and generally awakening and reawakening those impulses and memories which would fire his imagination and energise his mind for months to come.

He was due to join up with his old friend Irving Layton again, and former professor F.R. Scott at New York's prestigious YM/YWCA centre on 92nd Street. Here they gave poetry readings in the 800-seat auditorium; a measure of the man he was becoming and of the distinguished company he kept. It was serious stuff, this poetry, Leonard's now suntanned complexion adding to the prophetic tones as he came, Elijah-like, out of his own wilderness experience. (Scobie correctly urges this background in prefacing his comments on Leonard's work, but fails to mention, alongside Canada's vastness, the particular Jewish motif by which all prophets found their calling; similarly he omits reference to Leonard's own 'wilderness experience' on Hydra.) Distanced from the day-to-day world of his youthful and not-so-youthful listeners, he could speak with all the more understanding, all the more authority, to their needs. He was already on the way to establishing his role as a leading spokesman for the 'sixties generation' – a generation that was forced to handle change as never before, as Bernard Levin commented, in *The Pendulum Years*:

'Fashions changed and changed again, changed faster and still faster: fashion in politics, in political style, in causes, music, in pop-culture, in myth, in education, in beauty, in heroes and idols, in attitudes, in responses, in work, in love and friendships, in food, in newspapers, in entertainment . . . What had once lasted a generation now lasted a year, what had lasted a year now lasted a month, a week, a day. There was a restlessness in the time that communicated itself everywhere and to everyone, that communicated itself to the very sounds in Britain's air, the stones beneath Britain's feet.'

And not just in Britain either, though it was now setting the pace – or at least contributing its own in all these fields. Though not in poetry, whose influence now chiefly came from America and Canada.

At such meetings he kept himself in touch with the constantly changing scene of poetry, the new faces which appeared, the old names which disappeared. And it was fast changing. Between 1959 and 1969 poetry production was to triple, thanks to the industrious imagination of such as Phyllis Webb, Eli Mandel, Daryl Hine and not least that battery-hen of poets, Irving Layton, to name but a few. Comparisons were now being made between it and that of Britain and the USA in the thirties, when names such as T.S. Eliot, W.H. Auden, Ezra Pound, Stephen Spender, Louis MacNeice, Barker, Karl Shapiro and Randal Jarrell were exerting a telling influence. Moreover, Canada itself was changing – in the great building programmes in and around Montreal (not least at McGill itself, one of whose schemes resulted in the superb McLennan Library) and, more ominously, in the growth of separatism that was about to rock, in Pierre Trudeau's words, "the smug complacency" of English-Canada, the Canada of the WASPS ('White, Anglo-Saxon and Protestant') and of the Roman Catholic Church, a party to the 'Quiet Revolution'.

Leonard was keen to assert his own lead in that movement, for it was during this time that he was compiling his second book (five years after the first) *The Spice-Box Of Earth*, which was published in 1961 to great critical acclaim. If *Let Us Compare Mythologies* is a young man's book, this is one (though still of a young man, at 26) that offers poetic maturity, whose lyrics are charged with that mellow wistfulness, that trembling of *angst*, that vibration of incipient guilt and the plunging sensuality of a knowing, searching man; a book whose range – for all that – is narrower than *Let Us Compare Mythologies*. As Professor Pacey then judged him, "easily the most promising in this group of young poets."

The spice-box itself is one of the most suggestive symbols in Judaism; one which forcefully elucidates the Sabbath festivities, or at least their completion. Whatever we may make of Leonard's Judaism, he is a man seized by its traditions, its scriptures and their imagery. His mind is replete with it, and no real understanding of it, as expressed in poetry or song, should omit it. In the simple Sabbath ceremonies, much of Judaism's genius finds expressive recollection. It is a wonderful experience to sit with him in the quiet peacefulness of his home, the table cleared (in addition to having had the house duly cleaned by his 'daily') to make room for the Sabbath candles, its bread and wine. Most of all to listen to that deep reflective voice reciting the blessings, in Hebrew; a service which touches the very soul of the traditions, as well as the souls of those who are privileged to share them with him. 'The Sabbath is made for man,' and with its unpretentious yet pregnant ceremony a special grace overcomes those present.

The incense-burner of old Israel, the *besamin*, is no longer; the violent fury of man against the Chosen People has done its work and eliminated many of the ceremonies and practices. Replacing them at a familial level, the spice-box has taken its place, sometimes simple, sometimes ornate; a witness to the fragrance of that Sabbath grace that lingers still. Whether Leonard shares the old belief that the spice-box also honours Adam, who was supposed to have been bestowed with a 'higher soul' on the Sabbath, we cannot say. But it is certain that he, like the Jews of old, knows that, 'we are the Adam of our souls'; each has its own opportunities, each its own triumphs, failures and guilts. He bears witness to this, and to the whole man (as ever), with particular distinction in this new book. Scobie is surely right when, with regard to *Let Us Compare Mythologies* he says that the title 'seems to indicate that Cohen himself regarded the religious sense as the primary one' – which in *The Spice-Box Of Earth* becomes completely explicit and even urgent.

The ceremony of the *havdalah*, the bidding adieu to the Sabbath, centres on the spice-box and the candle. The blessing itself is made over a cup of wine in honour of the day ('Blessed art Thou, O Lord our God, King of the universe, who createst divers kinds of spices') which adds to the light of the Sabbath, symbolised by the candle, offering a fragrance and a beauty all its own. Leonard extends this sense here in this book – to those who will read and ponder. The book was offered with a sharp recollection of his own family, not only regarding his father's absence of many years (whose duty it was, formally, to say the prayer), but in the dedication of the book, another link with the past broken, another mainstay, albeit distant, removed: 'This book is dedicated to the memory of my grandmother Mrs Lyon Cohen, and to the memory of my grandfather Rabbi Solomon Klinitsky.' The familial links are not wanting in the poetry either. Beautiful is the one titled 'Priests 1957' (in honour of the family name, as well as its traditions and responsibilities; *The Spice-Box Of Earth*, p78):

> *'Beside the brassworks my uncle grows sad,*
> *discharging men to meet the various crises.*
> *He is disturbed by greatness*
> *and may write a book.*
>
> *'My father died among old sewing machines,*
> *echo of bridges and water in his hand.*
> *I have his leather books now*
> *and startle at each uncut page.*
>
> *'Cousins in the factory are unhappy.*
> *Adjustment is difficult, they are told.*
> *One is consoled with a new Pontiac,*
> *one escapes with Bach and the folk-singers.*
> *Must we find all work prosaic*
> *because our grandfather built an early synagogue?'*

His tone is one of sadness, of a great day now passed, of his uncles' and cousins' deep sense of loss – which he shared – of the death of his father (again), and of the disenchantment with their present, pedestrian lives in the light of the splendid triumphs of the past. (The reference to one escaping with 'Bach and the folk-singers' is to himself.) It haunted, it *tyrannised* their lives, not least his own. As he said (through the journal of his grandfather) 'I will never be free from this old tyranny: I believe with a perfect faith . . .' (which is how the statement of faith called the 13 creeds begins). But we should also note (as the critics largely did not) the positive values he inculcates in such reflections, with which he concludes his piece: 'Must we find all work prosaic . . .?' It is typical of him to assert, as Judaism does roundly, that all work is honourable; and deny that the reliance on special work and destiny ('God's work') elevates a man *per se*. Not so! asserts our poet – there is *no* difference between the sacred and the secular, prayer or work (which have the same root in Hebrew); 'oneness' will out!

If *Let Us Compare Mythologies* marks the awakening of his poetic consciousness when the city of Montreal (and all that was in it, not excluding its female charms) 'began to jump at me,' *The Spice-Box Of Earth* marks the heightening of his Jewish consciousness which he encountered in young adulthood, as a free agent abroad in the world, having to establish his own identity at a time when his own Tradition, and his position in it, began likewise to jump at him. Noteworthy is a second dedication in this regard, of a single poem to Marc Chagall (also a Russian Jew of hasidic extraction) whose rich symbolism entranced Leonard. (Nearly 30 years after writing it Leonard was enthusiastically recommending our attendance at a Chagall exposition on Sherbrooke Street.) Aniela Jaff has spoken of 'the mysterious and lonely poetry,' which she finds in Chagall's art, a 'ghostly aspect of things that only rare individuals may see,' which very much encapsulates Leonard's work, too. Commented Chagall himself, 'Everything may change in our demoralised world except the heart, man's love, and his striving to know the divine. Painting, like all poetry, has its part in the divine . . .'

Leonard's poem, 'Out Of The Land Of Heaven' majestically captures that noble spirit, as it does the depth and beauty of human love and the song to which it gives birth. It was a consciousness of joy and pain, of celebration and concern, of thinking and feeling, of hope and despair. Through it all the words dance like butterflies and dart like wasps.

Sandra Djwa argues that 'its lost ideals' are reworked as a Neo-Hasidic myth, and comments that 'the poet as priest is forced beyond Genesis' (sic); elsewhere she adds a description of Leonard as 'the exiled poet priest of *The Spice-Box Of Earth.*' Commented Al Purdy, 'with (this book) Cohen brought to near perfection the techniques and rhythms of his first book'; Eli Mandel – one of Canada's most astute critics – speaks of it as 'a kind of gloss' to the Sabbath service, noting its rich diversity in subject and tone, and emphasising that it is 'not a random collection of lyrics. It is unified, powerfully, by recurrent patterns and an informing theme.' But he is wrong to say that it is a gloss – especially as a rabbinic *scholium*! – on the Sabbath service only, and to hang (as he does) all his review from it. Leonard makes his own point powerfully enough by placing that very reflective ode to freedom, 'A Kite Is A Victim', first in the collection. That is the emphatic point; the tone of the book, its whole direction, is thereby established. Mandel is right about its being 'unified powerfully', but the principle of unity centres on 'freedom', not the Sabbath ceremonies (intrinsic, as they are, to Leonard's conception of freedom); which merely *protects* (when allowed to do so) that freedom.

The kite is the representative image of freedom, of which Scobie commented, 'it is one of Cohen's most successful and most richly complex images'; which Ondaatje highlights as 'symbolic of our ego and our ambition, of all that is original and free in us.' To a child of the thirties and forties there was no better symbol. The kite is 'a contract of glory', a signing between heaven and earth, which *needs* both parties for its sustaining. Though *apparently* free, it needs its controller; but the controller must release it to the natural powers, the wind and the air-thermals, if he wants to enjoy its flights. It is a picture of interdependency, not mere independence; it is a freedom of restraint, not unconstrained licence. As T.S. Eliot remarked in another regard, 'No association is free for the man who wants to do a good job,' for the 'religious' man not least, and for a Cohen most of all. The second poem, 'After The Sabbath Prayers' is placed second in deference to this, directing and interpreting the symbolism of the kite.

Wholly in the spirit of that imagery is his vision of the Baal Shem's butterfly – so much like a kite! – which followed him down the hill. A more powerful figure it would not be possible to evoke from one of Leonard's background, for it captures a significance which the kite could not: that man is only one of many free creatures, subject with them all to a higher power and influence. The name 'Baal Shem' means 'Lord (or Master) of (God's) Name'. Though applied to others of a given authority or holiness, it refers principally to one of the most influential personages in Ashkenazi (eastern European) Judaism, who followed the Palestinian traditions (as opposed to the Babylonian ones represented in its version of the Talmud): Israel ben Eliezer (Leonard's spiritual forebear, after whom he was named) – an 18th century Pole, the founder of the Hasidic movement; one whose religious awareness was very close to that which inspired Leonard, his mother and his grandfather Klinitsky-Klein.

(This represents another divergence between Masha Cohen and her sisters-in-law. They, as became self-conscious representatives of the Cohen tradition – austere, genteel, 'polished' – were not taken to the spontaneous expressions of liveliness which Masha's Judaism exhibited. Indeed, they could be offended by it. Masha merely felt put down by the *hauteur* she felt, even if not intended.)

And we may see another reason for the ambiguity in Leonard: Ashkenazi Jews expressed themselves in Yiddish, which was not merely their language (resting on 16th-century Middle High German and many Slavic loan-words) but in a particular sense a reflection of their world, their universe. Sephardic Jews, who are descended from Western Europe (Spain and Portugal; but also the Middle East and North Africa), expressed themselves through their own languages, but were always more 'intellectual', more philosophical – in the Aristotelian sense – more scientific and commercial, and more open to syncretism (e.g. with Islamic and Christian modes of thought) than their Eastern brethren. But it was that cultural *milieu*, as expressed through the left-wing Federico García Lorca, that Leonard reacted to and espoused in his youth! In it collided two incompatible forces, mental and emotional, alienating him from his own tradition – to which he was deeply fettered.

The BeSHT – ben Eliezer is known by that acronym – produced a shock-wave of such proportions in Judaism that it has still not recovered from him. It is said that his influence came through his extraordinary power, both learned and 'uncanny', to rearrange suggestively the letters of the divine Name (the Tetragrammaton: YHWH), which are so sacrosanct that they are considered to be unpronounceable. 'The Name' has been the Holy of Holies to all Jews since it was given to Moses as a special revelation of the divine essence; all other holinesses merely subserve it. We find allusive reference to it from time to time in Leonard's writings and songs – always with a *frisson* of awe. Ben Eliezer was able to channel some of that power, by which Jewry worldwide was hugely influenced. He was by profession a *melamed*, a Hebrew school-teacher, not even of rabbinic standing. But so seized was he by the divine knowledge, so 'evangelistically' fixed with its potency, that his exploits on its behalf quickly created his legend. In essence his message was very simple, as the products of such geniuses tend to be. It was, 'Love God, love the Law, love mankind.' It gave rise not only to a new religious movement of tremendous vitality, but also to tales of miracles and wonders.

Moreover, he was a warm-blooded man, who respected and enjoyed his humanity, and sought to encourage his followers to do so too. Judaism, as we have seen, has always emphasised the wholeness of man's nature and sought to sustain it. The BeSHT did more; he promoted it to a higher level of importance; he confirmed and extended the principle of enjoyment, bringing it much more centrally in to the people's worship as a sense of divine gladness. With his teachings and observances they could sing and dance, laugh and exult before God – as David did of old, as other psalmists did, as Miriam the prophetess and Moses himself did in his own Victory Song over the Egyptians. The everyday things of life were the greatest gifts to ben Eliezer; even as the human heart was the most appropriate place of worship.

Two Hasidic sayings exemplify this particularly: 'The best synagogue is the human heart,' and 'The heart is half prophet.' Jonathan Eibeschutz, a Polish authority on the Cabala, similarly commented when he said, 'Man's heart is the holy of holies.' It adds significantly to Masha Cohen's constant advice to her son throughout his life: 'follow your little heart.' Prayer itself therefore had to be personal, spontaneous and joyous. The felicity of God was not a piece of theological reasoning, but an essential part – a large and essential part – of God's being and the world's essence. So *The Spice-Box Of Earth* teems with this joyous response; it fills one's nostrils with its fragrance; it delights one's palate with its savouriness. Even as the BeSHT delighted his listeners with his pearls of wisdom, his stunning turns-of-phrase, his aphoristic acuity, so Leonard was learning his own, parallel metier; the butterfly was following him down the hill.

The negative side of all this was ben Eliezer's polemics against straight-faced, over-serious rabbinism; against those whose understanding of God's nature was austere and unfatherly; those who, while seeking to elevate the Most High, merely put him out of touch with his own children; debarred them from his welcoming presence by a system of learning that became 'frivolous' in its intensity: not that its perpetrators could be frivolous: black was their colour, even as severity was their posture – as becomes the frozen-in-soul. For such, God only frowns on the world, and stirs it to judgment; the butterfly cannot break loose into flight; it merely expires, as Leonard expressed it, ending 'its life in three flag-swept days.' 'It was hard for Satan alone to mislead the whole world,' declared the grandson of the BeSHT, Nachman of Bratislava, in one of his more caustic diatribes, 'so he appointed rabbis in different locations.' And not only rabbis, one might add, but priests and nuns, monks, ministers and bishops! The BeSHT became so influential that the leaders of the people, the power-manipulators and self-appointed guardians of the Law, had no alternative but to do what their like has always done to those who broke loose, butterfly-like: They excommunicated him; marginalised his usefulness; neutered his religious potency: 'A prophet is not without honour . . .'

Now one of the interesting cameos of God's providence, prominently found in the Talmud and among the Hasidim, is the idea that in every generation are 36 *tsadikim*, pious or righteous men, who (though unknown) keep the world going. The Hasidim idealised them, regarded them as intermediaries between God and his world. They are the Saints (the *Lamed-vov tsadikim*, the 36 saints) who perpetuate the principles of compassion and kindness which sustain life. This pity, compassion or mercy, is quintessentially Jewishhasidic; to such God is essentially the God of Mercy and Compassion. As against that central epithet of the rabbis, the justice of God, they posited the creative, life-giving and life-nurturing aspect of *mercy*.

Sainthood and mercy are entities of the most considerable sort in Leonard Cohen's work, as we shall see. Stephen Scobie, in emphasising the motif of sainthood in Leonard's writing, completely omits reference to this key Jewish emphasis, which would have prevented him from some of his more questionable comments, such as the reference to them as 'social outcasts'. Whether that is so in other societies, which is highly questionable, is irrelevant. Their rejection did not make of them 'social outcasts' (save to the unseeing) but raised their mark intensely: they were closest to God. In Judaism they were *venerated* – which is the position they obtain in Leonard's writing.

It is difficult to comprehend to what extent Leonard felt the sense of this over-arching, life-elevating principle. But it is very clear that it is present, though at times its influence waxed and waned. It is surely part of the ambiguity of his person, as well as of his work, whether 'priestly' or 'prophetic'. What, after all, is the difference between a priest acting in the highest sense of his vocation, or a prophet compelled into declamation, or such a saint (even unknowing), opening himself up to the mercies of God, becoming a channel for them to the world? One thing is certain, that those of them – priests, prophets or saints – who did so respond, were usually rejected. Not made 'outsiders' as Scobie argues, but marginalised, neutered: precisely because they were too near the centre of things; dangerous catalysts. 'It is better that one man should die . . .' was not infrequently their lot. Said Leonard, at the point of disclosure ('After The Sabbath Prayers', *The Spice-Box Of Earth*, p10):

'*And how truly great*
A miracle this is, that I,
Who this morning saw the Baal Shem's butterfly
Doing its glory in the sun,
Should spend this night in darkness,
Hands pocketed against the flies and cold.'

It was never different.

It is difficult to react adequately to George Woodcock's silly comment that in Leonard's first two books of poetry 'the thirties urge to relate the imagery of poetry to the world we live in, as the world we dream, might never have existed.' Spender's and Auden's world for example, as well as their views of it, were broken on the anvil of history; that ideology was bankrupted – and they themselves acknowledged it and moved on. Poets do not *necessarily* have to be commentators on the historic present; there is a world within as well as a world without. Leonard believed that they interconnected more than he is given credit for; he chose to speak of that one within, though not absolutely. The generation that rediscovered the *existential* was precisely the one best fitted to look and think 'within', which is not unrealism, but a different form of realism – and one unavoidable to such as Leonard, given the horrors inflicted on his own people by the most 'culturally advanced' nation of the day. A.M. Klein, a Jewish Montreal poet of considerable skill understood the matter, as Woodcock could not:

'*Not sole was I born, but entire genesis:*
For to the father that begat me, this
Body is residence. Corpuscular,
They dwell in my veins . . .'

('*A Psalm Touching Genealogy*')

If Leonard appeared in his first book to invite comparisons, now he made statements, claims, and most of all, confessions. Ondaatje perceived this and described the book as being 'far nastier and more frightening' than *Flowers For Hitler*; but the choice of words is unjust: there is nothing nasty or frightening about honest observation. Such value-judgments surely arise out of the critics' disappointment at finding negative aspects in an otherwise positive projection, an all-to-human aspiration for avoiding reality which Leonard refuses to do, to his great cost.

Manzano has drawn attention to a real difference when he says (of both these first books), 'In general Cohen is lyrical in his writings when he refers to himself, and anarchistic when he confronts the outside world,' a comment which becomes more fully justified as time goes by, though Leonard's anarchism remained personal and mainly verbal. He is wont to talk of the new vision that Lorca's poetry gave to him; 'here is my landscape,' he exclaimed repeatedly. But that other 'landscape', quieter perhaps, but like an underground stream, unconscious and very persistent, never failed to obtrude itself on him: 'It is strange that even now prayer is my natural language,' he said, in 'Lines From My Grandfather's Journal' (The Spice-Box Of Earth, p10) which powerfully reflect his own self-questionings; the 'tyranny' was asserting itself. He went on to speak of it thus:

'My journal is filled with combinations. I adjust prayer like the beads of an abacus . . . Thou . . . The language in which I was trained: *spoken in despair of priestliness* (our italics) . . . In my work I meant to love you, but my voice dissipated . . . I played with the idea that I was Messiah . . .' And yet he speaks with painful recollection of the sense of alienation he felt at times, '. . . I stood outside my community, like the man who took many steps on Sabbath'; (concluding) 'I will never be free from this tyranny.' But it is not a conclusion: 'All my family were priests, from Aaron to my father,' suggesting that on the family's spice-box should be inscribed (as was the old custom):

> 'Lead your priest
> from grave to vineyard.
> Lay him down
> where earth is sweet.'

Even in death he is willing to work at the vine (the biblical symbol of the Chosen People), suggesting in 'Credo' that the work, however unlikely it appears, is going on; 'the holy promised land' is being peopled: 'the feet of fierce or humble priests trample out the green'; he among them, despite putative evidence to the contrary.

We should note that it is the spice-box of *earth*. Among the exquisitely pungent thoughts of self, of responsibility and tradition, stands the one who was powerfully driven by his sensual nature, by his personal loneliness, by the intense need to be one not only with the One, but also with the many in human completion. Indeed, as we shall presently see, the two great intimacies – as ever – sharply reacted with each other, strengthening the conflict, heightening the ambiguity, posing in ever more painful interjections the question, 'Who am I?' One cannot write of 'the real world' till such a question has been answered. It is this question which is the ultimate one; the others are a screen to hide modern man from his real self, as T.S. Eliot found. Yet there is a deeper, yet more exultant sense of the delights of love, of its mellifluous sensuality, in this second book than in the first; though Scobie overstates his case when he claims it as 'nothing more than a joyous celebration (of love) richly seasoned.'

(His view of sex seems to suffer from the same 'Pharisaical' constraints that ben Eliezer fought against, when he condemns 'Celebration' as 'a failure of tone,' 'portentous . . . imagery and the reality of the blow-job.' It is, as is so often the case in criticism of Leonard's work, a travesty of Pope's high standards, a supra-imposing of the critic's personal standards not dispassionate appraisal.)

There are fine expressions of true sensuality in this book, and great gratitude to those he left behind: Anne (in 'For Anne'); Annie (in 'Now Of Sleeping'); Betty (in 'The Boy's Beauty: *For Betty*, his italics); and beyond those unnamed lovers of yesteryear, not a few who responded to his charm and wit. Longing was the key: 'I long to hold some lady,' a longing that was inexhaustible, tumultuous and yet ardently romantic. It finds full expression in 'When I Uncover Your Body' (*The Spice-Box Of Earth*, p39):

> 'When I uncovered your body
> I thought shadows fell deceptively,
> urging memories of perfect rhyme.
> I thought I could bestow beauty
> like a benediction and that your half-dark flesh
> would answer to the prayer.
> I thought I understood your face
> because I had seen it painted twice
> or a hundred times, or kissed it
> when it was carved in stone.
>
> 'With only a breath, a vague turning,
> you uncovered shadows
> more deftly than I had flesh,
> and the real and violent proportions of your body
> made obsolete old treaties of excellence,
> measures and poems,

and clamoured with a single challenge of personal beauty,
which cannot be interpreted or praised:
it must be met.'

In its fulfilment Leonard found solace from the *angst* which gnawed at his soul, a sublime escape from the rigorous demands imposed upon him. He is the poet *par excellence* (and later, the singer/songwriter *par excellence*) of the two great intimacies – woman and God – because he found refuge from the One in the other; when *accidie* impinged, Cupid intervened. Eros is, after all, not so far from Agape in the pantheon of the heart. Another expression of this psychic force is found in the cynicism and bitterness he displayed from time to time when he grumbles about the dark, the flies and the cold; but other references are very much stronger, e.g. 'The Cuckold's Song' etc).

This is not new to Canadian poetry, as Desmond Pacey declares, not least of A.J.M. Smith's poetry. 'Smith's chief themes are loneliness, and death, fear and renunciation . . . nowhere in modern poetry can one find such concentrated agony.' An aspect omitted by Dudek in his description of Smith's work. In a later book (*Book Of Mercy*, 1984) Leonard speaks of 'the two shields of bitterness and hope,' once again contradictions emerging, complementaries offered, by which the psychological and spiritual mechanisms of 'balance' and 'equilibrium' are secured.

The reason for the exultation, the explanation of how this sense of craving had been mollified and a sense of sexual peace bestowed on the lyrics was simple: Marianne had come into his arms; that golden apparition of loveliness, that lithe, sensuous, intelligent being of intuition and sympathy; a gift of the gods to rank – and outrank – anything so far told in the surrounding mythology of his adopted Greek homeland! He has memorialised their encounter and its temporary effect upon his deeper self, the depths of feeling he had for her, in his significantly titled poem 'Destiny' (*Flowers For Hitler*):

'Destiny has fled and I settle for you
who found me staring at you in a store
one afternoon four years ago
and slept with me every night since.
How do you find my sailor eyes after all this time?
Am I what you expected?
Are we together too much?
Did Destiny shy at the double Turkish towel,
our knowledge of each other's skin,
our love which is a proverb on the block,
our agreement that in matters spiritual
I should be the Man of Destiny

and you should be the Woman of the House?'

Perhaps nowhere else is the mood and tone of love more beautifully expressed than in his poem 'Beneath My Hands' (*The Spice-Box Of Earth*):

'Beneath my hands
your small breasts
are the upturned bellies
of breathing fallen sparrows.

'Whenever you move
I hear the sounds of closing wings
of falling wings.

'I am speechless
because you have fallen beside me
because your eyelashes
are the spines of tiny fragile animals.'

The sense of delight, of gentle wonder, the startled realisation of his sense of her bodily perfection and spiritual grace is consummated not merely in their mutual passion but more enduringly in that oneness which is beyond time and space, which understands the fragility of love as well as its strengths, its ethereal qualities as well as its physical needs. To the musician in Leonard she was a melody, to the poet a lyric, to the singer a song: poetry in motion and melodiously sweet. It is not surprising that he found in addition to writing about her, he had to sing about her, too.

Irving Layton found it too much, this eximious union of contrasts. Even his extraordinarily fecund language struggled to reassert the recollection: 'the ideal couple,' 'the beautiful inspiration,' 'illusion and reality,' (by which he meant that it was simply too good to be true; too perfect to last – a forbidding afterthought). For her intelligence, beauty and charm he had the highest admiration; it evoked a poem 'Party At Hydra: *For Marianne*'. She was the sort of woman to evoke poems, from Leonard not least, and lastingly.

The spice-box is delectable in its fragrance, Chagallian in its rich mixture of images and responses. As Leonard expressed it in the poem which – in title and texture counterbalances the title of the book:

'Out of the land of heaven
Down comes the warm Sabbath sun.'

As in Jacob's dream of old the movement is from earth to heaven. The words he uses leap and tumble over each other to catch the exultant mood: 'dancing', 'brandishing', 'chanting', 'leaping' and – most important of all – 'gathering'. The questor was beginning to find, the traveller beginning to arrive, the searcher beginning to secure. Or was he?

word as meaning

'Words should be weighed, not counted.'

HASIDIC SAYING

'Breavman wished to say all there was to say in one word . . . to say 12 things at once.'

LEONARD COHEN

'The question is,' said Alice, 'whether you can make words mean so many different things.' 'The question is,' said Humpty Dumpty, 'which is to be master – that's all.'

LEWIS CARROLL

peripatetic
poet-novelist

The impression is sometimes given – one of the many false impressions, often by journalists who fail to do their homework and idly reuse the scribblings of their files, thus perpetuating the myths – that, having left Canada in 1959, Leonard settled in Hydra for six or eight or 10 years (the dates are confused, not infrequently by Leonard himself, not always self-contradictory). It is wholly to misunderstand his life; most importantly, his character. Leonard was never – nor could he be – one to settle down. He was always the wandering Jew! the wandering troubadour, long before his musical career blossomed.

His life is a sort of itinerary; a ceaseless web of comings and goings; a restless, moving sea, which illustrate the unresting nature of his mind and spirit. Most poets suffer from it; surrealist poets most of all; and Leonard more than most. The changing scenes, the altering moods and landscapes, the various stimulations he gained from such journeyings, all fed his mind and quickened his eye. The whole man was involved: body, mind and spirit; in his hearing and seeing and touching, his feeling and his tasting. And we shall shortly see that an involvement with Zen Buddhism adds a further 'sense' to these; for 'thinking' is posited by it as the sixth *sense* though it is the thinking appropriate to the east, not the western style which Leonard detested, a reference to which is made in his poem 'Last Dance At The Four Penny', in which he decries the 'logical shrouds' of the cynical and world-weary rabbis.

Montreal is his real centre, to which he must return periodically. Not merely out of loyalty and affection to his mother and family, and those friends such as Morton Rosengarten, Derek May ("the most irreverent person I know" Leonard once remarked), Robert Hershorn, an accomplished manufacturer, Henry Zemel and Henry Moskowitz, his former school-friends to whom he preserved deep attachments, but also because this was the place where he renewed his 'neurotic affiliations,' where he most belonged. As he commented in *The Favourite Game* 'No one ever leaves Montreal,' it stays in the mind of her citizens as an ongoing, ceaselessly challenging reality; thus the youthful Breavman was made to exclaim, 'My city, my river, my bridges . . .'

Unlike many places in which he had stayed – New York, London, Athens – Hydra had become his home-from-home; the home of his dreams with a dream of a woman. It was a place where they luxuriated in the sun, mesmerised by the blue of the Aegean and the splendour of nature – a swooping gull, the rhythm of waves, the gambol of the dolphins, the dark green foliage of the orange tree set off almost psychedelically by its bright fruit. It was a place where they could also enjoy the works – and the idleness! – of man, his mastery over the sea, the rocks, his exploiting the world's resources for his food and sustenance, transport and company. A red-tiled roof here, a whiter-than-white wall there, the cultivation of a vine, a plant, a white sail on the horizon; or just the sheer spontaneity of life in a taverna. If he renewed his neurotic affiliations in Montreal, he found a fairyland of peace and contentment in Hydra, among friends, with work flowing easily and smooth, in the company of that greatest of all marvels, a stunningly beautiful and sympathetic woman. Yet he expressed another aspect of it in his poem 'Hydra 1960' (*Flowers For Hitler*):

> *Anything that moves is white,*
> *a gull, a wave, a sail,*
> *and moves too purely to be aped.*
> *Smash the pain.*

> *'Never pretend peace.*
> *The consolumentum has not,*
> *never will be kissed. Pain*
> *cannot compromise this light.*

> *'Do violence to the pain,*
> *ruin the easy vision,*
> *the easy warning, water*
> *for those who need to burn.*

> *'These are ruthless: rooster shriek,*
> *bleached goat skull.*
> *Scalpels grow with poppies*
> *if you see them truly red.'*

That other aspect, fruit of the Holocaust, the nightmares of the endocrinological rush, is bleak and unnerving. It is, nevertheless, quintessentially Cohen: a man of opposites, of dark ambiguities, of reality; not the smoochy reality of the stupid, who pretend that 'All's well . . . God's in his heaven,' nor the myopic pretences of those who avert their eyes from reality. It is the reality of the seer, the true prophet; one whose word scars.

But the need for travel, to be stimulated, always persisted. And so it was that he found himself, in 1961, having just launched his second book, on another island, on Cuba, 4000 miles away. One at the very centre óf the world's excited and anxious attention. Revolutions, mental and spiritual, moral and anarchic, civic and political, always fascinated this man of moods and changes. As did that of Fidel Castro. It is wholly in character that Leonard went to see what was going on, and thus found himself to be 'The only tourist in Havana,' as he described himself in a poem; and the only Jew in the Bay of Pigs! It could very well have been his ultimate moment, for at one point he found himself surrounded by belligerent troops on the beach, held on suspicion of being in the van of the American invasion!

But his intentions were more modest, if less careful, and he was able, as a Canadian citizen, to assure them of his peaceful intent. He was there long enough to be presented with a copy of the Prime Minister's and President's *Declaration* which displayed their revolutionary credo: 'The Republic of Cuba: our country or death.' He has it still, that proud, impudent document. The events of which it boasted had arrested the imagination of the world and brought it very close to nuclear destruction. It asserted pride in the new-found 'universal suffrage,' the 'effective exercise of their sovereignty,' their pride in the memory of Jose Marti. It condemns the documents, protestations and paranoia of its northerly, imperialist neighbour, and it sides with – and for – the peoples of Latin America, and those governments that were forced to kowtow to its mighty neighbour. It affirms its democracy, its freedom, its self-worth. And so on, and so on; through 13 pages of call and challenge, renunciation and claim. A short statement in the light of Castro's speeches later!

Leonard seems to have been more amused than harmed by the incident, and certainly found it a useful accretion to his own developing mythology. It fostered his sense of rebellion, which was not small, as when he commented to William Kloman of *The New York Times*, "I've been on the outlaw scene since I was 15." He had, though there has probably never been a more courteous and charming rebel! And he was getting an even bigger taste for it at 27. The establishment-minded priest was becoming an anti-establishment prophet; the natural conservatism of his mind was experiencing its own daring liberations. And if his youthful enjoyment of it was condemned by some, at least he could claim honourable antecedents, such as the similar experiences of Pierre Trudeau, who also enjoyed 'tempting fate' by searching out the trouble spots and centres of agitation. As the charismatic Prime Minister of Canada ruefully confessed, "I did it a little deliberately."

On Leonard's return to Canada, where he poetically decided not to govern Canada, dump asbestos on the White House, make the French talk English or, even more revolutionary, make the CBC talk English, he was fêted for somewhat different reasons. In May the Canadian Conference of the Arts took place at the O'Keefe Centre. Leonard was there reading his own and Anne Hubert's allusive and symbolist poetry (in French). They had much in common, the poetry apart, for both were from privileged backgrounds, held friendship with F.R. Scott in high esteem, wrote novels – Leonard's were still gestating – had an interest in the theatre, and were more moved by the music of language than its precise meaning. The day was stolen, not for the first time, by Irving Layton, who stunned the gathering with an eulogy to Jacqueline Kennedy, 'Why I Don't Make Love To The First Lady'.

Back on Hydra, Leonard was able to settle into his questing, reflecting and writing roles, the real business of his life. Others, apart from Marianne, were there to help. Two of his best friends at the time were the Australian writers George Johnston and his wife Charmaine Clift, who enthused him for the land 'down under' in a way that was to remain – for this incorrigible traveller – a temptation for over 20 years. George Johnston (not he of Canada, author of *The Cruising Auk*) was the author of *My Brother Jack* and *Closer To The Sea;* his wife that of *Peel Me A Grape;* all three influential novels of the sixties.

Together, they swapped stories of their lives and homelands, drinking large quantities of *ouzo* at the rear of the nearby grocer's shop, talking, gambling and singing well into the night – and beyond it at times. This was the beginning of the sixties, when personal freedom and self-valuation were at their height, the payment often being in life's ultimate currency. Both George and Charmaine were to forfeit their lives a little later, as did not a few of Leonard's companions. But may they rest in peace, for theirs was the mettle that helped remake the disordered, dull and pointless postwar world, and their lives will live on through their literature and that personal investment they both made in generous, uproarious friendships. In addition to the residents, many passed through Hydra, such as the Americans Allen Ginsberg and Gregory Corso; the Swedish poet Goran Tonstroum and the British painter Anthony Kingsville.

When things got too fraught, Leonard was always there with his guitar and a song, ever needful himself of the soothing, provoking presence of music, inspired by such as Ray Charles, though long before him the 'sweet psalmist of Israel' archetype of all true 'soul' singers. At such times he began to consider more urgently the possible fusion of his poetic insights with the country and western music that was constantly broadcast through the American forces' radio programme from nearby Athens or played by him at home; that of Ray Charles not least (one of whose records actually melted on his turntable!)

Another major influence on him was the Greek composer Mikis Theodorakis, whose own political style and courage was to land him in prison and internal exile in nearby Zatouna, in the Peloponnese. In his courageous book *Music And Theatre*, written on scraps from prison, like a Paulian epistle, he describes what a fruitful period this was in Greece musically – which seems to flourish best in adverse conditions. He had perceived that if poetry and traditional Greek music were combined 'a genuine style of music can be produced.' By such a combination he sought to achieve the unity between *logos* (word), *mousiki* (music) and *orchesis* (orchestra or group). He also placed great stress on two further traits which Leonard himself would seize on, albeit independently. First, the importance of the melody in song, that 'living intellectual organism' by which character, point and direction are given to life. And second, the element of theatre not least in setting Lorca's poetry to music, through which *catharsis* – a cleansing of the emotions through high emotional crisis and experience – is achieved.

These were very important perceptions that Leonard made during these years. He was forming his own musical style and theory, advancing from that foundation he laid with The Buckskin Boys. He was moving to a position in which the powerful *function* played by music was recognised as such, not merely using it as an enjoyment or a means of relaxation. Just as the logical had given way to the spontaneous and intuitive in his poetry, so now the language of the heart and soul was displacing the literary forms to which he had been educated. There was still a long way to go, but the first steps had been taken; he had got the message. As had composer Manos Hatzidakis, who had just released a double album of Lorca's poetry under the title, 'The House Of Bernarda Alba', the performance chiefly of the actress Katina Paxinou at the National Theatre, directed by Alexis Minotis as, indeed, Theodorakis also did.

In 1962 Eli Mandel and Jean-Guy Pilon edited *Poetry 62*, to which Leonard contributed five new poems: 'My Mentors', 'For Marianne', 'On The Sickness Of My Love', 'Action', and 'The First Vision'. The first three were to appear in his next book of poetry, *Flowers For Hitler*. He also wrote the piece 'The Drawer's Condition' on November 28, 1961, which also found its way into that volume. This latter emphasises how much Leonard then lived on a shoestring. Commented Sigmund Petersen, "He was very poor in those days." A situation that was to last for two or three more years despite the occasional dollar bills his mother quietly slipped in his direction.

'My Mentors' (*Flowers For Hitler*, p62) is particularly interesting, for it makes explicit his interest in far-eastern 'mythology', Zen Buddhism in particular:

> '*My rabbi has a silver buddha,*
> *my priest has a jade talisman.*
> *My doctor sees a marvellous omen*
> *in our prolonged Indian summer.*
>
> '*My rabbi, my priest stole their trinkets*
> *from shelves in the holy of holies.*
> *The trinkets cannot be eaten.*
> *They wonder what to do with them.*
>
> '*My doctor is happy as a pig*
> *although he is dying of exposure.*
> *He has finished his big book*
> *on the phallus as a phallic symbol.*
>
> '*My zen master is a grand old fool.*
> *I caught him worshipping me yesterday,*
> *so I made him stand in a foul corner*
> *with my rabbi, my priest, and my doctor.*'

A short series of dated poems bearing the date July 4, 1963 – American Independence Day – was written about this time (published in *Flowers For Hitler*). Only one (titled 'Independence') seems to have anything to do with that celebration, though a Canadian would not normally be expected to have such an interest in old taxation disputes and tea parties. He refers to it obliquely in 'I Had It For A Moment', but as he was apparently suffering from double-focus at the time, the main centre of his interest being a woman's body which naturally 'eclipsed' the other matter entirely ('. . . Now I'm getting into humiliation/I've lost why I began this . . .') we cannot be sure. He was not in any case in the States then, as his second poem, titled 'Island Bulletin', clearly reflects Hydra. In it he appears more concerned as to where he stands in the pecking order ('In my journey I know I am/somewhere beyond the travelling pack of poets/. . . a man of tradition . . .'); the reference to 'the tradition' reflects the ongoing conflict within. In the fourth one he dreams that his lover was 'Buddha's wife and I was a historian watching you sleep . . .' which has nothing to do with American self-assertiveness, even less with history, but at least has the advantage of revealing what he was doing during the day! (It also presages a scene or two in *Beautiful Losers*, as we shall see.)

If the last verse of 'My Mentors' (above) suggests a certain lack of commitment, it was not to last long. The creedless style of Zen, with its concentration on one's own self-consciousness (but in an alogical, unsystematic and detached sense), became more and more important to him. Judaism is a way of life more than a system of faith, but in Zen he found a way of life specifically refuting *any* system or credal affirmation. Along with George Johnston and his wife, Evan Wentze, Marianne and one or two others, he was making a careful scrutiny of some Tibetan texts translated by Wentze. It was the start of a much more vigorous journey into one aspect of 'comparative religion' and mythology, which added stern discipline to his needs for self-knowledge, solitude and a sense of direction. It reinforced his suspicions over scholars and their learning, as Bahya ibn Paquda said in his *Duties Of The Heart* (a significant title!): 'Some scholars are like donkeys; they only carry a lot of books.'

By far the most important piece of work on hand, however, was his continuing manuscript *Beauty At Close Quarters*, a raw, dazzling and uproarious piece of fiction drawn from his own life and imagination. His London publishers found it too raw, and so he had to put it back through the mill before its texture was sufficiently ground to suit their – and what they thought was the public's – taste. (It actually went through at least five recensions; another title was *Ballet Of Lepers*). The novel had not flourished well in Canada; fault, Pacey says, of two powerful inhibiting factors: a distrust of abstract thought, and the legacy of puritanism. Leonard certainly shared the former, and it is interesting to see how in his novels he overrides the traditional inhibitions, especially the pseudo-morality of puritanism (WASPish and Catholic) and launched himself in a highly personalised style against both.

His first novel finally appeared in 1963 under the title *The Favourite Game*, and while Leonard mourned the cannibalist recensions which reduced it to its present shape, it projected a novelist of no ordinary talent, variously linked with such heavyweights as James Joyce, Henry Miller and the like. As one review exclaimed, 'James Joyce is not dead. He lives in Montreal under the name of Cohen . . . writing from the point of view of Henry Miller.' It has to be said that he shared much in common with Joyce, who appears to have deeply and powerfully affected him. (His classic *A Portrait Of The Artist As A Young Man* had a specific personal influence, which we will encounter later.) Sharing the Dubliner's revulsion of bigoted Catholicism, a sort of self-exile from his own country, Leonard became a poet–novelist, under such influences, not least that of Yeats and Pound, yet without losing his taste for Romanticism, e.g. Keats and Shelley and other Romantics, among whom Lorca should also be cited. It was time, as Soren Kierkegaard once remarked, to 'get out (of) the poetical into the existential' (though Auden always understood this comment as a call to a finer style of poetry rather than a wider use of literary style); to explore the man rather than exploit the muse, to test himself in prose as opposed to poetic expression; and even embark on social comment *en passant!*

In it he also explored the so-called 'interior monologue' style of the Irishman, the 'stream-of-consciousness' method which has revolutionised much of modern novel-writing. The method was important for Leonard not only as 'technique', but as a means of distancing himself from 'history's crushing daisy-chain' (as he called chronological sequence and exactitude in 'The New Leader' – part of that despised scholarly apparatus), an aspect of fundamental importance to his writing and imagination. We shall see further – and maturer – use of this in his second novel, and not least a Miller-like use of historic events to portray modern problems. (This had long been done by his fellow-Jews, who frequently took biblical and liturgical texts and themes and transmuted them into lessons for their own day – a significant 'prophetic' technique.)

But he does not trust mere effect to make his point. His words are empowered with their own ability to create meaning, to build substantive ideas, to 'make' sense. It is a very Hebraic concept, which predated the *logos* (word) doctrine of Philo. Behind all this lies the oracle, mediated by the priest, which became the prophetic word: a word that scars. As he said in 'Lines From My Grandfather's Journal', 'I could imagine the scar in a thousand crowned letters.' (At the end of the novel the Wurlitzer effects a 'neon wound' on its much greater public – 'everybody'! – by which Leonard perceives and anticipates the greater influence of poetry-in-song, if we may use such a phrase of pop music. As Joyce himself wrote, 'In the virgin womb of the imagination the word was made flesh.')

In the wake of the 'legalisation' of *Lady Chatterly's Lover*, his novel was claimed as a harbinger of the New Fiction in which his zestfulness, eroticism and sheer zaniness were combined in a rollicking account of maturing manhood. As *The Guardian* remarked of it, 'a song of a book . . . a lyrical and exploratory bit of semi-autobiography.' And it was exactly that. Scobie is quite wrong to deny this (he was 'not really an autobiographical writer'!), and he misinterprets Leonard's irritation at his reviewers' attempts to decode his story. Leonard always suffered more at the hands of Canadian reviewers and commentators, and was concerned to protect his relatives and friends by various smoke-screens; to which should be added a certain blimpishness – itself a large and autobiographical, feature of the book.

Daniel Stern was more cautious in the *Saturday Revue*, 'Breavman . . . appears to be that familiar figure, the maverick artist, rebellious and restlessly in search of his soul . . . The vignettes grow more serious in tone as Breavman's 'sentimental education' continues . . .' However, he found 'the total effect . . . somewhat insubstantial. Mr Cohen has told his personal story in a succession of loose, brilliant sketches, often vague in their direction. Perhaps next time he will weave a tale that will more firmly bear the weight of his undoubted talents.'

The novel is structured in 91 numbered parts, of four 'books', with a deliberately disrupted time-sequence, a technique that not only helps to disguise the familial and social setting of the author, but heightens the drama of the story too. It creates a Zen-like disruption between thinking and feeling, and recalls Eliot's 'dissociation of sensibility' theory, whereby poets – and novelists! – 'thought and felt by bits, *unbalanced.*' (In his next novel he fulfils Stern's hopes in this regard extravagantly, as we shall see.)

The story-line follows the maturation of 'Lawrence Breavman', who is placed within Leonard's own family tradition in Montreal, offering, as we have already seen, any number of connections with Leonard's own upbringing. The book is devised in terms of Breavman's failed love for Shell, his greatest love, whom we encounter on the first line of the book: 'Breavman knows a girl named Shell . . .', from whom he walks away in the last section. But the connection is to remain: 'He must always be connected to her. That must never be severed. Everything was simple as long as he was connected to her, as long as they remembered.' Between the two references, the 'gamesmanship' (using the word Leonard offers in the title) of Breavman, the formation and projection of his character, his responses to life – at home and among his friends; not, significantly, at school or university – is displayed, riotously and simply. But it is not that simple. The whole point is to make it sound simple. It climaxes in the effect it has on them both: 'One day what he did to her, to the child, would enter his understanding with such a smash of guilt that he would sit motionless for days, until others carried him and medical machines brought him back to life.'

The 'favourite game' is not therefore sex, as some reviewers (and even the blurb writer to the American paperback edition) have asserted, but the 'games' people play with each others' lives, with their own. The favourite game is – in a book full of *jeux d'esprit*, not merely 'games of the spirit', still less witticisms, but *spiritual* games, meanings of the deeper sort drawn from a serious (if playful) experience of life: the landscape of the heart – is life and relationships; and our essential irresponsibility with them.

'Breavman' could well be a play on the word 'Briefman', by which the insubstantiality – the transience to use his word – the *fragility* of life and relationships, are suggested. (From *brevis*, 'short', especially in the musical sense of a breve.) For 'time' and its cognates are important to Leonard, despite his apparent antipathy to history. Scobie – who favours 'bereaved man' for the origin of the name – declares that 'flesh' is Leonard's 'most important word,' which is just as wild a statement. 'Time' in fact appears much more often, and there are many words that are more important to Leonard's vocabulary, not least love! He speaks, for example, of Breavman's efforts to get at history; of Rousseau's pictures delighting him by 'the way he stops time.' 'Rust, rust, rust,' he wails in 'Front Lawn', 'in the engines of love and time.' A rabbinic story makes the point: 'Life is a passing shadow,' says the Scripture. 'The shadow of a tower or a tree?' one asked. 'No' came the reply, 'the shadow of a bird; for when a bird flies away there is neither shadow nor bird.'

This *leitmotif* runs through the book, as it does through much of his work. We see it in the sickness and death of Breavman's father; later, of his mother through madness. We see it in his whole family: they were the conscience of the Jews; they built Canadian Jewry; yet they were in decline. Even the fragility of divine ceremonies and services is asserted to that end. We see it in the constantly changing, always impermanent love-life of Breavman; we see it in the failure of his great friendship with Krantz, which ends in their fighting; we see it particularly and tragically in the apparently pointless life and gruesome death of 'the mad-child' Martin, of whom Leonard commented to us that it was merely 'an unfitting addition'; that his approach to it was 'mytho-poetical', that it 'didn't work', 'it evaporated'.

But it *did* work! It adds a particular strain to that ephemeral consciousness which pervades the book, now wistful, now poignant, now hurtful, now unfulfilled. The very naïvety of Martin highlights the insubstantiality of other figures. Is the 'mindless' game of counting grass or mosquitoes any different, at death, to any other game that is more rationally played? Does not the game Breavman played with him – in taking him seriously – cause to stand judged against the irresponsibility of Martin's mother, and the camp leader and counsellors who refused to play it with him? And is Martin not a figure for those 'simpletons, children, madmen of various sorts, saints,' of which Empson wrote in his account of Erasmus's *The Praise Of Folly* which did for his generation of church-leaders what Leonard does for his, in both synagogue and church, Catholic and Protestant? Empson comments, 'We could indeed say that the simpleton is *innocent and natural;* this sums up most of the conception.' And most of Leonard's use of the concept here (and later of 'saints' in *Beautiful Losers*).

There are other Aunt Sallies, to be sure, more provoking targets, and a great surge of *angst* as to his own being and his own guilts, as we shall see. The book positively overflows with games – Scobie's 'excess' is surely right. They prepare us for the climax of it all: He commences the penultimate section (29) with the words, 'Let us study one more shadow,' which turns out to be an account of his love for another beautiful woman, Patricia, with whom, however, he could not consummate his love, for 'there was no desire in the touch . . . his room was never emptier or a woman further away.' But it was not so with Shell: 'The need for Shell stabbed him in a few seconds. He actually felt himself impaled in the air by a spear of longing. And with the longing came a burden of loneliness he knew he could not support.' Love – the greatest of all games, real or illusive – is thus portrayed; but *not* sex! Shell is forsaken, the one who most brought him to his senses, by which smash of guilt he spoiled for ever the possibility of full self-realisation. So he passes to the ultimate statement:

'I just remembered what Lisa's favourite game was . . .' Not sex, not passion, not carnal delights, none of which satisfied or fulfilled the thoughtful, yet thought-fearing man, but a child's game of patterns in the snow. It had all come down to impressions, symbols; elusive statements from an author who discovered his world in the surreal: excess confounding reality, as satiety always does; and never more so than in the realm of feelings. The impressions are made – 'a lovely white field of blossom-like shapes with footprint stems' – but they are made of snow . . .

As Job had it, in a mood of utter realism, if also of blank despair, 'Man is born unto trouble, as the sparks fly upward.' Without that realism Leonard Cohen cannot be understood. It is not that he is a despairing man, but that he is essentially a realist, far too much the 'seer', who refuses to filter out of life's realities the negative or the black things of ultimate reality: man's days, man's games, are numbered. And out of such 'depressive' realism he is forced to bear witness. Like Jeremiah of old, it is not a message, a witness, his contemporaries wish to hear, those fed on show-biz patter and hollow happiness, those sustained by professional jargon or guru-wisdom. It is a measure of the man that his art is true to his experience, and his apprehensions.

So Dudek is both right and wrong when he says 'the new generation of Canadian poets (he was referring only to the poetry; he has failed to take cognisance of the prose, so far as we can see) is not even capable of social anger, or of pity . . . The frame of the new poetry is tragedy; the tragedy of life itself, of humanity, suffering an incurable condition.' He is right insofar as he perceives it to derive from the tragic human condition; he could not be more wrong than when he puts it down to unbalanced, disorderly or morally enfeebled thinking. Leonard's so-called 'total negation' (the phrase is Dudek's; we dissent from its totality), is in fact the regular negation in man's experiences, now and always.

It is the apprehension of Qoheleth, the Preacher – who follows the *Lamentations* 'of Jeremiah' in the Jewish Bible. He, too, was a son of David, but his refrain, unlike David's 'Hallelujah', was: 'Vanity of vanities, all is vanity.' He recognised that there is, indeed, 'a time to weep and a time to laugh; a time to mourn and a time to dance.' It was Leonard's triple burden to apprehend, live and speak of it in a multiplicity of forms, through many changing modes and fashions.

new sounds – but
beware of the con!

According to the rabbis a Talmudic Jew 'entered his full strength' at 30 years of age. He came into manhood traditionally at 13; by 18 he was expected to be married, earning his living; by 30 he was ready to play his full part in the community. By contrast, according to Professor Dudek, Canadian poets are then past their best; they 'become sclerotic with their 30th year.' The Russians recognised this in their saying, 'Poets should die young.' Leonard, with two books of poetry behind him, having found for himself a point of tranquillity wherein to recollect himself, was about to break free of all sorts of traditions and be himself: independent, observing, audacious, and defiant.

Flowers For Hitler was the first instrument of this. Its title deeply upset some with a more direct awareness of the Nazi leader than Leonard. He was prepared to take the risk. Milton Wilson, who described Leonard as 'potentially the most important writer that Canadian poetry has produced since 1950 – not merely the most talented but also, I would guess, the most professionally committed . . .', described the book as 'a version of the poetry of guilt.' But to argue thus is surely to misconstrue the meaning as well as the psychology behind both the writing of the poems – by definition, isolated and independent units without the sequential drive of the paragraphs or chapters of a book, and the editing, which is given to thematic gathering but has a limited resource from which it may cull its materials.

The question of professionalism versus talent is interesting, for Leonard was an inveterate 'scribbler'. Unlike those authors who 'never had an unpublished thought' he wrote and revised, and revised again. His unpublished material is in excess of his published! And in much of this he was tasting and experimenting with form as well as meaning. Sandra Djwa comments that his technique is more complex than either

Dudek's or Layton's, and that is certainly so; more complex than Dudek's because he seeks not poetic purity but realism ('accuracy'); and more complex than Layton's because the font of his imagination lies deep within himself and his experiences, increasingly so, whereas his friend has worked from a broadening horizon, geographically and historically.

Leonard's aim, as represented sardonically by the title, was to taunt Hitler and his like: 'Flowers for Hitler the summer yawned . . .' (in 'Folk') is a heavily sarcastic example of this, which has a human response, unlike that of mute nature, in the poem 'Opium And Hitler':

> '. . . He fumbled
> for his history dose.
> The sun came loose,
> his woman close.
>
> 'Lost in darkness
> their bodies would reach, the Leader started
> a racial speech.'

His scorn reaches its zenith when, in the most trenchant poem, 'A Migrating Dialogue', he cannot even bring himself to name him: 'He was wearing a black moustache and leather hair,' concluding (via an apology to his readers for the tastelessness of the point) 'Braun, Raubal and him . . .' Similarly, he exhibits him as being yet '. . . alive/He is 14-years-old. He does not shave./He wants to be an architect.' (in *Police Gazette*). It is no different when it comes to speaking of Eichman and Goebbels, his henchmen–in–crime. (Somehow that phrase seems to read very lightly for the malignancy they personalised; but criminals they were, against humanity itself.) The former is dismissed in eight words, five of which are the same: 'medium'; the latter by deriding the 'light' of his propaganda:

> 'Ah my darling pupils
> do you think there exists a hand
> so bestial in beauty so ruthless
> that can switch off
> his religious electric exlax light?'

For the sake of such moral nonentities, he can pour scorn on the whole subject: 'History is a needle/for putting men to sleep' ('On Hearing A Name Long Unspoken'); or 'I think we should let sleeping ashes lie/I believe with a perfect faith in all the history/I remember, but it's getting harder/to remember much history' ('A Migrating Dialogue'); which reaches another climax in 'Now let him go to sleep with history/the real skeleton stinking of gasoline' ('Hitler').

Already we have overstepped the purely personal in his diatribes and contemptuous disparagements. He is not merely talking of the Nazis; who would want to? he seems to ask in his preface, offering 'A note on the title'. 'A while ago,' he explains, 'this book would have been called *Sunshine For Napoleon* and earlier still it would have been called *Walls For Genghis Khan.*' It was, pointedly, a book not about guilt, still less a version of the poetry of guilt, but a condemnation – at once ironic and contemptuous – of those tyrants who set themselves against humanity, of whatever race or creed.

Curiously, Leonard's present recollections appear to all but disavow this. "I was not touched by anything I wrote about," he said. "I don't recollect caring about anything. I did not seem to suffer. I was writing as response. In later years I am having to pay for every word." It is a precise example of the crypto-amnesiac factor that affects all writers, especially poets, by which subconscious ideas obtrude into the conscious. In Leonard these factors and their archetypes are of an immense antiquity, and very important for the understanding of his work. Eli Mandel once asked him why the concentration camps – that ultimate symbol of lostness, not merely lost freedom – appeared in all his books. Said Leonard, "Well, because I would like to be free of them." He was thereby claiming that freedom – the freedom of 'a bird on the wire . . . like the drunk in a midnight choir . . . like a worm on a hook.' He added that whilst he found the poems 'linguistically mature' he came late to their moral level. But there can be no doubt that this is too harsh a judgment of himself (as he is wont to make), and that real involvement, at all levels, was present.

He went on to speak of a later experience which cut him off from previous memories in that staccato way into which he sometimes lapses when recalling the painful: "Everything passed me by. A sense of personal mess (intervened). (I had) no understanding of the process. (I was) without ideas, roots. Somewhere along the way I got blasted. It's like being in a mine without a perspective of the earlier period." He wrote of it in 'To A Teacher':

> '*Hurt once and for all into silence.*
> *A long pain ending without a song to prove it.*'

It is, in fact, a book about freedom – like its predecessor, *The Spice-Box Of Earth;* but the other way on. The former was positive, assertive, appreciative; it lauded the creation and its fruits – the spiciness of earth. This book is the opposite of all that, in being negative, condemning, expurgatorious; it held its subjects to open ridicule; it poured contempt on their names; it belied their humanity. In the first we see life; in the second, death; one witnesses to goodness and charm, the other to evil and stinking corruption; the first is a crowning act of Jewish

sensitivity and enjoyment; the second of Nazi grossness – a paroxysm
of hateful repugnance; the one was symbolised by the spice-box; the
other by the swastika and the ovens.

Leonard knew the risk he was taking. But what is poetry, if it is
not to take a risk? Incidentally, it is another refutation of George
Woodcock's empty criticism that in his work we fail to find involvement with modern society. For Leonard modern society had no greater
problem than that of the Holocaust and the racial bigotry that inspired
it. Ironically, Stephen Spender, as early as 1939, spoke of being 'sick of
the public events being dealt with in a public manner in plays' – and we
may add poems, too. Professor Pacey, as we saw earlier, said the same
thing in identifying the poetic watershed of the fifties, in its movement
from the social-urban to the mythopoeic. The Depression, the Spanish
Civil War, the stark evil of the Third Reich, all surfeited the artistic
intelligence. In writing his blurb for the book, Leonard sought to pre-
empt the criticism he knew he was provoking, and in so doing, provides
us with a side view of his own response to the popularity and adulation
that he was securing:

'This book moves me from the world of the golden-boy poet
into the dung-pile of the front-line writer. I didn't plan it this way. I
loved the tender notices *Spice-Box* got but they embarrassed me a little.
Hitler won't get the same hospitality from the papers. My sounds are
too new, therefore people will say: this is derivative, this is slight, his
power has failed. Well, I say that there has never been a book like this,
prose or poetry, written in Canada. All I ask is that you put it in the
hands of my generation and it will be recognised.'

The man who, with Irving Layton, had known the bitterness of
rejection for writing plays for his generation, anticipating the events of
that generation by several years, who had seen his first novel filleted by
hands too delicate to touch raw nerves, and souls too timid to plumb the
real depths, was not going to be ignored twice round. Leonard was not
so much rising to the challenge of his own generation as putting down
the apathy of his peers. Naturally, he did it audaciously – how else is a
young man to do it, surrounded by grey-beards, know-alls and the
retirement-conscious? But, just as naturally, they sought to put *him*
down. That was their 'favourite game'; after all, they made the rules
and moved the goal-posts when necessary.

The book, in one sense oddly, was dedicated to Marianne. But
not so oddly, really. She was the light of his life, her beauty
transformed the ugliness of the world; her laughter peeled forth like
Westminster chimes – regularly and jubilantly. And she could look
reality steadily in the face. If he was ever tempted to be drawn under by
the anguish of the events-behind-the-names, if oblivion ever sought to
take over from the unreal grotesqueness of the history, she was there

with a sunny laugh, an uplifting encouragement, the deep consolation of her bodily presence which kept the demons at bay. Naturally he included a poem about her ('For Marianne') which reveals how important her presence was to his world and work:

> *'It's so simple*
> *to wake up beside your ears*
> *and count the pearls*
> *with my two heads*
>
> *'It makes it so easy*
> *to govern this country.*
> *I've already thought up the laws*
> *I'll work hard all day*
> *in Parliament*
>
> *'Then let's go to bed*
> *right after supper*
> *Let's sleep and wake up all night.'*

Theirs was that kind of sharing, that kind of love, that kind of passion. It is shown in a different light, in 'Promise':

> *'To love you*
> *is to live*
> *my ideal diary*
> *which I have*
> *promised my body*
> *I will never write!'*

But, as the rabbis said, 'One drop of love can create a sea of tears,' and for them both, now and later, there were times for tears, both of the inner and the outer sort. For one thing they both needed to travel – he to the north-west, to Montreal, his family, his publishers; she to the north-east to Oslo, to her family and friends. Sometimes they would travel together, and that was fine; sometimes it meant separation and heartache, and fear too. As Leonard expressed in 'Waiting For Marianne':

> *'I have lost a telephone*
> *with your smell in it*
> *and if it won't come back*
> *how will you phone to say*
> *you won't come back*
> *so that I could at least argue?'*

The book moves from the evil, the ridiculous, to the sublime, and the lovely; its natural *ambience* is a curious juxtaposition of 'decadent' Berlin (we shall encounter it again as a symbol of inhuman evil and undisciplined emotion) and the light and loveliness of the Aegean. And there is much more in the book than flowers for Hitler and bouquets for Marianne. As with all his books of poetry, there are many references to family and friends; to favour, fortune and human fiascos. A poet, more than any other writer, needs to feel the sharpness of angst (from which guilt is not necessarily absent). It is that which fuels his poetic consciousness. He does not write out of a vacuum; he needs to feel alienation, longing, desolation, desertion; as well as elation, fulfilment and peace. He can be wholly a poet without being whole; he cannot be wholly a man by not being whole; and he certainly cannot be wholly a Jew – especially a Cohen – without being wholly dedicated.

If their absences caused disquiet, their illicit relationship (in the eyes of the law and the legalisers, not to say family) caused even greater pain, and deep guilt. For Marianne was not only of the *goyim* – a Gentile – she was also a divorced, or at least, a separated woman. And no Cohen can marry a divorced woman. Their delight in each other over several years, a delight which the observant Layton could only liken to an illusion, so beautiful was it, was destined to fail.

While together, they lived and loved and savoured life to the full; but in the shadow was their own cross: the power of the Law and the Tradition. As he says, with wretched self-awareness in 'The Way Back' – a truly prophetic premonition 25 years before its time: 'I know you call me traitor/because I have wasted my blood/in aimless love.' And he went on to admit – one might say with the sadness of despair, '*and you are right.*'

If there was 'ambiguity' in Leonard at this time, if his 'two heads' collided, it was because his destiny had plunged him into a heart-searching, a guilt-stricken morass, from which he could not extricate himself without the most painful consequences, a living torment. He knew the reality of the wiser rabbis: 'Whether Jew or Gentile, man or woman, rich or poor – according to a man's deeds does God's presence rest on him.' The Presence, the *Shekhinah*, the 'glory' of prose and poetry (and soon) song, were threatened by this calamity. He had 'entered his full strength', and it threatened to tear him apart. The 'golden boy' felt his feet were indeed 'turning to clay.' He was made for love, and it was being denied him. Its joyfulness he felt deep in his spirit; its transience he felt in his bones.

Other influences were also at work through this book: his father, whose memory he idealised, is seen in collusion with him in his veneration of Queen Victoria (just as much the Queen of Canadians as of any in the then Empire, of course): 'my father and all his tobacco loved you . . .'; also in the 'disguise' of the rich man who 'must go/and his house become a hospital,' to which he adds his love of his father's wine, his contemptuous servants, his 10-year-old ceremonies, his car, and his wife. To that wife, his mother – still very much part of his life, but necessarily separated by 4000 miles of water and a millennium of culture and temperament – he speaks of 'the hours she puts into her skin . . . the industries that served her complexion.' He can write of 'My old mother/sits in her Cadillac/laughing her Danube laugh . . .' a rare jewel, undoubtedly; but somewhat tyrannical, nevertheless, as became an anxious, caring mother. The uncles came in for a familiar rejection: 'I'd rather sleep with ashes/than priestly wisdom' he exclaims in 'Police Gazette' (the ashes being those of the victims: I'd rather be dead!) and in 'Alexander Trocchi, Public Junkie, Priez Pour Nous' he speaks of his 'Uncle's disapproval of my treachery/to the men's clothing industry,' but hiding a more ambitious thrust as we shall see. He may demonstrate, in a wonderfully humorous and pointed piece ('The Project') his *gauche* involvement in that industry, but it is certain he felt the criticisms against him for not following in his father's footsteps; for not playing his proper part in the family business. If the uncles' shadow of censure fell across him at this time, causing him pain, the non-tyranny of his 'little female cousin/who does not believe in our religious destiny' rode 'loyally on my nostalgia' ('Streetcars').

His first book of poetry was dedicated to his beloved Grand-mother Cohen; a woman of great personal virtue, who was well equipped to partner her larger-than-life, wholly successful husband, Lyon. She, true to character and station, had not only splendidly reared her sons (single-handedly, one might suppose, given the unceasing commercial, religious, charitable and communal activities of her energetic husband), but found a special place for Leonard, her firstborn's firstborn son. We may not be far wrong in assuming that it was mainly her nurturing that produced the deep-seated recognition of 'priestly' status and function – not to mention their commensurate responsibilities.

She has more mentions in this book than any of his family save his father, and was clearly an object of his devotion and appreciation, even as she had been a pillar of comfort and concern, and perhaps of tyranny, too, in that very acceptable manner of doting grandmothers. His 'other' grandmother, Klinitsky-Klein, also has a mention, albeit in her final sickness, in 'I Wanted To Be A Doctor'. She also suffered from arthritis, but even in her discomfort high thoughts of Prince Albert, the Flanders Field (where her son-in-law was injured? by bullets? by shrapnel? by gas?) obtained, as 'The Millennium' makes clear. But most of all, in a curiously titled piece 'On The Sickness Of My Love', he refers to her agony, and her arthritis.

Other 'tyrannies' be they friend or foe also find expression, such as the late E.J. Pratt, one of Canada's foremost poets, who died in 1964, just in time for Leonard to include his salutation 'To E.J.P.' alongside another poem to his friend Irving Layton: 'For My Old Layton', which is almost an *apologia* for him – perhaps a celebration of his independent spirit would be a truer description – in the face of the difficulties and not infrequently the downright opposition meted out to this most out-spoken of men. And there were less personal ones, such as the city of Montreal itself ('Montreal 1964'); or the poem 'Three Good Nights' (a reflection of that nocturnal *angst* which ever threatened) which spoke of his '10 years sealed journeys/unearned dreams' which ends by celebrating that virtue of virtues of the poet: 'The Power of Eyes.'

Another form of tyranny was his financial situation, though he was more fortunate than some of his fellow-writers. He had a sound domestic base to which he might return should some calamity overtake him; and while it may have been death to his soul, the family business would have made room for him. Moreover, he had an annuity of $750 p.a. which, if not a king's ransom, at least ensured his supper. Despite this, and the Canada Arts Council, which had enabled him to travel to Europe, he was now on his own, with the additional burden of long-distance travel, Marianne and Axel to consider. The situation was drolly commented on in his poem 'The Suit': 'I am locked in a very expensive suit/old elegant and enduring . . .'; it had to last. The perplexity was more concisely summed up in his poem 'The Drawer's Condition On November 28, 1961':

> 'Is there anything emptier
> than the drawer where
> you used to store your opium?
> How like a blackeyed Susan
> blinded into ordinary Daisy
> is my pretty kitchen drawer!
> How like a nose sans nostrils
> is my bare wooden drawer!
>
> 'My hand has explored
> my drawer like a rat
> in an experiment of mazes.
> Reader, I may safely say
> there's not an emptier drawer
> in all of Christendom!'

The Coleridgean reference to opium – another tyrant – is important. The Devonian was virtually at the same age as Leonard now was when he fell under its addictive power. The use of drugs was popular among artists and writers, as Leonard well knew. Their popularity had never waned, though wartime conditions rendered usage scarcer. By the mid-fifties it began to reassert itself; and not just the opiate narcotics (such as opium, heroin, etc), but the non-medical use of sedatives and hypnotics (the barbiturates and minor tranquillisers – which technically include alcohol); especially the stimulants (the amphetamines; but technically coffee, tea, cola and nicotine are also included); and – the source of even graver concern in some quarters – the psychedelics and hallucinogens (in particular LSD and mescaline). For writers and artists there were special incentives. The common belief as to their usefulness attached to cannabis – marijuana – expressed in such phrases as 'the heavenly guide', the 'poor man's heaven', the 'soother of grief', 'the liberator of sin' – was growing. And acid diethylamide-25 (LSD), was fast becoming *the* consciousness-enhancer, which many writers thought they needed, perhaps 'sclerotic' poets most of all.

He refers to the habit specifically in 'Indictment Of The Blue Hole', where the repetition of the dates – January 28, 1962 – emphasises the reality; not least the 'De Quincey hairnet'! (of him whose *Confessions Of An Opium Eater* had been classic fare for more than a century). Drugs' usage in literature had enjoyed an ancient role and was well-known to the moderns, such as the Huxleys, the Lawrences, the Bloomsbury Group. Leonard was not one to follow the crowd; he led the way – and it was not inexpensive. So the exquisite 'My hand has explored my drawer like a rat . . .' – for one who had kept and known rats – says it all.

Behind all this moved a shadow of intimidating and awesome threat to the seeing; the arch-tyrannies of men, sometimes 'good' men, who will stop at nothing in order to preserve their world, their *status quo*. Ezra Pound felt it, and misjudged it calamitously, as William Empson said of him, 'The way his mind decides for him is rather too much above his head'; for which Pound was accused of treason, though politically found guilty of 'insanity'. Thereby America itself used the 'games' it condemned in the USSR, and for the same reasons of political expediency!

Pound knew it as fascism and, like many others in Europe and America at the time, believed it would prevent the communist and similar menaces from taking over. But 'fascism' in the hands of Mussolini, as in those of Franco somewhat later, and Hitler and his 'mut and jeff henchmen', became uncompromising, authoritarian, militant. As naked power always did; whether in the murderous régime of Genghis Khan, the proto-imperialism of Napoleon, the *fascismo* of Italy, the Nazism of Germany, the Iron Guard of Romania, the BUF of Mosley in Great Britain, McCarthyism in the USA or Peronism in Argentina. Liberalism was its great opponent, however interpreted, whether socialist or democratic, avant-garde or merely open-hearted. And it quickly became racist, not least anti-semitic, against which the majority in art rebelled, wrote, spoke, painted, and through it all, warned.

Alexander Trocchi was one such, of whom Layton wrote in his *Collected Poems;* as did Leonard in his latest book: 'Alexander Trocchi, Public Junkie, Priez Pour Nous'. 'You leave behind you a fanatic' (Leonard wrote of him) 'to answer (Royal Canadian Mounted Police) questions.' But there was much more than an exponent of the 'Underground Poetry' movement in this book; and many more causes by this ultra-quiet revolutionary-cum-fanatic. They *were* new sounds! they would not like them! it needed his generation to understand it – not that of Lester Pearson *et al.* Hence his satire against City Hall; the anti-racism of 'The Bus'; the ominous presence of 'the Kerensky of our circle'; but most of all the thoughts of the only tourist in Havana who turns them homeward in warning.

Such pressures do not explain his move to prose – we have already seen that he had very early interests in both prose and drama (not to mention his prosepoems, the first of which he published in 1954). But it certainly enhanced its need. He knew before he went to London that he could not enjoy the lifestyle he wanted by being a poet only. So in the wake of *The Favourite Game*, he set his hand to another and more ambitious work of fiction.

The materials for this new project had been with him for years. Always observant; naturally somewhat suspicious of how-and-why-people treated him; situated in divided Montreal where the WASP versus French cultures – perhaps we should say mythologies – clashed and jostled; and aware of the Indian/Eskimo/Intuit presence, he had lived for years with the makings of his plot. The problem was that Hugh MacLennan, his former professor of English Literature had already done it in *The Two Solitudes;* or nearly done it. A novel of brilliant evocation whose characters (in the first part at least) are worthy to stand alongside any in literature; whose revolutionary 'message' – discreet, yet unambiguous – was to set the tone for decades, had nevertheless not succeeded.

And so it was a sober yet hopeful Leonard who returned that autumn to Canada, to gather his materials for a new and even more outrageous book and to promote his latest volume of poetry. For this his publisher – Jack McClelland of McClelland and Stewart of Toronto – had arranged Leonard's most ambitious promotional package to date, along with several of his fellow-poets. It was a poets' tour, no less, whose itinerary below shows how well poetry was being received, if misunderstood:

ITINERARY FOR POETS' TOUR – 1964

Sunday, October 25

12 noon	Poets check in to Inn On The Park
1 pm	Meeting in Sherwood Room at Inn On The Park for rehearsal and checking of itinerary. Photographs by National Film Board and *Weekend Magazine* and Ontario Government photographer. Buffet lunch.
6 pm	Interview with Norm Perry of CKEY
8 pm	Poetry reading at North York Public Library. This reading is to be covered by *Globe and Mail*, *Telegram* and CBC *The Learning Stage* and *Weekend Magazine*.
9.30 pm	Reception at North York Public Library.

Monday, October 26

11.30 am	Monday morning free for radio and TV taping.
11.30 am	Leave for Kitchener-Waterloo in limousine accompanied by National Film Board.
1 pm	Lunch at University of Waterloo
3 pm	Autographing at University Bookstore
4 pm	Reading at University
6 pm	Leave for London
7.15 pm	Reception buffet supper at James Reaney's home.
8.30 pm	Poetry reading at University of Western Ontario
10 pm	Reception arranged by English Department, University of Western Ontario

Tuesday, October 27

	Stay at Inn On The Park or Hart House. Birney to CBC at 10 am for radio interview 'project 65'
11.45 am	Meet at Warden's Office, Hart House
12 noon	Luncheon as guests of Mr Culley at Hart House
1 pm	Reading at Hart House
3 pm	Leave for CFTO and taping of Berton Show
5 to 7 pm	Reception at Queen's Park. Donald H. Morrow, Speaker of the House.
9 pm	Reception at 151 Inglewood Drive. J.G.M.'s home

Wednesday, October 28

	Morning free for promotion, publicity.
12 noon	Autographing at University of Toronto Bookstore
1 pm	Luncheon at Gaslight Restaurant
2 pm	Leave for Kingston
5.45 pm	Reception at Royal Military College. Host – R.E. Watters

8 pm   Reading at Queen's University in Dunning Hall. Organiser
            Tom Eadie.
            Accommodation arranged by Queen's University.
            Reception to follow reading at Queen's.

Thursday, October 29

            Morning free for Kingston or Ottawa TV and radio
            promotion. Leave for Ottawa at approximately noon.
            Accommodation at Talisman Motel.
            Reception by Lester Pearson (Prime Minister) in late
            afternoon or early Friday morning.
8.15 pm   Reading in Alumni Theatre at Carleton.
            Reception to follow reading.

Friday, October 30

            Leave for Montreal. Accommodation arranged at Queen
            Elizabeth Hotel.
2.10 pm   Arrive at CFCF for one-and-a-half hour radio interview –
            Lee Dunbar, 150 Ogilvie St.
4.30 pm   Autographing party at Eaton's
8.30 pm   McGill University reading, Auditorium, Humanities
            Centre
10 pm   Party at Classic Bookstore as guests of Louis Melzack.

The foregoing shows in what distinguished company he now
moved – the best hotels; the foremost interviewers; cared for by such as
the Canadian Broadcasting Corporation and the National Film Board
of Canada; an *entrée* into the leading library centres and university
campuses; celebrity autograph exposure, as well as signing sessions;
guest of the most prestigious citizens and government officials, such as
the Prime Minister's residence in Ottawa and its official photographers,
and so on. And not least of all, among poets of the stature of Earle
Birney, Irving Layton and Phyllis Gotlieb; the first had worked in
Montreal for some years, as supervisor of foreign language broadcasts
for CBC. He was one of those hugely influential figures in Canadian
letters, and once broadcast a controversial 'Why Is Canada Still Banning
Joyce's *Ulysses*' which he rated as 'the most influential single novel of the
20th century.' Years earlier, he had made heavy criticisms of the
Governor-General's Award, with which his young companion would
soon be contentiously involved.

What was becoming apparent before was now stoutly confirmed
on this tour among such elevated individuals: Leonard was not only a
first-rate poet, admired by his colleagues and a great commercial
success, but he was a born performer, too. He had poise and style, and
expert-timing; on several occasions Leonard managed to reduce his

audiences to paroxysms of 'clean laughter', though his own style was much nearer to Shelley's, 'Our sincerest laughter/with some pain is fraught.' He was highly personable, conservatively dressed (though no longer in that old elegant suit; but ever elegant), very handsome, with a voice like rich chocolate sauce. It was a winning combination, not least as a natural modesty overcame any resentment felt by his peers. He was not merely Canada's youngest man of letters, he was its best representative, too. The National Film Board of Canada latched on to this, and made him the centre – the star, indeed – of a film: *Ladies And Gentlemen: Mr Leonard Cohen*, which was scripted by Donald Brittain, directed by him and Don Owen, and which is still in demand today, 25 years after its release. (Leonard, whose interest in film goes back to boyhood roots, an interest learned from his father, had already become an active participant in the new school of Canadian film.)

The film opens with Leonard appearing on stage before a large audience of mainly young people, to great applause. He is relaxed, well-dressed and coiffured, and full of good spirits. He opens the proceedings with an account of his visiting a friend – in a mental hospital, and describes his experiences there. Seven times in the short post-production script (kindly made available by the NFBC, who also made available a private showing at their Montreal studios) he was interrupted by laughter. The commentator states, "He is not primarily a stand-up comic (sic) but a novelist, a poet, and a very confident young man." He was all of these things. He had actually worked a few times as a comedian, and those who know his poems, his novels, his plays or his songs will understand that his sense of humour, not infrequently of comedy, is as well tuned (and timed) as any professional, a *manqué* Woody Allen of the Canadian Film Board!

The film proceeds by a series of recitations and voice-overs to a sequence of Leonard going about in Montreal – its streets, shops, restaurants and hotels. He speaks of his family background, his habits and his need for escape:

"You always have the feeling in a hotel room that you're on the lam, and it's one of the safe moments in the escape; it's a breathing spot . . . the oasis of down-town; a kind of temple of refuge, a sanctuary. A sanctuary of the temporary kind, therefore all the more delicious . . . the little place in the grass, and the hounds are going to go by for three or more hours. You can have a drink, light a cigarette and take a long time shaving."

In such exchanges his vulnerability is frankly stated. A vulnerability which is kept in check by his recourse to solitude, which is immensely important to him and moulds much of his life and habits. 'A man is weaker than straw and stronger than iron,' said the rabbis; it is in that ambiguous composition that Leonard's strengths and weaknesses are exhibited. As is often the case, a man's weakness is his strength, for thereby he fashions himself to live and work; thereby he apprehends reality – or sees through its vacuities; thereby he most expresses himself. As Rabbi Zusya said before his death: "In the world to come they will not ask me 'Why were you not Moses?, but 'Why were you not Zusya?'" Leonard, be it said to his great honour, was never anyone but himself, even if that self was sometimes weakened by pressure and circumstance.

Shortly before the film was made, a Winnipeg journalist described him as 'having the stoop of a crop-picker and the face of a curious little boy' ('furious', oddly creeping into the unedited script here!). It was the sort of thing to catch the imagination – to Leonard's regret, no doubt – and he has had to live with it for many years. But it was nevertheless a telling portrayal, despite his confidence in projecting his material. He does have a characteristic demeanour – not of a crop-picker, but of one both humbled by the *grandeur* of his vision, and weighed down by its responsibility. But he was *curious*, too, in an all-absorbing, ever-aware, reflective vision of man, his world and his affairs. It is the curiosity of the poet, of the seer.

Part of the film included a press conference, presided over by the highly influential Pierre Berton, plus two unnamed journalists, Irving Layton and Leonard. We saw, earlier, Leonard's 'celebration' of his friend's independence, his 'muscular grace', as well as his *penchant* for courting abuse and vilification. Something like that opened the conference, which demonstrated Leonard's unwillingness to be pushed into saying things he had no wish to comment on to experienced journalists. (Manzano describes the confrontation as 'a reincarnation of Laurel and Hardy' – *el Gordo y el Flaco* – though it was a 'fine mess' that the journalists got themselves in that day, not those inimical comics of yesteryear.) They continued:

First journalist: "All right. As far as you're concerned, your concern is Irving Layton and his survival, even more than the survival of the masses . . ."

Layton, intervening: "And Cohen's concern is my renunciation of the Canadian public." *First journalist:* "Is this true, or do you have some other concerns, Mr Cohen?"

Leonard Cohen: "I haven't a single concern!"

Berton: "Well, come now! What do you care about, really? Don't you care about *anything?* How can you be a good poet and not care about something?"

Leonard Cohen: "No! No! I do the poetry, and you do the commentary."

Berton: "Let's get this straight. Are you telling us that there is *nothing* that worries you? Nothing that bothers you? How can you write poetry if you're not *bothered* by something?"

Leonard Cohen: "Well. I'm bothered when I get up in the morning. My real concern is to discover whether or not I'm in (a) state of grace. And if I make that investigation, and discover that I'm not in (a) state of grace, I'm better (off) in bed."

Berton: "What do you mean by a state of grace? That's something I've never understood."

Leonard Cohen: "A state of grace is the kind of balance with which you rise to the chaos you find around you. It's not a matter of resolving the chaos, because there's something arrogant and war-like about putting the world to order . . ."

Berton: "You have lost me."

Layton: "What Cohen is trying to do right now is to preserve himself. That is his real concern . . ."

Following this exchange was another, which preceded Leonard recording his 'A Kite Is A Victim'. (The University of Toronto having bought his manuscript, decided that a phonograph should also be made for posterity: shades of the McGill Poetry series here!) The soundman said, "We have to cut out the dirty words." Leonard's reply was fast and definitive: "In poetry there are no dirty words – *ever*," a point then exercising his mind powerfully, in view of his projected second novel; a point of principle with which he was to deal boldly.

There followed an excursus in a local restaurant/café, Ben's, then a 70-year old institution on Maisonneuve, famous for its hickory-smoked meat sandwiches, the talk of Canada, not merely Montreal; at which four generations of Cohens – it lies in the heart of the clothing trade area – recalled high times and low times; not least those back in Europe from where Ben Kravitz also came. Al Palmer called it 'the unofficial heart of Montreal . . . where everybody meets everybody.' Said Emeritus Professor Alec Lucas, "It is an oasis of good talk, good cheer, good service and good food . . . where all . . . can feel at home away from home." It was such for Leonard and his friends – for his biographers, too! And not merely food but, touched with Lithuanian magic, it somehow becomes soul-food – available day and night.

The film goes on to incorporate more of his father's film (happily so, as the rest was accidentally destroyed). Leonard supplies the commentary for this, in language which is virtually identical with that of *The Favourite Game*, even as his reply to Berton above has close parallels with his second novel (yet unwritten, which offers a key to his technique, by which ideas and themes are ruminated upon, discussed widely, and only then find their way into final form, be they poems, novels or songs).

It then continues via a shot of his ordering sandwiches back at his hotel in impeccable French, to a discussion on the *I Ching* with some friends. *The Book Of Changes*, to give the oracle its more informative name, is of immense antiquity. Its present form dates back to circa 3000 BC. Both Taoism and Confucianism – China's main philosophies – have their source in its wisdom, which centres in man's oneness with the cosmos, and the principle of complementarity between male and female (*yang* and *yin*). It is developed over 64 ideograms which represent the full expansion of this complementarity. Each ideogram represents a change (hence the name of the book) in the cosmos, and therefore in humanity; the numbers are secured by either casting special sticks or – more usually today – tossing coins. Carl Jung 'rediscovered' the *I Ching* for modern man through his principle of synchronicity. Other leaders have been more cautious. Rashi, Rabbi Solomon Yitzhaki, one of the most influential commentators in Judaism said, "So it is with all astrologers; they see something, but do not understand what they see." Leonard, too, was cautious over occult matters and so played things safely. He viewed its 'messages' as aspects of personal insight; not indications by which one might plan one's life; an amusement by which one may learn of oneself, rather than an authoritative word – as with his response to many differing 'mythologies'.

The film offers more clips – of his life in Montreal, detailing *en passant* the process of events which led from his home-town to Greece; reciting appropriate selections of his poetry by way of extra illustration, and offering various items of interest. For example, it produces a comment on his experiment with vegetarianism: "Since I stopped eating meat I feel a lot better about animals . . . I can be much more honest when I pat a dog!" It offers a comment on his willingness to be photographed, in which he recognised its importance for his poetry . . . "Such material will some day be of value." He waxes eloquent on the theme of vital importance to him and his friends, human sexuality and its link with the other great intimacy: "That is something, happily, for which we must bend our knees (in thanksgiving) all the time. Sexuality is general, and although one man may be receiving the favours of a woman, all men in her presence are warm. That's the great generosity of women, and the great generosity of the Creator who worked it out that way . . ."

Proceeding to shots of an academic gathering from the earlier poets' tour, it provides Leonard with the opportunity to deliver himself of a broadside against academic and literary pretence – his *bête noire* – insisting that "Poetry is not an occupation but a verdict." He admits, too, that his own background and lifestyle is in danger of ruining the usual image of poets: He had even been able to play a little hockey at school! The unnamed commentator showed the skimpiness of his research, as was frequently the case, when he comments, somewhat contradictorily, "He has not read extensively . . . He has a hyper-sensitivity and an enormous curiosity." Leonard had an immense cultural interest and, according to Dr Johnson's admonition on friend-ship (which he also follows) kept it in good repair.

In speaking of his visit to Cuba, at the time of the missile crisis, he confessed to . . . "A deep interest in violence. I was very interested in what it meant for men to carry arms and to kill other men . . . The real truth," he continued, "is that *I* wanted to kill, or be killed . . ." To some extent this explains his use of the language of military weapons, ranks and ideas (though as a child of the thirties and forties that was a normal backcloth to his life), though he does not disclose, here, his strong antipathy to such things. But there is a *limit* to his use of them. Nowhere in his writings do they have the same intensity that he gives, for example, to loving or sexual encounter; nor do they possess the same explicit detailing which they have in Layton. Leonard does not glorify war even when he uses its experiences to evoke a sense of violence. There is no place in his thinking for that exalted 'mystical' experience of war and its brutality by which the heroic virtues are tasted and sung that we see, for example, in Ernst Junger.

In closing the film, a sequence of his watching himself in it was added. In full view of the cameras, Leonard writes *caveat emptor* on the wall for all to see: 'Let the buyer beware.' This is – and by it his legal studies protrude through his disaffirmations – a principle of commer-cial law: 'Be careful what the salesman tells you!' He said to the bemused cameraman, "I thought I'd make this little 'beep' and let those watching me know that this (film and commentary) is not entirely devoid of the con . . ." (An even more subtle comment was implied, to those who knew Hebrew, which is written without vowels, for his name – Cohen – then becomes chn!)

He might be the golden-boy poet, now producing new sounds: their value they must judge for themselves. He would have no part in guru-status, not now, not ever.

koan of cohen

His anticipations of reaction and misunderstanding were not long in being fulfilled. A particularly strident one came from his former mentor, Louis Dudek, to which Irving Layton offered a characteristically vehement reply. But regardless of the antipathy it stirred, or the apathy in certain quarters, the film was hailed as an important step in the poet's rising status. Another breakthrough, of a totally different sort, was made in the form of the Quebec Literary Award, a pleasing experience in the light of his second novel, now under way. Yet another was the offer to write scores or theme-music for National Film Board programmes, such as his friend Derek May's *The Angel*, and Don Owen's *The Ernie Game*, in which Leonard also performed. (May's film won a special prize at the Montreal Film Festival in 1967.)

But, "It was time to write a book," he told journalist Andrew Tyler, "so I locked myself in a room and got down to it." To Mandel and Webb's question about the book he replied, "I was writing a liturgy, a big confessional oration, very crazy, but using all the techniques of the modern novel . . . pornographic suspense, humour and conventional plotting . . . I gave it my all, because I had nothing to lose. In reality I was not interested in keeping anything to myself." To Susan Lumsden in Paris, he said, "It was written in blood. It took me nine months and at the end I was writing 20 hours a day and (kept) going only on pep drugs and hashish." To Jacques Vassal he confided: "I gave everything I had to that moment, the total gift. Sometimes I fail, but it is always a test of character. I want to master myself."

Beautiful Losers was the result, and if *Flowers For Hitler* stirred some, this one caused a *furore*. It was the novel whereby Leonard best became known. It was both a continuation of *The Favourite Game* and a divergence from it. It was a continuation in terms of method and style, the novels abound in luxuriant word-play, spirited comment, inventive imagery, as well as being quintessentially Canadian – all the main activity takes place there, with the exception of an important incident, if couched in unreality, in Argentina; a divergence inasmuch as the personalised element now becomes the *avant-garde* instrument of a different aim.

If *The Favourite Game* is semi-autobiographical, *Beautiful Losers* is its unlikely folk-political successor. If the first was joyously explosive, the second was positively Vesuvian. If the first centred on a game – even The Game, the second pivoted round a carnival. If the first was saucy, the second was outrageous – and some reviewers could hardly wait to dip their quills before condemning it outright. We spend time on it because it exposes Leonard's mind as well as any other piece of work. So much so that Scobie believes that he will never produce better, not even with his brilliantly popular songs.

It is a story about loss and losers – daring at any time. John Henry Newman's *Loss And Gain* comes to mind for a frontal display of such a theme – and it would be harder to find a less likely comparison! (But not so unlikely if we consider the influence of James Joyce on Leonard, and Newman's on Joyce.) Who would have thought that a book about so negative a theme would have sold over three million copies, and be translated into 20 languages? (Bob Seger even produced an album using 'Beautiful Losers' as its title.) Admittedly the characters are presented as *beautiful* losers; but the reality is that 'beauty' – by any normal standard – has superimposed upon it the opposite, in form and essence.

There is a deliberate tension throughout the book between 'appearance' and 'reality'; the book rests on their frequent conflicts – oneness again obtruding. But an innate cynicism also pervades: 'The very words you use are shadows on the sunless ocean floor. None of them carries a lesson or a prayer,' he says in commentary towards the end of the book. Such equivocation recalls his use of games in *The Favourite Game*, and it is not surprising to read in this new book that 'Games are nature's most beautiful creation.' Yet games are not meant to be taken seriously; they can only supply divergence – or manipulation. In that sense, it might be said to be based on Jean-Paul Sartre's comment that, 'The real is never beautiful,' though that conflicts with what Leonard says elsewhere, for beauty, glory, gold etc are sub-themes of his work. Here they are taken as the unreal, the shadow; perforce the distinctive qualities of the loser – in a transient, superficial world. 'Beware of the con' thus pulsates below the surface.

Some of the reviews were stunning: 'Gorgeously written . . . overwhelming . . . a prose poem,' (*The New York Times*); 'A fantastic eroticism which is wildly funny . . . an exciting book,' (*The Sunday Times*); 'The literary counterpart of *Hair* on the stage and *Easy Rider* on the screen,' (*The Daily Telegraph*); '. . . swirling, hallucinatory, heraldic, squirty, an intensely physical, tensely metaphysical novel,' (*Book Week*); 'a wild psalm to all the beautiful losers of sexual, racial and political exploitation,' (*The Listener*). Professor Desmond Pacey described it as, 'The most intricate, erudite and fascinating Canadian novel ever written,' which in the light of his encyclopaedic surveys is a remarkable judgment.

Alongside such we have to place the comments of those who were not enamoured of it: '. . . this curious novel,' commented 'Bannerman' of *MacLeans*, who went on to state that 'there are overtones of lavatory scribbling throughout the book . . .' and added, 'more psychotic than pornographic . . .' He spoke of Leonard as 'a young Montreal poet with a message that gets lost in sex,' – for all of which he was rewarded with a letter of protest from Leonard's solicitors (it was a very silly and ignorant piece of literary criticism) and a threat of legal action for not taking the book and its author seriously enough – or taking himself too seriously, perhaps. 'Dirty, for the sake of being dirty,' commented an Australian judge from behind the moral barricades of the Bench in New South Wales, in so doing confirming doubts as to his dubious profession. ('Sir,' commented Dr Johnson, 'I do not like to talk behind anyone's back, but I do believe the gentleman is an attorney.')

We saw Leonard at the National Film Board of Canada defending the use of 'dirty' language by denying that it existed in literature: "There is no such thing as a dirty word in poetry," he said Wilde-like ('There is no such thing as a moral or an immoral book'), adding with great emphasis, "ever!" He now puts that theory into practice, in bold fiction and resonant prose. It is a parable of a History Man which out-Bradburys Bradbury – 10 years before Howard Kirk appeared, though not a campus novel (that life being too artificial for Leonard's imagination).

It is a *tour de force* of sexual and social congress which sparkles and fizzes and explodes incandescently. It is a sybaritic saga which uses the new-found sexual freedom of the sixties (still seething and arguing in the wake of the trial of *Lady Chatterley's Lover*, *A Clockwork Orange*, etc) to the maximum – and then extends it unmercifully, in a way that grates, and shocks and unnerves. It is an onanistic pageant of febrile intensity; a brilliant display of William James's concept of 'stream of consciousness' *à la* Joyce and Virginia Woolfe. Brierre is surely wrong to posit the drama in schizophrenic terms; streams-of-consciousness (the plural is demanded by its sheer excesses) are more appropriate.

But much more important than these, it is a perfect example, if long, of the Zen-Buddhist *koan:* it breaks through our normal comprehensions; it paralyses our usual definitions and usages; it forces us to think paradoxically. Such thinking is not completely new to one of Leonard's tradition. The Hebrew *chidan* – the 'riddle', sometimes 'dark saying' or 'hard question', which is frequently used in parallel with 'proverb' – stands very close to some aspects of the *koan*. For example, Samson aims to confound the Philistines by the posing of his riddle; the Queen of Sheba comes to ask Solomon the Wise 'hard questions'; Daniel was known as 'a declarer of riddles'; and the prophet Habakkuk speaks of 'a taunting riddle'. There are differences of emphasis, but nevertheless a definite community of thought exists between the two concepts, which is all the more interesting when one considers that their usage in biblical literature is limited to foreign involvements: the Philistines, Sheba, Babylonia, Persia.

By contrast, and for Israel itself, God says that Moses is specially chosen, close to him, so there is no need to speak to him 'in dark speeches'. A counterpart to this is found in the teaching of Jesus, who declares: 'Unto you is given the mystery of the kingdom of God: but unto them that are without, all things are done in parables: that seeing they may see, and not perceive; and hearing they may hear, and not understand . . .'

It is given even more meaningful expression in the incident known as the cursing of the fig-tree, in which the tree is 'cursed' so that it dies immediately – talking to plants is at least as old as this! – because Jesus was hungry and the fig-tree was bare. The point of the story, not missed by his disciples, was that it was not the fig season. Jesus knew that, it was a particular lesson in the guise of 'prophetic symbolism', in which a *koan*-like paradox was intended. And Paul, too, can speak in ways recollective of the *koan*, as William Johnston has made clear in his *Silent Music*.

Moreover, surrealism itself presents the logic-breaking patterns, in words and paintings. John Ash accordingly, in his tirade against 'that most irritating of modern tropes, the Surrealist Genitive,' adduces Dali's 'sex organs of breadcrumbs' or Lorca's intimate tenderness of volcanoes.' To a decade which was becoming sated by the unbelievable, Leonard offered yet more; to those who believed in gorging themselves, he served an overdose; to those who demanded freedom, he demonstrated unrestrained licence. It is the ultimate of overkills: the literary equivalent of ECT. 'To ignore form – what gives beauty and artistic quality to a message,' comments Professor Byron Raizis of Athens, 'and to focus solely on meaning amounts to reducing a work of art to a merely functional communication . . . (It is) like noticing individual trees while failing to perceive the forest they belong to.'

So here Leonard has always acknowledged the gratification he obtained from this work because of its *technical* merits, in which his form almost eclipsed his meanings and contentions. We need to remind ourselves of his deliberate choice of method here – as well as the fact that elsewhere (for example in *Death Of A Lady's Man*) he castigates such a device as 'a filthy oriental idea, obsessed as they are with what is limited and what is not limited, or what is both limited and unlimited, or *neither* limited nor unlimited,' (his italics). How to 'break the mould' except by *breakage?* In *Beautiful Losers* he smashes through our preconceptions and nice preoccupations, and shows what real 'gamesmanship' can do.

So forceful and 'surreal' is it at times, that one wonders if some of it were not written under the influence of LSD, or one of the other hallucinogens. And yet there is an underlying 'logic', a masterly control of character and 'development', a stunning and inescapable destiny that grounds it in the almost-possible, the 'if, but . . .' area of life. It is not so much entertainment as entreaty; not so much wild extravagance as earnest warning; not grotesque immorality, but highly imaginative *fin de siècle* mores, though without moralising. To such a book the climax is all-important: what point the *koan* without the spine-rattling jolt? Without the profound discomfiture of being shaken loose from one's safe moorings? In such a book there are many climaxes, the following is one of them in which his much underrated sense of humour is finely demonstrated:

> '*Action was suddenly in the streets! They could all sense it as they closed in on the Main: something was happening in Montreal history! . . . Poets arrived hoping to turn the expected riot into a rehearsal. Mothers came forth to observe whether they had toilet-trained their sons for the right crisis. Doctors appeared in great numbers, natural enemies of order. The business community attained the area in a disguise of consumers . . . It was the Revolution! It was the first night of spring, the night of small religions . . . The Army hovered over the radio, determining if the situation was intensely historical, in which case it would overtake Revolution with the Tortoise of a Civil War. Professional actors, all performing artists including magicians, rushed in for their last and second chance . . .*'

The path to that culmination had not been easy, for reader and participants alike. 'Revolution' implies a revolt, and that demands turning full circle, in expectation and disturbance. At one point the story is referred to as a 'pilgrimage to lust,' but it had taken place in a 'nun's democracy' and therefore the revolution was deliberately unreal, cataclysmic, soul-shaking. It focuses on the 'ambiguities' within Leonard, his (Coleridgean) tendency to seek to reconcile divergent and discordant elements, his determination to find a path through his own dark cloud of unknowing. As Nicholas of Cusa found, 'I have learnt that the place wherein Thou art found unveiled is girt round with the coincidence of contradictories, and this is the well of Paradise wherein Thou dost abide.' His road to truth also led beyond reason; it included the principle of contradiction, and settled on 'intuition' as a safer guide; 'opposing coincidences' meeting in the divine, as Leonard's frequently does.

It is, in fact, the mind – rather than the body (though some have failed to see this) – that is the centre of the activities: it deals with issues that take place on the periphery of sanity. (In that sense Bannerman's perception of 'psychotic' is nearly correct, but sadly he could not – or would not – see beyond it.) Insanity is but one step away throughout the book; not infrequently the point is over-reached and madness, quite deliberately, prevails. The tone of the book is not so much Dada as ga-ga. But the line between the two is always fragile, its crossing can produce masterly periods. Hence, the key figure in the book – though not the central character – is made to say in one of its most elegant passages (of which there are many):

> 'Sometimes my mind seems to go out on a path the width of a thread and of endless length, a thread that is the same colour as the night. Out, out, along the narrow highway sails my mind, driven by curiosity, luminous with acceptance, far and out, like a feathered hook whipped deep into the light above the stream by a magnificent cast. Somewhere, out of my reach, my control, the hook unbends into a spear, the spear shears itself into a needle, and the needle sews the world together . . . it goes through everything like a relentless bloodstream, and the tunnel is filled with a comforting message, a beautiful knowledge of unity. All the disparates of the world, the different wings of the paradox, coin-faces of problem, petal-pulling questions, scissors-shaped conscience, all the polarities, things and their images and things which cast no shadow, and just the everyday explosions on a street, this face and that, a house and a toothache, explosions which merely have different letters in their names, my needle pierces it all, and I myself, my greedy fantasies, everything which has existed and does exist, we are part of a necklace of incomparable beauty and unmeaning.'

In answer to this vision of – or is it a prayer for? – unity, a frenetic wail echoes through the book, from the lips of the central character though not the key figure: 'Connect nothing,' he screams. The necklace is torn from the throat; the pearls of unity fall and scatter; lunacy impends – and then conquers.

But it is a lunacy which is fashioned of *clair de lune;* which is characterised by the dominating character of the feminine; for without the evocation of the female, without her paradoxical temptation to intense sexual release and virginal benignity the story would fall apart. The moon, *Genesis* makes clear, was made 'to *rule* the night', and much of the crucial activity here encountered takes place at night, as ever was the case in Leonard's own experience, 'demons' ever threatening. Lust and insanity are juxtaposed, for example, in the poem 'Why Did You Give My Name To The Police?' in *Flowers For Hitler* in the phrase 'the lust-asylum universe', passion being an emotion, an element of 'unreason' therefore.

But there are connections here of a deeper sort. *Angst* is never more evident than in the sleepless night, when sleep is difficult, and night-time terrors obtrude. It is then that the person (can we rightly call him a depressive?) is at his most vulnerable; when his mind is tyrannised by that emptiness, that *accidie*, that sheer vacuous absurdity. As Leonard describes poignantly of Breavman, 'He was alone with his insomnia . . .' Later he tells Krantz, unbelieving, disinterested Krantz, 'The last refuge of the insomniac is a sense of superiority to the sleeping world.' His secret of positive thinking – if it can be sustained! (Later, we shall find Leonard's songs replete with such references to the night.) But he moves into deeper reflection when he draws attention to that deepening of woe felt when one's partner is soundly asleep; her comfort becomes his greater discomfort – a regular point of emphasis in Leonard's poetry and prose alike. 'Her sleeping seemed like a desertion,' he wrote earlier of Tamara and Breavman's nocturnal separation. And cold separation it was. His poem, in solemn dual columns to represent the division, 'Two Went To Sleep', is a brilliant evocation of this. Togetherness has gone, the 'one heart' – 'the engine of our energy' – has been broken.

A different view of it is offered in 'I'm Your Man' in that his passion itself keeps him awake: 'The beast won't go to sleep.' A distant voice is heard through all this: 'It is not good for man to be alone,' but the experience is not always commensurate with the voice; sometimes it leads away from the voice and then greater alienation than ever supervenes. Loneliness can give birth to longing; sometimes it is reversed. He needs, he fears, his lover. In her solemn gaze is indeed 'incomparable beauty' and yet 'unmeaning' too. But the experience here, it should be noted; is post-orgasmic, as if Leonard were deliberately directing our attention to that particular feeling of mental and bodily awareness that subvenes, which the French characterise as *le petit mort* ('the little death'), directing us by a different means once more to the wisdom of the East. 'You dare to interview me on the matter/of your loathsome destinies/you poor boobies of the North,' he was to exclaim in *Death Of A Lady's Man* later, his Middle-Eastern pride asserting itself!

The book is fashioned in three disparate parts: The History Of Them All; A Long Letter From F; Beautiful Losers: an Epilogue In The Third Person. The characters involved are as few as their adventures are numerous: there is 'F', the central figure, wild and wilful, free-loving and fast, ardent and ambitious; the typical leader because he has the more urgent ideas, the more facile Tongue (the capital is required, as we shall see); a latter-day Sam Slick, whom Vassal audaciously suggests was modelled on Layton!

There is Edith, the young, inexperienced, out-played and ultimately suicidal woman of innocent virtue, who forsakes her virtue in order to retain her lovers' affections. And there is the Dallyer (no such name occurs in the book, Leonard simply refers to him as 'I' – the subject of the 'inner monologues'; the one carried away on the stream of consciousness which first floods, and then breaks all over him – but it keeps the reverse alphabetical sequence going F, E, D; Leonard would never be that obvious!); a history buff who was somewhat tyrannised by his subject.

One who is both amused and diverted by the allurements of 'F' and his own otherwise repressed inner makeup, who merges into the one by losing himself in the 'all'. Some commentators have seen in the use of the first person singular – 'I' – throughout the book and the otherwise anonymous emphasis on 'F' who appears to mesh with the 'I' at the end, the creation of a different character – a lost and compound personality: 'IF', whose 'lostness' is mainly the result of his religious formation, founded on the great 'if' of *deo volunte*, which features from time to time in the initial letters of the Danish Vibrator. But this is not convincing, though it secures a bizarre unity, and one of appropriate schizophrenic proportions!

And there is finally the sainted Catherine Tekakwitha who inspires the Dallyer, and ridicules F's feckless failures by her own tenacity and single-mindedness; who leaves judged the earthly Edith; a passing cloud in the hinterland of their experience, whose shadow challenges and antagonises them all by its solidity.

Despite the siren-calls of F, the Dallyer is provoked and titillated by History, which at once inspires and bemuses him. Without question, he is seriously involved with the past, his own not least. But that elusive thread which he seeks outwits him, except in stark failure – when he loses all. He is too ready to forego the application required for passing fancy; F's allurements easily tempt and mislead him from his path. Appreciative of the present, he foregoes the past in order to indulge his appetites to the full. By the time he has woken up to the realities, he has become 'orphaned'; overtaken by unmeaning; he has lost his individuality. He is the very epitome of Robert Frost's 'Hired Man': 'And nothing to look backward to with pride/And nothing to look forward to with hope.'

F fares even worse, for he proceeds from mere garrulity to political success, in the process of which he also loses everything, becoming not merely disgraced but mad. His was the vision, his the programme, his the means – and his the ultimate unreality. His world became a theatre, then a cell, and thence his tomb. But what flights of fancy he envisaged! What mind-spinning contrivances to achieve his end! How extraordinary his imagination to foster such fecundity; and how amazing that others could listen and be won – even though the winning is but temporary, and the subsequent losing overwhelming!

Catherine – *Saint* Catherine – is the substance to which much of the other characters' meaninglessness is related; she is the enduring presence in their insubstantiality; the reality in their shadow-like existence. She *is* the matter of History! they merely of uncertain existence, mere 'chronicle'. Lacking in every type of advantage and sophistication, she nevertheless endures and influences; from her slender resources eternal realities were fashioned. She is the one loser who wins; the ugly who discovers real beauty; the physical invested with the spiritual.

Despite the high-octane level of the book's sexuality, its rollicking extravagance – indeed, because of these things – many readers have missed the seriousness (not its gravity: that was Breavman's uncles' mistake), of purpose. But this is not a tale which provides answers. That is not Leonard's way. He does not readily don the teacher's mantle, save that of the autodidact, even when his work is charged with prophetic insight and implication. But here he wrestles with issues of high seriousness, content to let the reader draw his own lessons, make his own judgments, or not.

We should note that the frontispiece caption commences with a quotation from the 1927 song of Oscar Hammerstein II's 'Ol' Man River': 'Somebody said, "lift that bale".' By it the author directs us to the sub-theme of the book; its gravitational centre. It is about slavery and servitude; the ordering of one man and two women's lives and activities by another – the owning of them, indeed. It is about their lack of genuine freedom, i.e. their inability to exercise it freely; about their ensuing constraints and subjugation. It could properly be described as a parable on this theme, though its rich depths – well below the dense erotica which adorn it – might suggest an allegory (i.e. a story with several symbolic meanings rather than a single one); never a Platonic myth! But in 'Ol' Man River' it was not merely an individual who was unfree, ordered to do the menial tasks; but an individual who stood for a people. So here, with deadly earnestness.

The first part of the story ('Book I') comprises the storyline itself; what follows is more or less commentary on it – a device Leonard uses throughout his work from this period on, a particularly interesting development in the light of his reply to Pierre Berton's exasperated questioning. That story is named, 'The History Of Them All' – of his main characters, that is; but by extension, those for whom they stood: us! (but primarily his fellow Canadians).

But for one such as Leonard, to whom Tradition and History are intensely important, the story had to have depth as well as weight. It could not have been the story of *four* individuals – Catherine, the Dallyer, Edith and F. That would have reduced its seriousness, trivialised life. So he took a *cause célèbre* – the beautification process, then ongoing when he wrote it, (it was actually completed in 1980) of Catherine Tekakwitha, 'the Iroquois Virgin,' the 'Lily of the Shores of the Mohawk River.' ('Lily' and 'Rose' were to become more meaningful yet to Leonard, not least as they are translations for the Hebrew name 'Susan' – literally 'trusting one'!) – and anchors their story in real History; emphasising the fact by representing the central character of the book – the 'Dallyer' – in the role of an actual historian: 'an old scholar,' 'a well-known folklorist,' 'an academic authority,' no less.

To Andrew Tyler, of *Disc*, he explained that his source-material for the book was a volume of history titled *Jesuits In North America* and the authorised biography of the putative saint: *The Biography Of Catherine Tekakwitha*, though he refers explicitly to Edouard Lecompte's *Une Vierge Iroquoise: Catherine Tekakwitha. Le Lis de Dords de la Mohawk et du St-Laurent* in the book itself. He also told Tyler that he depended on a wartime (1943) comic book, *Blue Beetle*, for aspects of his characterisation; which may account for some of its zanyness. But behind all this, as is characteristic of Leonard's writing, lay a more personal interest. He explained it to Michael Harris on the *Saturday Night* programme of 1969 that has been so much quoted: He had a friend, Alanis Obamsawin, an Abenaquis Indian, who had many pictures of Catherine in her apartment, which he came to like 'over the years.' It was she who lent Leonard the 'very rare book' mentioned above – which Leonard subsequently lost – disconnections made permanent!)

In that statement/unstatement rhythm that characterises his work – the statement/commentary aspect just mentioned, which frequently calls the statement into question, and sometimes actually negates it – he accentuates the 'inner monologue' and outer dialogue aspects. The rhythm, we might add, recalls the dialectical nature of reality he was seeking to understand from his studies in Eastern mysticism and philosophy. It also signals man's defeatism – his first emphasis on loser status in the book – by speaking of the Dallyer's 'dusty mind full of junk.' He who could not sleep at night; who had 'forgotten most of what he had read,' and, 'frankly, it never seemed very important to me or the world,' and that he was 'so human as to suffer from constipation, the rewards (the plural identifies its chronic condition) of a sedentary life.'

To all this he adds – it is the second emphasis of loser status – that, unhappily, the subject of his expertise – Catherine and her people – had a 'brief history' which is characterised by 'incessant defeat.' 'This unfortunate people never won a single battle,' they were, in fact, a 'pack of failures.' The story is posited in a sea of failures; and it gets worse!

However, the Dallyer has a mission: he aims to rescue the Virgin from those who would have her beatified. He seeks to do so by *rescuing* her full womanhood. Church authorities wished to promote her saintliness by highlighting her virginity (even though she lost it in her youth); he wishes to restore her to a truer position by allowing the flower to blossom. They called the loss a deflowering; he asserts the opposite, it is a true burgeoning. They promote her interests by sterilising her womanhood – 'sublimating' it would be their preferred expression; he by causing it to reach its full and natural potential. He wished to liberate her from the bondage of artificiality, to the ordained fulfilment of all 'real' women.

The particularity of the *koan* is here manifested: true sainthood via sexual fulfilment; 'knowing' her spiritually by 'knowing' her physically. (A concept that is well known in other religions, Hinduism and the Inca cults for example.) In it both Zen Buddhism and Jewish theology converge to overthrow the centuries' old claim (not least of the Catholics, but of all downgraders of the physical) that a sexual life is less than holy; that virginity is a degree of human excellence beyond the ordinary. 'Rot,' claims our author, loudly and persistently. That is a misconception, another species of ultimate *loss*. (For such Buddhism as he had mastered – and it was not small – would not merely assert the 'connection' between the dualities which is germane to his native Judaism, but would drive beyond them towards that state of unitary consciousness which there exists.)

He enforces the point by exclaiming that 'desire changes the world,' calling on Catherine Tekakwitha herself to recognise 'how I want to be mystical and good' – not by negation, not by abstinence, but by fulfilling the divine command to honour their sexuality; by following the (Zen) path of 'transcendental ordinariness' (another *koan*).

The matter is accordingly summed up, provocatively, in the ultimate question of the book, the ultimate question of man's nature, indeed: *Is matter holy?*, a question that totally undermines (if answered positively) the duality under which Catherine has been placed – against her nature, against the 'primitive' teaching of her tribe, against the 'natural theology' of her caring sponsor's convictions. Their placing of her in history threatens to encapsulate her in an all-comprehensive loss: a necklace of . . . unmeaning. Vassal is correct therefore to emphasise how important 'matter' is to Leonard (whether gold, clay, wood etc), even as he is right to underline 'his most famous accusation in the book,' i.e. 'I accuse the Church' – the Church which has demeaned matter, undermined its reality by a false duality, and thereby diminished the world (of sense not least), of time and history, too.

Throughout these opening, subject-focusing paragraphs, another story-line has been intimated; it is one which is introduced by means of a series of quotations from F, the Dallyer's erstwhile friend and self-appointed mentor, who 'died in a padded cell, his brain rotted from too much dirty sex.' The story proceeds by a series of numbered sections, each representing a day in the Dallyer's life. There are 72 of them, significantly in agreement with the mystic number of man's life (see our comment regarding the telephone-dance). These quotations, which show that F was essentially a self-serving demeanour who always opposed what others wished for the sake of opposing them, by which he sought to establish his own superiority in their eyes, opens the History of the first Book into its full theme – their sordid and tumultuous, and essentially meaningless escapades; itself an essay in loss. By this the Dallyer is diverted from his own cause, his wife corrupted from her true nature to the point of suicide, and F himself reaps the just deserts of his insane visions and ideology, paying the awful price of the all-time loser in the process.

The story-line follows a Joycean stream-of-consciousness method, as with *The Favourite Game*, rather than a chronological sequence as we saw earlier, despite the numeration. (It is interesting to recall that both A.M. Klein in *The Second Scroll* (1951) – of whom Leonard had written in 'Song For Abraham Klein' in *The Spice-Box Of Earth* – and Henry Miller, had followed this. Miller, whose influence is detectable at several points, himself a visitor to Hydra and its *environs* – spoke of Joyce being a 'surrealist of sorts' as Leonard is here.)

The story is constituted by the piecemeal recollections of the Dallyer as he plunges in his cuckolded misery from one episode to another, his mind rolling forwards and backwards in agitation over his aspirations and losses – of profession and cause, marriage and friendship.

Space forbids the delineation of these, but suffice it to mention that, apart from tracing that the subjugation of the Indians by the French, and their spiritual ideology by the Jesuits (two critically important sub-themes), he scores *en passant* a few hits against other 'lost causes'. For example, he makes F compare the lost state of the Indians to that of the Greeks, among whom Leonard was living when he wrote, of course! (This was more perceptive than many realised, or gave credit for. A year after the book was published a *coup d'état* brought Greece to a standstill, under the right-wing 'fascist' power of the colonels. It recalls his and Layton's prescience in the matter of the rise of drugs, the hippies and violence in political life, as reflected in their 'failed' plays.)

Of the various subjects handled, there can be no doubt as to their importance, whether we talk in terms of human bondage or the emancipation of matter. More questionable, however, was the manner by which he examined them; the sheer extravagance by which his views were projected. Some authors, knowing the risk, may have dared to take one or two episodes and endue them with the sexual excess that Leonard gives to virtually every page. Not so, our author! It highlights both his obsessive qualities – surely one of the classical signs of genius, whatever else we may think of it – as well as the importance he attaches to them. As politics are too important to be left to the politicians, so he seems to say, sexuality is too sacred to be left to the priests; too serious to be left to the judges and law-makers. Matter matters, and mind should mind the actualities, not avoid them.

But there are indications, intimations, that he introduces to dissociate himself from the extravagances. This should be unnecessary in any case, given the book's fictional status, but he was too knowing to risk that. If some such association – at once loose and carefully controlled – be permitted, it is clear that the archivist-historian is close to Leonard's own role. Very significantly F calls his friend 'Larry' – as if in specific admission of his likeness to Lawrence Breavman; and a little later he comments that 'a kind uncle took the orphan in.'

How he suffers and writhes in the story! Not only with his own sensuous nature and entrapment therein, made all the more poignant as it both follows and clashes with the clear teaching of his faith and its 'natural theology,' but in the aspects it raises: the holiness and wholeness of matter, not least; but also his hopes for the world to be 'mystic and good'. His living 'meanly', and his forcing of his young wife; his (scholar's) pettiness of mind; his intense dislike of his own crudity ('Aren't I meant to speak of God?' he distraughtly exclaims – a Cohen of *koans*); his failure – another, agonising loss – to 'make connections'; his hopes to unify the world of his experience; his guilt over the homosexual practices of his youth, as well as his repeated expressions of disgust at his friend F's behaviour, and so on.

F, we should observe, was not merely the devil's advocate in all this: he was the devil personified. His madness showed itself ultimately, but it develops throughout the whole story – and especially in Book II which is something of a commentary on Book I by way of a letter of explanation from him. His loss of touch with reality manifests itself in ever wilder language and action, wildness that sucks in both his friend the Dallyer and his innocent but curious wife, Edith. It is, after all, F who tried to get him to 'love appearances' more than reality; it was F who said that, 'a strong man cannot but love the church' (perhaps merely a self-contradiction, rather than a *koan?*). It was F who commented that he had never heard of a single female saint that he wouldn't have liked to take to bed; it was F who cuckolded his friend – and grossly corrupted his wife in so doing. He is the *reductio ad absurdum* of the sensual man; the true 'sex maniac' because maniacally obsessed. The high principle which motivates his friend in matters sexual – the holiness of matter (i.e. the body) – and the divinely ordained sanctity of loving and its proper sexual expression – are not merely absent in F, but totally mysterious to him. 'Connect nothing' he screams out, and out again, while 'connecting' with everything and everyone gluttonously.

The sexual excess – graphic, intense, unsparing – is apt, for a *koan* would not be a *koan* unless it contradicted logical reasoning; disengaged the mind from its habits; jolted the consciousness into a new mode of awareness; and pitched the senses through pain and the *shock* of pain (a distinctive form of Leonard's Rinzai Buddhism). And a Cohen would not be a Cohen unless that which was ordained was not carried out in total obedience to that which is laid down: one cannot be merely devoted – one has to pursue, and consummate, one's craft.

A *koan* (the word simply means 'public case', from *kung-an*, as if a piece of case-law; that is, an issue of public record, a precedent) has been described by Professor Suzuki as 'a divine mirror that reflects the original face of both the sacred and the secular.'

In this entangled story Leonard asserts in all its brash rawness the clash between sacred and secular, holy and profane, saint and sinner, mystic and politician. He argues – it is the existential fact of his life – the divine face that each bears. We reel from its encounter, we doubt its wisdom (and its morality); and F whispers still: 'Connect nothing'. . .

But even the raw language used by him is not needed for the book merely in the symbolic sense (a usage we shall see him questioning – and rejecting – later), but also in a 'technical' sense then appropriate to the drug conscious sixties. It takes an explicit form, actually subjoining footnotation to it on pages 188/9, which form the Dallyer's commentary on F's invocations to history. 'Shit', for example, far from being a vulgar expression raised to the level of an expletive, is defined as 'Originally heroin and the hard drugs, but now in general use for any euphoriant, from the harmless Indian hemp to the innocuous aspirin . . .' Its use, therefore, is in itself a *koan*-like (certainly Cohen-like) usage specifically made to emphasise the *paradox* between that which 'elevates' the mind and that which destroys it; between the euphoria of the spirit and the excretion of the body. Leonard is nothing if not subtle, and ambiguous in his references. Indirectly, he urges us to connect all: oneness predominating . . .

There is one aspect of *Beautiful Losers* to which Leonard particularly drew our attention, surprised that it had gone unnoticed by reviewers and critics alike, and of great importance. (He had also made the point to Vassal: 'Cohen regrets that not one of them who had read it had seen what the novel was about,' a *roman à clef*.) We have made a number of comments emphasising F's curious control over the Dallyer, how the latter was comprehensively in his control, how subservient he was to his strange and mindless teachings; how willingly he risked all – career, home-life and future – for his friend. The relationship is as overdrawn as the sexual encounters are wild and the politicking unrealistic. It was precisely drawn to create that reaction. Leonard was making of it a strong point.

At the time of writing, all sorts of 'gurus' abounded – in religion, meditation, consciousness-enhancement, philosophy, mysticism, politics, art, and so on. Thousands of young people, and many not so young, placed themselves under their tutelage; gave them money; slaved for them in all sorts of ways; left home, parents, loved ones, jobs and future; and travelled the world at their behest. Such were found strewn all across Europe, North America, and not least India. Not so much the Klondyke Rush as the Hippie Trail. Not a few died on it. They carried the biggest 'bale' of all: false hope, which they, on lifting, were broken under its weight.

And for what? Never was Leonard so explicitly didactic as he risked being in the descriptions of this relationship between F and the Dallyer. He did so specifically to offer the warning: beware! As he said, in seeing the film of his life, *Ladies And Gentlemen: Mr Leonard Cohen: caveat emptor!* He was as adverse to anyone following *him*, as he was to hearing them follow any alleged sage, mystic, guru, teacher or more honest madman or self-delusioned visionary.

It was the natural precursor to his poems 'I Met A Woman Long Ago', later a very successful song, and his 'I Believe I Heard Your Master Sing' (also a successful song). Such were the carpet-baggers of the mind, the parasites of heaven – after whom he called his next book.

However, there is a bolder chain of significances throughout the book, which reviewers – the more discerning, that is – have not been slow to recognise. It reaches its own climax in section 15 of Book I, where Catherine is spoken of as having developed 'a hatred for finite shit' – i.e. for human euphoria and that which produces it; stating that the name 'Tekakwitha' means 'she who, advancing, arranges the shadows neatly'; that is, that she has made progress in the real order by a proper ordering of the appearances. The sacred has, in her case, given way to the secular. 'The girls' (that is, Catherine's friends, Leonard informs us) 'are spending too much time on tomorrow, but Catherine is gathering her days into a chain, linking the shadows.' She was *connecting*.

It paves the way for the first explicit denunciation of modern society, but more so, of the Church which has – through the use of main force when it wished to – fashioned it, in the book (though not in his poetry); naturally, it is an extravagant denunciation:

> '*I don't like what's happening to Montreal architecture. What happened to the tents? I would like to accuse the Church. I accuse the Roman Catholic Church of Quebec of ruining my sex life and of shoving my member up a relic box meant for a finger, I accuse the RCC of Q. of making me commit queer horrible acts with F., another victim of the system, I accuse the Church of killing Indians, I accuse the Church of refusing to let Edith go down on me properly, I accuse the Church of covering Edith with red grease and of depriving Catherine Tekakwitha of red grease, I accuse the Church of haunting automobiles and of causing pimples, I accuse the Church of building green masturbation toilets, I accuse the Church of stealing my sun and tan, of promoting dandruff, I accuse the Church of sending people with dirty toenails into streetcars where they work against Science, I accuse the Church of female circumcision in French Canada.*'

A denunciation that leads back into the story of Catherine; born, we are told, in virtually the same year that Canada's colonisation by the French started (1656 and 1664 respectively).

Something was afoot: Nature itself was poised; Catherine wept; strange doves wheeled in the sky; the 'Heart' – which was 'neither new nor old, nor indeed any prisoner of description,' listened; Catherine was about to be forced to marry. A fish (the sacred Ichathus?) leaped out of the Mohawk River; Catherine discovered her womanhood; the luminous fish smiled; Catherine fled, was chased, outwitted her would-be husband; the fish continued to smile; Catherine returned home; she was roundly beaten: 'Catherine Tekakwitha smiled cheerfully'; praise and meditation broke out! The rape of Canada becomes a reality. The political *dénouement* unfolds; the double-edged attack – against false spirituality and wrong-headed materialism on the one hand; against political rapine on the other – becomes clear.

It carries a veiled criticism against the consumer society (see the reference regarding Joseph 'the acquirer'), against the transitoriness and gloss of the movie industry, against all that glitters and glistens meaninglessly. A gloss, one might add, that arises out of America's own Declaration of Independence, which promised 'Life, liberty and the pursuit of happiness.' Such 'utilitarianism' is based on an ideal that is plastic in essence, never more so than when in the hands of unprincipled money-makers. As the Hasidics said, 'While we pursue happiness, we flee from contentment.' It was never better encapsulated than in the tragic life of the great exponents of the jazz age, Scott and Zelda Fitzgerald, the former Leonard first encountered at McGill in his English Literature studies, an influence that followed him to the Aegean. (He was actually reading Fitzgerald's collected works about the time of this novel.)

We are moving from the personal to the communal; from the individual to the social, and that at a time when anti-American feeling was rife in Canada. The Dallyer's involvement with F reaches a new height; he is invited to share the latter's political success, and sit in on his maiden speech in parliament. It was he, F, who had recommended him to have sexual relations with a saint, which had earlier disgusted him – and then caused him to ask whether in it he had 'stumbled on the truth about Canada.' (The political reality, that is.) 'Am I any closer to Kateri Tekakwitha? (he questions), which now inspires the all-important reflection on what a saint is. In so doing he discovers the real essence of true saintliness, which is somewhat different from that Buddhist definition – 'those who have won the Path' – that Leonard was presently studying. Scobie has drawn attention to the image of the saint in Canadian literature (e.g. in Robertson Davies and B. P. Nicol), but there are much more important connections, as we shall see. The saint in this work has a distinctive function: she is the kernel of the *koan:*

> *'A saint is someone who has achieved a remote human possibility. It is impossible to say what that possibility is. I think it has something to do with the energy of love. Contact with this energy results in the exercise of a kind of balance in the chaos of existence. A saint does not dissolve the chaos; if he did the world would have changed long ago. I do not think that a saint dissolves the chaos even for himself, for there is something arrogant and warlike in the notion of a man setting the universe in order. It is a kind of balance that is his glory. He rides the drifts like an escaped ski. His course is a caress of the hill. His track is a drawing of the snow in a moment of its particular arrangement with wind and rock. (An almost specific throw-back to Lisa's favourite game.) Something in him so loves the world that he gives himself to the laws of gravity and chance. Far from flying with the angels, he traces with the fidelity of a seismograph needle the state of the solid bloody landscape. His house is dangerous and finite, but he is at home in the world. He can love the shapes of human beings, the fine and twisted shapes of the heart. It is good to have among*

us such men, such balancing monsters of love. It makes me think that the numbers in the bag actually correspond to the numbers on the raffles we have bought so dearly, and so the prize is not an illusion.'

The very act of defining – of reaching such perception – only emphasises how far he is from it; how difficult the perfection for which he yearns; even 'a kind of balance' is impossible: 'The pursuit seems such nonsense. I'm not happy here, in F's old treehouse,' which earlier he had called 'a shit glory tree,' using one of the codewords specifically placed and interpreted, i.e. that which induces an artificial sense of spiritual euphoria, that most deluding form of 'appearances'; a word which could not be used publicly – i.e. in the *New York Times* – as late as 1983. 'My brain is ruined. My career is in tatters . . .' Yet reality is intervening. The parallels between this passage and Leonard's replies to Pierre Berton are patent. It is the reformulation of the lifelong quest, in almost identical language.

Earlier the Dallyer had wanted to be 'a mystic wit,' now the levity has given way to a due seriousness. We should note that, whatever his definition is, it is localised in the real world: the saint can exercise 'balance in the chaos of existence,' a balance 'that is his glory.' He loves the world, and so can give himself to it – to its 'laws of gravity and chance,' the 'solid bloody landscape,' though 'dangerous and finite,' it *is* his home. He loves the people, be they fine or twisted. '*It is good to have among us such men, such balancing monsters of love,*' he concludes. But why make love to one? It is, as he recalls his loving of Edith his wife, *the* time when his loneliness, his alienation was least felt: 'for a blessed second truly I was not alone.'

That is what it was all about – love as company, love as family, love as the neutralising agent of solitariness, the existential pang of solitariness. 'How do I get close to one?' he asks, especially a dead one? He's not happy here . . . But he has discovered the secret, if not appropriated it. Whatever the degree of possibility – 'remote' or otherwise, he has grasped the energy of love; he has learned to love, to love the world, to love people. As R.S. Ingersoll perceived, 'Love (is) the only priest.'

He refutes F's 'cheap *koans*'; he is brought to the realisation that he wanted to achieve his goal instantly, without the pain and trouble involved. It was an important moment in self-understanding. But an even more important realisation awaits him, the realisation of the book, which takes place at a public demonstration. He is earthing the high voltage of his energies. It has nothing to do with 'flying angels': 'History decreed that in the battle for a continent the Indian should lose to the Frenchman. In 1760 History decreed that the Frenchman should lose to the Englishman!' The Dallyer was pleased. The speaker continued: 'In 1964 History decrees, no History commands, that the English surrender this land, which they have loved so imperfectly, surrender it to the Frenchman, surrender it to us.' A new 'Laurentian Republic' is stirring . . . The first Book closes with F stating that the new scheme requires some blood to be spilled – a martyr's (his own!) – and the Dallyer beseeching the Virgin everywhere.

The second Book constitutes the aftermath and the commentary, by means of a long letter from F from prison, but read posthumously. It achieved its own climax in the latest region of fascist expression – in Peronist Argentina – amid wild, sexual extravagance, an extravagance that demonstrates that a development beyond mere 'secular pleasure' is possible; an understanding that goes beyond one's 'tiny swamp machinery' to greater heights and pleasures; experiences realisable only via the Danish Vibrator: the *DV*, which has a life as well as a will of its own, and a power to fulfil it.

But not before Edith has protested to F over 'what you've done to me and my husband,' and emphasised that that which is mediated comes via a member of that régime: a waiter in the form of 'him' 'the brain mole,' 'the new leader,' 'the leader (who) started a racial speech,' whose 'black moustache and leather hair' are precisely attended to before departure, after they had been washed in soap made of 'melted human flesh.' He is here in Argentina! Little has changed; tyranny is universal – 'he' misses the newsreels, the parades, but 'everything else is available.' Not only 'everything' but 'everywhere' – a pansophic warning! – which is made in the appearance of Isis, the present reality of Edith as transformed by the waiter: the goddess who was 'all things to all.'

In front of such, F declares 'I'm only fit to suck your toes,' but, says Leonard obliquely: understand the game, observe the pattern, 'beware of the con'! F confessed that it was he 'who feared the rational mind, therefore I tried to make you a little mad.' He asks whether his friend is now 'disarmed and empty, an instrument of Grace? Can you stop talking? Has loneliness led you into ecstasy.' He moves to 'the sweet burden of my argument,' to which all his own speeches had been mere preface, the Climax of it All, (a piece Buffy Sainte-Marie set to music, titling it 'Magic'):

> *'God is alive. Magic is afoot. God is alive. Magic is afoot. God is afoot. Magic is alive. Alive is afoot. Magic never died. God never sickened. Many poor men lied. Many sick men lied. Magic never weakened. Magic never hid. Magic always ruled. God is afoot. God never died. God was ruler though his funeral lengthened. Though his mourners thickened Magic never fled.*

Though his shrouds were hoisted the naked God did live.
Though his words were twisted the naked Magic thrived.
Though his death was published round and round the world the
heart did not believe. Many hurt men wondered. Many struck
men bled. Magic never faltered. Magic always led. Many stones
were rolled but God would not lie down.'

Significantly, though undoubtedly deviously, as became a politician F admits that he wanted his friend's 'confusion to be a butterfly net for magic.' Wherever 'magic' appears we should read 'mystery' and, where appropriate, mysticism, which Leonard uses as a synonym for them, though Jean-Dominique Brierre (who wrote on *Beautiful Losers* in Vassals' book) is utterly wrong to say that 'one is obliged to mention that if one wants to understand the conception of mysticism that he develops . . . one must understand magic.'

It is unnecessary so to speak, given the high religious background of Leonard's mind, not only in the Cabalistic writings but especially in that element of surrealism which adorns – and informs – such writing as this novel. Brierre has failed to observe, as many commentators have, the deliberate interplay between 'God' and 'magic' and ignores Leonard's poetic use of parallelism, after the Hebrew style. 'A diet of paradox,' he asserts, 'fattens the ironist not the psalmist,' how much more a diet of *koans!*

word as song

'Music, as everybody knows, is a delicious pleasure . . . It forms part of every social gathering, and of every entertainment as a sheer delight.'

ARISTOTLE

'Discoursed with Mr Hooke about the nature of musical sounds, and he did make me understand the nature of musical sounds made by strings mighty prettily . . .'

SAMUEL PEPYS

'God respects me when I work; he loves me when I sing.'

TAGORE

'The curious thing we call song is satisfying . . . A lot of us don't know how to sing according to certain standards, but there is a whole tradition of music where you just want to hear the man telling a story as accurately and authentically as possible. That is why there is a place for singers like me.'

LEONARD COHEN

the sound of
many hands

By this time, and through this process of searching and writing, Leonard's mind (once 'cleansed' of the effects of writing *Beautiful Losers*) had achieved its permanent lineaments: the recognition that he had something important to say; a discontentment with the narrower confines of Judaism as sufficient to encompass his understandings, to which his gleanings from Christianity added very little; and the realisation that in Eastern philosophy – not *so* different from Jewish at some important points (especially in its Hasidic/Cabalistic forms) – was particularly congenial.

We have seen how his Zen Buddhism found a real place in the expression of this in *Beautiful Losers*. Its dialectical nature of reality and the *koan* principle, in particular, were extremely important. "I like Zen," he commented. "(It's the) personal practice of letting the mind drop." But this particular effort was not without a price. After he had finished *Beautiful Losers* he fasted for 12 days as the writing of the book had caused him to 'lose his appetite'. Unfortunately, he was sunburned at the same time. He ended up with a temperature of 104, which required intravenous feeding, and two months' forced rest.

One of the best known *koans* is offered in the form of this question: 'What is the sound of one hand clapping?' The provocative questioning inherent in such challenges now began more earnestly to inform and formulate his work, and also to disengage him from previous understandings. In particular, the music and song which had been such an important part of his life hitherto forced itself upon him, purposefully. From a distance we can already hear, not the sound of one hand clapping, but many hands, as a brilliant and rewarding future slowly unveiled itself.

We have seen that in both his novels, as in his poetry, Montreal occupied a position of some importance. It could not be otherwise for this 'Jerusalem of the north', as Leonard called it. As E. A. Guest sighed in 'Home':

> *'It takes a heap o' living in a house t' make it home A heap o' sun and shadder, an' ye sometimes have t' roam Afore ye really 'preciate the things ye lef' behind, An hunger fer 'em somehow, with 'em allus on yer mind.'*

Things were happening in Greece, menacingly; and in his native city, reassuringly. In July 1965 there had been the brutal suppression of left-wing demonstrations in Athens following a ferment that lasted for 70 days, in which 200 were injured and up to a million gathered in its streets, frequently orchestrating the chorus, 'King! Take your mother, and go!' – but one indication of the deep unrest in that deeply divided country. Not least among the powerful influences ebbing and flowing was the poet-composer Mikis Theodorakis, whose music and courageous activities had profoundly impressed Leonard. "My people have been told that they are nothing," Theodorakis had said, "but through my music I tell them that our country is great and beautiful, and that we can do anything. Greece can live happily."

Throughout Leonard's time on Hydra the folklorist/popular traditions of Greece were being taken by Theodorakis and given a new dynamic, which became immensely popular achieving no less than 60 per cent of the country's record sales, not least in featuring the bouzouki. (So characteristic did this become, as a sort of signature-instrument of the new and highly politicised agitation, that the authorities actually outlawed it, so ensuring that it became an even deeper part of Greek consciousness.) For five years a tug-of-war took place, between scholars and artists, oligarchy and populace, crown and people. In the dismissal of George Papandreou by King Constantine the fire was ignited, the Greek army put on full alert, and the way paved for the Colonel's coup of April 1967. At the heart of the ferment was Theodorakis's vision and music. Leonard was impressed, and motivated still further towards a life of poetry-in-song. Scobie's view of Leonard's motivation is simply absurd at this point, and unworthy of the serious critic; especially when left to cover the man as well as his art:

'Pop art is to become an increasingly important image for Cohen: he embraces it because it is itself a loser (sic), despised by the critical élite, essentially ephemeral, and energised only by the immediate emotional charge it provides: cheap thrills.'

We ignore the sheer *hauteur* of the criticism, as we do the foolish imputation of motivation to the world of pop art, and his unknowing condemnation of it as ephemeral – as if the only measure of art is its ability to last! Coming from a critic who did not see the need even to interview his subject, this is a species of flippancy that out-ranks even that of the hack-critics. 'Cheap' is his word for it. More realistic is Leonard's own comment in 'Lot' (which combines origin and destiny):

'Tell me master
do my lips move
or where does it come from
this soft total chant that drives my soul
like a spear of salt into the rock . . .'

Meanwhile in Montreal, other voices were commanding: As Breavman said in *The Favourite Game*, 'In Montreal there is no present tense . . . only the past claiming victories'; it was, as Krantz once exclaimed, 'bloody beautiful'; now feeling the pulsations of a rising generation, the challenges of post-war freedoms. For more than 20 years there had been open political discussion which sounded to British ears – and not a few WASPS – like revolution. It had, in fact, gone on for years, the First World War had raised the severe question of dying 'for someone else's war', which was strongly exacerbated by the Depression, and rapidly accelerated by the Second World War. Mac-Lennan's *Two Solitudes* highlighted its particularity, if it did not actually precipitate matters. Men like Pellatier and Levesque had been meeting for more than 10 years – oddly enough, in Westmount itself – 'to test Liberal policies.' The time for change was upon them. Canada was beginning to assert the feeling that this should be her century: a feeling – as we saw – that Leonard expounded in *Beautiful Losers*.

The turning point was reached in the urbane, highly intelligent shape of Pierre Elliot Trudeau, a French-Canadian of partly Scottish extraction, who was elected to Parliament for the Montreal riding in 1965 (an interesting constituency which boasted almost an exact split between English – and French-speaking voters, about one third of whom were Jewish). Commented Leonard to Elizabeth Thomson in 1979: "He is probably one of the greatest figures we've ever produced. He dignifies the country with his presence."

Not only dignified it, indeed, but electrified it. It is not surprising that he so influenced Leonard – and millions besides, within and outside of Canada – for 'the only constant mental factor' he gave expression to in himself was 'opposition to accepted opinions.' Here was Canada's answer to John F. Kennedy; and more so. A devout Catholic who detested both clericalism and nationalism (he once attacked the hierarchy calling its members 'the frogs from holy-water basins,' *and* poured scorn on the separatist movement, then rapidly gaining ground), a brilliant scholar, bilingual, with a truly mondial culture grounded in French sophistication; a lawyer-teacher (but Leonard could forgive a genius!), who was attracted to 'the religion of love' as represented by the best of Eastern religious philosophy, and hence against legalistic ethics or credal limitations.

(To Trudeau's own world-travels and adventures, we might add the coincidental arrival in America of A.C. Bhaktivedanti Swami Prabhupada, by which the Hare Krishna movement was begun – and much more besides, for with his arrival psychedelia took off). Trudeau was still a bachelor, shy, but devastating with women, a man of *renaissance* mind, an alluring sense of *fantasie*, flamboyant, sentimental; a lover of brilliant talk, music and poetry, who – like Leonard, as in so many ways – needed solitude 'to replenish my emotions, to find my inner directives.'

Needless to say this rising star exploded on the scene, causing the largest political crowds to gather in Canadian history – Trudeaumania they called it, in the wake of The Beatles. Within a year he was appointed Minister of Justice, in which office he introduced the most forward-looking moral reforms – which the traditionalists said could not be done, to which defeatism he retorted, "Government has no business in the bedrooms of the people." But separatism was moulder-ing in the bars and clubs, on radio and television, and throughout the eastern townships. One government minister in Quebec was heard to say that his government 'will have to take steps *forcing* immigrants to integrate with Quebec's French-speaking population.' Within days a Declaration was signed by over 150 intellectuals, urging the govern-ment to make French the official language of Quebec. The exciting sixties! Little wonder Leonard felt the need, yet again, to return home. He recognised in Canada, as in Montreal, the excitement as well as the danger.

1966 was a very good year for Leonard Cohen. In addition to *Beautiful Losers*, he also published his fourth volume of poetry: *Parasites Of Heaven*, a counterpoint to the alleged irreverence and immodesty – some said stark immorality – of the novel. Professor Dudek, in editing his *Poetry Of Our Time*, also published that year, spoke of Leonard being 'beyond classification', yet known for 'his lyrical verve, his spon-taneous frankness, (his) engaging personality,' and drew attention to the 'modernity of outlook' he projected: 'He belongs to the new generation which includes the beats, The Beatles, and the *boîtes à chanson*.' (The latter a café with a corner or stage for singing. Rumours of Hydra, and elsewhere, having clearly percolated through!)

But, apparently unbeknown to Dudek, it was changing, dramat-ically. George Bowering hit the mark when, in a review which suggested that Leonard 'could become the Jewish Kahlil Gibran,' he spoke of him as being 'After all (or before all) a serious writer with a vision of himself that is more enduring than Kodak . . . The newest book . . . is his least important, but in it one may find his greatest strengths . . .'

Himself a poet of almost exactly Leonard's age, Bowering was highly complimentary to him, not uncritically, happily; and spoke of him as an 'ultimate lyric man,' 'the epitome of Western man, formed by post-Hellenic European modes of perception and thinking.' But that is to misread Leonard. His ambiguity, his deep, driving need to connect – through history and in history, albeit in a supra-historical way – is deep precisely because he is *not* 'Western man, formed by post-Hellenic European modes of perception and thinking.' If he had been that, how easy would his life have been! How simple then the *angst!* As Mr Bowering quotes the poet of himself, without understanding the point he makes: 'Leonard hasn't been the same/since he wandered from his name.'

He was a Cohen, root and branch; brought up, *formed*, as the French say, of the pre-Hellenic as well as the 'post-Hellenic, European modes . . .'; a mixture – not a blending – of the two worlds: the old, Middle-Eastern world of *Hebrew* perception and thinking: concrete, intense, graphic as in hyperbolic – surreal, one might say, risking the anachronism; a believer in 'magic' – rooted in the precept that 'the fear of the Lord is the beginning of wisdom'; unitary therefore, and inextricably wedded to the concept of word; and that of post-Hellenic European man, with his demand for logical, scientific and modular perceptions, disunifying reality therefore into molecular blocks or chromosomal pairings, a demand for economy in matters of the spirit: 'Small is beautiful'!

Moreover, as we saw with the novel, far eastern modes and techniques (notably Japanese) were also apparent, though Manzano is wrong to say that they emerged in this new book of poetry. 'Summer Haiku' had been published in *The Spice-Box Of Earth* (a poem dedicated to F.R. Scott and his wife, Marian); *tankas* – a five-lined poem, as opposed to the *haiku* which has four lines – appeared in *Flowers For Hitler* ('Old Dialogue') and *The Energy Of Slaves* (such as 'I Don't Know What To Call It', 'Each Man', 'This Is A Threat', best of all, 'Love Is A Fire').

Perhaps his best known *haiku* is 'They Locked Up A Man' which probably refers to himself, although it was Ezra Pound who was 'locked up'. It is even more concerning that not one of the professional critics – the gurus of English Literature – have noticed his experimentation with this (and other) forms of poetic utterance; even those who, like Woodcock, go out of their way to emphasise his conventionalism, his reliance on derivation! Can it be true that an expert is one who knows 'more and more about less and less' – until, finally, one presumes, he knows nothing at all – and writes about it in ever larger volumes? Leonard had to 'wander from his name,' in so doing he could not swim smoothly in the stream of his Nature – especially in its stream-of-consciousness – still less 'live but one man.' But its cost was enormous, its pain incessant, its guilt irresolvable.

So *Parasites Of Heaven* is both his least important (*qua* poet), and his most important book (*qua* man – and, of extreme importance, this as commentator on man's lot). For him, as we shall presently see, it could only be done through the prism of his self-hood – he is a man not a lens, a psychosomatic unity (when he keeps it together!) not a catalytic agent – recollecting, exploring, organising even, the world as it appeared to him, this man of 'the stony Semitic stare,' this man of high perception, this Rodanesque thinker, ever seized by the *angst* of his own vision and feeling.

For once his publishers caught the mood of the occasion exactly right in their selection of its cover picture: Leonard in profile, with his hand over his brow, pensive, strained even – but immaculate, in a quality suit and double cuffs, duly cuff-linked. ('Poems', the *Dictionary Of Literary Biography* says, 'that had been rejected by (previous) publishers.') A man, moreover, who was already showing signs of deep distress in his personal life and most intimate relationships – a sure sign that something less than magic was afoot. Through it, however, he was connecting, along the narrow highway, ever driven by curiosity; a lover of life, but always aware of that which was out of reach and his control; promising at times to sew the world together, at other times threatening – as did the political situation – to tear it apart. Sometimes he heard 'the comforting message, a beautiful knowledge of unity' – seeing the disparates achieve oneness, the paradoxes unite, the questions resolved; at other times stark *unmeaning*, as had happened from early youth when his world collapsed with the death of his father, the piercing depth of Francis Thompson's reflection (in 'Daisy'):

> 'Nothing begins, and nothing ends,
> That is not paid with a moan;
> For we are born in another's pain,
> And perish in our own.'

The Talmud is a much wiser book, a surer guide, than many ever experience. One of its profounder sayings is, 'Happy is he who knows his place and stands in his own place.' It was a lesson Leonard was learning during these years. Years that were, despite everything to the contrary, happy and fulfilled, as he found his *metier*, though ever conscious of the fragility of life, not least of public opinion, on which he depended for sustenance. That happiness found expression in this last book of poems, yet without beclouding the greyer reality. 'The nightmares do not suddenly develop happy endings,' he wrote in echo of this greyness; continuing:

'And should love decide
I am not the one
to stand scratching his head
wondering what wall to lean on
send King Farouk to argue
or come to me dressed as a fast.'

His great inspirer, Nachman of Bratislava, once commented that 'Freedom is the world of joy.' This was unquestionably both the heart of the ache in Leonard's soul and the goal of his religious and philosophical searchings. It is one of the most important tenets of Judaism, man's freedom of will, from which is derived all other freedoms; and yet its history was a contradiction of the principle, and its literature very largely a cry of pain. Not surprisingly, it was part of Leonard's great quest, too.

The measure of happiness Leonard felt reflected his varying sense of freedom, now ecstatic, now bowed down by its absence. Who could be truly free with such a nature as his, at once finely tuned to spiritual realities and energised by carnal desire? Who could be free in such a world as this, glorious in its beauty yet corrupted by the selfishness and ambitions of men? Who could truly be free when hounded by the distress, the suffering, the pain and – not least – the actual captivity of so many good men? The confrontation found present expression in his prose-poem, 'Here We Are At The Window':

'Here we are at the window. Great unbound sheaves of rain
wandering across the mountain, parades of wind and driven silver
grass. So long I've tried to give a name to freedom, today my
freedom lost its name, like a student's room travelling into the
morning with its lights still on. Every act has its own style of
freedom, whatever that means. Now I'm commanded to think of
weeds, to worship the strong weeds that grew through the night,
green and wet, the white thread roots taking lottery orders from
the coils of brain mud, the permeable surface of the world. Did
you know that the brain developed out of a fold in the epidermis?
Did you? Falling ribbons of silk, the length of rivers, cross the
face of the mountain, systems of grass and cable. Freedom lost its
name to the style with which things happen. The straight trees,
the spools of weed, the travelling skeins of rain floating through
the folds of the mountain – here we are at the window. Are you
ready now? Have I dismissed myself? May I fire from the hip?
Brothers, each at your window, we are the style of so much
passion, we are the order of style, we are pure style called to
delight a fold of the sky.'

Three times the reference to freedom – that teasing, challenging concept in Leonard's work – is made: he tries to name it – it loses its name; everything has its own style of freedom – 'whatever that means,' he adds sardonically; it lost its name to the style with which things happen. *Angst* pervades; the chimera expands; 'lift that bale!' reverberates through his mind still.

The same thought is continued in his poem, 'He Was Beautiful When He Sat Alone', in which he reviews himself in the third person – this man who needed to sit alone; another prose-poem in which the dialectical statement-and- commentary, statement-and-unstatement, of his assertions and his disavowals, is very prominent: 'He sat alone because he was beautifully dressed . . . because he was not a civilian,' (i.e. unfree); he is not sure whether he even likes himself any more (this golden-boy poet); 'you' (changing from third to second person and thus accusingly) 'didn't expect to fall in love' – 'at the same time I answered gently, "Do you think so?"' and so on, through humming, through desertion, through his pain, his changed pain, through his dancing to the spirited climax: 'And he thought that she thought that he thought that she thought that the worst thing a woman can do was to take a man away from his work because that made her what, ugly or beautiful?' It is his ultimate predicament: he delights in her presence; his work suffers! He feels most himself; his soul is engulfed! Freedom is consummated; servitude ensues . . .

'And now you have reached the mathematical section of your soul which you claimed you never had,' he reflects Dylan-like. It is the one-to-one reckoning, the way of easy formuli, at once algebraic and geometric. His own I-and-Thou clash (Martin Buber was himself a devotee of Hasidic literature, a non-traditionalist Jew, who worked assiduously at claiming – or preserving – his faith for today's world.)

Such thinking could only produce 'the last line of each verse of the song' (such was never far from his mind) but he didn't have any other lines; and the last line was always the same: *Don't call yourself a secret unless you mean to keep it.* In one sense it is the reiteration of the *riposte* to Pierre Berton: 'I write the poetry; you do the commentary': he knew who he was, he had something to say; he knew that both came together in generally unwanted – and certainly 'uncommercial' form, aspects not merely disconnecting, but thereby neutering each other. His search was not merely about himself but, much more importantly, about his *role*, his function. It provoked him to think about singing as well as life – but, 'if there actually is such a condition, is anybody in it, and are sadists born there?' Answering, 'It is not a question mark, it is not an exclamation point, it is a full stop by the man who wrote *Parasites Of Heaven.*'

Those who think that Leonard moved from being a poet to a novelist, and thence to a 'pop singer' are not only showing their ignorance, but their naïvety, too. From early days he had been tormented by what he *felt*, the potential of his own tradition to help heal that rift, the limitations of his own tradition to do so completely. But more than that he searched for a means of capturing the essence of what he felt – of being able to express it, not merely precisely and economically, but in such a way as to get it across to the hearts, as well as the minds, of those around him.

At first poetry appeared to supply those means, but then there was the risk – the debilitation of getting lost in arty, academic (or at least pseudo-academic) discussions; certain that he could not be a Layton, ever protesting, ever bombarding academia with incisive – sometimes insulting! – criticisms and warnings. So *not* abandoning poetry, even if it threatened to abandon him, he took to writing fiction, thoughtful, reflective fiction; despite its frenetic sexuality – the means, he thought, of arresting attention, of disengaging minds – even (in that sense) didactic fiction, whose limitations quickly became apparent. Worse, he was threatened therein to be not merely neutralised by academic discussion, but relegated to smutty entertainment, the school-boy giggle, the prude's sciolism.

The burden he felt, of knowing and perceiving, was already beginning to get away from him – by failing to be heard, to be understood. His message was becoming still-born, rather than misunderstood; aborted, rather than rejected. The priest who had turned prophet was feeling the ultimate in prophetic dilemmas: he was failing to get his message across. Paralysis was threatening to overcome perturbation.

If *Beautiful Losers* explored the national predicament in which he was plunged by reasons of patriotism, *Parasites Of Heaven* explored the personal predicament by reason of his deeper national identity, his name and his destiny; the inner voice that would not let him go. It reaches a conclusion in his poem 'I Am A Priest Of God', which in fact is not a conclusion, merely a part-summing up in this present *fin de siècle* mood:

> 'I am a priest of God
> I walk down the road
> with my pockets in my hand
> Sometimes I'm bad
> then sometimes I'm very good
> I believe that I believe
> everything I should
> I like to hear you say
> when you dance with head rolling

upon a silver tray
that I am a priest of God

'I thought I was doing 100 other things
but I was a priest of God
I loved 100 women
never told the same lie twice
I said O Christ you're selfish
but I shared my bread and rice . . .'

In it convictions are jostled, thoughts are jumbled, vision is obscured. But the voice – Bath Qol or Bath Cohen? – persists: he *is* a priest of God. Jacob quaked on hearing that voice; Moses trembled, and hid his face; Isaiah cried, 'Woe is me!' and Jeremiah exclaimed, 'I am a child, I cannot speak.' Leonard Cohen, in the 32nd year of his life exclaimed:

'. . . I was alone and a priest of God
making me so empty
that even now in 1966
I'm not sure I'm a priest of God.'

Jacob hobbled for the rest of his life in the wake of his questing; Moses suffered – and was excluded from entering the Land of Promise because of his temper; Isaiah suffered his burnt mouth (and according to tradition, was sawn in two); and Jeremiah was thrown into a pit and exiled. The mills of God grind slowly, and very small . . . As the rabbis said, 'God is our Father, destiny our step-father' and 'the man who is destined to drown will drown in a glass of water.' But we are mistaken if we think that this was the only consideration of his life. The pain had remittances, the cloud its silver lining, the gloom a ray of sunshine – and that in the form of Marianne, the kind and the beautiful, never less so than on Hydra:

'In almond trees lemon trees
wind and sun do as they please.
Butterflies and laundry flutter
My love her hair is blonde as butter . . .'

The beauty of the words merely reflects the beauty of her person, and that contentment he felt with her. But the 'vocational' torment would not stop, it continued:

'Clean as the grass from which
the sun has burned the little dews
I came to this page
in the not so early morning
with a picture of him

> *whom I could not be for long*
> *not wanting to return or begin*
> *again the idolatry of terror.'*

The dialogue with himself, against himself, continues. He speaks of engineering 'various shames' against his innocence, against their love. Was there ever a more Kierkegaardian figure? Marianne, herself Scandinavian, in place of Regina; the 'hunchback' of Montreal in place of he of Copenhagen? Both came of families in the clothing business; both had their childhoods spoiled by parental death; both found university irksome; both wrote books early – and were panned by journalists and critics; both distrusted dogma; both were vehement social critics; both highlighted – and lived – in the light of authentic choice, needing its counterfeit freedoms for the true expression of their natures. Leonard's plot against himself, he tells us, arising out of their love, her involvement with his work:

> *'. . . documenting the love of one*
> *who gathered my first songs*
> *and gave her body to my wandering'*

She is, as Irving Layton states: the muse beautiful, the inspiration of his earthly self, the prism of his terrestrial vision, the catalyst of his natural world. Happy the man to find such a place, to be able to stand – and lie therein. But there he could not remain; the voice, the need, was too persistent; the still, small voice of prophetic command would not allow the repose, the sirenic whispers. 'I am too loud when you are gone,' he wrote, in the poem that bears that title. He speaks of his 'longing' – so different, so more enduring than mere desire – 'not for music' but 'longing, longing to be Him/I am diminished, I peddle versions of Word/that don't survive the tablets of broken stone/I am alone when you are gone.' Crisis was breaking out – and breaking into the peace and contentment he found with her. He agonises, he bids:

> *'Live for him, huge black eyes*
> *He never understood their purity*
> *or how they watched him prepare*
> *to ditch the early songs and say goodbye*
> *Sleep beside him uncaptured darling*
> *while I fold into a kite . . .'*

(A kite, we might add, which is a *victim* . . . a fish you have already caught . . .) And he goes on to explain that in the battle he was having with himself when he was 'wondering what adventure is/ wondering what cruelty is,' when he sought to 'bargain with fire/which must ignore both of them.' She is his 'uncaptured darling', because he cannot pay the price:

> '*Now you want to marry me*
> *and take me down the aisle*
> *and throw confetti fingerprints*
> *You know that's not my style*'

To marry a Gentile, a divorced woman – was the very antithesis of priestly standing! His 'blood' was *claiming* him, even as it was wreaking havoc in his life:

> '*Claim me, blood, if you have a story*
> *to tell with my Jewish face,*
> *you are strong and holy still, only*
> *Speak, like the Zohar, [s] of a carved-out place*
> *into which I must pour myself like wine,*
> *and emptiness of history which I must seize*
> *and occupy, calm and full in this confine,*
> *becoming clear like good wine on its lees*'

(The *Zohar* more correctly, the *Sepher-ha-Zohar* is the 'Book Of Splendour', the most important book in the Cabalistic tradition. It is a 'commentary' on the Talmud which incorporates a Pandora's box of mysticism, folk-tales, superstition and numerology, much of which is tangential to the Talmud, though highly reflective of the 'theology' of cabalism with its dreams and codes, its doctrines of man, the angels and the devil, as well as a 'system' of ethics, a collection of prayers. 'F' was merely reflecting the current wisdom as well as his own fears when he said to the Dallyer that 'the Jews didn't let young men study the Cabala. Connections should be forbidden to citizens under 70.'

The impinging emotions were formidable; amid the crises of mind and spirit the body was also seeking to have its say. In a volume in which 'Suzanne Wears A Leather Coat' and 'Suzanne Takes You Down' (later to achieve classical status as a song), in which the poem 'I Met A Woman Long Ago' gives voice to the clash within himself but also – tellingly – between the fair and the dark woman – which may well have their counterparts in 'I Believe I Heard Your Master Sing', 'Clean As The Grass From Which', and 'Give Me Back My Fingerprints' – we see a little of the searching dilemma confronting him.

'The kindest adjective that can be applied to (*Parasites Of Heaven*)', said Stephen Scobie, is 'uneven'.' But the emotions at this time were not uneven; they were tumultuous, as Alberto Manzano suggests – verifying Landor's epigram, that 'No truer word, save God's, was ever spoken,/Than that the largest heart is soonest broken.'

'The nightmares do not suddenly/develop happy endings/I merely step out of them . . .' Leonard wrote significantly; adding, 'Love wears out/like overused mirrors unsilvering/and parts of your faces (the plural bears emphasis)/makes room for the wall behind.' It reaches a climax in the convulsed prose-poem 'I Guess It's Time To Say Goodbye', which is as convulsed in emotion as much as in its failed structure, thus standing the previous piece 'It's Not So Hard To Say Goodbye' on its head. As Scobie rightly detects, 'the main thematic preoccupation is, once again, the subjective self' – but in the absence of a burning bush, what better substitute than a burning, divided heart?

bringing back
the word

The deep questioning as to message and method, which resulted in a new emphasis on the former and a new vehicle for the latter, were strongly evident in *Parasites Of Heaven*. Indeed, in the poetry-form which they exhibit, no less than five of his songs were already published: 'I Met A Woman Long Ago' (known later as 'Teachers'); 'Suzanne Takes You Down' (which became 'Suzanne'); 'Give Me Back My Fingerprints' (sung as 'Fingerprints'); 'I Believe You Heard Your Master Sing . . .' (the 'Master Song'); and 'I Stepped Into An Avalanche', ('Avalanche'). There is at least one 'song' present that never reached its potential in music: 'I've Seen Some Lonely History', which is nothing if not a classic Cohen-song, unifying the natural and the carnal with the spiritual and the divine, and always with a touch of self-deprecating humour; not just unifying those disparates, but 'confusing' them – and subtly, as was ever his way:

> '*I've seen some lonely history*
> *The heart cannot explore*
> *I've scratched some empty blackboards*
> *They have no teachers for*
>
> '*I trailed my meagre demons*
> *From Jerusalem to Rome*
> *I had an invitation*
> *But the host was not at home*
>
> '*There were contagious armies*
> *That spread their uniform*
> *To all parts of my body*
> *except where I was warm*
>
> '*And so I wore a helmet*

With a secret neon sign
That lit up all the boundaries
So I could toe the line

'My boots got very tired
Like a sentry's never should
I was walking on a tightrope
That was buried in the mud

'Standing at the drugstore
It was very hard to learn
Though my name was everywhere
I had to wait my turn

'I'm standing here before you
I don't know what I bring
If you can hear the music
Why don't you help me sing'

The *koan* must startle and disrupt; the parable must not be too
easy of comprehension! Moreover, the subject of 'Suzanne Takes You
Down', as we saw earlier, has another poem in her honour, which
speaks of the impressions she created in the Montreal of 1963 (when the
poem was written):

'Suzanne wears a leather coat.
Her legs are insured by many burnt bridges.
Her calves are full as spinnakers
in a clean race, hard from following music
beyond the maps of any audience.

'Suzanne wears a leather coat
because she is not a civilian
She never walks casually down Ste Catherine
because with every step she must redeem
the clubfoot crowds and stalk the field
of huge hailstones that never melted,
I mean the cemetery.

'Few serve the lilac,
few heal with mist.
Suzanne wears a leather coat.
Her breasts yearn for marble.
The traffic halts: people fall out
of their cars.
None of their most drooling thoughts are wild enough
to build the ant-full crystal city
she would splinter with the tone of her step.'

So here, in this fourth book of poetry, in this his most successful year to date, financial and literary, he has intimated his move. Not from poetry or from literature; but with it – to song and stage and an even more public arena. It is not a change of direction, merely a change of his means of communication. The mood in which he made the change is recorded in his poem 'Your Eyes Are Very Strong', in which he refers to himself in the third person: 'as you go *hopefully*/from profession to profession.' But it is important to emphasise that this was an *extension* of his role, not the shouldering of a new one.

The *dilettantes* and purists may sniff – and did so, loudly and discourteously – but they fail to understand that poetry and music have ever gone together, need each other, reach their separate perfections in each other's company. The muses are not consistent because they, unlike the specialists of literature and history, do not recognise the artificial boundaries placed by these moderns – curiously those mainly of the universities whose worlds are anything but universal! They are untouched by the presence of music in the poetry of ancient Greece or Rome, Jerusalem or Babylon, and understand its music even less.

By this time his location in Hydra had been displaced for one in New York, thanks to a loan from his old friend Robert Hershorn. (Hershorn sadly died in Hong Kong from a heroin overdose, in circumstances that were always mysterious.) He had actually left the former to stake his claim in Nashville, the home of country music which had been claiming his attention through recent years with ever greater demand, not least through its persistent exposure on the American Armed Forces' radio network based in Athens, to which he listened avidly. The 'folk boom' had reached its zenith and he was intrigued by its successes; music had reasserted its power over the masses and was claiming for itself a position as the most vital form of communication on a broad scale, not least to the young.

It was through this medium chiefly that such great entertainer-communicators as The Weavers, The Kingston Trio, 'the Queen of Folk' Odetta, Pete Seeger (who broke away from The Weavers) – Mr Folk himself, the long established Carter family, The Memphis Jug Band, John Hurt of Mississippi, Blind Lemon Jefferson, and the grandfather of them all, Woody Guthrie, made their mark. Not least at this time, of course, occurred the successes of Joan Baez and Bob Dylan, then Bob Dylan and Joan Baez, as the latter followed him into rock, whose musicality and poetry, respectively, became one of *the* sounds of the sixties, at least in thinking circles. (Leonard said that he was unaware of Joan Baez and Phil Ochs when he first came back to the States.)

Leonard was very aware of Bob Dylan and commented that he saw him "as a very accomplished poet," contrasting his style with the 'verbosity' of Whitman and emphasising that his skill with words was 'beautiful'. He appreciated the hidden depths in Dylan (who does not even get a mention in *The Oxford Companion To English Literature,* unlike Whitman, Ginsberg *et al;* poets-in-song are evidently *infra dig.* Better to have pure poets, even if inferior!) In particular he found him "well read . . . and his grasp of musical idioms is vast, he synthesised so many traditions." He was "the Picasso of the scene." Moreover, he sympathises with Dylan's social conscience, noting that "he was seized by everything" and confessing that "I had a vision when I was very young. It's not been realised yet . . . Dylan was able to create this complete identity, but I have not achieved it yet . . . The vision includes society, but it is beyond it and has to do with 'elemental' relationships which can inform all societies."

To these classic folk-singers mentioned above must be added the names of the great blues singers – Erich von Schmidt (including his so-called 'white' blues) and Huddie Ledbetter's (later, Leadbelly's) 'black blues'. (Not only the names indeed, but also the sociological realities. As Myra Friedman commented in her moving biography of Janis Joplin, *Buried Alive* – as true a descriptive title as any book of the era, to be sure – blues 'spoke the pain of the young generation' – and the not-so-young, too!)

Alongside such were individual musicians like the brilliant Bob Gibson (12-string guitar and banjo, brother of Ralph who was later to perform on Leonard's fifth album) whose virtuosity precludes easy classification, and Lester Flatt and Earle Scruggs whose 'bluegrass' playing added an important dimension to the developing scene. They also performed with Leonard later. And Ray Charles was now celebrating his 20th year in showbiz! They were exciting, inventive days – whether one thought in terms of such phenomena as The Beatles, whom even Leonard Bernstein applauded as pacemakers, or the King of Rock, Elvis Presley, whom Leonard rated as a musical genius.

Another influence on Leonard from this time was fellow-Canadian Gordon Lightfoot (who performed at Expo '67, alongside Don Messer and his Islanders, Ian and Sylvia, and Les Feux Follets), who along with Carole King and Kris Kristofferson would be among the first non-classical artists to perform at New York's famed Philharmonic Hall.

These were the days when Greenwich Village all but ruled the world of American music – 'pop' music, at least, much to the chagrin of San Francisco and other great centres of music. Men of the stature of John Hammond of CBS, and Albert Grossman, impresario-manager of Bob Dylan, Peter, Paul and Mary and Janis Joplin; Maynard Solomon of Vanguard, and 'Colonel' Tom Perkins (who perhaps did more for the scene in recognising the need to unify 'black' and 'white'

sounds) gathered in the cafés to spot, and quickly tie-up, rising talent;
when Washington Square would explode into spontaneous song and
rhythm; and when 'spots' along MacDougall Street or Bleeker Street
such as The Bitter End, The Café-Wha and The Gaslight showed the
way forward, and offered unique opportunities to perform for
would-be artists.

There was also the New York 'Y' on 92nd Street – where Leonard
would be welcomed and enjoy considerable success. At the same time,
in San Francisco, the beat-culture of Ginsberg *et al*, also influenced
Leonard in terms of the potential to move people through a poetic,
involved, medium and was now giving way to the music of The
Beatles, Dylan, The Byrds and The Rolling Stones. By 1966 there were
1500 bands operating in the area!

One of the key centres of artistic New York was not a café but a
hotel with a notorious past in literary circles, the Chelsea; at whose
doors guests are reminded that within its confines there resided in days
gone by such luminaries as O Henry and Dylan Thomas.

Leonard had originally set out to make Nashville his base, but, as
he often commented, he was 'highjacked' on his way there by New
York, and New York won his heart, as it always had and always would.
Characteristically, he had asked around to find 'where the musicians
stayed,' clearly intent on a role as songwriter. But more interestingly, he
stated, 'as an antidote against isolation' – from him the lover of solitude!
It recalls his comment in *The Favourite Game* that 'a community is an
alibi for the failure of individual love.' Music was, clearly, not the only
motivation. He was not disappointed, at one time he stayed there in the
company of Joan Baez and Bob Dylan, Jimi Hendrix and Janis Joplin.

There is something different about New York. Here one
experiences a rush of blood – red blood – to the head; it consumes the
whole body, all of it, organs internal and external; senses five, and so
much more! 'Little old Noisyville-on-the-subway' (to use O Henry's
description of it) was not merely good enough for the ex-convict who
added a spectacular dimension to the word 'coincidence' (in Leonard's
view, a diminution of the idea of providence), but the maternity ward
of almost everything that has inspired, accosted and insulted taste and
art over the last few decades.

Walt Whitman had to write verse about it ('Of hurried and
sparkling waters! city of spires and masts/City nested in bays! my city!'
said he, pre-echoing Leonard's – or at least Breavman's – delight in
Montreal); Frank Sinatra had to sing about it; Harry Leon Wilson had to
inveigh against it ('a little strip of an island with a row of well-fed folks
up and down the middle, and a lot of hungry folks on each side') and
Leonard's erstwhile guide, Henry Miller – he of the lovely, if quixotic,
Colossus Of Maroussi – could call it 'the grandest and emptiest city in the

world' which is true, so long as the two epithets are juxtaposed. And the city with the greatest (as in 'largest', which stands at the pinnacle of American epithets of appreciation: 'Large is Beautiful'!) human symbol of freedom. 'Liberty made her home here,' declared President Grover Cleveland in 1886, when he unveiled the Statue of Liberty, 'her chosen altar' – in ironic commemoration of the centenary of the French revolution for *liberté*, itself a joint venture between France and America. Its fame will never cease, and its wildness as well as its superb cultural life will never diminish.

Formerly the tallest building in New York (at 11 storeys, but that was in the 1880's!) the Chelsea is still 'making the scene like a grandmother in a miniskirt' as Richard V. Schenkel reported in *Art Times*. It was built at more or less the same time as the famed Dakota Building where John Lennon lived and, met his pointless death. To the illustrious names of yesteryear – Mark Twain, Sarah Bernhardt, William Burroughs, Arthur C. Clarke, Virgil Thomson, Sandy Daly, Rene Shap Shek, Jimi Hendrix, Edie Sedgwick, Thomas Wolfe, Brendan Behan, Edgar Lee Masters and Arthur Miller and so many more, Leonard now added his own; quietly as was his style, modestly, as was his manner.

Stanley Bard was manager when Leonard appeared on the scene, he and his father had ensured that the ambience remained the same, as it does to this day. It needed a Bard to house a poet, especially one now destined to be a troubadour! If Montreal represents the old-world of French-Canadian society, and Hydra that of the buccaneering-maritime world of Greece, the Chelsea represents that of arty-literary America, and exudes its charms and eccentricities. From the cavernous hallways and reception rooms, to the small individual bedsits and the elegantly high reception rooms. From the rosewood beamed bedrooms, to the small, intimate lifts – ideal for striking up such an announcement as 'Little lady, I'm Kris Kristofferson!' one of Leonard's humorous introductions to the song 'Chelsea Hotel No 2' which he wrote in memory of the sad and reckless Janis Joplin. At one point she stated that there was not sufficient room on the music scene for her and Judy Collins: it would be one or the other that made it to the top, not both!

It has known every passion and feeling experienced by man – from the tenderness of illicit *amours* to the murder by Sid Vicious of his girlfriend, Nancy Spungeon. And, not surprisingly, going bust *en route* (Not as a hotel, however, but in its 'pre-classical' times, when it functioned as a new cooperative housing society – one of its many claims to fame.) The heights of *Under Milk Wood* were reached in Room 206 – from which the great poet was carried to his alcoholic grave, not the first to die there.

Arthur Miller, playwright, political commentator, former husband of 'Lady Marilyn' (Leonard's title in *Beautiful Losers*, for one of the all-time beautiful losers) spoke of it as being 'a ceaseless party,' and so it was; yet a party that worked, that perceived, that spoke of real things – at the highest levels of imagination. It is one of America's answers to left-bank Paris, or London's Soho – a haven of bohemian styles and freedoms – and just as legendary. Perhaps the wildest occasion was when the choreographer Katherine Dunham – at the time Leonard was about – took over the Chelsea for a rehearsal of the opera *Aida*. Not knowing what was to transpire, Mr Bard had given his go ahead – only to find his elevators closed off, the police cordoning the building and the Mayor's office all but hysterical. Live lions and tigers had been brought onto the sixth floor – Leonard's floor! – and the rehearsal was under way, a roaring success, apparently.

Chris Turner interviewed Leonard there for *New Musical Express*, finding him in his room, of 'small, large cupboard-size, and most of the room taken up with two single beds.' But however surprising the internal arrangements, it was both home and launch pad, as well as the scene of one of his greatest turning points to date. The launching took place thanks to the good offices of Mary Martin, a Montreal agent who was known to Leonard and Judy Collins. Ms Collins described it thus in *Trust Your Heart*, her very moving and candid autobiography:

'He came down from Canada one night, and I listened to his songs in my living room. He sang 'Suzanne' and 'Dress Rehearsal Rag' that night, sitting on the couch, holding the guitar on his knee. I was moved by his singing, and by the songs, and by his whole presence. There was something very ethereal and at the same time earthy about his voice. When Leonard sang I was entranced: I became immediately devoted to him, and soon we were friends.'

In an interview on BBC television she talked of 'the charming quality of his voice.' This needs to be emphasised, for few singers have suffered from such jaundiced, uncritical comment as Leonard has. 'If you can't, you teach; and if you can't teach, you teach others to teach,' goes the old saying. To which we should perhaps add 'and if you still can't, become a hack music critic.' She goes on to talk of their regular meetings, having tea with him, and their walking around Greenwich Village together; of her recording 'Suzanne' and 'Dress Rehearsal Rag' for her album 'In My Life', which was released in 1966 – and went gold in 1967. (Others followed, such as Chad Mitchell, Spanky and Our Gang, Leon Bibb, and Noel Harrison.) Out of this success, she suggested, he made his début as a singer. It was a fulfilment of his plea in 'I've Seen Some Lonely History', which ends:

'I'm standing here before you
I don't know what I bring
If you can hear the music
Why don't you help me sing'

But it was also the bracing of himself to take the final leap, of
which he had written in 'He Was Beautiful When He Sat Alone': 'He
thought he knew, or he actually did know too much about singing to be
a singer; and if there is actually such a condition, is anybody in it, and are
sadists born there?' It was, indeed, his 'full stop': the terror of which he
wrote about and has often commented on; which would ever remain a
terror to him, as he endured the birth-pangs of his vision and hopes –
from one concert to the next, across America, Canada, Europe, the
Middle and Far Easts.

It was not only Judy Collins that 'went gold', thanks to his
brilliant mind and facile (but not easy) pen. A whole generation – two
generations in fact – of singers and would-be singers followed her lead
and his genius, from Buffy Sainte-Marie to Nick Cave, wedging
between them such names as Joni Mitchell, Jennifer Warnes, Ian
McCulloch, Julie Felix, Morrissey, Tanita Tikaram, Fairport Convention, Blixa Bargeld, Bono, Coil, The Sisters Of Mercy (who took their
name from his song), The Stormy Clovers, Spanky And The Gang,
Rita Coolidge, Suzanne Vega, The Flying Lizards, Tracy Chapman,
Foetus, Mr Mister, The The, and many more.

Leonard's songs on Judy Collins' album caught the attention of
John Hammond, doyen of A&R men at Columbia Records, the man
responsible for signing Bob Dylan and who had in the past nurtured the
careers of many distinguished jazz performers. In years to come
Hammond would also 'discover' Bruce Springsteen. Ms Collins was
also responsible for introducing Leonard to the singer/songwriter's
circle in New York, notably Bob Dylan, David Blue, and also to Andy
Warhol and The Velvet Underground. Like many others Leonard was
somewhat enamoured of Nico. Leonard became Hammond's latest
'catch', but not before he had lost the recording rights to 'Suzanne' –
'duped out of his rights,' as he commented to Mick Brown of *Sounds* in
1976. Such experiences led to the formation of his own company
Stranger Music Inc. Though a major figure in poetry and literature, in
the smart, back-biting music industry he had learned his first hard, and
expensive, lesson. The man who had warned of the con, had himself
been conned.

Back-biting is by no means reserved for the music industry,
however. 'Hell hath no fury like a woman scorned,' and if that scorned
woman is the poetry muse herself, woe betide the poet who rejects her!
From this time on Leonard was forced to listen to many voices of

criticism, of contempt, of hollow laughter and heavy sarcasm – from people who could not understand his songs, his specific *genre* of music, its practised intonations; the careful modulation it required to preserve his meanings, and its moods – usually in the subdominant and dominant keys (respectively, higher fourths and fifths). The style of his clothing, the brand of his cigarettes, his (then) vegetarianism, the way his hair was cut – or left uncut, his suits, his lack of suits, the contours of his face, the colour of his skin, the shape of his nose, his ears, the colour of his eyes, the way he stood, walked, sat. And – perhaps most wounding of all – the criticism of his former companions in poetry – they of the perceptive eye, the attentive ear, of the delicate and subtle nuance – or the paroxysmal turn of phrase – who simply and wilfully, refused to understand what he was seeking to do.

Vassal quotes him saying before one poetry recital in New York of this time (of 500 people), "I am the most distressed person here." They constantly called attention to the conservatism of his poetic form, of its mythological and ideological nexus; they asked why he was not more adventurous – criticisms that were in any case overdrawn; and when he did something extraordinary for poetry, when he broke new ground and incurred the wrath of the music critics for so doing, they rejected him! They seemed to believe the world-weary cynicism of Beaumarchais, when he foolishly ventured the non-thought: 'That which is not worth saying is sung.' Commented the suitably anonymous *Times Literary Supplement* reviewer in the 'In Haste' column, on the publication of his *Selected Poems 1958-1968*:

'Leonard Cohen . . . in other incarnations for some of the more trendy lady folk-singers, a novelist famous for the Danish Vibrator and other fetching creations . . . a vocalist of dubious attainments – is lavishly treated by his British publishers to what must be the classiest presentation for a young poet in recent years. The lyrics are well-meant but thin. Undergraduates get drunk on songs like 'Suzanne Takes You Down', but the same sort of thing has already been done better. More concentration needed.'

As this was indeed a very 'classy' presentation of Leonard's best poetry to date – heralded as such across Canada, America and many parts of Europe and well beyond, for which many accolades were offered as well as literary awards made, we may well treat it with the contempt such asininity and condescension deserves. But it is typical of the type, who could neither understand the best of his poetry nor the poetry-in-song to which he was now turning. Said his former professor, Louis Dudek, about this time, '. . . it's a critical delusion that folk-poetry is the mother-tongue of the human race, or that the immediately popular is the touchstone of art. We're still suffering from this delusion.'

About its finality hovers just a whiff of the academie-gone-sour, the faintest suggestion that 'little books of poetry' are intrinsically better than big books, that there is a greater artistic integrity in failure, or at least in belated success, than that which is gained in one's own lifetime to worldwide esteem, if not adulation. So many brick-bats; so few bouquets! 'L'amiti,' exclaimed Napoleon in such a condition, 'ce n'est qu'un nom.' ('Friendship is but a name.)

Many of the commentators know nothing of the long history of folk-song – from Moses and Miriam through David and Solomon to the unknown author of *Lamentations* – and cared even less. Strangely, they rejected – ignored, rather – even the comments of their peers, such as Percy Bysshe Shelley who, uniting two elements of Leonard's songwriting, commented, 'Our sweetest songs are those which tell of the saddest thought' – or for that matter the broad history of the bards and troubadours, who frequently highlighted their verse with simple melodies, musical intervals – from semitones to compounds.

But Leonard knew, and was serious about joining one of the greatest traditions in human artistry, as well as one of its most eccentric. As he commented on more than one occasion, "I sometimes see myself in the court of Ferdinand, singing my songs to girls over a lute." The connection was as precise as the intention was strong, though other similarities might have come to mind, not least from his own Bible (from which everything ultimately stemmed with him) in which 'song' alone occurs 80 or so times, a third of the occurrences referring to psalm titles, and all of them demanding musical accompaniment: a very appropriate background for this grandson of one of the foremost 'hirers-and-firers' of cantors in Canada and North America!

Mendele Mochar Sefarim – Mendele the Bookseller – said, 'A man can detect a speck in another's hair, but can't see the flies on his own nose' – which is even more difficult if that nose be raised in an arrogant sniff. And Leonard was about to see many flies on the parasites of earth as well as those of heaven. One such fly came on the nose of Richard Goldstein in his put-down article entitled 'Beautiful Creep', which appeared in *The Village Voice* in December 1967, even before Leonard's record was released. He had taken the description from a letter Leonard showed him, which had been received from a tormented female who felt 'frightened' by his poetry and offered to pray for him. Goldstein finds little to praise; the Chelsea is in 'steep decline', its corridors are 'long and lit occasionally'; he found 'humid ladies in black lace seeming to peer at him from every transom'; and old men, he imagined, 'with their backs turned lurk in every shadowy corner'; he knocked at 'the wafer-thin door' ignoring 'the smell of stale cigars, or is it piss?' and found, much to his dismay it would seem, Leonard in the throes of a heavy cold, which he found a suitable subject for further disparagement.

He pours scorn on 'the boog-a-loo of modern verse' he found in Leonard's poetry – 'perfect for pressing roses,' he stated; he does not find it surprising that Allen Ginsberg 'huffed out of a meeting with Leonard Cohen, muttering, "This place looks like a ballet set" (in an otherwise unknown accident for which Goldstein offers no detail)'; he castigates his interviewee as 'a Visceral Romantic' who 'suffers gloriously in every couplet' – unaware, apparently, of the many poetic forms that Leonard used, though he actually quotes from some of them. He suggests disbelief over Leonard's claim to have 'always written with a typewriter for a guitar,' his eyes sagging 'like two worn breasts' (sic), his voice fading 'into an echo of itself,' and so on. Throughout the piece the reporter struggles to find a compliment, and quickly undermines the risk of one by adding another schoolboy tee-hee. It is redolent with high-school newspaper cracks, the sort one usually outgrows before graduation, and worthy of a bucolic – not a Village voice. He is the epitome of what Myra Friedman referred to in her *Buried Alive:*

'The media works like a monster computer . . . receiving, coding, indexing, slotting, programming, dividing, multiplying; it condenses and subtracts, then collapses with simplicity, the process of it all too exhausting for its resources, the immensity of size an obstacle to nuance.'

Leonard, in particular, would suffer from this 'computerisation' syndrome, the shallowness of informed outlook and the betraying simplicity of journalists who were content to regurgitate old information, at once rancid and undigested.

We must thank Goldstein for eliciting one piece of information that is easily worth the five pages he needed for his otherwise myopic piece. He quotes the self-understanding which haunted Leonard since childhood, the conviction of his vocation, which is particularly interesting in the light of this recent change of *métier:*

"I had a very Messianic childhood. I was told I was a descendant of Aaron the High Priest. My parents actually thought we were Cohenim (sic) – the real thing. I was expected to grow into manhood leading other men."

Hence his move from Montreal to London, to Hydra, to New York – always with Montreal cushioning and inspiring him. We should be aware of 'the con' in these interviews; a notable feature in which he sends up the less aware who are ready to take anything down from him. Layton was a past-master of this and openly spoke of 'those singular lies with the power to get themselves believed' – meaning his poetry, of course – but could also speak of his own 'messianic sign' in his being born circumcised: *asinus asinum fricat!*

The interviewer left him 'slaving over the songs he calls "Eastern Country-Laments," trying to make them sound the way they read.' An honest slavery; he ground out the words like fresh cora, 'one word at a time'; they are too precious, too *accurate*, to be discharged like some common emission. He decants his words – bread and wine! – savours the bouquet, rolls the sacred nectar around his palate, sips at it contentedly if it works – or writhes in discomfort when it does not, endlessly experimenting with the formula; revising, renaming and rebottling it.

And the music, by which he composed the words, revised them, and revised the revision, also had to fit. The words-in-song must be heard 'the way they read.' Even as he slaved to ensure that his poetry scanned, so now must the music flow, not just melodiously but appropriately, projecting the words, bearing them like some sacred ark, exposing them dutifully. It was the craft of devotion all over again: a 'priesting' of the word.

More lately he has changed his description of them. He no longer favours 'Eastern Country-Laments'. For one thing, the appellation is too general. They are not merely 'eastern' but Jewish; not merely unwestern – and the point is extremely important if we are to understand him adequately – but Hebrew, in origin and tone; in direction and goal, if not in morality. And that is why he could call them 'Country-Laments'. Many of them do partake of that specific form, a *very* important aspect of Hebrew experience and the literature it produced. But not all can be so named, hence the change; not 'white' blues or 'black' blues, but *Jewish* blues; an independent, self-justifying, serious art form which challenges the critics to meet it on its own terms, and not in the second-hand way inflicted on it from a late-night dose of Laine or Leadbelly, Leary or Lennon – or even Litz.

It is deliberately simple in its musicality. Theodorakis may well evolve and sustain a 'mathematical' logic for his music, Leonard has evolved a mode of basic chords *deliberately*. The censorious may laugh, make a few jibes, disappear below the froth of their beer that produces ultimate froth – a journalist's 10-minute stint at his typewriter – but Leonard soldiers on, refinding his art, and finding the voice within it. It would be a battle of over 20 years' length, and even then not understood in some quarters, perhaps deliberately, and certainly not always professionally.

His aim was expressed even more carefully in referring to the first album in the programme of his second British tour, in 1974. After six years 'on the road', having listened to innumerable critics applying worn-out clichés and methods brought in from different traditions, and been amazed that his carefully framed replies, his confidences, could be so amateurishly bungled by those who failed to note distinctions, trod rough-shod over ideological and personal egg-shells, had difficulties in the orthography as well as the meaning of words and the grammatical nuances he employed, he spelled it out: "The aim is to bring the word back to the jukebox, which is really where you have to have it, or at least where I like to have it."

Not words, but 'the word' – a concept of technical proportions, with a history, a development, a meaning. He thereby announced his vision, drew attention to his plan, stood up for what he was really about. The priest was responding to his prophetic burden. But, as with all prophets, it would be borne at a cost: 'A scar is what happens when the word is made flesh.'

the mystery
of song

'Rien n'est plus mystérieux que le chant' ('Nothing is more mysterious than the song') the French daily, *Le Figaro*, commented on one of Leonard's songs in 1985. It was this mystery which had been imposing itself on Leonard for four decades. The magic of his mother's singing, the Yiddish and the Russian songs heard in his earliest days – happily before commercial radio forced everything into a stereotype – created patterns of music in his subconscious. To which the soul-stirring singing of the cantor in his synagogue – which in post-Lyon Cohen days became more of a virtuoso performance, when the emotional intensity of the 3000-year history charged the congregation with its high voltage.

Such cathartic experiences reinforce the old saying that there are 'three pillars of Judaism: the *Torah* (law or instruction/learning); *avodah* (worship); and gemilus *hasidim* (works of kindness)' – which all feature in Leonard's life and work notably. (These three correspond, with significant differences, to the Greek trilogy of word (*logos*), music (*mousiki*) and group (*orchesis*), in which a receiving is transformed into a response which issues in communal expression; *logos* is used technically for the words in a line of a song.) It was partly this, and partly the inherent musicality of words, that made him such a splendid poet.

Between his birth in 1934 till the end of the war, in 1946, when he was 12 (and coincidentally about to become 'a son of the command-ment,' a major turning-point in his life) the sound of Jewry, eastern Jewry, had predominated. He was captivated by it, and its rhythms and sounds came easily to him, which he reproduced on his harmonica, his Jew's harp and his flute. A.M. Klein refers to it as music in essentially a 'minor key (with) its gesticulative cadence . . . with cantorial frills and tremolos . . . lingering recitative upon a middle path . . . with meditative mournfulness . . . the accents of forgotten kinship.' It is

only one description, of course, but that which appears to have touched
Leonard most deeply. Significantly, in his first European tour in 1970,
the first song that he sang was 'Un As Der Rebbe Singt': 'As The Rabbi
Sings'.

The burden referred to above denies a man his freedom at the
same time that he feels its powers most strongly. It framed his words
and his music; it provided them with their strong constraints. The
Beatles could hammer out a song, a tune, in open studio – simply by
'messing about' with ideas, words, phrases. It worked. And it
revolutionised modern music (and studio usage). Bob Dylan could
rattle off a song – a brilliant, riveting song – in 15 minutes in the back of
a taxi, or on his horse or motorbike, and it would *work*, sensationally.
Leonard Cohen broke rocks to get at the silver in his mine, laboured to
release the thin veins and pea-sized nuggets. They, too, worked
brilliantly; they made his name; they made fortunes for others, but it
cost him dearly, this smelting of the ore; this servitude of the mine. As
he said to Billy Walker of *Sounds*, in early 1972:

"I've never written with the luxury of choice . . . My songs have
come to me. I've had to scrape them out of my heart. They came in
pieces, at a time, in showers and fragments . . . I can't dispose the song
to any situation or anything in the political realm. (My work) has always
been torn from myself . . . If it has any value, it's because it's been
created in a certain kind of furnace that gives it a certain kind of quality,
and it's nothing I can determine."

The potential of music for 'his work' had always been there, at
times quiescent, at times unstoppable – as when he became captivated by
the guitar heard in his local park, and immediately had to arrange lessons
for himself; it was there in composing, and even in the reciting of his
poetry, at events small and large; it was present in the quieter poetry
moments at University, when the editing sessions would finish and he
and his friends would relax to the sound of his guitar and singing. It was
there, memorably, on the steps at McGill, conducting his spontaneously
assembled 'choir' and at New York in a similar gathering, on the steps
of the International Friendship Centre on Riverside Drive, and in
London at Stella's; not least – and unsparingly – on Hydra, when its
promptings became relentless, clamant, and then unstoppable.

It was the summons to his major work, which brooked no excuse
nor permitted any rival, whether literature, or leisure, or companion-
ship. If his poetry came 'from the gut,' then his music originated in the
heart, with all its compressed and rhythmic force – which beats in
harmony with the cosmos, at 72 beats per minute, with time and
history, with the movement of the heavens – lip to lip, heart to heart;
mind to mind.

The phrase – 'lip to lip, heart to heart' – so important for understanding his espousal of song as the vehicle of his main work from now on, as well as the mechanism by which it was fulfilled, comes from an otherwise unidentified Spanish poem Leonard quoted in an interview in 1970 in Paris. As Vassal quotes it: *'Le Chant Vrai passé de lèvre à lèvre et de coeur a coeur, et rien ne peut le mettre en cage, ni l'arrêter.'* ('True song passes from lip to lip from heart to heart and nothing is able to restrain or detain it.') It is 'True Song' of which he speaks, which cannot be 'caged' or 'impeded'. The word may produce scars, but it gets through, inexorably. As he said to Karl Dallas of *Melody Maker* in 1976, reinforcing the seriousness with which he pursued his *métier:*

"I have always felt that the nature of a song was a movement from lip to lip. That's the nature of the thing. It's built somehow into the design of a song, the fact that it moves around. And if it doesn't then it really isn't that thing that we call a song. It could be something else pretty excellent – it could be a poem designed to stand on a page, or an esoteric document, or a kind of paradox that doesn't exist on parchment. But you *know* a song. Its nature is that it *moves.*"

He was signalling the completion of his career as a pure poet, one who sees and hears and produces meaning and significance in a particular way, who was unwilling to entomb his vision even in sparkling words; he was signalling the cessation of his work as a novelist, who creates a story-line by which he can unfold his view of man, his world, in entertainment or in commentary. In moving to poetry-in-song, Leonard was moving to a more active, a more involved means of communication; he was no longer content to perceive and describe, in order to 'arrange' reality, but intent now on influencing it. The priest was indeed becoming a prophet. Not merely a hearer of the word, but a proclaimer. His path was taking him beyond the Cohen, far from 'the con', behind the *koan*, to frontal confrontation; he was about to perform. It is a point that has not been missed by one of the more discerning of his critics, as Elizabeth Thomson said in 1979, 'He has made a whole generation of listeners search for some *real* meaning in songs.' (Her italics.)

Professor Louis Dudek, in a different context, differentiated between 'art songs and rough popular music,' and though Leonard has never sought to be 'arty' in that sense – indeed he has had to struggle against his natural disposition for a cerebral emphasis in favour of one that would touch the broader market – the point is well made. True folk had more or less disappeared, and in any case his songs were not it. As Tom Cokeson once remarked: 'folk they are not.' But they are art-songs, or as Mike Jahn prefers to call them 'a hybrid that has come to be called art-folk – Brecht with an acoustic guitar.' There is at times something genuinely Brechtian in Leonard's performances, but very little of that alienation technique so important to the German. Moreover, Leonard was always struggling with his producers who frequently sought to bowdlerise his work by inappropriate sound (Phil Spector's 'Death Of A Ladies' Man' is the epitome of such vulgarisation.)

Similarly the record company and ad-men who could not believe in the mass of people sufficiently as to credit them with the understanding of his songs, which *The New Musical Express Book Of Rock, II* mirrors: 'He is too self-consciously a poet ever to develop into a first-rate song-writer'!

But it all depends where you stand. The mindlessness of punk seems to be too much for some. Leonard was determined he was going to do it with style – his style – from mind to mind and lip to lip. Cokeson articulated it, in that August 1970 interview in *Sounds* just mentioned, when he commented that 'Cohen has brought back to rock music an awareness of the more formal disciplines and the more classic themes of poetry.' Michael Watts was wont to refer to him as 'the literary lion,' whose 'literaryness (sic) leaps from every page . . . few writers have his feel for language and his gift for mystery.' And not just in literary style, but in content too; culling from the past – from history and Tradition, and making it an appropriate vehicle for the present; though without that particular reference that would tie it to the present. 'The Story Of Isaac' is a good example of this: from Abraham to Vietnam (or wherever the next imbecility of ambitious frightened men takes us) in one song; and finely literate withal!

Leonard Cohen, without question, is in the tradition where songs last for millennia, not months; and his popularity is to be measured in endurance, not short-term emotional response – like the 'sweet psalmist of Israel' whose songs (i.e. psalms) are still best-sellers, whose son Solomon composed a thousand songs which have reverberated round the world – from Sheba to Siberia, from the Temple Mount to Mont Royal – and thence to Mount Baldy, Makalu and Melbourne. It was their power to *work*, not their mere popularity, that drew him. As *The Zohar* explains, 'There are halls in the heavens above that only open to the voice of song.'

It was Solomon who wrote the *Shir ha-shirim*, The Song Of Songs (or Canticles), also called the Song Of Solomon. Appropriate that he of a thousand wives, who wrote a thousand songs (one for each?) should write the world's best known love-song! Appropriate, too, that our author of 'messianic upbringing' should also tread that path and further that tradition.

Despite the beauty of his songs, their rhapsodising of nature and human love, they are also replete with the down-side of life, its weals and woes, its hurts and disappointments. In that Leonard is a faithful communicator, an *accurate* conveyor of mood and meaning, to use his preferred word. 'Accuracy,' reported Karl Dallas in the interview already cited, 'means a lot to Cohen, and though some may complain that his lyrics are sometimes obscure, to him the use of an intensely personal poetic metaphor is strictly in the interests of getting across an experience *in almost documentary fashion.*'

But honestly 'reporting' and speaking of life in the round; not merely the joys and successes, but the grimmer aspects of reality which touch us all at one time or another. Indeed, emphasising more the grimmer side as an appeal to sanity and balanced outlook. As one reviewer remarked: 'Leonard Cohen has killed cool. Killed it with warm. And he might even teach us to cry out again, if we don't watch out . . . Sometimes when he's talking very slowly and picking out his words as carefully as a kid at a penny candy counter, he sounds like he's talking from another world – or maybe just letting you catch a smoky glimpse of that private world behind the black eyes!'

'Another world' indeed; far from that of candy-floss America, where coffins become caskets and cancer is secreted behind 'the big C'; where pain is glossed over and death camouflaged behind smooching unreality. In that respect, for sheer candour and integrity, for serving men and women's real needs, and sustaining them in their darkest hours, Leonard Cohen may well go down as the most influential songwriter of the century – not in box-office counts, not in gold discs (though his successes in both should not be discounted), but in the steady year-by-year, ache-by-ache *secours*, over nearly 30 years, in which he offers genuine 'acts of kindness' (*gemilus hasidim*) which he writes – and sings – deep into countless lives.

Judy Collins recognised this quality from the first: 'His songs carried me through the dark years like mantras or stones that you hold in your hand while the sun rises or the fire burns. They kept me centred as I stood in front of thousands of people, my eyes closed, my hands round the neck of a guitar, my voice singing to his ethereal lyrics . . . The songs were like water to a person dying of thirst. They were songs for the spirit when our spirits were strained to the breaking point.'

And in her *Judy Collins Songbook* was placed the dedication against one of his best known songs, 'To Leonard, with love; singing 'Suzanne' gets me higher than anything.' For those with a bent for literary or at least bardic criticism, a comparison between Ms Collins' version and Leonard's shows major changes, as well as not a few insignificant ones. The conclusion of the first and last verses, for example, have *reversed* Leonard's meanings. (Joan Baez also liked the song, and included it in her set at Carnegie Hall in April 1968, though 'with credits given to Judy Collins' according to *Billboard*'s Aaron Sternfield.) Another long-time enthusiast and well-known singer, Jennifer Warnes, said a similar sort of thing in her own enthusiastic way on BBC television (edited):

"It's because he *dares* to talk about sorrow. Americans in general, not the Europeans but the Americans, like you 'to keep the sunny side up' – you know, put on your smile and come out swinging no matter how ruined you've been. Leonard will say, 'Look at the shreds of my heart; it's in shreds! You pulled my heart out with a pair of prongs!' They dislike acknowledging that the whole act of living contains immense amounts of sorrow and hopelessness and despair. And also passion; high, high hopes and deep and eternal love. Leonard has images that are spiritual, with all this . . . His songs always have the *full range* of emotions . . . I'm an intensely complex person, and in order to be honest in song I have to have complex lyric that speaks about the complex mixture of God and sex and spirituality and myth, forgiveness and lostness – all in one song! He's been able to do that, to write these lyrics."

It is significant that it is the American singers who call attention to these traits. Leonard did so himself, in the 1970 interview with Cokeson, mentioned above, even if he underestimated the resilience of the image-makers: "I am sure the era of glossy, artificial show business is dead. It is being replaced by religion in the broadest sense: religion as a way of seeing things through unclouded eyes. That, I believe, is what gets through with my songs . . ."

Gravity was to be his mark, not levity; he who observed through Breavman's eyes that 'his uncles were not grave enough'; who saw through what 'gravity' they had, and perceived it was merely strictness (the mark of the legalist – Jewish or Christian) was not going to make the same mistake, even if at times his gravity evinced a funereal tone. And it is doubly significant that it is mainly women who make such perceptive comments, as many women the world over perceived the depth and sensitivity of his songs. At one time, indeed, he used to say that he wrote poetry because that was the surest way of winning a woman's heart. But while there is some truth in the statement, we should not be put off by his own put-downs; he was far too serious about poetry for this to be the real, still less the main, motivation; though typically, some journalists took it for real, and still retail it rather than do their own thinking.

It is not simply a sexual thing. It is more that women have greater sympathy for spiritual realities, are closer to pain – and more ready to expose themselves to it – than men. They allow more room for the left-hand side of the brain – the artistic, feelings-related sphere, than 'rational' men. It is not so much a question of female, as 'feminine'; not so much the *yang* – the male principle – as the *yin*, the female principle. And woman – i.e. the feminine principle – is of inestimable importance to Judaism, from which Leonard derived his main inspirations. 'Man is not even called man,' says the *Zohar*, 'until he is united with woman.' And *Genesis* establishes before anything else that 'it is *not good* for man to dwell alone.'

The 'not good' is meant to contrast sharply with the 'it was good' refrain that runs throughout the listing of the created order: light, land, seas, trees, grass; the heavenly constellations; fish, birds, mammals and man himself; then woman – a deliberate enhancement of man, as the crown of creation, who named her Eve: 'the mother of all living (creatures),' towards which everything climaxed, at which point the refrain changes – thanks to the presence of woman and becomes 'behold, it was *very* good'!

Her presence is so important that at Sabbath-eve it is the woman of the household who lights the candles and says the benediction: she is the priest on that important occasion. Long before other nations and cultures had made wife beating illegal, the Jews had ordered punishments for such – and, if unrepentant (i.e. if the husband did not cease from it) the culprit was to be anathematized, i.e. excommunicated, the direst punishment in Israel, worse than capital punishment itself. As the commentary (*midrash*) on *Genesis* says, in stark unambiguity: 'Everything derives from woman' – everything: life and art and understanding.

It is precisely because of this that the *gemilus hasidim*, the works of kindness, are important – the 'soft' virtues by which sympathy is retained, and hardness kept at bay. In the same way that the woman is seen as the 'crown of her husband,' so the acts of kindness are to be seen as the crown of life itself – of which she is the mother. As the Talmud stated, asserting its rigorous rationality in balance with its inner logic, 'The highest form of wisdom is kindness,' and Nachman himself said, 'Where there is no truth, there is no kindness.'

All this is no digression from Leonard's work, still less his personality. He is consummately kind because he is wise to the spiritual realities. He finds room for the feminine in his life not out of any effeminacy, but through 'balance,' keeping 'a state of grace.' "I've always depended on the kindness of women," he admitted. Such things halt interviewers in their tracks: Pierre Berton admits incomprehension; others merely giggle like school-girls; yet others shake their heads and deride. But many understand, and follow; the women not least, who comprehend.

It is not surprising, then, that in this first album the emphasis should fall on women – their charms, their allurements, their passion, their honesty, their strength, their wisdom; but also their fragility, their weakness and their need. The songs of Leonard Cohen are songs about women, about love, about relationships (sexual and spiritual, carnal and sacramental – there are no such false dichotomies in his world-view), about caring and passion, trust and its breakdowns, fulfilment and desolation: the whole gamut of life is there; for in that man/woman relationship – the male/female rhythm – we have a microcosm of the universe itself. It is a central part of 'the word' that he has heard; the word he now delivers – in song.

The first album 'The Songs Of Leonard Cohen' was recorded in New York, at Columbia's 'E' studio, in 1967. It was produced by John Simon, who had been a major factor in levering Janis Joplin from Big Brother, arguing that her former group were good for live perfor-mances but not good enough for recording. Simon offers an interest-ing explanation of it in *Buried Alive*, marking the differences by description of 'studied music and tribal (sic) music.'

Gifted with perfect pitch, Simon could be a mandarin in the studio, forcing the complaint from Leonard that . . . "CBS tried to make my songs into music. I got put down all the time," although he told Manzano that Simon was "truly magnificent." The recordings ran into trouble from two different angles: John Hammond had a heart attack in the middle of things (Manzano says it was Hammond's wife that took ill), which caused the first problem; then Leonard found he disliked 'the original guitar soundtrack.' Their work pattern, in any case, was disrupted – 'not a daily one' – and so Leonard felt that . . . ["I] was losing contact with some of the songs . . . There was a conflict over aesthetics. I did not want drums for 'Suzanne' – that would push it into popular music." So he said he was allowed to mix it himself, shades of *Let Us Compare Mythologies* production, perhaps! It was from this early point that he decided he wanted to use women's voices – a marked trait of his albums.

Of the 10 songs on the record, four refer to women in their titles ('Suzanne', 'Winter Lady', 'Sisters Of Mercy' and 'So Long, Mar-ianne'); four have women as their central characters, either in his life or just out of it ('Master Song', 'The Stranger Song', 'Hey, That's No Way To Say Goodbye', 'One Of Us Cannot Be Wrong'); leaving but two, which offer the more socio-political themes: 'Stories Of The Street' (which nevertheless finishes by his telling his partner – female, to be sure – to steal away with him and avoid all the hassle; an action one might identify as a Cohen-like commentary on Jean-Paul Sartre's theme 'Hell is other people'). And 'Teachers', which introduces one of the ignored themes of *Beautiful Losers*, that of spurious gurus who take everything, negate everything, disrupt and ruin others' lives – and leave their victims puzzled and empty: 'Some Joseph (the name means 'acquirer' in Hebrew) looking for a manger.' But even this one, naturally! has a woman, several women, involved.

His problem was not that he felt 'unbalanced' without them, that went without saying; the real problem is how to be balanced *with* them, how to maintain the equilibrium when open to their enchantments, the passion they induce. The problem of the woman is really the problem of the female principle writ large, and honestly spoken. (A full 'commentary' on the songs is being produced by the present authors, under the title *Leonard Cohen: Troubadour Of Truth*.)

The cover-blurb of the album homes in on his individuality and the variety of subjects covered: 'Leonard Cohen continues to move in a direction distinctly his own. The lyrics are startling juxtapositions of natural speech with formal metaphor. Pain, loss, fear, guilt, loneliness, are unashamedly admitted; yet there is no trace either of self-pity or ironic posturing . . . Ultimately, the songs are religious, in the most profound and mystical sense of the word . . . Those with ears will hear.' An astonishing admission from the leader of the music industry, secular man at his most competitive point, and biblical with it!

Two things stand out in this ad-man's synopsis: one, the highly personal tone recognised in the songs; and, two, their 'religious' content. They lock together, these entities, as Alfred North Whitehead perceived long ago: 'religion is what a man does in his solitude.' Leonard's next album, in fact, was to make an even profounder statement on this theme, as we shall see – and we must view each album, not as a collection of eight or 10 songs, but as an *arrangement*, an *étude*, on certain themes, a gathering together of not only complementary but also disparate aspects of reality which nevertheless, when viewed together, produce a view, or at least a viewpoint, rather like a tapestry which tells a story – the overview – but also offers individual themes, identified by their colours or their smaller gatherings.

Leonard was thus 'connecting', going out on that path 'the width of a thread and of endless length,' seeking 'to sew the world together,' yearning 'to be filled with a comforting message, a beautiful knowl-edge of unity . . . a necklace of incomparable beauty.' But all too often, in the jarring and clamour of 'greedy fantasies' – our human condition – breaking up on mere 'unmeaning'. Little wonder at times that the ghost-land response was a shout: 'Connect nothing!' *Billboard* observed that his main market was adult; he was not yet reaching the younger segment, despite creating 'a splash in the consumer press.' It also noticed a much better response in Europe, particularly the United Kingdom, than in the USA.

The 'personal tone' is characteristic of everything Leonard wrote. He is one of our most personalised, self-reflective writers – as becomes one whose life is suffused by *angst* and the existential awareness that produces it. American critics labelled it 'Introspective Rock,' 'Self-conscious poetics,' 'Autobiographical Reminiscence,' but all of this later – of the songs of Joni Mitchell, James Taylor, Dory Previn, Laura Nyro – but Leonard had led the way nearly a decade earlier with his 'Jewish Blues'. But it is self-reflective without being self-absorbed or cloying. And it is disarmingly honest in its revelations, without feeding off them in any exhibitionist sense.

It is the perfect example to which Professor Dudek, in a very illuminating series of broadcast talks on Canadian radio, and later in a book titled *The First Person In Literature*, called attention: 'All the problems of modern literature turn on this split between the universal and the particular or private . . . The conflict between these two poles of possibility explains the anguish and the energy of modern literature.' The point re-emphasises both Leonard's close involvement with literary problems and his determination to air them on the widest possible front; his was not a 'running out' on his responsibilities, but hanging-in with them, in the most difficult areas, boldly drawing attention to them. And his view was getting across, to some. The poet Robert Graves, for example, a persistent critic of pop music words was rumoured to be working on his own collection of lyrics for his first recording. Poetry-in-song was taking off!

But much more importantly do they highlight the role of the individual – if willing to go through with it – as a symbol of broader humanity. To use a biblical metaphor, it is the stance of the suffering servant: the one who is willing to stand *for* (and sometimes *against*) his people; a role which in Hebrew literature was deemed to be messianic. Whether consciously or otherwise, Leonard was fulfilling the pious hopes of his parents, and those of his ancient people. Not as Messiah! but in a 'messianic' service which gathers priestly and prophetic roles together.

(Such roles were 'messianic' by virtue of their 'anointing' – *mashiach* – hence messiah), which could only have 'energy' to accomplish their work by virtue of the suffering – the anguish – that the subject endures. That is part of the immense power behind his songs: he willingly offers his heartaches – 'accurately' describing them; and by identifying with him, others' pain is resolved.

Some empty headed journalists scoffed at this, and at the honesty and the style of suffering entailed, but tens of thousands the world over *know* the utter relief, the singular disburdenment, that comes through his words and music, both. This is why it can be described as 'religious', 'profound' and 'mystical'. It *is* a mystery to him! And he is profoundly moved by its effects. He is also aware of the dangers, and has no interest in forming a cult with Cohen at the centre. He sharply reacts to any such nonsense, for life is much too serious for such frivolity. He is a true prophet pointing to the Word behind the word, the Source back of it all, though discreetly, not crudely.

We had a particular experience of this in his favourite café in Montreal. In the middle of one of our interviews, presiding over the omnipresent bowls of *café au lait* – the Gentile equivalent to the spice-box? – a fan rushed up to him, seized him by the hand, and thanked and praised him for his music. Leonard thanked him very politely, but continued as if nothing had happened; moreover, he refused to be drawn by our questioning on these interruptions to his life. They existed, they were gratifying, they were necessary – but the forward movement of his work-in-hand was what really mattered.

The anguish was real: the love of his life, Marianne, was barely in his life when he recorded the songs. "We simply drifted apart," he commented, down-playing the immense regret they both felt in their parting. 'So Long, Marianne' daringly tells all – at least, all that is required for the song to be the vehicle of the loss; the loneliness that ensued, the sheer pain of ruptured love. (On the album the backing track is played by the psychedelic group Kaleidoscope, which highlights the mood, if not the depths of the relationship.)

Begun on Aylmer Street in Montreal, and completed at the Chelsea in 1966 a year later, it captures the spirit of the partings – the partings of all upright people who so suffer. "I didn't think I was saying goodbye," he mused, "but I guess I was. She gave me many songs . . . She is a Muse."

He explained that during the recording he had been writing to her, and she came to stay with him in New York. By now he was living in the SoHo area, close to Clinton Street (actually it's in Brooklyn Heights), around the corner from the home of Thomas Wolfe's, author of the appropriately titled *Look Homeward, Angel!* Leonard informed Manzano that after he had sung this song, Marianne said to him (they were still seeing each other, off and on), "I am pleased that you did not write this song for me." Leonard expressed some surprise. Marianne continued, "Yes! because my name is Marianne!" Commented Leonard, more in relief than confusion, but pleasing the Scandinavian, "It is a song for the perfect woman."

The honesty, the conflict, almost unnerves him: he used to think that he was some sort of gypsy-boy before she found him; she knows how much he loved to live with her – but: 'You make me forget so very much . . .' to pray in particular. It is not a criticism; it is a statement of broken-hearted fact. They had met 'when we were almost young,' and her letters speak of their continuing closeness – but: 'Why do I feel alone?' He knows it cannot continue; he is on a ledge of despair; they are bound together – by such a fine thread that it cannot hold; he still needs her, but it will have to be her 'hidden love' – now that she's changed her name again. He knows this just as he has got over the first, depressing assaults – 'this whole mountainside.' Significantly, the album does not include the seventh verse which was printed on the sleeve, for in it the loss, the grief, the regrets, give way to recrimination:

> '*How come you gave away your news to everyone*
> *That you said was a secret for me?*'

But the song, as is so often the case in Leonard's writing, had a dual focus: the chorus originally read, 'My father is falling/but my grandfather is calling,' in which he tried to convey the idea that 'the sixties were about return, bypassing parents, to a previous generation. Yet people were generally dismissing the elderly!' His blood, his destiny, were obtruding restlessly upon him. As he regretfully expressed it in one of his new poems in *Selected Poems* ('The Broom Is An Army Of Straw'):

> '*Beloved of war . . . beloved of my injustice . . .*
> *Forgive me the claims I embrace*
> *Forgive me the claims I renounce.*'

He could say 'goodbye' – he must say it – because of those claims: the voice of his grandparents had won. 'Return' was now a meaningful path. Despite this the same spirit of graceful parting, on the basis of fondly remembered love, continues with great vigour in 'Hey! That's No Way To Say Goodbye'. A song written at the Penn Terminal Hotel on 24th Street, New York. ('Terminal' as condemned prisoners stayed there before execution.)

The sense of grievous loss is here, too: 'And now it's come to distances/And both of us must try/Your eyes are soft with sorrow/Hey that's no way to say goodbye!' Even as in the first he tried to turn the disappointments around, and tried to get Marianne to think positively, as the delightful and clever refrain reiterates: '. . . it's time we began/to laugh and cry, and cry and laugh about it all again.' There will be tears, but the smiles must win! He assures her that 'I'm not looking for another . . ./Our steps will always rhyme/You know my love goes with you/As your love stays with me . . ./But let's not talk of love or chains/And things we can't untie . . .'

A sense of loneliness pervades the album: man in his cold solitude. The 'Stranger Song' (which Vassal says demonstrates his sense of being an outsider; marked off from others by destiny, we might add) takes up the ignored theme of *Beautiful Losers* regarding would-be gurus, whom Leonard refers to as 'some Joseph' (i.e. some *acquirer*), 'a joker,' 'a man who talks his dreams to sleep.' To link this with Breavman's severance from Shell, as Vassal also suggests, is surely to misunderstand Breavman's failure of nerve: he gets cold feet just at the point where their relationship is about to deepen inexorably. She was the great 'connection' in his life, the one he could not afford to sustain.

In 'Sisters Of Mercy' it is 'your loneliness that says that you've sinned.'
Even Jesus 'spent a long time watching/from his lonely wooden tower'
– he 'who was broken . . . forsaken' – the suffering servant, *par
excellence* the illicit romance took place in 'The Master Song' in 'a lonely
lane.' In 'Teachers' she woke up alone one morning; and despite her
assurances, he cries out in 'So Long, Marianne', 'Why do I feel alone?'

Other matters are more peripheral: 'Suzanne' the memory of a
hapless woman, a ballerina for all that (hence 'her perfect body') who,
unaware of her own vacuity, is nevertheless kind and responsive, who
holds out 'the mirror' to those 'leaning out for love' who fascinated
Leonard, as she has many of his listeners. Manzano was informed by
Leonard that she was "the wife of an old sculptor-friend in Montreal.
She had a lot of courage, and in such a repressed society she used her
courage to express what she wanted. She was a ballerina and on one
occasion she invited me to eat oranges by the river." (Leonard told us
that it was *Constant Comment* tea which is made of tea and orange rinds,
that she gave him to drink; though the song states 'she *feeds* me tea and
oranges . . .'

Scobie finds in 'the exotic tea and oranges' a reference to
marijuana, for which 'tea' stood as a synonym. Marijuana came mostly
from Mexico, however; it was hashish that came from the Far East,
according to a REMP report of 1969. Manzano challenged Leonard as to
the Suzanne of the two already published poems in *Parasites Of Heaven*,
and the matter was agreed to be left suspended with some emotion.
Mike Jahn identifies the river in 'Suzanne' as the East River of New
York City, which was near to Clinton Street, on Lower East Side,
where Leonard lived for a time, Leonard has stated that it was, in fact,
the St Lawrence of Montreal; 'Our Lady Of The Harbour' being a
reference to *La Chapelle de Notre Dame de Bon Secours*, which has been a
place of pilgrimage – to fishermen and travellers particularly – since
1673. Moreover, the Suzanne who appears to have entered his life at this
time was an American and had a relationship of dependency – guru
dependency? – on Leonard: "You've taught me most everything I
know," she commented to him in front of Paul Saltzman of *MacLeans*.

Similarly, 'Winter Lady' can only know him as 'just a station on
your way'; beautiful as the moments are, she is merely an interlude – a
reminder of 'the child of snow' he once knew: one moment there, the
next gone. And the 'Sisters Of Mercy' are even less substantial. They
merely encountered him when he felt his life was but 'a leaf/that the
seasons tear off and condemn.' It was 'comfort' – such a key word in
Cohen! – they brought him, but of a passing sort. When he 'thought
that I just can't go on' – he who knew the agony of having to leave
everything (the comment demonstrates a great need in him) that he
could not *control*. So they sweetened his night, but that was all.

The 'Master Song' encounters something very different: he has been jilted, when sick. He had to endure the pangs of his love going off with a lesser man, who misled and maltreated her, and then ruined her. Interestingly, Manzano provoked more emotion from Leonard when questioning him about it. "The theme still evokes the dramatic infernal triangle of *Beautiful Losers*," said Leonard. "It is a song which deals with the trinity, but that is for the learned. Above all, it is (about) three people."

He has got used to 'this empty room' (loneliness, as ever), but he is still her 'prisoner', to whom she brings – he hopes – a little brightening fare: wine and bread. (A reminiscence of Abraham rescuing his nephew Lot, celebrated similarly with Melchizadek, the priest.)

Likewise, the song 'One Of Us Cannot Be Wrong' echoes the bleak experience of desertion, though with a different outcome. For here it ends not in hopeful expectation but in pleading for the impossible, despite his attempts to win her back (lighting the thin green candle): she has gone. He had endured 'the long sleepless night,' and so he resorted to 'torturing' the dress with which she used to provoke and seduce others; knowing that she had ruined them – the doctor, the saint, the Eskimo – all of them false to themselves! – knowing that she is resolute in her defiance of his love – 'your blizzard of ice' – he yet pleads, not for her to come in, but to allow him to join her there, in the storm! The song ends in despair, fading out as the voice wails on unmusically with a last shout of tortured emotion.

In all this the voice is soft, reassuring, comforting. He accompanies himself on a guitar, with Willie Ruff on bass and Jimmy Lovelace lightly supplying rhythm on drums, with some backing voices and sundry musical accompaniment. A positive and agreeable commencement, tentative perhaps (he told Goldstein that he feared the album was "going to be very spotty and undistinguished," explaining that the studio "tried to make my songs into music"). But nevertheless a great success! The word had gone out.

'a great writer
and a fine singer'

Writing in 1967, George Bowering referred to 'the Leonard Cohen boom,' by which he meant the growing response to his poetry and the reprinting of his four books in a series edition, virtually a matching set, not the release of his album, 'The Songs Of Leonard Cohen'. It was not only these and the album's appearance that lionised his name, on both sides of the 49th parallel and well beyond, but the recognition of him as a brilliant songwriter and the covering of his songs by others, too. Joe Cocker, Diana Ross and Neil Diamond all covered 'Bird On The Wire' with great success. Excerpts from his second novel *Beautiful Losers* were recorded by Buffy Sainte-Marie on the Vanguard label; she was becoming known as Leonard's first means of folk-projection, according to *Billboard*, who described Leonard as 'the new patron saint of the non-hippie hipsters.'

'Bird On The Wire' marked, in a dramatic way, an ending and a beginning. Begun in Hydra, it changed some lines in Oregon, and was finished "along with everything else," as Leonard remarked semi-obscurely – in a Hollywood motel. Kris Kristofferson, Rhodes scholar, songwriter, singer and actor, one-time companion of Janis Joplin, said he was going to put the first two lines on his own tombstone, to which Leonard replied, "I shall be hurt if he doesn't." It is Leonard's most performed song, with which he usually opened his concerts – to thunderous applause – because, "It returns me to my *duties*," an informative comment in the light of its words:

> 'Like a bird on the wire
> Like a drunk in a midnight choir
> I have tried in my way to be free
> Like a worm on a hook

Like a knight from some old-fashioned book
I have saved all my ribbons for thee
If I have been unkind
I hope that you can just let it go by
If I have been untrue,
I hope you know it was never to you.

'Like a baby stillborn
Like a beast with his horn
I have torn everyone who reached out for me
But I swear by this song
And by all that I have done wrong
I will make it all up to thee.
I saw a beggar leaning on his wooden crutch
He said to me, 'You must not ask for so much.'
And a pretty woman leaning in her darkened door,
She cried to me, 'Hey, why not ask for more?'

'Oh, like a bird on the wire
Like a drunk in a midnight choir
I have tried in my way to be free.'

At first blush it appears to be about freedom, and many have understood it to be so, but the smallest concentration emphasises its nature as an *apologia*, and a pained 'apology' most of all. Mike Jahn, in his excellent *The Story Of Rock*, misses the point of the song completely when he offers the explanation that it is, 'A glorious expression of the *Beautiful Loser's* theme: the man who tries and tries to make it, but always fails, and always in a bumbling way, a stupid way, but in the end, a way easy to pity.' It might fairly be said that in so commenting, he has missed the point of *Beautiful Losers*, too. It makes one realise the elegant truth in Archibald MacLeish's comment in *Ars Poetica:*

'A poem should not mean, but be' *con brio* the song. Its open nerve lies in the key words, 'If I have been unkind.' Kindness, defined by the rabbis as 'the beginning and the end of the Law,' is the ultimate virtue; its negation a matter of the gravest import. Such had been the commitment, such the ardour behind its execution, not merely 'obsessed' but at times 'manic' (he once threw his typewriter out of the window, so great his distress and burden), such the 'rage' in fearing that he was failing to fulfil his duties, that nothing could be allowed to stand in his way: he acted 'like a beast with his horn/I have torn everyone who reached out for me.'

Its heartache lies in the pain he had caused to Marianne especially, and the hope that somehow he could 'make it all up to (her)' one day.

But it was double-edged, this pain. To have hurt her was to have failed in his solemn duties – to have failed God. The 'thee' is deliberately ambiguous. It is therefore an apology and a declaration to both. In the line 'I have torn everyone who reached out for me,' another signal appears, which we see elsewhere in his work; namely, a reluctance to be loved and cherished, perhaps a fear of it – of its entangling propensities? As if long-term closeness suffocates or deprives him of that 'freedom' his psyche demands. It is very close to his need for control and dependency that we see manifested in the production of his books, his albums – at times, even his interviews. It throws an interesting light on his later phrase, 'a *sovereign* state of common grace' (our italics) by which 'freedom' is specifically linked to equilibrium.

That heartache was formidably deep. To not a few he represented it as 'a breakdown', and in view of the high emphasis and importance he gave to 'balance', maintaining his 'state of grace,' it was, indeed, just that. There were other factors, not least the drug-taking, which had been a feature of life on Hydra and more so in New York. What started as experimentation became an ambush and then a master. One of the best known drug habits of the day went under the name 'electric cool-aid' – fruit juice spiked with LSD – by which more than a few came unstuck mentally, so savage was its effects. (It was not until October 1966 that the US government officially declared LSD 'a dangerous and illegal substance.')

In New York, drugs were so prevalent that he felt that he must leave the Chelsea Hotel and find respite from its dangers at the Henry Hudson Hotel on 58th Street (after a brief sojourn at the YMCA), never knowing what was 'spiked' or what was not. LSD appeared in everything, even in fried potatoes. "It was best at times not to order anything," he told Alberto Manzano. The atmosphere was less openly 'arty' than the Chelsea, which pleased Leonard, who goes out of his way to deny artiness, planning or programming in his work – even meaning at times! He still met "a few interesting people" there. But he had sowed the wind; he was now reaping the whirlwind. He has admitted that his use of 'speed' brought his weight down to 116lbs at this time and he . . . "Didn't look very good. I was very unhealthy . . ." (The Henry Hudson was a sort of home-from-home as it evoked memories of the explorer of that name who discovered Hudson Bay and much of the Canadian Northland.)

He was not the only one by a long way to be caught out by this wilder lifestyle. Tragedy was on the increase, for all sorts of reasons. His idol, Ray Charles, was presently undergoing hospital tests to determine whether he had abstained from 'narcotic drugs'; and Richard Farina, brother-in-law of Joan Baez, died tragically in a motorcycle accident on his way home from a party. Bob Dylan crashed on his

Triumph 55 near Woodstock, and disappeared from the scene for many months – amid rumours of being comatose, permanently brain-damaged, draft-dodging, or so drugged-out that he would never perform again; some even spoke of his death. Sadly, there was no such exaggeration in the news of Woody Guthrie's death from Huntington's chorea, nor that of Otis Redding in a plane crash.

Not a few pop stars found themselves on the wrong side of the law, then being tightened in the face of the growing dangers of drugs. The Rolling Stones made the headlines – fairly and unfairly – frequently, which did not prevent *Rolling Stone* magazine of San Francisco from offering a free roach-clip with its first issue!

In August The Beatles announced that they had given up drugs. "We don't need it any more," commented Paul McCartney, somewhat prematurely. Within days of the statement, Brian Epstein, their manager, died of an overdose of Carbirol; and the Maharishi Mahesh Yogi – to whom The Beatles had offered themselves as disciples, a guru of gurus, informed them that his death was 'not important'. It served, however, merely to nerve them for greater involvements with him, for a month later Lennon and McCartney publicly espoused his doctrine of Transcendental Meditation. *The New York Times* suggested that such involvements in non-Western culture and music was a sign of youth's moral, aesthetic and psychological 'revolution', others thought 'degeneration' more appropriate.

In San Francisco, the first 'Human Be-In and Gathering of the Tribes' took place. A forerunner of rock festivals (as late as January 1967!), it was led by such cultural pacemakers as Tim Leary – 'father of the drugs cult,' the amphetamine (speed) rage, which gave way to heroin (smack), reached its heights in 1967/8 – Ken Keasey (famed for his acid-test house band), Allen Ginsberg – 'father of the Beat Generation' (who turned the Angels on to (acid) and used to perform on his harmonium in Tomkins Square Park, New York, with George Harrison and Prabhupada, which instigated group-chanting, another lively feature of the times) – and Jerry Rubin – soon to announce his Youth International Party.

Twenty thousand young and not-so-young people gathered, delighting in the music of Dizzy Gillespie, The Grateful Dead, Jefferson Airplane and Quicksilver Messenger Service, among others. Ravi Shankar – who had introduced the sitar and its music to the scene – admitted that he was 'disturbed' by the adulation he was receiving, especially from the hippies. (The word comes from the American slang 'hep' or 'hip' meaning knowledgeable; much of their activities have an uncommon resemblance to the gnostic movements – and before them the 'mysteries'; 'gnostic' also meaning knowledge, of course. True hippiedom was short-lived: it arose in 1966 and was ceremoniously bidden farewell in the 'Death of Hippie' parade in 1968; needless to say, the traditions of the young proved as unchangeable as those of the old!)

Meanwhile, Judy Collins covered Leonard's song 'Priests' (which Richie Havens also covered in 1969) though Leonard never performed it publicly. She had won great acclaim at The Troubadour in Los Angeles, singing 'The Sisters Of Mercy' as an encore, which called attention to her penchant for 'sad songs' and 'the *new* folk-poet, Leonard Cohen.' They performed together at the Rheingold Music Festival in New York. 'Priests' was due to appear on his second album, its words were published in the song book: *Songs Of Leonard Cohen* – covering the first and second albums – but it was omitted, perhaps simply through lack of space. Its title and contents are so close to him that one wonders if there were not other reasons. (He astutely side-stepped our questions on this!) Clearly set in Greece, where highway shrines are more regular than milestones, at which the dead are honoured publicly, it dramatises Leonard's more self-indulgent side in a soliloquy of hope and caring concerning himself and his beloved:

'And who will write love songs for you
When I am lord at last
And your body is some little highway shrine
That all my priests have passed
That all my priests have passed.

'My priests they will put flowers there
They will stand before the glass
But they'll wear away your little window, love
They will trample on the grass
They will trample on the grass.

'And who will aim the arrow
That men will follow through your grace
When I am lord of memory
And all of your armour has turned to lace
And all your armour has turned to lace?

'The simple life of heroes
And the twisted life of saints
They just confuse the sunny calendar
With their red and golden paints
With their red and golden paints.

'And all of you have seen the dance
That God has kept from me
But He has seen me watching you
When all your minds were free
When all your minds were free.'

As with so many of his poems and songs, the earthly is 'confused' with the heavenly, the divine with the human, the secular with the sacred. What is clear is that, as in 'Bird On The Wire', he gives voice to his aspirations, his *unfree* status: God, no less, has 'kept him from the dance.' Nevertheless, 'he has seen me watching you/When all *your* minds were free . . .'

He was continuing to write poetry, although the pace – and some of the style – had gone. Several of the pieces which would appear in his last book of formal poetry were penned at this time, in Hydra, in New York, and especially in Montreal. The video *Poem* was made there, too. It offered an extract from *Beautiful Losers*, beginning with the turbulent repetition, 'My mind, my mind, my mind . . .' which emphasised his ongoing strain, and his inner struggles; but in a particular way, for the photographic sequence that goes with it is of the work of Goya, Dali and reportage from the Spanish Civil War, in which the juxtapositioning of his work with Lorca's obtains its first, 'public' exposition.

It was the time of the World Fair in Montreal, which inspired Canada in its growing self-awareness, not least its young people. In addition to enjoying his share of the laurels for writing the score for May's *The Angel*, he performed at the celebrations of Canada's Centennial, which raised fond memories as well as proud hopes – not least for the separatist cause. Curiously, at the Centennial Conference at Kingston, a large majority of university professors expressed strong opposition to a larger place being found for modern culture, art and creativity in the universities. Such reactionary behaviour was the seed-bed for the students' revolt; they felt let down – as truly they were – by this resistance to the 'cultural explosion'; 'revolution' was simmering below the surface in more ways than the obvious, albeit quietly.

Much more serious, however, was the military *coup* in Greece, on April 21, which led to the seven years' dictatorship. It was widely believed that the US government was involved – aiming to divide Cyprus and thus serve its interests in the Middle East; and elsewhere too, some argued, as a diversion to its government's rapidly growing unpopularity over the Vietnam War. This was, after all, Leonard's second home, where many of his friends lived, and poet-musicians of the calibre of Mikis Theodorakis were exposed to every danger and brutality.

Perhaps of even graver concern to such as Leonard was the outbreak, on June 5, of the war in Israel. The concern was precipitated a week or so earlier when the surrounding Arab states issued their infamous Declaration committing themselves to 'the destruction of the State of Israel' (which they did not recognise!). Israel retaliated by warning that it would defend itself with *main force:* 'Not war to kill,' the government declared, 'but war in order not to be killed,' and its embassies around the world quickly filled with volunteers willing to fight for it. The predominant sense of fear throughout the young nation was transformed into a sense of purpose and even victory by the appointment of that military genius, General Moshe Dayan – 'the greatest Prime Minister the young state never had' – who created order out of chaos, resilience out of fear, and victory – in six days – out of what many feared was to be certain death. It was a proud time to be Jewish.

Meanwhile the Vietnam war rolled on, its horrors and toll in human misery ever-escalating, its sapping of the nation's vitality and resources ever deepening, its bitter criticisms – at home and abroad, not least in the artistic and intellectual communities – ever mounting.

It was a very busy as well as an anxious time for Leonard, with poetry readings, concerts in Central Park, New York (an open-air festival), and at the famed, if short-lived, Newport Folk Festival. (It was here that Arlo Guthrie – son of Woody – introduced his well known 'Alice's Restaurant' which was later filmed as well as released in record form.) In September Leonard featured on *Camera Three*, a Sunday morning cultural affairs' programme in New York, when Leonard sang some songs, read some of his poetry and was pictured staring into various Broadway windows, all somewhat tawdry, as became a poet! This, his début on American television, produced the largest audience-response in the programme's 14-year history: a sure sign of his huge influence on youth of the sixties.

He also took part in a videoed programme with Gwendolyn Macewen, in the *Modern Canadian Poetry Series*, recorded by the CBC at Toronto. Later, the World Poetry Conference took place, in early September, as part of the 'Man and his World' theme – ironical in the light of the revolutionary and war-like vibrations that were being felt. Denise Levertov threw the conference into confusion by her vociferous appeal for 'engaged poetry', urging her *confrères* to prepare to make 'the ultimate sacrifice' against the horrors perpetrated in Vietnam.

Canada, of course, was an able and persistent critic of the war, and aided those 'draft-dodgers' who wished to register their opposition by refusing to fight, by keeping her borders open to them. When challenged by state officials on the issue, Pierre Trudeau merely replied that it was America's problem, not Canada's, thus demonstrating what a man of steel this Renaissance-man truly was.

Curiously, it was this very war that aided Leonard's career: his introduction to 'the big time' was facilitated by Judy Collins, though it was by no means his public début. It actually took place at the New York Town Hall on West 43rd Street, round the corner from Times Square and in the heart of theatre-land. It was, in fact, a concert

organised on behalf of Sane, one of the protest movements against the
Vietnam war, which took place on April 30, 1967 and broadcast by New
York's Pacifica WBAI. (One of Leonard's direct involvements in
protest, which would consummate shortly in his 'signing-up' to fight in
Israel in the early seventies!) Ms Collins, not sparing Leonard's blushes,
described his reaction to her invitation, and its consequence, splendidly
in her book, *Trust Your Heart:*

> *"'I can't do it, Judy, I would die from embarrassment."*
> *"Leonard, you are a great writer and a fine singer (she always
> made that point, against his critics), people want to hear you."*
> *He finally agreed, reluctantly. When I introduced him, he
> walked on to the stage hesitantly, his guitar slung across his hips,
> and from the wings I could see his legs shaking inside his trousers.
> He began 'Suzanne' with the hushed audience leaning forward in
> their seats; he got halfway through the first verse and stopped. "I
> can't go on," he said, and left the stage, while the audience
> clapped and shouted, calling for him to come back. "We love you,
> you're great!" Their voices followed him backstage, where he
> stood with his head on my shoulder, my arms around him. "I
> can't do it, I can't go back." He smiled his handsome smile. He
> looked 10-years-old. His mouth drew down at the sides, he
> started to untangle himself from his guitar strap. I stopped him,
> touching him on the shoulder. "But you will," I said. He shook
> himself and drew his body up and put his shoulders back, smiled
> again, and walked back onto the stage. He finished 'Suzanne'
> and the audience went wild. He has been giving concerts ever
> since.'*

In her BBC television interview she added a few more details: he
appeared in an elegant suit for this occasion, a peace-protest, which
became his style from now on: and his hands were shaking as much as
his legs! Moreover, it was the audience as well as Ms Collins who incited
him to go back: "Come on, Leonard, you can do it!" they shouted. As
she went on to say, "It was the beginning of this gruelling life as a
travelling troubadour. He is, in fact, a wonderful performer . . . He
sings very well; he's quite mesmerising as a singer . . . He may not
thank me for setting him on this road!"

But 'on this road' he was, and he was beginning to enjoy it. A few
weeks later, still plagued by stage-fright as he always would be, he
performed in Central Park, at one of those immense rock-rallies that
were so much a feature of the period. And then at the Newport Folk
Festival nearby, just four years after Dylan's own début there. At both
his songs and singing were met with huge applause – they were
applauding a new voice, a new message; the word was being heard. (Ms

Collins was a director of Newport, responsible for some of the more imaginative changes such as square-dancing, story-telling and highlights; Leonard among them.)

In fact the year marked a double celebration. In addition to Leonard's successes, his 'old Layton' won the Governor-General's Award for poetry for the second time (the first was in 1959); now for his book *An Idiot Joy* which re-established him (if that were necessary!) as 'the most important poet of the sixties . . .' 'one of the most powerful, accomplished and controversial poets writing in Canada today,' to quote Eli Mandel.

As the latter said of him: 'A darker spirit enters the poetry of the sixties, almost despair in *Periods Of The Moon* (which has been a symbol of the feminine, and constantly a female deity; it is a powerful Lorcan theme, and a key symbol in Leonard), close to savagery in *The Shattered Plinth*, and in some way connected with the intrusion of Europe into the poet's line of sight. It may be that the Hellenic world of sea and light and form and sensuality equally pervade the later poems.'

The same goes for many writers, not least Leonard himself. Marshall McLuhan had his famous work *The Medium Is The Message* recorded at this time; even its successes did not prevent some academics from sourly referring to it as the Mess-Age of the time. The sixties saw something ferocious enter and destroy man's spirit: the use of naked power on a scale beyond our conception, by politicians and 'military scientists' (sic) who perfectly fulfilled the ancient's comment that 'those whom the gods wish to destroy they first make *mad*.' Not just in the 'carpet bombing' of North Vietnam but in their general cheapness of life, as illustrated by the monstrous outrages in the Generals' coup; Arab fanaticism 'in the name of Allah,' as if in total ignorance of its roots and real meaning; police brutality and all forms of political cynicism: unkindness not only achieving supremacy but being boasted of by its practitioners.

The Jewish sages had warned: 'One is a lie, two are lies, but three become politics.' They all do it, these leaders of peoples; they do it until caught out in their duplicity, and then resign with honour! Self-satisfied, no doubt, but unaware of the moral turpitude they create. Poets do it, too! but those of integrity – such as Layton and Cohen – at least admit to it:

> '*I do not know if the world has lied*
> *I have lied*'

But his 'do not know' is not rhetorical; it is part of his detachment – not his moral insensibility – in which he 'scorned the fraternity of war.' To those outraged by the sheer obscenity of violence, ambition, blood-lust, official murder – all the nauseous follies of war – this alleged silence of his was a major problem. Why could not Leonard say more, he of the seeing eye, the rapier-like word and phrase? He has yet to speak of it, but two things, perhaps three, are obvious: One, at this time he was extremely busy, 'embattled' with the tasks of career-building which he never quite seemed to win, despite his many successes, and that in a broken relationship. There is a Kierkegaardian self-destructiveness about some of his actions, as if success had to be 'balanced' by pain and self-sacrifice. (When asked about this, he merely replied, "I liked one of his titles: *Fear And Trembling!*") He appears to need the torment, not because he enjoys it, but as a sort of hair-shirt, keeping him in contact with his vocation, ensuring his equilibrium.

And it is that vocation which is the second point: that if we claim prophetic status for his work, and we do (he does not, nor would not), it is because he is in that old tradition of being powerless before the 'imperialism' of the word, the voice. Not in the *political* tradition of Moses, or Elijah or Isaiah or Jeremiah, whose 'word' was very largely political, national; but in that of, say, Micah or Ezekiel, who were intensely personal and individualistic. He writes and sings from heart to heart, lip to lip – not as in addressing a public gathering. It is a different, but surely equally valid service. We shall shortly see that some journalists referred to it as a meditation, others as an incantation; whatever the terms used few would be prepared to deny its spiritual power even though it is immensely entertaining, sometimes cathartically, sometimes humorously but always melodiously.

This is of extreme importance for understanding Leonard Cohen, not merely in the personal expressions of his poetry and songs, but overall. What is a nation, after all, but the sum of its individual members? And what is its value, save that of the totality of each of the citizens within it? The disgust we see writ large in *Beautiful Losers* – compressed in the conglomerative smut of F's deranged mind, 'made mad by too much dirty sex,' from which 10 days of fasting were not sufficient to cleanse Leonard – is levelled chiefly at his fears of Canada being taken over by America: the capital of capitalism; where money talks, where its power is the one necessary say-so to becoming somebody; where nobodies are the poor, the powerless, who literally don't count – they have nothing to count. The individual is entirely lost in the rapine of the rich and the corporate; where a man is merely a cog in some power-manipulator's wheel, where his hunger, his need, his ill-health, is someone else's problem not least his own, for not 'getting up and getting on'!

Concentrate on the individual says Leonard; then you will get your priorities right. As the great Hillel questioned, 'If I am here, all is here; and if I am not here, who is here?' As Nachman himself said, 'The I is the soul, which endures.' If a man, even a prophet, starts to understand such things, he has enough to do, without trying to order or correct the world. Leonard so understood: 'I-Thou' had become his sufficient objective. It may be a long haul, it may even be ineffective, but it was his dutiful way:

> '*He sang and nothing changed*
> *Though many heard the song.*
> *But soon his face was beautiful*
> *And soon his limbs were strong.*'

There is, however, a third possible explanation for this reserve. Leonard has never shied away from his Jewishness; indeed, he has glorified it and gloried in it, as well he might. But he came to maturity – his education began, he said – on seeing the horrors of the death-camps, the extermination ovens of his own people. Through parts of his poetry and at least his first novel the smell of burning flesh hovers, as does the gas of the chambers. His soul was seared by those experiences. Professor Dudek is surely wrong to see that strain of cynicism developing merely from the ongoing situation. Leonard came from something far worse, and he saw very little real concern for it about him. Six *million* of his own people died horrendously at that time.

His cynicism, which appears in the near-tasteless essay we discussed earlier, gets fuller expression in *Let Us Compare Mythologies*, and reaches a climax in the consummate scorn of *Flowers For Hitler*. But it is there enduringly, a scar in his psyche, a scar made more permanent by hearing the word accurately. Since Masada, and well before, his people had been dying unjustly. Not because they did wrong, not because they weren't useful, not because they were selfish, not because they were crude or callous; they died simply because they were Jewish. Beside such inhuman crime – from which many of their contemporaries simply hid their faces, be they popes, politicians or the military – how can one speak?

Others have spoken, but what came of it? And what did the world do more recently but stand by and watch, when the Arab Declaration of May 29 was issued? Has anything changed? Leonard had good reason to emphasise the high, high importance of the individual, for only when the individual is prepared and mobilised will society truly change – as he, more than most so wished:

> '*Like an empty telephone booth passed at night*
> *and remembered*
> *Like mirrors in a movie-palace lobby consulted*
> *only on the way out*
> *Like a nymphomaniac who binds a thousand*
> *into a strange brotherhood*
> *I wait*
> *for each one of you to confess.*'

'Ονομα : *Leonard*   (1)

'Επώνυμον : COHEN   (2)

Τόπος γεννήσεως : KANAΔΑΣ   (3)

Χρονολογία γεννήσεως : 1934   (4)

Κατοικία : KANAΔΑΣ   (5)

Westmount High School, June 1950. Leonard is on the middle row, second from the right.

Busking in Hydra.

The Buckskin Boys, with Leonard on guitar.

With Marianne and friends in Hydra.

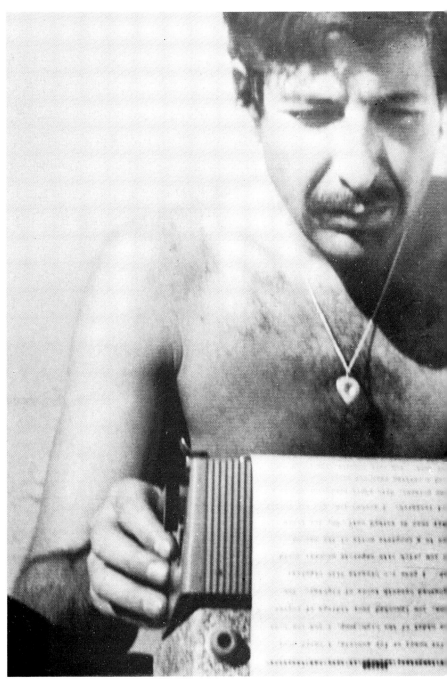

At work in Hydra and, inset, in Toronto. *Author 's collection*

With John Hammond, the legendary Columbia Records A&R chief, who signed Leonard to the label. *David Gahr*

With Judy Collins. *David Gahr*

Barry Plummer

Receiving a gold disc for ' Various Positions ' from CBS Germany. *Dag Thorenfeldt*
Inset : *Rex Features International*

The Chelsea Hotel, New York. *Author's collection*

Professor Louis Dudeck, Leonards English tutor at McGill University, and lifelong friend. *Author 's collection*

Michael Ochs Archives

James Wigler

word as life

'*They looked in vain to history for an explanation of themselves: more and more it appeared that the meaning was not to be found in theology . . . Thereupon these citizens found that they had no other place to search but within themselves – even though, at first sight, that repository appeared to be nothing but a sink of iniquity.*'

PERRY MILLER

'*Perhaps a mind will open in this world perhaps a heart will catch rain Nothing will heal and nothing will freeze but perhaps a heart will catch rain.*'

LEONARD COHEN

'*The heart is always involved with wishing, wanting longing, possessing, holding, losing. That's the* landscape *of the heart . . . It's important that the* real *feelings in society and the life of the heart be affirmed . . .*'

LEONARD COHEN

people-poetry, and
public recognition

The New York Times hailed him in 1968 as 'a major spokesman' of his generation. It, at least, was listening! Whether he liked it or not, and most of the time he appears to have liked it, he had obtained cult-status. That is, his voice was distinctive, real and honest; and people were responding. He may have upset 'the cool' of many, but they liked 'the warm' which he put in its place. The word was getting through.

In a curious but valid way, Stephen Williams made the point in *Newsday* when he said 'perhaps (it's) because in style and content he's closer to Berlin or Zurich of the twenties than to the SoHo of the eighties.' A half-truth, to be sure, for at the very time this was being penned Leonard was establishing his own rapport with the ho-ho of SoHo by getting involved in Ron Hubbard's 'dianetic' discoveries (actually made in 1948 when Orwell was fashioning his own, more robust fictions). For one of Leonard's cast of mind, there were obvious spears of interest – even if this particular spear was devoid of that ability to 'shear itself into a needle' and sew the world together. Not least among them was the concept of preconceptual memory by which an individual may find his freedom to develop by returning to his distant past and rediscovering himself within it: connections ever resonating. In this case, a very brief connection.

That barometer of humanity, the *New York Times*, made the point in a different way when, in August 1968 it drew its readers' attention to the 'new emphases' that were becoming apparent, the confluence of poetry and pop music which was taking place in the works of Bob Dylan, Paul Simon, Laura Nyro, Rod McKuen – and Leonard Cohen. (Leonard's poetry was regularly placed alongside McKuen's, whose *Lonesome Cities* was rated as one of the two best-selling books on poetry; the other was Leonard's own *Selected Poems: 1956-1968*, discussed below.)

MacLeans magazine did similarly, hailing him specifically as Canada's answer to Bob Dylan, which was particularly interesting for Canada was now producing more records, and greater record sales (at $44 million, retail prices) than ever before. And *Village Voice* offered its own perception, 'His voice has been called monotonous, but it is also the most miraculous vehicle for intimacy the new pop has yet produced.' The intimate sound – of the two great intimacies – from lip to lip.

And not merely for 'new pop' and 'intimacy' but for poetry, too – ever his first love, even if his sphere was changing and he now worked with it in a different medium. The 'cult status' of the man now produced the need for a summation of his poetic work, which had actually been on the go for two years already, in the form of his *Selected Poems: 1956-1968*. It quickly established itself as a best-seller, an enduring monument to his art and sensitivity. At 246 pages, it was his most extensive work to date, and probably his most important.

The selection was actually made by Marianne's hand and shows her sensitivity to his work. Her writing is strong and bold, like her character, and shows a purposefulness in selection of great understanding. Not surprisingly, poems concerning herself were gathered up at the end, as if in humble protest at their possible inclusion – a judgment happily over-ridden by Leonard, to our great pleasure. Moreover, it had a short collection of 'New Poems' appended to it, in which tranquillity of the poetic sort lies alongside the harsh judgements (and self-judgements: we should not forget the importance of the symbol of the mirror in Leonard's work, now and later).

The mood is one of pure romance ('Wherever it is we meet/I can't go far from'); of loneliness ('Don't they know what it means/to be lonely . . . and an explorer'); of ambition in art ('The reason I write/is to make something/as beautiful as you are'); of philosophical detachment ('A person who eats meat/wants to get his teeth into something/A person who does not eat meat/wants to get his teeth into something else . . .'); of alienation, even poignant despair ('Marita/Please find me/I am almost 30'); of crucifying self-doubt ('Do not trust him/unless you love him'). Most appropriate of all, it commences with a poem to Marianne, 'This Is For You' in which he delights to make the connections, substantiate the history: 'All this happened/in the truth of time/in the truth of flesh . . .' Nevertheless, 'Now I am a shadow/I long for the boundaries/of my wandering . . .'

It sold nearly a quarter of a million copies in the first few months after publication – rare for any book in those days, and unheard of for poetry for a very long time, and a reprinting was soon put under way.

(An abridgement of it was published in 1969, under the title *Poems: 1956-1968*.) Commented Kenneth Rexroth, perfectly making the point:

'Leonard Cohen's poetry and song constitute a big breakthrough . . . This is certainly the future of poetry – people poetry – direct, one to the other, I to Thou. Cohen accomplishes what the surrealists failed to do – his poetry is fundamentally subversive of the human sensibility. It is the voice of a new civilisation.'

Subversive or not politically, it is curious that Rexroth – a leader himself in the fifties and sixties by virtue of his brilliant fusion of poetry and jazz (he was, with Kenneth Patchen, its third-generation standard bearer) – should be content to talk *simpliciter* of 'human sensibility'. He meant the old human sensibility, the staid and essentially dualistic forms (not to say 'male, white and American' – which includes the WASPS of Canada, so long as their independence and superiority was allowed!) by which Catholic and Puritan Victorian values were protected and projected. It reached its apogee in McCarthyism in the States, and produced the Underground Poetry wave associated with Alexander Trocchi, its oldest exponent.

We saw Leonard expressing his views of this in *Flowers For Hitler* (if somewhat covertly); more explicitly in *Beautiful Losers* (if sardonically); and now we find him hailed by one of its most seeing practitioners for subverting 'fundamentally' that wrong sort of sensibility, and its subconscious and subliminal ideologies. Perhaps Rexroth had in mind Vachel Lindsay, the founder of jazz-poetry's incantatory ballad 'Bryan, Bryan, Bryan, Bryan', who wrote '. . . Candidate for president who sketched a silver Zion,/The one American Poet' – Leonard was nearly that, and he did get F to say 'I long to be the President of the new Republic, who could sing outdoors' – but whatever, the die was now cast. Leonard felt its weight, assented to its responsibility – and made the biggest gesture of his life, the most public and the most influential. He stood up, was counted, and acted with astonishing *bravado*.

The Governor-General, or rather his literary minions, whose job it was to make the selection, failed to understand him, to their own enormous embarrassment; so much so, in fact, that the rules were changed in the wake of Leonard's refusal of the Award they offered. (From henceforward those selected for the honour were to be politely asked, in confidence, if they would receive it.) To the proffered honour Leonard cabled a terse reply: 'No; the poems themselves forbid it absolutely.'

It had repercussions, did this reply (and surely its boldness and honesty are sufficient answers for those who criticise his detachment from politics as being 'gutless'.) By some quirk of mischief, he invited himself to attend the ceremony at which the award was due to be presented, to the further embarrassment of many, some of whom wished to forget he existed altogether, poets among them. Some of his fellow-poets had of course laboured for years without recognition, still less reward. Some had given their finest labours to establishing its importance in literature – in society.

(Leonard's *riposte*, had he needed one, would have been a Kierkegaardian *caveat:* 'a poet's sin is to poetise instead of being'; 'being' required decision, commitment, action: 'political' or not.) This was treason! One was so excited apparently, that he tried to punch Leonard's elegant nose, untranquilly, forgetting his *tier* and style; made mad by the gods, perhaps? In other, less violent, circles – where love was understood and politeness and gentleness appreciated, not merely discussed – it established his credentials still more.

Another matter, not unconnected, was carefully investigated as well as discussed in some written replies offered to *The Jewish Telegraph*. (For some reason he started to refuse interviews about this time; a transitory decision.) The replies were then put to a consultant psychotherapist, whose own reply was, 'Obviously he is very deep-thinking and interested in sublimative writing.' (sic): ('If you can't . . . become a trite and inarticulate expert!'). But Leonard's replies, albeit deliberately cryptic (*à la* Pierre Berton interview again) are very interesting. We repeat the questions and answers below:

Q. *"Do you manage to retain your Jewish teaching in spite of your fame?"*
A. *"If I forget thee?"*
Q. *"Do you ever find that your Judaism is a hindrance? Do you come across any anti-semitism?"*
A. *"Let them be ashamed and confounded together that seek after my soul to destroy it."*
Q. *"Does your Jewish background influence any of your writing?"*
A. *"From the roof he saw a woman washing herself."*
Q. *"Does your Jewish background in any way help your writing?"*
A. *"And the woman was very beautiful to look upon."*
Q. *"Where were you born? Was your Jewish upbringing strict?"*
A. *"Montreal. Just balances, just weights."*

We should note particularly that the second part of *Psalm* 137:5 which we italicise is left implied: '*If I forget thee O Jerusalem/Let my right hand forget her cunning.*' His métier is considered less important than his Jewish identity! Similarly, in avoiding the direct reply to the question of anti-semitism, he reaffirms his identity by quoting *Psalm* 35:4: his

Jewishness – whether 'hindrance' or not – is not a negotiable trait, whatever the outcome.

In three he is even more elliptical, referring to 11 *Samuel* 11:2 in which King David succumbed to the temptation Bathsheba put in his way by washing herself publicly. An influence as well as a warning for all male Jews, of which Leonard was only too well aware; a confession (soon to reappear in song-form) as well as an influence.

So with the next two questions. The double question was answered: a) explicitly (Montreal), and b) quintessentially Jewishly, in that in the answering he honoured his parents' wisdom in finding that very difficult mean between 'strictness' and 'understanding' with a reference to Mosaic law (at *Leviticus* 19:36; *not* the misquoted book of *Exodus!*): in which justice is inculcated . . . 'Just balances, just weights' refer to righteousness (*tsedeq*) by which exactness and kindness are commanded.

Said the untherapeutic psychologist, unable to express either accuracy or justice, apparently: 'Leonard Cohen does not express physically to the outside world that he is Jewish, but philosophically he does.' No one could have said this who had read one of Leonard's books, or listened to either of his albums that had appeared to date. It is a blatant example of that empty-headed twaddle that sometimes goes under the name of learning, expertise or scholarship which disgusted Leonard. Journalists were not exempt from it either, hence his strictures. But what of the imprecations he calls down on his denigrators (in an almost unique mood) Ah, sings Leonard later, his Jewishness clear and unashamed, 'there is a judgment coming . . .'

We should note that Leonard nowhere shows a reaction to anti-semitism (Leon Pinsker's 'demonopathy'), one of the questions he deliberately avoided above. His youthful irritation at Pound reveals as much as we can find anywhere. In *Flowers For Hitler* he deals with the picture of its resultant genocide, rather than the essence of the matter. There he does so either by pouring scorn on its perpetrators – the immature and boring Hitler, his 'Mutt and Jeff henchmen,' the 'average' Eichman, Goebbels the failed novelist etc. – or by sharing the recitation of his people's suffering and humiliation in general terms. As against the anger of his confrères (which Leonard rarely expresses, rising to pained complaint or argument, at most). He seems to embody the philosophical truth of Sartre (who could express things physically) that, 'If the Jew did not exist, anti-semitism would have to invent him.' The world needs a scapegoat, especially when its complacency and incompetency is revealed!

The BBC, regardless of the alleged snub, and perhaps misunderstanding the point he was making, invited him to take part in four programmes that year: first, to appear on the *Julie Felix Show*, singing

'The Stranger Song' and – with Ms Felix – 'Hey! That's No Way To Say Goodbye'. Then to appear on *Top Gear*, also presenting two songs: 'You Know Who I Am' and 'Bird On The Wire'; which was followed by his own two-part show (In August and September) in which he offered 12 songs and some musical improvisation titled 'No, It Wasn't Any Good'. It was a sort of *mise en scène* for his second album, also released that year, to great acclaim. Before long it had reached the Number 63 spot of *Billboard*'s Top 200, an incredible achievement given the individuality of his style and – if one dare say it – the rather laboured, not to say funereal pace of the music.

He achieved more than commercial success with this album. It was the fulfilment of a long-held ambition: to be recorded in Nashville, the home of so much good music, the best, in fact, in country and western. For other singers, long established in New York or other recording cities, Nashville was – in Mike Jahn's phrase – 'an escape to the country,' a return to the roots of the matter, often from slums and ghettoes and stultifying suburbs or downtown dereliction. For Leonard it was quite different, his arrival and triumph – at the Mecca of music, 'music city' no less; in the wake of such champions as Joan Baez, Bob Dylan, Buffy Sainte-Marie, Ramblin' Jack Elliott, Judy Collins, Kris Kristofferson, Johnny Cash, Hank Williams, Elvis Presley and Dolly Parton, to name but a few.

He has often commented on his 'deep abiding affection for Nashville music' – a relic of his youth, and much more. But somehow he got it wrong. It did not come quite right even under the expert eye of producer Bob Johnston, himself a Nashville man, who produced albums by Bob Dylan and Simon And Garfunkel. (He was called 'the first of the super-producers' by the *New Musical Express Book Of Rock, Vol II*.) The studios had only just been opened and Dylan had been thrilled with the surroundings.

The album's tempo, or rather, lack of it, is the most obvious fault. There are only eight songs instead of the usual 10: 'Bird On The Wire', 'Story Of Isaac', 'A Bunch Of Lonesome Heroes', 'The Partisan' (actually written by Anna Marly and Hy Zaret in 1944, and taken from Leonard's treasure-trove *The People's Song Book* which he had devoured in 1949 at the Ste Marguerite Summer Camp in Quebec – the one from which the report mentioned earlier is derived), 'Seems So Long Ago, Nancy', 'The Old Revolution', 'The Butcher', 'You Know Who I Am', 'Lady Midnight', and 'Tonight Will Be Fine'. Perhaps the presence (and the responsibility) of his own group The Army contributed to this, or perhaps it was the excesses of the last eight years or so catching up with him. What is certain is that the heartache of the broken relationship was carried into this new album; Marianne could not be so easily forgotten; her photograph adorns the album sleeve.

'Songs From A Room' effuses a mood of deep reflection. 'The Room' – a Room – is a concept very characteristic of Leonard, which he explores in 'Tonight Will Be Fine': 'I choose the rooms/That I live in with care,/The windows are small/And the walls are only bare/There's only one bed . . .' He is a man of deep – and high – sentiment. It was a particular place – Hydra, of course; a particular time, and a particular moment he wished to capture, and convey. And despite its slowness, he does so, thanks to the guitar work of Ron Cornelius and Bubba Fowler (who also played the banjo). Charlie Daniels (who was to form his own band later) added bass and guitar and violin – a very important 'mood' instrument for Leonard, and producer Bob Johnston supplied the keyboards and some guitar. Corlynn Hanney and Sue Mussmano were the vocalists.

But memories of the room serve only to evoke the one who is no longer there: in this place of sparse decoration 'there's only one prayer/ and I listen all night/For your step on the stair.' It underlies the saying that 'it is good to hope, but bad to depend on it'; that 'hope is a liar.' The 'fine memory', the 'thinking of the past' – despite the chorus of hope that 'tonight will be fine' even 'for a while' – is all to no avail; the album ends with him humming, then whistling, then silence. Sometimes silence speaks more powerfully than words – even *the* word.

It is no different in 'You Know Who I Am', for the very knowledge the song encompasses precludes the continuance of their relationship – though here it is the man himself, not his 'mission', who creates the problem: 'I am the distance you put between/All of the moments that we will be.' And she knows it, too: 'You know who I am/ You've stared at the sun.' But the burden of it has been welcomed, nevertheless: 'I am the one who loves/Changing from nothing to one'; for in that role, in his becoming the one he was always meant to be, his zero-status finds worth: he becomes himself, someone. And the one, surely, part of the One to which philosophers, prophets and sages had all aspired. In which a haunting particularity is gladly surrendered for unity.

The point was made in the first two songs – in 'Bird On The Wire' in a mood of anguished regret that his duty remained undone; and in 'The Story Of Isaac' in an opposing mood of willingness to go, Isaac-like, through with the sacrifice: 'he knew I would not hide.' It is given extra weight in 'The Butcher' who conveys to his 'only son . . . my only child' the world itself. Puzzled by his father's torturing of the lamb, insufficiently helped by his recourse to 'the silver needle'; confused by the appearance of flowers in the place of bloody sacrifice; perplexed that he might have to offer there 'praise . . . a joyful sound'; he is forced to view the futile path his life has taken: 'Listen, listen to me now/I go round and round'! And worse, he is 'broken down/From a recent fall/

Blood upon my body/And ice upon my soul . . .' Whether in brokenness or in radiant obedience to the vision, the choice is the same: the 'freedom' is non-existent. As he remarked to Manzano, "Freedom for me is something more than the possibility of choice . . . it is a moment of pure experience," a comment that recalls Hegel's own definition – for all Kierkegaard's protestations! – that 'freedom is to be in possession of oneself.'

Scobie, one has to say characteristically, misunderstands it; reading into it merely the sentiments of a love song. 'Like a bird on the wire/Like a drunk in a midnight choir . . ./Like a worm on a hook/Like a knight from some old fashioned book . . ./Like a baby stillborn . . .' It explains why the relationship ended – he was Another's; how the relationship ended – guilty and indebted; and in what spirit of contradictoriness it ended:

> 'I saw a beggar leaning on his wooden crutch
> He said to me, "You must not ask for so much."
> And a pretty woman leaning in her darkened door,
> She cried to me, "Hey, why not ask for more?"'
>
> (Copyright © 1968 Stranger Music Inc, New York.
> Used by Permission. All Rights Reserved.)

That spirit of contradiction, so characteristic of this ambivalent man, is seen elsewhere in the relationship: 'I need you to carry my children in/And I need you to kill a child'; 'You kept right on loving/I went on a fast/Now I am too thin/And your love is too vast.'

But there is far more in this album, which positively aches with human need, grief and loneliness. For it moves – from start to finish – between the personal and the communal, between the divine and the human. As Allan Jones said of it, 'It is one of the few albums to try to approach the implications of contemporary violence and despair in relation to the European holocaust.' We do not ourselves see much of the holocaust here. But we do see the dark shadow of Vietnam, of Greece, of Israel – but most of all of the sheer waste of any 'sacrificed' life, wherever and whenever wasted – across its lines.

The regret of the first album has here become despair, its hope turned into despondency, its day a long night naked of comfort and warmth. The prophet is standing up and, through the lens of his own individuality, is focusing on aches in the body politic. In the interview with Jones he said that people would respond to the album 'as they went through the kind of psychic landscape he had explored in the creation of it.' He agreed that 'the most important aesthetic question of these days' was whether rock or art could be adequate to the totality of the European breakdown. "One feels, in the face of these massacres, disasters and human humiliations, 'What are you doing singing a song?'

But the worse it gets the more I find myself picking up a guitar and playing that song." – 'The Story Of Isaac'.

Some will find it astonishing that it became Number Two in the charts in the UK, but one reviewer (in *Sounds*) commented that it is 'probably the most beautiful album that anyone could own.' The 'beauty of the word' was clearly becoming evident. (Both Vassal and Manzano, believe that this was due to the disaffection from Dylan that his 'Nashville Skyline' album caused – not least for its alleged sentimentality and mawkishness – its intranscendentalism, to use the latter's phrase. But this is unconvincing, and is disputed by Leonard himself.

To Mark Paytress he later commented that it was after his 'having gone through a mental breakdown' that he recorded this album. As such, it is even more remarkable that the focus can be so objective of the situation: 'A scheme is not a vision' whether social or military; they have 'never been tempted/By a demon or a god': and yet lives have been damaged, ruined, annihilated in their causes. Their presumptions of brotherhood remain open to doubt: 'Just according to whose plan?' And the contradictoriness of the situation, once more, breaks in: 'I will kill you if I must/I will help you if I can.' The tragedy is their greed and ambition, their self-serving, self-vaunting ends, whether they be 'Men of peace or men of war' the reality is pure vanity: 'The peacock spreads his fan.'

Similarly in the story of 'Nancy' the questions, not of nations and schemes of nations, but of relationships and individual self-worth are raised. The word of the age was alienation; not the passing feeling of loneliness, but the undying sense of personal alone-ness, the acrid sense of estrangement, of depersonalisation, it vibrates disconsolately through it. Though the daughter of a Judge – (Sigmund Peterson, a school friend of Marianne's no less, knew Nancy well. His recollection is quite different from Leonard's in historical terms. But Leonard's technique was not to follow a story-line pedantically but to embroider it artistically, *à la* Miller, and draw out his own implications thereby) who presides over 'the House of Honesty'! – she is the perfect example of the one used and abused, loved and left, in an age empty of real relationships, of real meaning: 'There was no one, at all.' She delighted in others' joy – 'she fell in love for us'; she delighted in their fulfilments: 'She's happy that you've come'; but for her, in that 'House of Mystery', where loneliness became isolation, and isolation despair, her only freedom was suicide.

In an age when folk-singers had turned to rock, 'folk-rock', and even psychedelic rock, he was proving that *words matter*, i.e. that mind – not just sound – matters. 'Less poetically,' commented his Spanish biographer – but surely more existentially! The challenge was out. To the comment that he was a new prophet of the age, *à la* Dylan *et al*, Leonard replied:

"My songs are inspired, but I don't aspire to be a guide. The only thing that I aspire to is to be an instrument for a certain type of information in determined moments, but not always . . . Look, I believe that these are difficult times, hard times . . . we are in a situation now in which men are becoming beasts, and beasts can become men; anything can happen."

It was about this time that Vice President Spiro Agnew let fly with one of his harangues at young people's involvement with drugs. The Vietnam war was poisoning the world, major industries were producing poisons – and drugs! – for it; it was the fault of the hippies! Of such are mice made. Ironically, a story a little earlier in *Billboard* had reported the diminishing numbers now attending The Beatles' concerts – still very impressive by any standard – suggesting acidly that perhaps it was because, in reducing the volume of sound, it was now possible to hear the words they were singing! It did not prevent Judy Collins from singing both Cohen and Beatles' songs at her concerts. On April 13, 1969 Leonard commented, in the *New York Times*, speaking of his own work that . . . "There is no difference between a poem and a song. Some were songs first and some were poems first, and some were situations. All of my writing has guitars behind it – even the novels." Even if there had been no mention of the unifying presence of the guitars, we should have expected Leonard to have said something like that, for he took his work very seriously – risking and even foregoing his personal relationships for it, no less. It would have been incomprehensible for it not to have had such 'connections'.

George Woodcock, in a much quoted article, was merely being disingenuous when he took Leonard to task in his article 'The Song Of The Sirens: Reflections on Leonard Cohen'. This is particularly curious in the light of Woodcock's ostensible affirmation of D.S. Savage's view of criticism: 'To interpret, elucidate and evaluate our literature, and in so doing to define, defend and expound the tradition. Not the literary tradition solely, but the whole cultural complex from which literature is one specific outgrowth . . .' To achieve his *coup de grâce* on the poet, Woodcock has to take with utter seriousness his 'admission' which at first seems astonishing; on reflection one realises that it is starkly honest', namely: "I don't think too much about the words because the words are completely empty and any emotion can be poured into them. Almost all my songs can be sung any way. They can be sung as torch songs or as gentle songs or as contemplative songs or as courting songs." In other words, comments Woodcock with all the alacrity of a schoolboy who thinks that he has noticed an error in his textbook:

'Cohen is creating forms of words which receive life and meaning from the singer's style; the essential emptiness of such writing becomes evident when one reads his verses away from his voice . . . There's no intrinsic feeling in such verses; that has to be simulated by the voice . . . one knows that it is not real love that is being sung about, or a real world, and the never-land that Cohen creates with his guitar and voice is precisely what attracts the masses, who, in this age as in any other, are inveterate escapists.'

Ignoring the sheer condescension, Woodcock's specious argumentation is capped with the quotation 'Marita/Please find me/I am almost 30,' which he offers as an example of 'neutral vehicles for the emotion a singer superimposes,' though never meant to be sung, was never in fact sung, and was merely a piece of graffiti Leonard supplied as an afterthought to *Ladies And Gentlemen: Mr Leonard Cohen* when sitting in his bath tub and warning his viewers of 'the con' implicit in such programmes. Little wonder that one once observed that no one has ever erected a monument to a critic!

Judith Skelton Grant offered maturer and serious reflection – real criticism – in her piece 'Leonard Cohen's Poems-Songs', which dealt with the serious business of taking 'the masses' needs' seriously, and not in the scornful sham of a would-be academic turned sour. She found 'interesting aesthetic implications' which yielded 'a fundamental understanding of Cohen's craft as both poet and song-writer' in the examination, which was a real examination of comparative texts, not second-hand borrowings from a journalist on a late-night show, which contented Mr Woodcock. The movement between poem and song (she dealt only with those that were written as poems and subsequently converted to songs) gave rise, she argued, to 'changes, both major and minor.' These ranged from 'little words to fill out the weak beats in his basically iambic rhythm,' to line-lengthening 'necessitated by the musical shape Cohen chose for his song.'

We saw how Judy Collins, without question a great songster and musician herself, changed a number of things in her own version of 'Suzanne'. More interesting is the point, very well made by Ms Skelton Grant, that her changes are 'not as tidy as his.' We would go further, for they are often clumsy and unmeaningful. But let Ms Skelton Grant have the last word: (Leonard's) 'awareness of his auditors' need to have verse units defined and a sense of ending established are met astutely . . . the shift from the formal statement of the poems to the casual conversation of the songs can be seen as a sensitive response to the more personal, immediate relationship between singer and audience.'

The Woodcock, though large, is a shy bird of uncertain intelligence, with a marked ability for self-preservation. In criticising its namesake's attack on Leonard we have no wish to berate or diminish him. But his is a good example of the sort of pseudo-scholarship which Leonard had detested from his youth, and the ego-centred criticism which – from learned and unlearned alike – was poured on him from time to time. In launching *Canadian Literature*, in the summer of 1959 (of which Woodcock was editor, finally 'arriving' on the literary scene of his own homeland after many years), he wrote of 'the arriving guest, anxious to exert whatever attractions it may possess on its potential host – the particular public to which it has chosen to appeal.' A comment which highlights the self-importance and the essential rudeness of those self-imposing 'guests', ever-anxious to exert themselves, invited or otherwise, on their 'hosts' heavenly parasites not infrequently. The problem was, as *Proverbs* asserts, 'a rebuke sinks deeper into a man of intelligence than a hundred lashes into a fool,' and these studied assaults – more so than the thrusts of hack newspaper critics – did hurt. Especially when they came from fellow-Canadians. As has often been remarked, 'no prophet is without honour, save in his own country.'

There is one final point of Ms Skelton Grant worth considering, an aside rather than a conclusion from her honourable and careful work. She found 'disturbing' the 'self-indulgent, self-pitying speaker that the songs reveal even more clearly than the poems,' and in addition to her strictures on him for not revising all his work as thoroughly as he did for these poems-turned-into-songs. Sufficient has been said, one hopes, to establish that they were *not* self-indulgent or self-pitying imaginings, but the aching reflection of a tender spirit, one that had been cauterised by historical events, in whose history he had an ongoing – and inescapable – share. He was a Cohen, from its thraldom he could not, nor would not, escape, even if his heart was 'torn out' in the process.

'mouthpiece of
confusion and
uncertainty'

Leonard's move to Nashville was a major turning-point in his life, a sea-change which produced some most important consequences.

Marianne had been left in New York, and was now engrossed with her son Axel who at seven-years-of-age needed her especially. The 'drifting apart' became absolute, and she gradually faded from Leonard's life, finally returning to her native Oslo to start afresh. For some time theirs had been an 'open' relationship, so it was not surprising that Leonard slipped into another which, if anything, had even greater influence on him and his work. The new love of his life was Suzanne Elrod (elsewhere Vaillancourt, per Scobie, who comments that Leonard was 'conjured' by the name; and Ozar per *Premiere* magazine. The first one, a Hebrew name, means 'lily' or 'rose'; both of them of high significance in his poems and songs). She was a brunette of conspicuous beauty, with whom he stayed for several years, fathering Adam and Lorca (representing his Judaic and poetic beginnings respectively), his two children by her.

His opening months in Tennessee were lived out in suitable poetic seclusion, for he rented a farm from Boudleaux Bryant, one of the first country songwriters to become established in the fifties, and the writer of many hits recorded by The Everly Brothers, including 'Bye Bye Love' and 'All I Have To Do Is Dream'. It was Bob Johnston who introduced Leonard to Bryant. There, in the arid plains of Tennessee, virtually on the time-zone change between Central and Eastern times, he found another lifestyle or, rather, a different locale for his now usual lifestyle of blackening pages and searching for those elusive melodies : 'Heard melodies are sweet , but those unheard / Are sweeter . . .' as Keats exclaimed.

For the first time in his life he was permanently based inland – millions of acres of it; deeply inland, with no water in sight. This may well have been a factor, if but a small one, in the disorientation that seems to have been gathering pace within him. The island feeling of Montreal, Hydra, New York – even London – was exchanged for unending roads, rolling hills and almost featureless plains. Where, in those islands, he could respond to luxuriant growth, bright colour and all-pervasive light (in Canada and Greece particularly), he now had to deal with scrub and dryness and universal austerity. The cosmopolitan sense which had fired and inspired him was also absent; now he listened – when there was anyone to listen to – to slow-speaking Americans with a swagger in their voices, not chattering, boisterous Greeks whose musicality of voice bore the wisdom of the centuries, the furies of history. Where his eyes had feasted on the stunning blue of the Aegean, he now faced dirt-roads – swirling dust and bleak horizons.

The farm – an expanse of some 1500 acres which Leonard rented for $75! – was scarcely worthy of the name, for no one attended it (least of all Leonard) and in any case the soil was poor. In fact the only thing that was regularly harvested was ginseng, which grew in the nearby hills. The location did, however, allow him to take up horse-riding again, which he had not indulged in for many years. Kid Marley, a local rodeo champion, actually sold him a horse, an unruly half-lame stallion that Leonard spent more time chasing than actually riding. In fact, he said he never caught it! (He wrote of its lameness in *Death Of A Lady's Man*, but unrevengefully). He also learned to shoot, raising his proficiency with a much-prized Winchester – known to all schoolboys as *the* weapon if one was to become a real cowboy! – by shooting cans in his own corral, and icicles when the heat of the plains was transmogrified into near-Canadian sub-temperatures. Shortly after this he began to appear at his concerts on a white horse, Roy Rogers' style, but it was not a very practical habit, and his image had been changing – from Buckskin Boy to Bloodshot Eyes!

But the external world was of less significance to him now, in any case. For several years he had been 'retreating inwards': retreating from perilous involvements which he was powerless to prevent, exploring the subconscious labyrinths and exploiting the subliminal in ever more urgent ways to hone his craft – all the time advancing to new spheres of influence in his new media. For every technical advance he made, there were at least two 'recusant' voices from deep within. He was embattled. He had never felt more ambiguous, never more at jeopardy. "Somewhere along the way," he said of that time, "my mind got blasted." Grim memories of the past crowded about him, wild pressures surged and receded and surged again like an advancing tide, and years of stimulants, depressants, anti-depressants, intoxicants and hallucinogens all claimed their merciless spoil.

In his poem 'I See You On A Greek Mattress Reading The Book Of Changes . . .' first published in *Parasites Of Heaven* though written three years earlier, he refers not only to the *I Ching* which we saw him reading alongside Wentze's translation of the *Tibetan Book Of The Dead* and various Buddhist texts, but to a young man who played a key role in their discussions, Steve Sandown – not the Steve Smith, to whom he dedicated *Beautiful Losers*, who died in 1964. (Wentze was actually on Hydra at this time, as was George Liallios.) A stimulating companion, he was ever-looking for that knowledge which can quench and satisfy the driving spirit of man:

> *'Once again you read how the pieces of the world have changed around your question. Did you get to the Himalayas? Did you visit that monk in New Jersey? I never answered any of your letters. Oh Steve, do you remember me?'*

Sandown had a major influence on him, then and later, for it was he who introduced him to Roshi – Joshua Sasaki, the Zen Buddhist who left his monastery in Japan to bring his form of Rinzai enlightenment to America. Rinzai Buddhism is one of the five 'houses' of Buddhism, named after its founder Rinzai Gigen who died in 866 AD. It distinguishes itself from the others by demanding genuine insight, not mere lip-service, in the scriptures, with a life consonant with that insight. He was totally against 'a knowledge of the words of scripture' which fail to grasp its deeper meanings and applications. A fierce, no-nonsense man, Rinzai used both physical and verbal violence – his form of Koan-like intervention – against his students to break down their apathies and to encourage them to persevere. His teachings are found in *The Record Of Rinzai*. A master's life develops in three phases: training under his master; wanderings 'to settle and test his insight'; his own teaching career. An interesting sidelight, perhaps, of Leonard's own life from now on!

So Leonard took himself to Mount Baldy in California, for a 'trial' lasting four weeks. He was not, in fact, over-enthusiastic about Zen during this time. The discipline was too tough, somewhat unreal, perhaps artificial for him. But 'something' had caught his imagination: the non-credal affirmations? The practice of taking everything seriously, but nothing too seriously? The liberating independence – of mind not least – inculcated? The need to think about everything *de nouveau?* The tranquillity of the place? Or merely – and more likely – the winsome character of Roshi and his extensive knowledge and under-standing. Whatever it was, it supplied a deep need, offered real sanctuary and inner satisfaction. He was back within a few months! this time staying longer; since when he has spent at least three months every year working at his reorientations, his self-discipline, but above all enjoying the wise friendship and mutual esteem and independence he finds with Roshi.

His routine there was as tough as for any student. He woke at three am and made his way to the *zendo* (the meditation hall) where he sat with 50 other students, working, for three hours. Each session commences with Roshi giving them a question (e.g. 'How can you be free of the wind?') on which they are to set their minds. At the end of the session, they each meet Roshi to give their answers, limited strictly to five minutes. The questions, however, are not important; the techniques, the mental procedures, are; it is that which inspires Leonard.

At six am they breakfast, sitting in silence 'ritualistically'. They take tea ceremoniously, and return to the *zendo* for a further 30 minutes. They are given 'house-tasks' following this – cleaning, preparing food, looking after the hens, which last till midday. (Leonard built a stone wall round the garden as part of his domestic duties!) A free hour is arranged after lunch, followed by more work till six pm, when they return to the *zendo* for a further hour's meditation.

Supper is offered at seven pm, after which formal *zendo* training takes place till 10 pm. So ends the day, save for Leonard, when an 'unscheduled' meeting with Roshi would take place which could last up to two hours, aided by an un-Zen-like bottle of Cognac. Roshi, apparently, liked to see his students go to bed happily!

Once a month the routines were deliberately broken by a three-hour sitting each day for a week in the Roshi – the master's place – in complete silence, meditating on their situation and progress; a vigorous time of self-appraisal and special discipline – aided by physical blows, in line with Rinzai's 'violent' system – which can be disorientating, sometimes causes depression and, strangely, that condition of 'boredom' which can lead to new orientations or meaninglessness.

The whole point is to examine oneself, what one is, what one is becoming; a process not all students can tolerate. Breakdowns have been known to occur. Roshi is careful to emphasise that the training is to prepare them for the outside world. He emphasises – and combats – the dangers of self-satisfaction and complacency, of beginning to enjoy the lifestyle there: 'God's world is good,' he will say, 'but you can't remain there for too long.' He constantly affirms the importance of 'the daily round, the common task' – washing, eating, working.

Not surprisingly, Leonard finds this ambience highly congenial for his work, his songs not least: "There are always things you want to say, and if you're quiet enough you can hear them, and write about them." Layton picked this up when he talked of Leonard now being 'well beyond concepts'; he thinks 'with his whole being' he added – oneness firmly asserted.

Leonard quickly found that this relationship went beyond that of master and student. They had – for all the disparities between them – much in common and, as had happened between Irving Layton and Leonard, the tie strengthened through mutual concerns. It is customary for the Zen Master to rename his disciple, and to Leonard's secular and Judaic names (which had their own connections), he added another: Solitary Cliff. Less obscure than the others, it encapsulates the man very well, underlining his essential strength of character as well as his solitary disposition.

Not least of Roshi's positive attributes, Leonard stated, was that he "hates religion." There is, Roshi finds, "something ugly about it. The armour of religion places people in hateful situations." What is required, Leonard believes, is for people "to find the positive values between the black and white; non-judgmental values based on real values; a position that acknowledges complexity, yet takes a strong stance." He finds no essential contradiction between the two – Judaism and Buddhism – but, unlike Ginsberg, his real and abiding loyalty is to the former and unquestionably, if subtly, traditional. "I would move to find a more overt, traditional position, if forced," he admitted.

It is all part of that intense mind of his, 'driven by curiosity, luminous with acceptance . . .' which had energised him since his earliest youth – mythologies ever asserting – and which had caused him and his friend Danny Usher to study Freud, which pushes him into literature ever more deeply: Jewish and mystic, the occult, magic, comparative religion, hypnotism, and so on – confirming Oscar Wilde's dictum, that 'literature always anticipates life. It does not copy it, but moulds it to its purpose.' It was, in fact, at Roshi's that Leonard met Suzanne, his new love, herself a follower of that form of Buddhism. She quickly became Leonard's student, as well as his lover.

In one of our discussions about this time in which we discussed motive and aspiration in the move, Leonard said: "The spiritual path led to annihilation. I had no psychic tools left . . . the dissolution of the personality which you can see in either a psychological or a spiritual way. The wilderness is real. There are no landmarks there." It is an important admission, critically important, for at this time the plunge into his 'breakdown' was nearing that abyss from which some never return. At several points he admitted to not having any memory of this period; which worries him. He even went to a hypnotist in the hope of recovering some threads by which he might retrace his connections, but – unlike Breavman's – the man's powers proved to be inadequate for the job.

Of the background and meaning of his song 'Priests', for example, he commented: "It was (the past tense is significant) a strange song. I never understood it . . . There's something heretical about it; it's an audacious claim: 'When I am lord at last'! Perhaps it was connected to my inability . . . I'm glad Judy (Collins) recorded it." His comments remind us of Robert Browning in a similar situation of being unable to explain his own verse. 'When I wrote those lines,' the poet said, 'two people knew what they meant: God and Robert Browning. Now only God knows.'

Something of the aridity of the Tennessee pastureland comes through such poetry as he managed at this time – not only in its barren sparsity, but in its formlessness, too. The muse was no longer amused:

> 'Each day he lugged
> a hunk of something precious
> over to his boredom
> and once or twice a week
> when he was granted
> the tiny grace of distance
> he perceived that he laboured
> as his fathers did
> on someone else's pyramid.'

Even more severe is his 'Picture Of The Artist And His Room':

> 'His first masterpiece, the painterly art
> invisible, detail photographic
> and accident, our newest rhetoric
> bravely absent, except that he had to start
> somewhere and it was this room that stopped him
> between women: that's all he owes to chance.
> He might be waiting for an ambulance,
> a naked woman, or the Seraphim
> of God. But he's not. He's going to get up
> and paint his room at midnight with himself
> in the corner saying, This is myself.
> This is the bed. This is the plastic cup.
> I am one, I am welcome, like the chair,
> the table, any of the objects there.'

Or, having spoken of his being listed in the books 'among the dead and future Dylans,' man's last itinerary, he suggests that:

> 'You can understand
> I am in no hurry to make the passage.
> The sunlight is old and yellow
> a flood of what I laboured
> to distil a tiny drop of
> in that shabby little laboratory

called my talent.'

And that point, 'I am in no hurry to make the passage' is important. Despite many rumours of attempted suicide, of persistent suicidal thoughts, he was hanging on to life, buffeted by it, dragged down in it, but still holding on. The pain could intensify to the violence of mental torture at times, obliterating everything:

'For a long time
he had no music
he had no scenery

'He killed three people
in the darkness of his greed
The rain could not help him

'Pass by
this is no vision offered
this is his truth'

It scorches, does this detritus of the soul. It was his 'dark night of the soul,' when the darkness was tangible, at times suffocating; it was his 'Cloud of Unknowing', when even the sharp darts of eternal love seem powerless to break through; his wilderness experience, which all true prophets endure – from Moses to Malachi and well beyond. In it there is something beyond mere *angst* – destructive as its barbs can be; it is the ultimate in that death-mimicking experience of *accidie* when one can only cry out with the psalmist, 'My God, my God, why hast Thou forsaken me?'

It is astonishing that those who claim sensitivity to literature, to poetry in particular, could interpret such musings as 'self-indulgent' or 'self-pitying'; could fail to understand that the resonant pain in his work – poetry and song – was simple honesty. Yet it was this experience which caused him to see beyond 'the panic of loss'; caused him to understand that many suffer; that a word – an accurate, faithful word – must be claimed and offered to them. If the servant must suffer, whether by his own follies or those of man's inhumanity to man, it was that the many, subsequently, be made whole. He hung on grimly, even though:

'Lost my voice in New York City
never heard it again after '67 . . .

'Lost my voice in New York City
Guess you always knew.'

As Dorothy Parker said wryly:

'Razors pain you;
Rivers are damp;

> *Acids stain you;*
> *And drugs cause cramp.*
> *Guns aren't lawful;*
> *Nooses give;*
> *Gas smells awful;*
> *You might as well live!'*

Towards the end of 1969 he took a small house in the 'Greek' district of Montreal, where Suzanne and he settled down together, a period of more stabilising happiness than the Tennessee experience, in which he was able to blacken pages more positively, and perhaps more effectively for several months.

The quiet was broken by criticism of Leonard for having stayed in Greece after the coup of 1969, a comment made by some more outspoken 'leftists'. Leonard observed that he was himself in some danger, one of his friends having been tortured for six hours 'on a terrace/above a well-known street.' (In the original version, in *The Energy Of Slaves*, it continues, 'I swore by the sunlight/to avenge his broken feet,' which he changed commentary-fashion on the facing page to the more diplomatic 'to take his advice:/remove all evidence from my verse/forget about his punctured feet'!) He was firm in stating that "I left Greece because I was ready to go, whether the régime changed or not."

In May 1970 he undertook his first European tour, in the company of his group The Army. (Graeme Allright, the New Zealand singer who had adopted Paris for his art, had in fact translated and sung some of Leonard's songs there from as early as 1968, as had Georges Chelon and Serge Lama. It was judged an important contribution to *la chanson française*.)

Compared to later tours it was a small involvement – seven shows, one of which was a poetry reading in London, at the Institute of Contemporary Arts, in seven cities: Amsterdam, Hamburg, Frankfurt, Munich, Vienna, London and Paris. But it was the start he had hoped and worked for, in which he was able to offer a 'set' of 20 songs – and sometimes some poetry. There were only minor changes in his programmes which are interesting:

> 1 *'Un As Der Rebbe Singt'* (*Sung as a solo, once or twice on this tour*)
> 2 *'Bird On The Wire'*
> 3 *'So Long, Marianne'*
> 4 *'You Know Who I Am'*
> 5 *'Dead Song'*
> 6 *'Lady Midnight'*
> 7 *'One Of Us Cannot Be Wrong'*

MOUTHPIECE OF CONFUSION AND UNCERTAINTY'

8 *'The Stranger Song' (sung as a solo)*
9 *'Joan Of Arc'*
10 *'Tonight Will Be Fine'*
   (Intermission)
11 *'The Partisan'*
12 *'Sisters Of Mercy'*
13 *'Diamonds In The Mine'*
14 *'Story Of Isaac'*
15 *'Famous Blue Raincoat'*
16 *'Sing Another Song, Boys'*
17 *'Celebration' (Poem)*
18 *'Hey! That's No Way To Say Goodbye'*
19 *'Suzanne'*
20 *'Please Don't Pass Me By (A Disgrace)'*

In later concerts 'Celebration' was exchanged for his poem 'Travel', but then the practice was dropped altogether. At the Royal Albert Hall 'Avalanche' entered his repertoire, but was dropped from it temporarily: too much perhaps, even if the boisterous sixties had just ended, even when offered as a solo by him. The tour was successful, in an age when many groups strove to establish themselves. It was the first international stage of his new career.

In Amsterdam he had actually led his audience through the streets, in an extended concert that went on throughout the night! In Paris, at the famed Olympia arena, he achieved the most outstanding ovation in its history, even after he had got the audience up on stage, which caused the police to move in. Leonard stayed obdurate – and won! *Le Nouvel Observateur*, a left-wing journal called him 'the folk-singer of the year,' and the French capital for once seemed to be united. (A little later he was to be a special guest of the President no less, Giscard d'Estaing; and his successor Georges Pompidou capped this by revealing that he took Leonard's records on holiday with him – some feat by the man famed in post-war France for a high-culture profile!) But he was still not satisfied.

In London, there was a similar positive reaction from the 4,000 who attended, but Leonard was devastated. "It was terrible," he told Tom Cokeson in an interview for *Sounds*. "A disaster. I am so ashamed . . . I failed. I want you to apologise to everyone for me. I want to atone. I feel like giving a free concert to make up for this." He got to the point he was trying to make: "I don't want purity any more. I want it dangerous, so that it will jeopardise me. I want to do something with people's emotions. I want to lift them, make everything nobler . . . That's why I feel so bad about the concert. It wasn't noble."

He had come unstuck on British phlegm! The prophet had sung, played, intoned, recited – raged, even! They sat there, politely; indifferently. They failed to hear the word. They had even been unmoved by 'Please Don't Pass Me By'. He had introduced it with a reference to the blind man on 8th Avenue, and the lame man round the corner from which he came across mentally disabled at the Young Adult Institute. He had warned his audience that they would have hard times themselves, and should be prepared. He had 'chanted, over and over again' the refrain 'Please don't pass me by.' They *sat* there! They simply enjoyed the rhythm, delighted in his style, but immobile! Finally he had shouted. "Kneel down," he cried, in an effort to produce a more appropriate response. "Take off your clothes," he demanded, hoping that would shake them out of their impassivity. The British Bulldog merely blinked.

He also appeared at the Forest Hills Tennis Stadium at its Folk Festival in July. And at the Aix-en-Provence festival he once again found great acclaim with the French, who enjoyed his formulations of Quebecan *liberté;* so much so that part of his show was broadcast on French radio. They loved the showmanship of his appearing on stage on a white horse, though whether the Hebrew symbolism was understood is perhaps less likely! But someone did get excited over his 'non-involvement' with the Generals' *coup* in Greece. 'Fascist!' cried one, and before the organisers recognised the dangers, pandemonium broke out. Abuse flew, then threats, then bottles. He got his danger, all right, that day. And his jeopardy. And what emotions he stirred, albeit unexpectedly! As to the nobility; well, that's another story. Like Tennyson, like Carmen he was learning a thing or two about democracy:

> 'We have scorned the beliefs of our fathers
> And cast their quiet aside;
> To take the mob for our ruler
> And the voice of the mob for our guide.'

He said, when refusing to condemn the Generals' régime, for not trying to stir up democratic fervour: "I am not at ease with any régime."

One other important performance took place at the Isle of Wight Festival off the south coast of England, where the bill also included The Doors, whose lead-singer, Jim Morrison, could turn on a crowd rather differently. In addition to the 14 songs that Leonard sang at this open air concert before a massive crowd, he recited three poems: 'Dead Song'; 'They Locked Up A Man' (which was printed on the sleeve of 'Songs Of Love And Hate'); 'A Person Who Eats Meat'; and offered two improvisations: 'They Gave Me Some Money' and 'Let Us Renew Ourselves Now'. Jimi Hendrix also performed, as did Miles Davis, Johnny Winter, Kris Kristofferson, Ten Years After, and The Allman

Brothers Band. At the time when he most felt that he was being disconnected, he was making real connections, inwardly, and with a following that would stay loyal for two decades and more.

On his return to Nashville, an important appointment awaited: the recording of his third album, to be called 'Songs Of Love And Hate,' part of which had already been recorded in March 1970, when 'Avalanche' was first laid down at the Columbia 'A' Studios in Nashville. The American Federation of Musicians' contract, cited as 'Project 06063', credits Bob Johnston again as producer, adding that 'no arranger, no copyist' was employed. Johnston played piano and keyboard for this new album, as well as producing it, and once again Ron Cornelius (on acoustic and electric guitar), Charlie Daniels (on bass, fiddle and acoustic guitar), and Bubba Fowler (on banjo, bass and acoustic guitar) featured. Bob Moore also played in one session, as did William Pursell. To this was added the strings accompaniment of Michael Sahl, and the now familiar voices of Corlynn Hanney and Susan Mussmano. Additionally, the Corona Academy of London were dubbed in on 'Last Year's Man' and 'Dress Rehearsal Rag' which needed children's voices.

On May 14 another event took place, of a very different order. Leonard appeared at the Convocation of Dalhousie University, in Halifax, Nova Scotia, to be capped Doctor of Laws. It was the fitting climax to the poet's career to date. Another was Eli Mandel breaking his own rule, in his volume *Poets Of Contemporary Canada: 1960-1970*, by which no one who had appeared in previous volumes was to be represented. The one exception was Leonard himself: 'It seems to me,' Mandel stated in his introduction, 'inescapable that in Leonard Cohen's work the sensibility of the sixties finds not only its most elegant but its most representative voice . . . In no other poet of this time is that change so clearly revealed as in Cohen . . . his career reads like a cultural history, it is virtually impossible to conceive of an anthology of this period that would omit his poems.' Others might have wished to blacken his character, as they did with Odysseus himself – unmusical echoes of the Woodcock there! – but it was by no means universal. He may not have recognised it himself, but his stock was growing: nobility will out.

In the Citation at Dalhousie, similar thoughts to Mandel's had been expressed by the Senate spokesman:

> '*Mr President,*
>
> '*For many young people on both sides of the Atlantic, Leonard Cohen has become a symbol of their own anguish, alienation and uncertainty. He is a Canadian, born in Montreal and educated at McGill University, and it is fitting that his*

remarkable popularity should be recognised by a Canadian University.

'The lyrical poignance which lies at the heart of his appeal has been apparent since the publication, in 1956, of his first volume of poems, Let Us Compare Mythologies. *Three more volumes have since appeared. In 1963 his autobiographical novel,* The Favourite Game, *was published, and in 1966 his controversial second novel,* Beautiful Losers, *established him as the mouthpiece of the confusion and uncertainty felt by a whole generation. This image has been confirmed in recent years. He has increasingly used popular media to convey his particularly personal nostalgia. As a folk-singer both at concerts and festivals he has had spectacular success, and his record albums are outstandingly popular with the young of the seventies.*

'In recognition of this achievement, I ask you, Mr President, in the name of the Senate to confer upon Leonard Cohen the degree of Doctor of Laws, honoris causa.'

But Leonard, true to style, was not in a self-congratulatory mood. The headiness of the doctoral award soon gave way to 'anguish, alienation and uncertainty,' and in his third album it had pellucid expression. Said Alastair Pirrie, in *New Musical Express*, 'Cohen became more and more dissatisfied with each LP he produced, culminating in almost dejection (sic) in 'Songs Of Love And Hate'. And Leonard later expressed agreement with this, 'regretting many things' about it: "There is something in the voice that is really wiped out; conflicts were arising; it's a disturbing voice; there is anxiety there. It was a tremendous effort to make the songs, the anxiety was paralysis-producing." He drew a distinction between himself and George Jones ('Drinking, divorcing and deep, deep sorrow on stage and off,' is how Ed Ward defines country music in *Rock Of Ages* – and Jones virtually defined the term so in the fifties and sixties), believing that if he had proceeded more slowly the angst he then endured would not have broken through. His songs would have been merely 'sad songs' like Jones', who 'managed to transcend himself.'

To Mark Rowland of *Musician* Leonard commented, "I thought I was one of those men that sang about his predicament, and that somehow everybody would connect with it. But I lost my way and began involving myself with speculations that I knew deep down were not really public concerns. The world was no longer attracting me. It wasn't very entertaining." And he added, "It was over-produced, over-elaborated; an experiment that failed." To Allan Jones of *Melody Maker* he merely said that its A-side was, "a little burdened and melodrama-

tic." He identified that failure with the 'collaboration' of his voice and
the backing arrangements, which produced a sort of inauthenticity in it
– to him, who emphasised 'accuracy', a cardinal fault. However, it did
spawn a single which offered 'Joan Of Arc' and 'Diamonds In The
Mine'. This proved to be popular and successful.

To sensitive souls 'Songs Of Love And Hate' is a more off-
putting, aggressive title than the first two, but it is in fact a better album
– at once more musical, and sung in better voice! The anxiety of singing
has ebbed, and that sweetness and charm of which Judy Collins (and
many thousands more) spoke is evident. At its best it is delightful; when
in his 'proto-punk' phase (as in 'Diamonds In The Mine') it becomes
more guttural, savage even – more appropriately dramatic; as was his
intention, (though Leonard's view is that the pain is evident, although
he was managing to resolve it 'in the making of the songs'). It has a
better tempo, too. The reflective, intoning qualities are still to the fore –
in some respects, they *are* the voice. Pitch and modulation vary
according to need, as do the tonalities, adding to the natural timbre. His
connections, outward and inward, were being achieved.

In March, despite Leonard delaying the album because he wanted
to see Paul Buckmaster, Elton John's arranger, in order to make use of
some of his idiosyncratic sounds (what Ken Tucker described as 'Soggy
string sections'!) *Billboard* announced that Columbia was 'Putting a
heavy commercial push behind the forthcoming release of the third
Leonard Cohen album . . .' noting that gold discs had been awarded
him for both the two previous albums in Canada (each achieving sales in
excess of 100,000). And it found 'Dress Rehearsal Rag' and 'Famous
Blue Raincoat' the most impressive of a good selection. Vassal makes
the interesting comment that the latter song and the first version of
'Chelsea Hotel' were written in Leonard's early and rather short period
in New York when he was – ostensibly at least – studying law; from
which period also came the last part of *The Favourite Game*, but it is
unlikely – for one thing he didn't own the Burberry raincoat then.

The contradictions were still there in the title and in the individual
songs, but overall he had realised a better unity. He admitted that the
experiences which had informed the album were still with him, but a
new note was emerging; whatever the pain of the past, Leonard
commented, "You can't take the past along with you. It has to be
discarded at some point if you are to move forward. You have to move
lightly and quickly." Manzano highlights the intimacy of the album,
the allegorical images, an obscure metaphorical language and the intense
existential experience of a man totally compromised at the most
exciting point of his life (*con la exaltacion de su vida*); a pilgrim in a
landscape of suffering, no less.

The first commenced in the buffetings of an avalanche, which had actually been written as a song, not a poem, but owing to his lack of material in *Parasites Of Heaven* it appeared there in poetic form! The tidying and tightening is well adjusted, but there is greater openness to his needs, the bereft sense has given way to an honest admission of his need, and longing for his woman has now become a more forthright asking. More importantly, the impossible two last lines of his fifth verse have become 'You say you've gone away from me/but I can feel you when you breathe.' Even more effort was needed with 'Last Year's Man', which took him five years to get right – neutralising, surely, suggestions of slap-dash work! It cost him a Mexican 12-string guitar, too, for he jumped on it 'in a fit of impotent fury' in 1967.

Part of the problem, as ever in this industry which credits accountancy more valuable than art, was length and the related problems of compression; even so it still has no less than 14 quatrains. Assonance of a different sort was showing at another point, too. He said, "I have always had an enormous appetite for religious things . . . But none of my work has been an argument for religion. Religion is one of those references which forms part of my life, my language and my culture, not one application to my work."

The tone of the song is derisory: of Joan of Arc, of biblical events and references, of Leonard himself. The discordancy of the jazz-lover (of Western African music married to American South) – was now merging with Eastern country laments, in word, if not in harmony. (Incidentally, the poetic forms of the songs are very varied on this album, which make reading lines a special pleasure.) Joan of Arc makes a second appearance in the song of that name, slyly sending up the women's libbers, while delighting his French (and other anti-English!) followers. It was not only her own soldiers that she treated well, this Maid of Orleans, but her Canadian admirer – 'who was not born to fight.' Vassal quotes from an interview with Allan Jones that Nico – Warhol's companion – inspired the song, as she did several of his poems of that period. It was certainly Nico that was asked by Leonard, "Did Joan of Arc fall in love?" To which she replied, "All the time!" But not even this irreverence could annoy the French, delighted at finding a modern defender of their famous Maid.

'Dress Rehearsal Rag' finds permanent expression here, too. It had been around for some while, and was first performed in 1968 on British television. It is the most savage of the personal *dénouements* on the album, and reveals how long he had been engaged in his fight, when life appeared to be meaningless and he was about 'to lose everything.' Leonard has said that this was one of the songs he sings only at moments of supreme happiness! by which he kept, presumably, his neurotic affiliations alive. He has retailed the story of the song as coming from a

Czechoslovakian milieu, originally called 'Gloomy Sunday', which the Czechs banned because of its ability to depress – and even cause suicide. A tragic song, which ended in tragedy for the composer who, apparently, took his own life. 'Diamonds In The Mine' is the social counterpart to this acute sense of personal devaluation. To social disorder and the cheapening of life comes the awareness that its little surprises – letters, grapes, chocolates and diamonds, are no more; the revolution's pride is washed up. 'That's all I've got to say to you,' he curtly asserts, as the refrain fades away.

The 'hate' side having been concluded, he moves towards the positive, in fulfilment of remade commitments and vows, finding in 'Love Calls You By Your Name' the astonished awareness that hope and love is stirring again among the embers of a shattered life: Love calls! 'Famous Blue Raincoat', one of the best known of all his songs, continues the upward movement in terms of a letter he wrote to a friend who had cuckolded him. Forgiveness is offered, for he recognised that his 'wife' is being helped – he had been so overcome by his own concerns that he had failed to see the trouble from which she was suffering. 'Sing Another Song, Boys' adds a note of sardonic bitterness – the bitterness of life, not non-life; of hope, not despair – in the infatuation of the young girl for the run-down man of yesteryear. But the future has to be left open! Sufficient the juvenile, unfulfilled stirrings, despite the intensity of their desires. In 'Joan Of Arc' a culmination is reached – of poetic and musical excellence, in an expression of amorous self-giving which leads to a destruction that ennobles, as true love must. The birth-pangs may not be over, but at least he has reached beyond the agony, aware that new life has come out of intense anguish and pain.

the evidence
of a life

The contradictoriness at this point in Leonard Cohen's life is as sharp, if not sharper, than at any other. Unquestionably, the tide had turned. His 'breakdown' was now behind him, diminishing if not resolved. But the undertow of its currents were still strong and, as any estuary swimmer knows, extremely menacing. The surface tide may be bearing him away to warmer, sunnier climes, but the anxieties below were by no means absent.

Of a time when the Georgia *Straight* spoke of him as 'unquestionably Canada's most important pop cultural icon,' and though anxious of the domestic ordeal, he played at Montreal to great acclaim towards the end of the year. That popularity was about to surge sensationally on the international front, as he planned his second European tour which would keep him and 'The Army' (now much changed in personnel) occupied for two months in late March and April, 1972. And not only in Europe, but in Israel itself; a late, but nevertheless fervent gesture of solidarity; fulfilling the hope of every Jew, pious or otherwise, of 'next year in Jerusalem.'

Before doing so he renewed his less neurotic affiliations in Montreal and Hydra, watching the old world throw off the deadness of its winter, and allowing the surge of new life to recharge his physical and emotional batteries. In Montreal he bought a house, alongside which was a smaller one he was making available for Morton Rosengarten's sculpturing. According to Paul Saltzman of *MacLeans* Leonard was now looking 'healthier than ever . . . in fine shape.' He had put behind him his drugs usage; practised yoga, meditation and fasting, spent part of each day working out. ("I had muscles then," he remarked to us!) He had placed on deposit at the University of Toronto his papers and manuscripts, and found that his relationship with Suzanne was now running smoothly. 'They're so fine together,' the reporter commented, 'warm and calm and loving.'

Nevertheless, other signs of stress were evident. "I'm just reeling, man," Leonard commented a day or two later. "Most of the time I'm staggering under the blows . . . There's no doubt I contrive these blows for myself." Comments which even a brief respite on Hydra in preparation for his tour could not efface. Henry Miller described it as 'Almost a bare rock of an island . . . (where) there are two colours, blue and white.' But that was never true of this ancient place of Greek mystery, save in the passing fancy of the writer who admitted that he had only stayed there 'a few days.' Miller, however, did acknowledge that 'aesthetically it is perfect . . . Hydra was entered as a pause in the musical score of creation by an expert calligrapher. It is one of those divine pauses which permit the musician, when he resumes the melody, to go forth again in a totally new direction.' Leonard was essaying both – to go forward, and change his direction, but finding a ground-swell running against him which threatened his nobler thoughts and deeper self. Saltzman thought that there were 'many parts of himself that he hates,' and questioned him on it. "I like my true self," Leonard admitted, after a long pause.

Leonard returned to the States via London, where he was interviewed by Billy Walker, editor of *Sounds*, at his 'smallish, unpretentious hotel' on the 'unfashionable edge' of the Kings Road in Chelsea. Asked why he chose such a dismal place, when clearly he could afford far better, he quoted the mystic: "If riches assist thee, acquire riches; if poverty assist thee, seek poverty. There are many styles of life. I don't think one is better than another. It's just that what suits me is a more modest style than generally could be discovered in a first-class hotel where so much is based on the good graces of the people around you being purchased . . . I looked into the 'high style' and I didn't find it high style. I found it a very degrading style . . . I found they didn't deliver what they promised . . ."

Walker commented: 'It's Cohen's ability to look reality straight in the eye and write and sing about it in complete honesty that makes him stand out from so many of today's performers,' a comment which shows he understood the man perfectly; not merely as a 'performer', but in his 'hidden' role as prophet, for the attributes he describes of Leonard are precisely those which fitted him for that higher role.

But Leonard was not in London merely to stay over and make such interesting self-examinations, still less to deliver baby clothes which he actually was doing on behalf of a friend, but to plan a second film which was to be of his tour. If The Beatles could do it; why not Leonard Cohen? And so they set to work, his producer Bob Johnston, Mike Machar and Tony Palmer. "I think it's going to surprise me,"

Leonard commented; words that would be written indelibly, and expensively, into his mind for all time. In so saying he showed that he could 'fore-tell' as well as 'forth-tell'.

In making the film, he said that he hoped it would be 'a kind of essay.' To do so, they were forming a new company, to be called – in line with Leonard's character and role – Sincere Productions; the name "represents the sensibility of the idea," he said; accuracy writ large, whatever the content.

"All my work is the evidence of a life, and not the life itself," he explained. "If I could live a life well and have the evidence of it turned into information and entertainment, that would be OK. If I could find a style which would enable me to do that I would be happy to embrace it . . . I don't know if I'm really interested in turning my life into palpable art . . . I'm interested in another kind of direction now."

This is not merely the dreaming of some would-be film-star, or film-director, a profession that he agreed interested and excited him. He said that he did not have 'the energy' for that 'wonderful notion'. Nor is it simply the poet-turned-songwriter who aspired to greater heights; one who realised that the logical outcome is still greater personal encounter and unveiling, pressing the Rousseau-principle (or is it Augustinian?) to its final point. Rather is it the donning, perhaps reluctantly at times, of the prophetic mantle, the realisation that the ultimate prophetic symbol is the manifestation – Jeremiah-like – of one's own soul. Not 'the life' *tout simplement*, but 'the evidence of the life.'

In other words, not life lived in this world, as a man among men – and especially women – but as one who lives at the bar of judgment, as a witness to what one feels, perceives and understands. It is to live life not in 'high' or 'modest' style, but sincerely – true to all one's convictions, sensibilities and responsibilities. Elsewhere he will speak of it as the need 'to be accurate'; a concept which recalls Dylan's emphasis on 'the clearness of sincerity.' To be a true witness, not a partial one. To be wholly true to oneself, not fragmentary; to be genuine, not superficial; to be earnest, daring, even; to be 'what thou singly art, and personate only thyself . . . and live but one man.' As Miller said of Leonard's adopted island, 'To recount the exploits of the men of Hydra would be to write a book about a race of madmen; it would mean writing the word DARING across the firmament in letters of fire.' Such was Leonard's commitment, albeit modestly:

"When you become the work itself then notions like uptightness and relaxation are irrelevant; when you are the work itself you don't just stand aside. You're just the instrument of the energy and there (are) no second thoughts. It's only when you are not working at your full capacity and you are not the work that those jewelistic notions of failure and excellence come in."

He has now pushed the notion into full light. And Walker was too good a journalist, too alert a thinker, not to rise to the occasion. He asked Leonard specifically if the 'energy' he talked of 'works in the way many artists use religion or mysticism in their performance?' Replied Leonard, in one of his most outspoken comments to date, at the same time refusing to be raised to the 'guru' status he had so often warned against: "There are many people who feel that we are now in the days of judgment, and in some ways I think we are; and we'd better be true! I think Dylan says it in one of his songs, 'Let us not speak falsely now the hour is getting late.' People have a sense that we are at the end of things and this is not the time to put anybody on. I think people have to go to their own sources of energy. I could never, in any way, evaluate sources people turn to . . . I wouldn't want to put people under any banner. But I note when I walk on the streets, as many have before, that there's tremendous agony around us and it's the agony of souls crying out for life."

George Harrison might comment that spirituality was 'driven underground' in the sixties, but it is obvious that in Leonard Cohen there was at least one authentic seer, willing to live above ground and honestly. Of its truths he could be disarmingly frank, even if it was at personal cost – momentarily and in reputation: Only someone who has been there can so write, and sing, and witness. It is not surprising that the explanation rises out of the context of spiritual 'energy' and is geared to religious conceptions. Once again we are reminded of his openness with Pierre Berton, of states of grace, equilibrium, and even sainthood. He could not escape the burden. Perhaps significantly he now sported a Buddhist haircut (in an earlier generation, it would have been called a military crew-cut: *plus ça change . . .*).

His second tour followed a geographical line – through Dublin (where he appeared twice, once with Amazing Blondel, exponents of Irish folk-song in which Leonard was becoming interested, thanks no doubt to such poetry as that of William Butler Yeats *et al*), Glasgow, Manchester, Leeds, Newcastle, London, Copenhagen, Stockholm, Brussels, Hamburg, Frankfurt, Dusseldorf, Berlin, Vienna, Munich, Geneva, Amsterdam, Paris – and then to the source of it all, so far as Leonard was concerned: Jerusalem; thence to Tel Aviv.

As mentioned earlier, 'The Army' had changed fundamentally, almost beyond recognition. Its combatants were now Bob Johnston (keyboards), Ron Cornelius and David O'Connor (guitars), Peter Marshall (bass) and, on backing vocals, Jennifer Warnes and Donna Washburn. Perhaps it would be truer to call it a Peace Corps, for its style and music had changed too. Leonard was now more self-assertive of this, more sure of what he wanted from it, how the word should be projected by it. In this Bob Johnston played an important part, not only of guiding and directing, but of listening and conceding – by no means an easy task for one so talented!

In it Jennifer Warnes also played her equally important part, for she added more than a beautiful alto voice – what someone with an ear for the finest things of life dubbed 'sensual alto' – but a depth of sympathy (empathy, rather) that conveys itself in the most delicate of nuances, the most precise harmonies. She had been performing since the age of seven, so she knew a thing or two about music and song, performance and delivery. Hers is not so much a voice as a perfect human instrument, accented to both feeling and spiritual values, that pierce ordinary sound like a crystal bell. If Marianne was the enchanting muse, Jennifer Warnes must be his symbiotic priestess.

The range, as well as the quality, of Leonard's music had altered, too. His repertoire was both larger and profounder: the word was getting through. His sets were also longer, richer and more varied. And he was unwearied in his self-giving, frequently offering on average a set of 17 songs – though at Munich he gave 22, no less – as many as six or seven solo pieces. In addition to the songs, a number of musical improvisations were offered: the 'Minute Prologue', 'I'll Mind You Coughing, Baby', 'I Don't Know Why I'm Scared Tonight', 'I Passed The High Buildings', 'I'm Trying To Break Free Myself', 'The Broken Lip', 'I Always Sing Alone', 'Take The Girls Down', 'If There's Anything That Doesn't Please You Tonight', 'There's A Forest Of Microphones', 'I Always Wanted To Sing For Naked People', 'I Just Can't Go On', 'Just In Case You Should Have To Break Down', 'Come On Speaker, Speak To Me', 'I Don't Care Any More', 'What Goes On Beyond The Song', 'I'm Just Your Mirror Now', 'I'm Glad It's You Out There', and some untitled pieces.

In offering such he was belying the silly dishonesty of those hacks who spared nothing to make the cheap crack about his musical accomplishments. He was not only 'blackening pages' incessantly but filling the air with melody, by which the word became a passage, the voice an arrangement – meanings and connections all the way. Only extremely rarely now did he interpose his poetry. (For Dublin, the cradle of Celtic couplets and balladry, he made an exception and recited 'Come Down To My Room'.)

The experience of the years was now showing. His performances were fully mature, with Leonard fully in charge, even when problems of sound developed, as happened at the Royal Albert Hall. "Is this an insurrection?" asked Leonard. "Choose a spokesman," he suggested. But there was no need. They were enjoying his concert, despite the p.a. problems, and his witticisms and close contacts with his audience safeguarded further unfortunate developments. The essence of the songs was getting through, too, not just in professional style, but by creating its own energies – no easy task when the songs have been played thirty-odd times in almost as many days. Such was their depth, however, and such his skill and integrity in leading his group that a mystical awareness was made to settle over the concert.

Answering Steve Peacock's question as to staleness (which produced wild behaviour in other groups, wholly inimical – and destructive – to Leonard's style, of course) he replied: "For the people in the band they've become a kind of – I hesitate to use the word! – meditation," which is precisely what many of his followers found – whether they described it as such, or as mesmerism or hypnotism – *Melody Maker*'s Michael Watts referred to it as 'a sweet hypnotism' – 'a mad mystical hammering,' or whatever. It brought the people to his concerts, captivated them whilst he sang, and sent them away cathartically renewed – and not infrequently 'addicted' to his music for ever.

The days on tour were an intoxicating mixture of travelling, setting-up, sound-testing and rehearsing, meeting the press, and – headiest of all – performing to live audiences that, again and again, confirmed that the word was getting through, that they too were being tapped into 'sources of energy' akin to his own. Such spare time left to them was taken up with that form of 'crashing out' common to all groups between gigs: sleeping and relaxing, loving and obliterating through various forms of pleasure, the anxieties and fears of failure and uptightness which, though irrelevant, nevertheless can assert themselves with destructive force, not least in the wake of silly and snide reviews with which all artists need put up with from time to time: 'He can't play,' 'He can't sing,' etc; things which his audiences do not notice or are not concerned with or totally repudiate: they hear him; they love him; they need him.

Some of his reviewers produced in him an even more circuitous method of dealing with the increasingly foolish – and loaded – questions, and so the cycle became even more evasive, more diversionary, more sterile. As when he answered Rob Mackie's question as to what he (who had been dubbed by the journalist, Captain Mandrax) had done after these two years; he simply replied, "Trying to maintain a balance between standing up and falling down." Needless to say, it was published – as the capping piece to the interview; *asinus asinum fricat*, indeed!

The aftermath of a tour can be engulfing in its anti-climactic force, and this one proved to be that, and more. During it he had felt the ecstasies of great insight, inspiring power and brilliant success; in its wake came the tiresome, unnerving despondencies of self-doubt, the enduring jibes of critics, the heightening of a sense of having done well, but not well enough. How that cantankerous thought could plague him! Self-preservation may be the first law of nature, as Samuel Butler asserted; but it is all too often the consequence of fear, self-doubt, the after-effect of a brush with the *néant* which pierces all defences and leaves a man trembling on the edge of his own personal abyss.

Leonard Cohen felt that and more during this time, to which was added the ongoing nightmare of another broken relationship, the unforgiving knowledge that the one which he was now in was breaking up, was breaking him up, threatening his balance, his state of grace, his work and commitment. As Ambrose Bierce commented, in *The Devil's Dictionary*:

> '*They stood before the altar and supplied*
> *The fire themselves in which their fat was fried.*'

It highlights Montaigne's observation in *Essays* that 'a good marriage would be between a blind wife and a deaf husband,' but when both are too seeing, too self-determined, when they are pulling in different directions, seeking contrary objectives or mutually exclusive paths, the result is pain and disaster. As he wrote and sang at this time, 'There is a *war.*'

He now gave up his Franklin home, and refound some pleasure in life again on Hydra albeit intermittently (Montreal was still his main base), as we saw earlier. To his home there, he now returned, to rest and recuperate, to think and reflect, to blacken pages and form new melodies, even though many in Greece writhed and suffered; as he did inwardly. He also spent time in Montreal, a more appropriate base for his family life, but the circumstances were difficult. He admitted to "a loss of identity when the children were born," that he was still working "but bewildered." He felt his freedom slipping away from him, and therefore his art, his destiny. He felt trapped, but there was as much exhaustion as disorientation; the touring had taken its toll, and once more insomnia and the nightmares struck. His present work was titled first, *A Woman Being Born;* then *My Life In Art* a blistering document of distraught emotions and shattered hopes, as we shall see.

Israel was once again reeling from Arab hatred and oppression, and so Leonard, in an effort to avoid confrontation and pain at the personal and domestic levels, offered himself – as many Jews from around the world did – to fight it. This was how, in September and October 1972, he came to be back again in Israel where only four months previously he had broken all records and raised his fans' adulation to near-hysterical heights. At Tel Aviv, where they had planned for an audience of between 2000 and 3000, 10,000 turned up. In an effort to ease the pressures, Leonard invited them to come nearer the stage, as he was wont to do – and even on it, at times. The result was chaos, a 'riot' ensued, according to some reports which required 'firm treatment' from the authorities, and not a few of those who came bruised in soul returned bruised in body. For two months he toured on various military bases, raising morale, diverting men and women from the boredom and terror of war, even coming under fire in a few nerve-wracking incidents himself when the external conditions matched the frenzy of the internal.

His return home found matters little different, though he had the pleasure of putting up Bob Dylan and his Canadian girlfriend for several weeks. Save for the Concert for Bangladesh in 1971, Dylan had not played an advertised concert since 1969, nor had he released an album of new songs for nearly two years. He did go, however, to the Mariposa Folk Festival with Leonard (Canada's equivalent of Newport), and so began to circulate again. Leonard recalls their discussing Christianity and Hasidism about this time, Dylan then being both pro-Arab and Zionist! (Dylan later moved from this 'mathematical phase' to his new-birth one, which interested Leonard – who regards Christianity as 'the missionary arm of Judaism' – and added spice to their conversations. Leonard favoured Dylan's new-found religious fervour.)

So he took off again, ostensibly to share in the launch of his latest book of poems, *Energy Of Slaves*, which reflects the draining conditions of his life, as well as his sense that formal poetry could no longer fulfil that to which he had hitherto aspired, still less effect its realisation. Stephen Spender speaks of this when he writes, in his *Journals: 1939-1983*, of 'the fatality of American poets: . . . I think the American poets, far more than English ones, cling to the idea that the poet is the 'unacknowledged legislator' . . . They have a public concept of the efficacy of poetry: and usually they accept blindly that the poet is quite inefficacious.'

Louis Dudek has spoken of it somewhat crushingly as early as 1967, at the World Poetry Conference, when he said, "Canadian poets can say anything they like, but they have nothing to say." It was a sort of swan-song for Leonard in that medium, in which he disconnects himself from it, at the same time lamenting his lost art, his failed abilities:

> 'The poems don't love us any more
> they don't want to love us
> they don't want to be poems
> Do not summon us, they say
> We can't help you any longer
>
> 'There's no more fishing
> in the Big Hearted River leave us alone
> We are becoming something new

> '*They have gone back into the world*
> *to be with the ones*
> *who labour with their total bodies*
> *who have no plans for the world*
> *They never were entertainers*
>
> '*I live on a river in Miami*
> *under conditions I cannot describe . . .*'

It comes out in even more savage vein in another untitled piece (few – 12, in fact – have titles), itself an indication of his heartache, the sense of desolation, anger and disappointment to which he had fallen prey:

> '*I have no talent left*
> *I can't write a poem any more*
> *You can call me Len or Lennie now*
> *Like you always wanted*
> *I guess I should pack it up*
> *but habits persist*
> *and women keep driving me back to it*
> *Before you accuse me of boring you*
> *(your ultimate triumph and relief)*
> *remember that neither you or me*
> *is f------[s] right now*
> *and once again you have enjoyed*
> *the company of my soul*'

(As he has now apparently renounced the use of coarse language, we do so here in anticipation of his new edition.)

And again, in similar style, not only turning on and berating himself, but attacking those he saw enjoying his misery:

> '*I am punished when I do not work on this poem*
> *or when I try to invent something*
> *I am one of the slaves*
> *You are employees*
> *That is why I hate your work*'

The sacred had become blurred, the secular had overtaken him, the connections with higher forms of energy were severed, and lower forms merely fuelled the anguish – and the unmeaning:

> '*You want me at all times*
> *without my prophet's mantle*
> *without my loneliness*
> *without the jelly girls*

You want me without my agony
without the risk
that my health insults you
without my love of trees
without my ocean hut
You want me to lose the thread
in my friend's conversation
without my memory
without my promise to animals
and come here and come here
and come here and come here
and come here and come here
and come here and come here
and come here and come here
and come here and come here
and come here and come here
and come here and come here'

He bared his soul in this book; and led with his chin. Not a few of his critics – learned and unlearned, true and untrue, obliged – and put him down: '. . . designed for the heat of adolescence,' commented David Lehman in *Poetry*. 'Prosy, inexpert, uncompelling,' *The Times Literary Supplement* pontificated, adding self-defensively, 'Teeny boppers of all ages will have the book on their shelves.' 'Apparently as shoddy a piece of work as one would find anywhere today,' said Eli Mandel, more in sorrow than in anger (to whom we must return; his 'apparently' being all-important). 'A collection of poetic fragments, failed poems, and anti-poems,' said Frank Davey in *From There To Here*. Scobie refers to 'lines which just sit up and beg to be quoted in negative reviews,' his own prelude to the attack, which he does not fail to press: 'blatantly bad . . . a tone basically one of disgust, especially self-disgust . . . deliberately ugly, offensive, bitter, anti-romantic.' True, of course, 'deliberately' being Scobie's parallel to Mandel's 'apparently', as we shall see.

Tom Wayman espoused contempt, dipping his pen in vitriol in order to match Leonard's tones, though he does it blindly, ungracefully; working more like an abattoir technician and with as little charm, he says: 'Women in Cohen's poems in this book primarily are holes, though sometimes they can be breasts or thighs or asses,' he speaks of him 'whimpering'; 'his whine-act'; 'the sententiousness of a Rod McKuen'; 'another, self-abasing spurt of ego'; this *pretence* . . .' He concludes his bitter, myopic scan by saying, 'Nothing inside that I can find will repay anyone – female or male – for the time necessary to read

through these poems, for the time necessarily spent in the company of
Cohen's soul.' As Shakespeare had concluded in *Othello:*

> *'Trifles light as air*
> *Are to the jealous confirmation strong*
> *As proof of holy writ.'*

It is useful to note that Wayman scorns in particular: 'the vague
idea of a revolution'; 'reducing women to mere bodies'; 'the war
between women and men'; 'the poet's style'; 'this *pretence* of discussing
politics.' He concludes, 'A kind of basic immorality has to be added to
Cohen's poetic faults as exhibited in this collection of tedious male
supremacy, vagueness, sententiousness and mental titillation . . . his
poverty as a writer is evident.'

Now it is a law of literary criticism that context is essential to
understanding any text. Structuralism, important as it is, is merely a
refinement of this. The sad thing about Wayman's piece is not whether
or not he has damaged Leonard's reputation with his petty-minded
superficialities, but whether he has damaged literature itself! And
whether the editor of *Canadian Literature* – Mr Woodcock, no less – has
done anything more than serve an equally petty vendetta in publishing
such purblind comment. Happily, literature is made of firmer stuff,
though its atmosphere can be polluted.

Professor Dudek suggested (in a different context) that, 'Perhaps no one so well as (Ezra Pound) epitomises the predicament of
modern poetry, the poet pitted against his age, and to all intents
defeated by the immense pressures of actuality.' But it is at least
arguable that Leonard also epitomised that predicament, and pitted
himself (if only indirectly) against his age: the genocide of Vietnam, the
false gurus (read prophets!), the 'discomfort' of modern, high-rise
buildings, the easy facilisms of the learned, the soulless pedantry of the
lawyers, the crushing power of the manufacturers and the bodies
corporate, their self-absorptions; and those of the fashion-makers – in
art and film, music and literature, and even journalism; but most of all,
against himself, his feelings of disquiet, inequilibrium, alienation. The
sense of ennui, nausea and angst – such key words which encompass so
much! – the failure to find or hold an integrated world-view which
includes the fruits of modernity without destroying the old; the art of
enduring relationships.

The Swedish publishers of the book expressed great acuity in
putting one of the shorter pieces on the back cover, at once exposing
such vacuities as Wayman's, and centring attention on the serious and
key problem exercising Leonard's mind:

> *'I make this song for thee*
> *Lord of the world*

who has everything in the world
except this song'

There is a religious dimension to the book, as there is in all Leonard's work. It appears as early as the sixth piece: 'I'd like to read/one of the poems/that drove me into poetry/I can't remember one line/or where to look' (itself a telling admission). It continues, 'The same thing/happened with money/girls and late evenings of talk' (by which he emphasises the utter destructiveness of his experience); going on to question 'Where are the poems/that led me away/from everything I loved?' (in which lines he demonstrates that the Tradition of his youth was not forgotten, merely displaced); and closes with a prayer, no less:

'to stand here
naked with the thought of finding thee'

What the title of the book has expressed obscurely – too obscurely for the shallow scanners, to be sure – here finds emphatic expression. It is a book of confession. Its very title challenges its readers so to think of it: *The Energy Of Slaves* – and white paper as much as 'blackened pages' hits the eye on opening it: the energy is all but absent! As honest as ever a Rousseau or an Augustine ever wrote; 'accuracy' writ large, and painfully.

He takes up the theme again: 'Keep the fire. Keep the fire./Your body is holy./Do not believe the truth . . .' And it has very beautiful expression in the piece:

'Stay
stay a little longer
timid shadow
of my repose
fastened so lightly
to the breath before
my first question
Thou art the hunger
can disarm
every appetite'

And in 'How We Used To Approach *The Book Of Changes: 1966*' it is dovetailed into the Tradition again. Addressing Abraham, he confesses:

'Good father, since I am broken down, no leader of the borning
world, no saint for those in pain, no singer, no musician, no
master, of anything, no friend to my friends, no lover to those
who love me only my greed remains to me, biting into every
minute that has not come with my insane triumph show me the

way now, tonight, to possess what I long for, to ensnare, to tame,
to love and be loved in the passion which I cannot ignore despite
your teachings give her to me and let me be for a moment in this
miserable and bewildering wretchedness, a happy animal.'

Even in the thought of such ecstasy he knows of only one true desire:

'moan for me
as I will moan for you my love
as I will moan for thee'

Even at the height of frustrated physical delight he returns to his roots, his calling, his destiny. Once again the knowledge of the human leading into a prayer for the divine.

Everything in the book is there – everything that Wayman *et al* have failed to understand: his lostness, his brokenness, his misery, his last wish to be loved by the woman of his dreams – not 'the hole' that Wayman nauseatingly crows about, but one for whom so much was given – who taught him 'to forget so very much.' But it is there *unstructurally*. For nearly 30 years Leonard had been striving for artistic excellence, following the rules, honing the discipline, honouring the forms and rhythms. What had been its first, heartbroken flowerings, when he wrote words on a piece of paper, slit open his father's bow-tie, inserted the now forgotten words (which remind us sadly of the Russian proverb that, 'He who forgets his own history is condemned to repeat it'), and buried it in the garden overlooking the park, where they had talked and played and walked, had turned into a long quest, had come to sensational fruition, recognised across the world. But the quest had run out of steam – as it does in so many poets – whether by sclerosis, to use Professor Dudek's word; by suicide to recall the fates of such as Hart Crane, Sylvia Plath, Randell Jarrell; or plain, disconsolate boredom which led some into alcoholism and others into insanity such as Dylan Thomas and Robert Lowell; which very nearly claimed Leonard, as we shall see: 20 years of it, no less.

Leonard had long recognised the signs – within others, such as George Woodcock, who virtually gave up poetry at the age of 39. (In later life he did start again, but flickering embers are even less warming than carbonised sticks – he wrote but seven of them – which made their appearances between 1949 and 1974.) Leonard still felt – knew – that he had something meaningful to say, a word to offer. The problem was, as with very many poets of his age, 'the poems don't love me any more.' The poetic muse had withdrawn. Worse, few people – especially young people – seemed to care, despite the so-called 'poetry boom'. The howl had become a howling. Leonard had risen to the Collected (or Selected) Poems level 15 years before Woodcock – who was 22 years older than he. He had *led* his own generation for 20 years. In *Energy Of Slaves* he was not giving up; he was persevering. But the poet had become a slave of his own craft, his own habits. He was no longer in the Promised Land, he was back in Egypt – working on someone else's pyramids, slavishly.

Now pyramids are among the most primitive of all building styles – they rely on pure gravity for their strength; they have no cantilever effect. Hitherto, Leonard's books of poetry had been 'structured'; their cantilever-effect works from the titles: mythologies for *Let Us Compare Mythologies;* the spice-box for his second volume; inhumanism for *Flowers For Hitler;* and various dependencies in *Parasites Of Heaven.* Here, too, there is a similar principle at work, but it is that, not so much of 'failed poems' as Frank Davey suggests, but (to use his precise phrase) anti-poems. In Scobie's telling phrase, 'either the poems are deliberately bad (*which is a form of aesthetic control*), or else . . . they are rhetorically impressive,' (our italics). Quite so. In other words, to revert to the principles of architectural structuralism again, unimaginative critics such as Wayman and Woodcock want isomorphic poetry: even their avant-garde wishes must conform.

(Not surprisingly, *Beautiful Losers* was also heavily – disdainfully – criticised; it, too, registered its protests and warnings by denying formal structures: 'unstructured' cried some unaware of a stream-of-consciousness method.) Leonard has gone beyond all that. He was offering purer feeling; he was stating that recollection in tranquillity is a *romantic* shibboleth, a destruction of art; its disciplines purely bureaucratic and therefore unreal for *this* situation, *this* experience. From within his own experience, enslaved by it no less, he yields to its demands. He is no longer 'free' to discipline his work, himself; he uses the mud and straw that is to hand: a true reflection of life, his life (and many others); *true* poetry, not neutered niceness, prettified to demonstrate egotistic wishes. The poetry of his tortured life; poetry that works – like the *duende* itself – 'from the gut'; genuine evidence of a life, no less.

That is why Mandel's 'apparently' and Scobie's 'deliberately' are so important. That is why Woodcock's or Wayman's strictures – or, for that matter, Dudek's refined élitism – are unhelpful. Art must convey life, demonstrate it; it becomes non-art when it becomes a didactic tool – still worse, a vehicle of snobbishness – to some vague appreciation of what life should be. Of such he writes expressly, on the very first page of this new book:

> '*We are alone*
> *until the times change*
> *and those who have been betrayed*

come back like pilgrims to this moment
when he did not yield
and call the darkness poetry'

Leonard, amid the sordid break-up, 'the panic of loss,' once more led the way. He did so with his mind casting itself back to his 'neurotic affiliations', to his destiny – sadly begrimed. At least he was man enough to admit it. And man enough to say of 'drugs and alcohol, sex and politics, of gurus and personal shabby plans-for-the-evening': that is *not* the way. The revolution has failed! But the war continues, at all sorts of levels – of relationships, of principles, most of all in life itself – the challenge to be free or unfree.

It is seen most poignantly in his beloved Greece: the 'man/ tortured on a terrace' (the infamous Bouboulinas Street, the police headquarters in Athens); or indirectly in speaking of the pyramids at the time of Israel's fear of war; in referring to the competitive, conform- ing pressures of New York, of Montreal; of the destructive pressures of unequal, multi-directional relationships – 'Can two walk together unless they be agreed?' But he can no longer care: 'I only sing this for the ones/who do not care who wins the war.' ('What war?' asks Wayman, astigmatically.) When the mind has been 'blown' by such total disasters, only the body's feelings seem true, only the appetites may be trusted: but 'I didn't like myself/when things went wrong . . . I learned to write/I learned to write/what might be read/on nights like this/by one like me' – written by one who 'hated the world on your behalf.' He has been reduced from 'golden boy' to a dwarf. In an age of demythologisation, he was demythologising himself! The pain is 'overheard on every corner':

'I was meant to be
the courtless invisible king
I am that
the clearest example of royalty
who serves you tonight
as he makes a bed for the dog.'

The dialogue with himself runs through the whole book – discussing, accusing, reminding, condemning, scorning (he can do that of himself with far greater grace and perception – and style, even when writing unstylishly – than the flotsam of academe, the jetsam of the literary world). He has stated his evidence; he challenges those who can see and hear to judge it. We stand with him at the bar of judgment. As Mandel concluded, the book 'elucidates with the precision we used to call poetry the failure of contemporary poetry.' Far more uncom- promising than Lee or Atwood or Bowering or Ondaatje, and more scrupulous . . . as becomes a prophet!

live songs –
dead heart

It was not all negative emotion that was felt at this time. In the manner that some of the most poignant psalms came out of broken dreams and destroyed lives, so Leonard was able to write and sing: the word still emerging.

His fourth album, which appeared in 1973 (to the accompaniment of a scare-story of his early retirement lionised by the press) did not please the critics but it did delight his fans. It was a compilation of songs, mainly from the recent tour, mirroring the mood he created throughout Europe.

The scare story arose out of an interview which Leonard gave to Roy Hollingworth of *Melody Maker*. Believing himself to be speaking in confidence, Leonard said, "I cannot stand to remain part of it (the music business). I've reached a state when I'm just not writing anything." A week later the theme was continued, "There are a lot of people who have suddenly found that they have lost themselves. There's much disillusionment about . . . I don't want to talk about it. I don't want it to be the substance of an interview." Naturally, it was published; as an interview. Leonard was actually in London to be presented with a gold disc. It is clear that his preoccupation was not with the industry itself (which he loved), but its effects on the artists' lives – and particularly those of their families. Leonard's not least. As Alastair Pirrie observed, on interviewing him for *New Musical Express*, "A large change had taken place in him; he smoked continuously; was much more withdrawn; he answered questions vaguely and lapsed into frequent silences. A man under pressure. A man seriously at risk."

'Live Songs' commences with his 'Minute Prologue', an 'improvisation' in the form of a somewhat world-weary plea:

> '*I've been listening to all the dissension*
> *I've been listening to all the pain*
> *and I feel that, no matter what I do for you,*
> *It's gonna come back again.*
> *But I think that I can heal it;*
> *but I think that I can heal it;*
> *I am a fool; but I think that I can heal it –*
> *with this song!*'
>

World-weary, even cynical as he felt at times, he nevertheless must go on, ever thinking despite his better judgement that he can 'heal it – with this song.' And he did! As thousands testified as the word was heard. Nietzsche had appositely remarked that, 'What is great in man is that he is a bridge, not a goal.' And a priest is, *par excellence*, a bridge. Leonard was the main contact with reality for some. He always found time for those whose grasp on life and reason was tenuous, freely visiting clinics, psychiatric wards and mental hospitals, offering inmates joy in his music and solace in his words. Vassall suggests that Leonard sees madness as 'another possible source of liberation' (read freedom), citing Breavman's mother in *The Favourite Game* and the schizophrenic language in *Beautiful Losers*.

Perhaps; but Leonard always sees the terrible price such unfortunates must pay (nowhere more movingly than in the depression/suicide aspect, as we see here or in 'Nancy' or in 'Chelsea Hotel'. Janis 'got away' but to what? Daphne was 'transfigured' but for what? If 'What am I?' is the ultimate question of his life, 'Why?' must rank as a close second. Leonard had certainly known the temptation to suicide, but he knew and thought too deeply about his own freedom through it. He preferred that of the bird, the drunk and the fish, even the kite.

Daphne Richardson, a minor artist of some note, had her daydreams printed in the album's sleeve. While in hospital she had told her attendants that she had been in contact with Leonard, but she was not believed. So she made further contact by letter and was overjoyed at his positive and welcoming reply. Unfortunately she did not live to enjoy the moment when the album was released: in a fit of depression she jumped off Bush House in London and ended it all, leaving her small contribution to echo its way – and his – around Europe:

> '*TRANSFIGURATION. That's what occurred the night of*
> *13 December*
> *Since then I am not just a human being*
> *I am inhabited by God, and love bleeds*
> *and burns within me, but what caused the*

TRANSFIGURATION
was the mad – mystic hammering of your body
upon my body, your soul entered mine then, and some
union took place that almost killed me with its
INTENSITY
I cannot justify my outrageous claims. I can only
relate what happened before the fire burns me . . .'

It is sensual, it is 'mystical'. It is Dylanesque. Its energy is as raw
as its feelings are honest. But not sordid, not cheap. Not a feeble joke
such as a Tom Wayman in his smutty perversity might make of it, not
warranting the 'scholarly' disdain of Scobie who unknowingly condemns it for being 'pretentious': 'unable to express her perceptions in
words of any precision or freshness.' As if such things mattered a damn
when one's life was 'hanging by a thread'! Piddling priestly wisdom at
its emptiest! It was a desperate attempt at psychosomatic fusion by the
longing soul – a religious soul – sensing its deep *alienation*, clinging to
that which it can feel, that which offers it some hope; its last remaining
contact with memory and life.

This is one of the strange things about Leonard's concerts, his
poetry, his art. They are mystically sensual, never merely physical. The
dichotomy – of spirit and body – that robs many people of their full
health is absent from his work. It challenges our falsity, it provokes our
awareness, it quickens our conscience; and, most amazingly, it nour-
ishes our souls. This is why he can pass so easily from body to spirit,
from woman to God, from the secular to the sacred: a true spokesman
of the two great intimacies; even from death to life, for some who
hear.

The music on this new set is excellent, especially the keyboard
work and vocal harmonies: quietly emphatic and harmonising beautifully with Leonard's voice which is strong and sweet – when
necessary, at other times, ringing in its tones of appeal and anguished
challenge. Perhaps one of the most charismatic aspects of his performance is the interpretation of songs which vary from concert to concert
and often differ markedly from the cultivated studio version. 'Beat
words' creep in, as do connecting links which enhance the rhythm and
give greater stress to the depth of poetry-in-song. More importantly,
the changes are fashioned out of his responses to the live audiences.
Together they feel, and together they respond.

This is the 'mystery' of song: lip to lip and heart to heart. It is also
the mystery of true poetry (structured or not, stylish or not) – for those
with ears to hear. The *energy* he channelled could be both hypnotic and
awe-inspiring. At times raw, at times *soignée*, the words resound
through it all, pulsating and alive, incisive and questioning, always with

feeling and that bedrock of knowledge – his knowledge of man's soul, which all prophets have. He searches them out; his words demand a response; only the feebler sort of critic can remain unmoved, lost in their superior judgements and supercilious posing. The voice is heard. It echoes through the songs. The authentic word of sympathy, hope and healing. Out of the fiery furnace – of a Daphne, a Steve, a Nancy – gold shines.

The album offers healing in its first lines, from the song 'Passing Thru', previously covered by many noted folk singers. (The sleeve credits Leonard with the writing, though it was written by Richard Blakeslee. But Leonard never took over someone else's song *simpliciter*, and this one was arranged by him, so the credit is justified.) 'I saw Jesus on the cross, on a hill called Calvary,/'Do you hate mankind for what they've done to you?'/He said, 'Talk of love, not hate' . . .'

Nothing could be more natural for Leonard, a Jew, to talk of Jesus thus; though others might express it very differently. The *San Diego Union* drew attention to this in an interview ('Cohen's most idiosyncratic – and controversial – view') which drew from Leonard a characteristic reply: "Yeah, I'm Jewish. So was He!" on which he broke into that well known grin. In more serious vein, he told his interviewer: "My admiration for Christ is on a completely personal level. Of all the people who left their names behind, I don't think there's a figure of Christ's moral stature. A man who declared himself to stand among the thieves, the prostitutes, the homeless. His position cannot be comprehended. It is an inhuman generosity . . . (which) would overthrow the world if it was embraced."

This rendition of 'Passing Thru' was taken from the March 1972 concert at the Royal Albert Hall, in which we hear Leonard's concern not just in the music or the words, but in his thoughtfulness for a late arriver. "Come a little closer, friend," he invites, between verses one and two. To verse two's 'I'm an orphan now and I'm only passing through,' he adds the warning, 'So are you!' And at verse four, when President Roosevelt is made to say 'One world must come out of World War Two,' he adds 'Oh! the fool!'

'You Know Who I Am' (taken from the Brussels concert a few days later), offers an interesting addition, as he paints a strained picture of himself, caught 'mid-flight' as it were in his perplexity, immobilised by life's traumas:

> 'I am not life, I am not death
> I am not slave or free'

(Copyright © 1972, Stranger Music Inc, New York.
Used by Permission. All Rights Reserved.)

In Paris in mid-April, he delighted his audience with his French introduction ('*Comme l'oiseau sur la branche,/comme l'ivrogne dans la choeur de la nuit,/j'ai cherché ma liberté*), in an extraordinary performance: of one who 'searches' still. The first verse differs from that given in 'Songs From A Room: 'Like a knight from some old-fashioned book,' has become 'Like a knight *bent down* in some old-fashioned book,' by weight of stress; and instead of the gallant, 'I have saved all my ribbons for thee,' appears the equally burdened explanatory note, 'It was the shape, the shape of our love that twisted me.' We should note particularly, as we did earlier, that 'thee' is reserved for a God-dimension, by which usage he frequently signals the *double entendre* so often found in his poetry and songs, switching thereby from the earthly to the heavenly, from woman to the divine.

Jennifer Warnes, in 'Famous Blue Raincoat', fails to observe this, and misses the point of the song; as many have. In so changing it, he has added to the song's pained freedom–cum–enslaved contradictions; he has rendered far more graphic the torture of their love: a torture that was 'twisting' him from his true shape, from his destined course. 'Nancy' terminates the A-side; taken from the London concert, in which he alters the opening line to, 'the morning had not come,' highlighting thereby the misery of her lonely vigils. The song concludes on a note of penetrating challenge: 'Why don't *you* look around you?' and 'Many of *you* use her body . . .' by which he intensified the use-and-abuse ('love 'em and leave 'em') habits of the sixties. In exact contradiction to the blind and demeaning comment of many, he exhorted his hearers to think about the effects that their freedom produces and those of free 'loving'. He has challenged again those who live 'in the House of Honesty,' warning all such *poseurs* that they are the ones on trial.

The 'Story Of Isaac' which follows was introduced by him concerning those 'who would sacrifice one generation on behalf of another' – whether in the Middle East, Greece or Vietnam, Canada, America or Europe. From the first it was a perfect instrument of warning: Abraham did *not* sacrifice Isaac. Why should they, who had not even had a vision, heard the voice of either a demon or a god? The only alteration of substance occurs in the final line, a very crucial heightening of the warning: 'The peacock spreads his *deadly* fan': it is of life and death that he sings. 'Please don't pass me by (A Disgrace)' is here offered for the first time, again from the London set of 1970. Then it had concluded his concert – to nerve-shattering applause, whistles, cat-calls and cheers, despite Leonard's own reactions; a stunning performance, manifesting Leonard's dramatic sensibilities as well as his integrity. The song is based on a simple quatrain format; which he raises to a pentameter by repetition of the first line in a blues-rock rhythm:

'Please don't pass me by
Please don't pass me by
I am blind, but you can see
I've been blinded totally;
Please don't pass me by.'

If ever he was possessed of charisma, it was on that evening. He took them through *10* repetitions of the song, each time ratcheting-up the emotions, the moral demands of the lines, the logical implications, their proper responses.

He commenced quietly, by simple appeal; became louder and louder, increasing the rhythm till his audience burst into clapping in harmony with him; they then commenced singing with him, carried away in the emotion. It was following this performance that he expressed shame that he had so let himself go – and that under the withering gaze of Queen Victoria! But his instincts were right, and happily we now have preserved this vital exposition of his social conscience and his challenge to selfish affluence – a rare but important work, which achieved special force when he explained that the man whose sandwich-board had jostled him was not, in fact, physically blind at all. It was ever meant to be a stroke against social inequality, injustice and greed.

'Tonight Will Be Fine' achieves, thanks to Bubba Fowler's banjo, an unusual and exhilarating 'hoe-down' effect, which enlivens the drama of a broken romance – but not too melodramatically. (Leonard expressed particular relish over this, as the country-music effect heightened the comradeship and 'masculine' tones, which he liked.) He heightened his last two verses to develop the mood of abandonment and all-round dejection:

'Ah! I've looked into the mirrors in numberless places,
they all smile back at me with their troublesome faces.
And the cards that they dealt me, there weren't any aces,
and the horses never listen to me at the races.

'There's still one or two of us walking the street,
no arrows of direction painted under our feet;
no angels to warn us away from the heat,
and no money to keep us where it is sweet'

Nevertheless, he knows that tonight at least, it will be fine – for a while, that is . . .

We have very little record of his time at Franklin, a couple of poems in *The Energy Of Slaves*: 'Overheard On Every Corner', when he recalled that 'I have been chosen to perfect all men . . .' and, adding to his dilemma of being torn in two directions: 'I Try To Keep In Touch Wherever I Am,' adding the *caveat* 'I live for you/without the memory of what you deserve/or what you do not deserve.' But on on this album we have a recording made in the solitude of that 'cabin' by the little creek, thanks to the tape-recorder loaned to him by Bob Johnston. It originated in his poem 'Queen Victoria And Me' and is redolent, not only of his father's tobacco (itself an interesting throw-back to the distant childhood days), but the whole Victorian/Edwardian scene. However, it, too, is a song of broken love, because 'my love, she gone with other boys' and which ends with their shared 'incomparable sense of loss': in bereavement and cold-blooded rejection.

> *'Queen Victoria. I am not much nourished by modern love.*
> *Will you come into my life?*
> *with your sorrow and your black carriages*
> *and your perfect memory?'*

(Copyright © 1972. Stranger Music Inc, New York and Music Sales Ltd, London. Used by Permission. All Rights Reserved.)

It is not easy to escape the conclusion that this period, once the tour was over, was somewhat desultory. Even parts of the tour reached zero-point in his emotions. In Jerusalem, for example, Manzano reports Leonard appearing on stage 'drugged'. By the time he came to sing 'So Long, Marianne' he was in tears, a mood exacerbated by the sentiments of the song, necessitating an unplanned interlude while he recovered. On returning he said, "There are nights when one is raised from the ground, and other nights when (one) cannot raise oneself . . . this night we can't get off the floor. The Cabala says, 'If you cannot raise yourself from the floor, you remain on it.' This night my masculine and feminine parts refuse to meet each other."

Rather little of 1973/4 has been left on record – save in the Notebooks, to which we must return. It was a bleak year, alternating between hope and despair; love and – that most painful of all experiences – love's remorse. As Heraclitus questioned, 'How can you hide what never goes away?' Leonard appeared on Swedish television in June, offering 10 of his better known songs, beginning with 'So Long, Marianne', plus 'Hey, That's No Way To Say Goodbye', which might well have been directed more to neighbouring Norway than its easterly neighbour. Other appointments included an interview with Christian

Heeb on DSRI radio, and one in Montreal following a mini-tour through Canada (Vancouver, Kingston, etc), also on radio, for the *Concert Canadien* on CKRY-FM. Rob Mackie was rather unimpressed with the output at this time, saying that 'it didn't amount to much.'

By far the most memorable part of the year was experienced away from broadcasting stations, and the disquiet of his weakening domestic life, in Israel where, being once more on the verge of war with her recalcitrant neighbours, Leonard decided to volunteer for service in her army, and was posted to its support-services group, in which his role was one of sustaining the morale of her troops by word and song. A believer in reconciliation – between nations as well as couples and families – his convictions were tested under fire as well as that attitude of all-out commitment necessary to an army in action. His beliefs did not waver; 'the golden age' of psalmists and prophets held strong in his mind: one day the lion would lie down with the lamb – a very different attitude to that youthful witticism which had obtained when he wrote 'Millennium'. And an idealism which was to surface pointedly in 'Book Of Mercy' several years later.

Like all soldiers, he knew fear in those days, as well as fierce nationalism, that determination to *win* of which *Beautiful Losers* is the foil. 'Let everything tremble' commanded that genius of modern warfare, General Arik Sharon, at the onset of battle in 1967. And it did; as did Israel herself; as did its enemy. As did this new combatant in 1972. They went, not to fight, but 'to win a war'; not to kill, but in order not to be killed; they went to settle an intractable problem. And win they did, as win they must.

The military texture of his next album, 'New Skin for the Old Ceremony', reflects the concentration of those days: the existence and language of war, of enemies and friends, aspects of rank and obedience, questions of bravery, of weaponry; life – and – death-making decisions. The fear he saw around him, the fear he felt, the brave talk, the earnest concentration and, most wonderfully, the power of song to penetrate the strongest heart, in the most horrendous situations; its preternatural ability to speak, and be heard. Said Leonard to Manzano, "I continue to believe in the reconciliation between Arabs and Israelis. It's something that has to happen. I may sound very romantic, but they are sons of the same God . . . I know that in Toledo or Cordoba (as elsewhere) Christians, Muslims and Jews live together . . ."

It reached a consummation in his *Book Of Mercy* when, at *Psalm 14* he – the Jewish priest – exclaims, 'Blessed be Ishmael for all time . . .' and in his *New Selected Poems* (1990) he will change the untitled *Psalm 27* to *Israel And Ishmael* in bold defiance of those who resent his gesture of 'ecumenical' peace.

The Talmud says that the age of 40 'is for understanding,' but while Leonard's exterior view fulfilled that observation, the interior one was very different. It was, in fact tumultuous. As he commented to Allan Jones of *Melody Maker*, trying to lessen the hurt: "I seem to give this impression that I've been recovering from some long and serious illness. The image I've been able to gather from the press is one of a victim of the music industry, a poor sensitive chap who has been destroyed by the very forces he started out to utilise. But that is not so; never was . . ."

To Mick Brown, of *Sounds*, he pin-pointed the real, internal problem, which centred in his home-life: the shape of their love, 'twisting him' beyond any possibility of serene self-understanding. From the Notebooks he wrote the experience up into a fourth 'novel' but, like the first (*Ballet Of Lepers*), it was never published in novel form. It went much further than the first, however, and required an actual and expensive withdrawal from his publishers at proof stage. It was not a pose, as Scobie asserts, once more overcome with subjectivism. Said Leonard to Brown: "It isn't any good . . . It's too personal, it treats people close to me in a way that is somehow inaccurate, one-sided. I try to be truthful in whatever I do in some kind of way – not so much truthful to the fact as truthful to the experience. The book was truthful, but it wasn't fair."

So back through 'the word factory' it went, finally emerging (in 1977) – and in a totally altered shape, in *Death Of A Lady's Man*, whose singular form (contrasted with the plural of the album of that title) directed its readers to the tortured reality he was experiencing. We shall deal with the book more specifically in the next chapter, but five dated pieces from this time are worth looking at here:

'The Promise' '. . . I eat too much when I'm with her. I become obscure,' which he glosses: 'In one form only does she recognise me, the form of wife. In every other form she is searching for her mate; she blunders past me like something going blind, a salmon or a sea turtle, and I am landscape and water, going the other way.' Domesticity, a denial of his more 'ascetic' aspirations, role-reversal, an inability to meet her need for self-fulfilment (as she sees it), all conspire to pull them, and particularly him, apart.

'A Modest Gift', in free-verse form: 'It was a modest gift/Five-foot-eight in the Age of Dwarfs/Those nostalgic for the future/those who mourned the ancient excellence/did right to ignore me/But you deluded darling/you died in captivity/believing you'd surrounded a poet.' The withdrawn novel had been titled *My Life In Art*, as we saw earlier, which reflected a somewhat Tolstovian understanding. He was aware of other characteristics of the Russian, not least his developing spiritual crisis and the conflict this produced with regard to women. So he glosses the entry by denying that it reflects 'the Russian's resentment of the woman's constant presence'; attaching it rather to 'the old interior quarrel (upon which the universe is sustained) of the limited versus the unlimited' – the poet, naturally, existing in a realm of unlimited, if disputed, vision. He describes the situation as 'a parody on the metaphysic of polarity' but the emotions referred to were not recollected in tranquillity, still less in detached ratiocination, but in an agony of mind and conscience, which is further developed under the heading 'Another Man's Woman'.

In this piece the attempt is made to goad himself into a different response – a response against his nature – by taking on a different form, 'in order that you may refine your love for me'; but it was to no avail: 'the Iron Guard marching between us/With your sweater and your coffee and your cigarette/and your plans for the morning.' It was in such clashes that he recognised the dangers of inaccuracy, one-sidedness, unfairness. He required a soul-mate; she looked for a sole mate. In 'Traditional Training And Service' he describes 'the Working of Marriage' which reveals how much he tried – or tried to try and meet her needs: 'I will go behind the mask of your anger/I will go behind the mask of your revenge/I will dwell in your heart and your halfness.' But the very suggestion of her 'halfness' emphasises a lack of mutuality. It was not a renunciation of love, but a declaration of absence – the painful absence of that true halfness which, with his, would have produced a wholeness of content and comfort for them both.

Such antipathy could not be hidden indefinitely. At a time when his whole being cried out to comprehend and express 'understanding' he found it impossible to deny his assertive nature; as he said in 'Which Is So Beautiful', 'the betrayal was not always deferred.' So he turned off the radio – 'It has to be quiet, so I can study what it means not to be forgiven,' that results in the heartfelt confession which recalls the first couple's expulsion from Eden: 'O love, there was/a flaming sword which turned everyway/when I tried to explain the sorrow.' The sword is that handled by the protective angel of *Genesis* 3, positioned so that the man and the woman cannot re-enter the paradisal garden. Defeat indeed!

The final dated piece, 'If I Am Not Her Servant' which is said to come from 'An Angry Conversation With Lilith' (the screech-owl of Jewish mythology), intensifies the misunderstandings by emphasising poetically the horrors of the situation – to no avail. So 'Finally she turned her back on him and he experienced her compassion' – the compassion of solitude, silence and a severance he hoped would be final: 'Goodbye, goodbye and goodbye.'

Listen as hard as he did; think as deeply as he could, he could not heal it. It was to come back again, and again, and again. Fool or not, he tried – in plea, in prayer, and most of all in song.

rediscovering
the word

'The real deserts are outside of Tradition.'

LEONARD COHEN

'All beginnings are hard. How is a person going to be stirred to return to God if there isn't a single spark of God's light inside him to wake him up? And how can God's light begin to dawn within him if he hasn't even started to return to him?'

NACHMAN OF BRATISLAVA

'. . . Biting my truant pen, beating myself for spite: Fool! said my Muse to me, look in thy heart and write.'

SIR PHILIP SIDNEY

the art of art

We have repeatedly seen that Leonard's art was fabricated of his life – his ancestral background, his people's anguish, his parents' suffering, his developments through school and university, from poet to novelist, from songwriter to singer, his life and loves and their crises. We have also seen how he switches, in the varying recensions of his songs (which he is sometimes content to acknowledge as a 'lightweight means of communication' – but beware of the con!) from the personal to the general application, e.g. from Nancy's experiences to her generation's easy loving; from Abraham's 'sacrifice' of Isaac to that of the sixties genocide of its youth. In all this he was engaged in enquiry – an enquiry after truth.

It is tempting to say that his data was only his own changing life and lifestyle, but that is both facile and unjust. His was an open-eyed journey of unending length, perhaps only the width of a thread, but always intercoursing with time and history – all those vibrant connections pulsating with the rhythms of eternity – through which he continued to make his own connections; always linking beginnings with ends, means with conclusions – seeking accuracy, truth, whose first and last letters in Hebrew equate with 'alpha' and 'omega' in Greek; by which he, consciously and otherwise, demonstrates his endless attempts 'to sew the world together,' as he unites the Hebrew origins of his soul with the wider cosmic forces of his life.

His is not a life of single dimension, but universal; it has not one meaning, for himself, but a generality of meanings – for many; it is not personal, but representative; it is not individualistic, but collective. It is not surprising, therefore, that his firstborn was called Adam, which simply means 'man'. Ever an attractive and significant name, it symbolises Leonard's own viewpoint and position; his hopes of broader usefulness. His is the artist's life – unconsciously directed, but consciously imagined and expressed; a life of art, and therefore a life of opposites – contradictions, if you will – of pain and loss; of gain and advancement; of hope and despair; a life of dark ambiguities, and clashing colours, both exquisite and raw; a life of beautiful losers and inglorious winners. Ten years earlier, speaking to Rob Mackie, he had discussed the risks of being a pop-singer: 'dealing with money, women and fame' – "a conventional reaction" Leonard exclaimed. To him the risk was deeper, and more insidious: "The real risk is losing your touch, risking the inviolable sanctuary from which your work emerges; an aspect of losing your virginity." It is a life in which the need for 'balance' is primary, as well as one which demands a constant infusion of new sights and experiences. It is a life of endless searching for comprehension, and therefore of limitless aspiration and suffering. It is very similar to the oft-quoted experiences that inspired, and frustrated Rousseau when he wrote:

> *'Two things, almost incompatible, are united in me in a manner*
> *which I am unable to understand: a very ardent temperament,*
> *lively and tumultuous passions and, at the same time, slowly*
> *developed and confused ideas . . . I feel everything, and see*
> *nothing. I am carried away by my passions, but (am) stupid . . .*
> *My ideas arrange themselves in my head with almost incredible*
> *difficulty; they circulate in it with uncertain sound, and ferment*
> *till they excite and heat me . . .'*

Professor Dudek, who quotes the foregoing (with some differences) in his brilliant broadcasts *The First Person In Literature*, comments, 'There is no real or absolute universality or objectivity possible in art . . . all art is admitted or disguised subjectivity, an individual conception of truth.' He is surely right and wrong. There is real – that is *authentic* – universality in art: that is what art actually is. And the more genuine it is, the more it conceals 'art' (as Ovid perceived), which thus lessens subjectivity – admitted and disguised. And so the more genuinely it reflects reality, whose essence is the compound of particulars raised to universals. But, by the same token, there is not, nor can there be, any 'absolute' universality or objectivity; for all things (as Hume perceived) are 'in flux'. The fault lies in Dudek correlating 'real' and 'absolute', 'universality' and 'objectivity'; it is a collation of antonyms – a false connection! Art is not *simpliciter* 'admitted or disguised subjectivity.' At its best it is the distilling of the universal from the particular or individualistic – whether it be in Michelangelo's *David* or Plato's *Republic* or Van Gogh's flowers.

Professor Pacey has voiced the view that 'a state of high excitement within the community, together with some powerful stimulus from outside, is likely to result in the creation of a vivid and vigorous body of writing.' He was speaking of a nation's literature, its written art, but the same principle surely works, and that primarily, at the individual level. Leonard's 'excitements' created his poetry, his songs, and his very powerful and moving performances for those with an ear to hear.

It is not surprising that Rousseau and Hume come together thus as an expression of art as well as human friendship, albeit doomed. Nor should it be thought surprising that Leonard's art – always more deeply enquiring and philosophical than his *confrères* in song – should reflect their views and experiences. The Holocaust and other experiences of loss and alienation had undermined his sense of providence (though he never became comfortable with mere 'coincidence'), and paved the way for his flirtations with the *I Ching* whose aleatoric prognostications both cheered and unnerved him; with astrology and dianetics, whose whimsical suppositions both excited and repulsed him. 'Fate' is perhaps nearest to his understanding, but – significantly – it has no specific usage in his work. It is as if he cannot bring himself to espouse so impersonal a concept, although this view is mirrored in the Yiddish proverb: 'God is father; fate a step-father.'

As a self-aware artist he was moving from the 'confused' and 'stupid' through the 'ferment' and 'heat' to his own perceptions and articulations. His life – or rather, his responses to it – were articulating a perception of reality of universal application: art in its profoundest sense; as tens of thousands of his readers and listeners around the world can testify. He was not merely 'pouring out his soul' in this or that circumstance, but exploring his soul in them; from which he extracted wider meanings. There is a clear development from the first loves and borrowed understandings to the stronger, firmer elucidations; even if they be the outpourings of a broken heart, disillusionment, and rejection. The failed union of male and female (in himself as well as in his romantic attachments), to which he aspired, exacerbated his sense of the failed union of human and divine; not least his own sense of failure.

It was not all guilt and failure. In these past two years he begins to show a new relish for life and love; borne out of failure, despair and even attempted escape. Some may condemn him for running away; he was actually running towards his destiny. These experiences were unfolding wider realities: his experiences were becoming theirs; his life, that of the world; his concerns, man's; and so on. It was never more cogently put than when he was 'carried away' at the Albert Hall in London, when he sang repeatedly 'Do Not Pass Me By':

'And you know as I was walking (along Seventh Avenue)
I thought it was them who were singing it

I thought it was *they* who were singing it
I thought it was *the other* who was singing it;
I thought it was *someone else.*
But as I moved along, I knew it was *me.*
That I was singing it, to myself.'

From which he passes from his own experience to theirs:

'*Now I know that you're sitting there in your velvet seats,*
And you're thinking, "He's up there singing something that he
thinks about.
But I'll never have to sing that song."
But I promise you, friends, that you're going to be singing this
song. Maybe not tonight, maybe not tomorrow.
But one day you'll be on your knees.
And I want you to know
the words when the time comes
because *you're* going to have to sing it –
to yourself, or to another, or to your brother;
    You're going to have to learn how to sing this
song . . .'

Afterwards, as we saw, he expressed shame over this performance. But he was right, intuitively and – dare we say it? –
prophetically. He *knew* it then, and those who heard it knew it: He *was*
articulating for them – from the particular to the general; from his life
to theirs. Despite the dangers, ignoring the ridicule, he was giving voice
to the word. Such is the ultimate in 'art', if not in 'performance'. And
what was then explicit has since been implicit. What was there from the
beginning, latently; what became a passive, even half-understood
element in his work, now found full flowering. But not without other
diversions, to be sure!

It was at this time that his lawyer, Marty Machat, struck out into
theatrical production and used Leonard's 'Sisters Of Mercy' in an off-
Broadway production. The review, by Clive Barnes of *The New York
Times* conveys the point similarly:

'It is all about a young man, a dissolute poet, a Bohemian in the
Montreal suburbs – and his difficulties with women. They find him
totally irresistible. But this is largely through a misunderstanding,
because he is, you must accept, a little boy at heart. Women instinctively
realise this. Also his emotional engagements could never hope to match
his perfectly phenomenal sexual prowess. Such a sexual paragon among
men would be almost certain to have difficulties with women. He is
surely a man to be pitied rather than blamed.

'One presumes – perhaps unjustly – that Cohen identifies with
this male fantasy-figure. His poetry would be difficult to explain if he

did not, and it seems that 'Sisters Of Mercy' is the kind of ego-trip that might be thought of as stylised autobiography.'

The critics responded very well to his fifth album: 'New Skin For The Old Ceremony'. 'A real record,' commented Rob Mackie in *Melody Maker*, '. . . way beyond the sparseness of the old . . . a surprisingly nice album, more reflective and self-pitying.' (Odd that the 'self-pitying' is seen here as a virtue: it was not that – but at least the effect of the word was getting out!) Michael Watts added, also in *Melody Maker*, '. . . a little more spirited than any of his past four . . . you suddenly find yourself swimming around in meaning that's hard to find but which draws you deeper all the same.' And Mark Paytress, reflecting on the record 12 years later, found that 'the desolate, intimate landscapes of his earlier work had now given way to the lush – dare I say it, complacent – sound which seemed to ensnare most singer-songwriters around this time,' linking with his own views with Leonard's comment that it was "much less neurotic" than the former albums.

In the light of the frenzied energy and depressiveness of some of the songs – by no means all of them – it may seem 'complacent', but that is not truly the case, as we shall see. The album is still a tour of his interior landscape, but the maturation of his understandings and his musical style – thanks, not least, to John Lissaeur's brilliant arranging and production, with which Leonard was closely associated – increased his ability to come out smiling (as well as fighting) from the recent tragedies. It was, indeed, 'new skin' for the old ceremony; and light years away from the experience of 'the sky-light is like skin, for a drum I'll never mend' in 'Last Year's Man'. Even though in retrospect Leonard commented, "There is hurt in the voice; the approach is hurt. The power is not there. I was weak. I was learning how to sing again; in different styles." However, it was new-style: ballad and folk-blues, a new dimension musically; a new musical phase which commenced his more personal, more Traditional style.

'New Skin For The Old Ceremony' was recorded at the Sound Ideas Studio in New York, with a much fuller musical accompaniment than hitherto: Jeff Layton on banjo, mandolin, guitar and trumpet; Ralph Gibson on guitar; John Miller and Don Payne on bass; Ray Markowitz on drums; Armen Halburian and Barry Lazarowitz on percussion; Lewis Furey on viola and Erin Dickins and Emily Bindiger as vocalists; plus Leonard and John Lissaeur, who played, respectively, guitar and woodwind and keyboard.

The album cover (which was censored in the USA and Spain, a suitable cod-piece being found by an angel's false wing!) uses the symbolic representation of the *coniunctio spiritum* of the *Rosarium Philosophorum* of 1550 to project the unifying idea of the songs, which Leonard came across in the Jungian centre in Los Angeles when, he explained, significantly, "I was looking for an image to represent myself."

We saw Judy Collins' and Jennifer Warnes' reaction to it earlier, but this is another direct admission he made of a particular conflict in himself – that of the male and female principle – and one of strong purport. In his poem – later a song – 'Death Of A Lady's Man' (but was the singular there originally? He acknowledges that it went through 'many variations') there is a reference to it in the lines 'She mocked his female fashions' and 'He was trying hard to get/a woman's education/ but he's not a woman yet.' We are not here discussing effeminacy – still less any in Leonard as commonly understood; but of the *anima*, the feminine side of a man's nature. In Jungian terms the anima – 'an inherited collective image of woman,' is usually projected onto one's mother, sometimes one's wife and, if of a creative disposition, one's art. How interesting that Leonard, whose life has been adorned by female companions of varying duration, and whose vocation – in which women have such a high profile – has been subjected to certain changes, should admit to this at this time. And how interesting is the first title of the book of that song, though early abandoned: *The Woman Being Born!*

In an interview for *Melody Maker* in 1988, Kris Kirk stated that Leonard was, 'The first man in popular music to evince a genuinely feminised or perhaps androgynous mentality,' though he spoiled the insight by attaching it to a question as to whether Leonard had been involved in gay relationships (which received a categorical denial).

He uses the representation of the spiritual union of the male and female principles because its negation is the essential message of some of the songs. The album's title glosses this to suggest new hope arising out of disenchantment, which couples with the prevalent notes of forgiveness and determination. Said Leonard wistfully to us over his own shattered expectations from which they were drawn, "I know what she did to me; I don't know what I did to her." And Manzano repeats Leonard's admission to him of "never before having behaved as badly as with my wife." We shall hear similar things again from him, but never as clearly, nor as regretted. His experience was the ultimate 'low' in his life.

The chorus of the first song provides the title: 'Is This What You Wanted?' – to live in a house that is haunted/by the ghost of you and me.' As with so many of his poems and songs, it has an inner dialectic, a twin set of attributes shared between himself and his lover which move from self-accusation ('You were the promise at dawn; I was the morning after' etc), through an equality of status ('You were Marlon Brando; I was Steve McQueen . . .'), to a claim for his own superior condition:

'You got old and wrinkled; I stayed 17
You lusted after so many; I lay here with one
You defied your solitude; I came through alone
You said you could never love me; I undid your gown.'

But we are mistaken if we limit its application to some lovelorn state. Leonard frequently drew attention to the song referring to *two* dialogues: 'your exterior lover and your interior lover' – by which he pointed to the profoundest union of all. Is the only thing left, he repeatedly asks, this ghost of their true selves? Is their house so to be haunted? The chorus, twice repeated at the end, with rising voice, fades away into the stillness of a desolating non-answer, the first of several unanswered questions.

'Chelsea Hotel, 2' changes locations and contexts dramatically, which is a marked feature of the album's composition: from low to high, from earth to heaven, from the human to the divine – and back again. To the austere emptiness of the house is offered the bustle of a busy hotel; to its lack of communication is juxtaposed a mutual, if but superficial understanding; to the bad tempered arguments and vindictiveness of 'Is This What You Wanted?' is paralleled the caring and consoling relationship of two lovers caught up in the money-scramble of the day, only one of whom 'gets away', albeit through a terminal 'fix'. Sadly he 'remembers you well,' even though – still caught up in the rat-race himself – he doesn't 'think of you that often.' It is the tribute of a fellow-worker in song to the lost yet talented Janis Joplin who, used and abused by the industry, was too unprepared (or immature) for its heavy demands and sacrificed her life to excesses of every kind, an excess of excess in fact. (An interesting correlation between them is that Janis Joplin claimed that liquor and drugs had destroyed her memory, though she – like Leonard – could recall what was necessary when necessary!)

'Lover, Lover, Lover', one of his most performed songs, follows. It came out of his brief, if alarming, sojourn with the Israeli army at the time of the 1972 war, and was actually written in Sinai amid bullets, Leonard informed Manzano. It posits the reason for the break-up of his love-life, which lies at the core of his being: his Jewishness, or rather, his sense of failure as a Cohen. The song is a plea – to Father Abraham – that his name be changed; the name which in Hebrew thought signifies the person. He wants out! He is guilty as to how he has behaved; how his actions have demeaned the name. The answer is not complicity in his demands, but explanation: 'I locked you in this body, I meant it as a kind of trial . . .' He who had been superlatively tempted in the story of Isaac now passes on that same lesson, which is taken up positively:

'Then let me start again, I cried, please let me start again!
I want a face that's fair this time; I want a spirit that is calm.'

To start again, but differently! It is but the repetition of the original plea, slightly recast. So he is reminded of the patriarch's persistence: 'I never turned aside,' he said, 'I never walked away.' To this is added the reproach 'It was you who built the temple; it was you who covered up my face,' (an old prophetic denunciation for disobedience, or for doing the right things in the wrong way or at the wrong time). You cannot win with the One who commands, 'Walk before me, and be thou perfect,' unless you are an Abraham (and even his perfection was marred), but still there is hope:

'May the spirit of this song, may it rise up pure and free
May it be a shield for you a shield against the enemy'

He who was called 'the shield of Abraham' (shield = *mogen*: the same word that is used of the Jewish hexagram for the 'Star' of David – whose own imperfections disallowed him from building the temple) is now offered in the song as a shield for this son of Abraham. And so the spirit of the song – the loving relationship with even a failed son – is perpetuated: 'come back to me.' The unanswered pleas of his human relationships finds a more positive, more healing, response from the battlefields of old Israel.

'Field Commander Cohen' has been described as one of the most incomprehensible of Leonard's songs. But the frame of reference, his self-awareness as an artist and the battlefields of modern Israel, its place in the modern world as well as the delusions of revolution that he saw in Cuba, make it clear. The rank he gives himself, despite his family's and his name's prestige, is really a *jeux d'esprit*. It is the infiltration aspect that is mainly operative: he lives to propound 'the new revolution' to which he has frequently referred – in diplomatic parties, in failed revolutions like Castro's. From this he is invited to return, to:

'Leave it all, like a man; come back to nothing special
Such as waiting-rooms, and ticket-lines, silver-bullet
suicides, and messianic ocean tides, and
roller-coaster rides
And other forms of boredom, advertised as poetry!'

A viewpoint he was to reassess in 'First We Take Manhattan' – in which boredom again occurs. The failed mission requires rest and recuperation: he needs his sleep now . . . his life's been hard . . . even though many men continue to fall where he promised – nearly 30 years ago – to stand guard. His selfish and self-seeking prayer has been heard: that he be allowed to be 'this and nothing more/than just some grateful, faithful woman's singing millionaire/the patron saint of envy and the grocer of despair, working (like Janis Joplin and so many other workers-in-song) for the Yankee dollar,' a new twist on the feared American domination. Failed missions and unworthy dreams still do not block the ever-persistent invitation – to let these 'other selves be wrong. Yeah! let them manifest and come/till every taste is on the tongue, till love is pierced and love is hung/and *every* kind of freedom done.' Then – and only then (it is implied) – he will get his rest, that *spiritual* condition repeatedly held out to failing Israel which can only be known, like peace itself, when all the right elements are in place; when all the duties are completed. That peace, like sexual fulfilment itself, is the opposite of self-serving; it is the union of the two principles – male and female; divine and human.

Side one finishes on a note of reconciliation. But reconciliation in terms of a cessation of hostilities, of recognised incompatibilities. She does not need him; he must be allowed to go his way. It is not a question of being unwilling to go together: 'I'd *like* to take you to the ceremony . . .'; but the experience of 'Jack and Jill,' who are about to 'join their misery,' who have 'finally taken cover,' who have 'agreed to obey' those difficult vows – the ones 'for each other' – is too accurate. Think of what they are doing; do not prevent or hinder them, but 'try to do without him' yourself is the message, the only way whereby he can be true to himself, which is the opposite of self-serving. Behind it all is the sense of lostness generated in the realisation that the effort and optimism of the sixties was itself a failure. For all his rejection of guru-status, he had to admit that they had found no better than Castro, Nassar – or any other of the would-be leaders of the new age. It even overlapped into the sphere of sexuality: the new woman was appearing, strong, self-assertive and dominant; the men were on the retreat, not least into homosexuality, weakened by the war, fearful of its outcome.

The second side takes us back to the war, not between the Arabs and Israel, but the interminable war of which some (such as Wayman) are ignorant: the clashes within society – between rich and poor, between man and woman; between those who know it exists and those who do not; between left and right; between black and white – between the odd and the even. *The Boston Phoenix* understood Leonard's existentialist position in the matter, in reporting of it that 'Cohen challenges us . . . believing that life is not worth living unless it is lived honestly.' It is not so much an invitation, this time, as a command: 'Come on back'! The excuses fly: 'I live here with a woman and a child/ the situation makes me kind of nervous' – the very situation which most prevents him from doing his duty, from rejoining the deserted forces. Yet she does not appreciate what he is doing: 'You call this love; I call it service.' She cannot stand what he is trying to become in order to be true to himself; she prefers the easier man, whom she can control – and thus defeat – by deflecting him from his true destiny. 'Don't be a tourist' is the injunction: come on back . . . 'pick up your tiny burden,' says the voice; 'can't you hear me speaking?' Be honest, painful as it may be, to your convictions.

Such challenges to his manliness and courage raise the inveterate problem of his truthfulness – his faithfulness to the alpha and omega of his understanding, and therefore of his real vocation. 'A singer must die for the lie in his voice' is the accusation. Only acceptance – polite, humble, and full – will do:

> *'And I thank you, I thank you, for doing your duty;*
> *you keepers of truth; you guardians of beauty.*
> *Your vision is right, my vision is wrong,'*
> *I'm sorry for smudging the air with my song'*

He admits, beyond the acceptance (within which veiled irony lurks: their doing their 'duty'; their keeping 'the truth'; their observance of the 'vision') that he took refuge in the love of a woman, and in that of a woman 'I would like to forgive.' But is it real, this accusation? Have they indeed the vision true? Is it not simple fear of them – the fear of man that operates a snare – that causes him to confess? Their actions condemn them; as does their unwarranted use of violence. The song breaks out into social protest. He betrayed *them*, not a higher power; *their* vision, not his own. Hence the heavy sarcasm:

> *'Yes! And long live the state, by whoever it's made*
> *Sir. I didn't see nothing (sic), I was just getting*
> *home late.'*

The mood of his next song 'I Tried To Leave You', the woman whom he liked to forgive, is totally contradictory. Caught as he is between loyalty and love, principle and purpose, he sought to leave her 'at least a hundred times.' Even though he knows she would be better on her own, he wakes up 'every morning by your side.' So the years go by, pride is lost, he stays at home, his work remains undone. But at least he's here, for her: 'a man, still working for her smile.' A tenuous position, given her inability to understand him, the narrowness of her vision.

From which, contradictorily, he catapults his listeners back to his higher duties.

'Who By Fire?', based on a prayer recited at the sacred time of atonement – when reconciliation is effected, echoes the response-to-the-voice that repeatedly finds expression in his later work. But the context to the original prayer is one of judgment; a call to self-examination. There can be no reconciliation without that, is the inference. In whatever experience or danger man faces – fire or water, sunshine or night-time, in high ordeal or common trial, etc – who can be said to be calling? Who? is the resonant question which throbs and trembles throughout this song. Whose is the unseen, ubiquitous voice? Who is calling? Clearly a power that dominates the experiences, that is heard over the dangers. But who?

And from such heights we are returned to the everyday experience of mankind, man's loving and his needs in love, by which juxtapositioning Leonard signals again the importance of the union – the eternal completion of body and soul, male and female, of God and man. 'Take This Longing' reflects the depths of longing that all feel, he appears to say, which are a signpost to something else, another voice, another calling. Man is not the measure of his own soul. Hear that longing well! Be true to that vision, that song! This is a song which long plagued his mind – from the mid-sixties, when Buffy Sainte-Marie covered his earlier version (called 'The Bells') through six or seven years of wanderings around America, Israel and Ethiopia, until it reached the present form 'in the shed on St Dominique Street in Montreal' in 1973. Whilst not performed so regularly as other songs, it may well be rated one of his best – in mood and tone, and sheer poetic depth:

> 'Your body like a searchlight
> my poverty revealed . . .

> 'Let me see your beauty broken down
> Like you would do
> for one you love'

Perhaps it was listening to Nico – the German model-cum-singer who recorded with The Velvet Underground and became a companion of Warhol – of whom Leonard was enamoured (though failing to win her charms), that inspired the poetic depths, even if the cynicism of the song is well-nigh crushing, both in its portrayal of her promiscuities:

> 'Hungry as an archway
> through which the troops have passed
> I stand in ruins behind you
> With your winter clothes
> your broken sandal-straps.'

And her loyalty to someone else:

'You're faithful to the better man.
I'm afraid that he left . . .'

He is caught up in the anguish of infatuation – or is it true love? – for which he will do anything:

'I'll even wear these old laurel leaves
that he's shaken from his head
just take this longing from my tongue
and all the useless things these hands have done . . .'

The same thoughts occupy 'Leaving Greensleeves' a song with a very long and honoured history, going back, some would say, to Elizabethan times (even to that all-time royal lover himself, Henry VIII), which completes the album, even as it turns full circle on the earlier themes of being wronged; offering love and forgiveness; yet, being rejected still, he too takes off. Within it he faces bluntly the experience of being 'wronged', cast out discourteously; he who had loved her so long, who had delighted in her company. Even her disdain of him awakens his heart – her lover 'in captivity.' He repeats, as in 'The singer must die,' that 'I sang my songs, I told my lies' in order to consummate their love, hoping that she would change, respect him, start to understand. But she has gone. And so, amid his futile appeals, 'I'm going, too.' Such agony! Such disruption! and yet: it's so easily done 'leaving the Lady Greensleeves.' The union is irreparably broken.

in dying, reborn

To Billy Walker, editor of *Sounds*, Leonard had commented a few years previously:

"An artist responds to necessities within his soul as everybody else does, or should. It takes you where it leads you. It can take you to a minor work; it can lead you into silence. It leads you into what it needs for its own survival, and if you're obedient or if you're sensitive to the sound of your own self then you'll follow it."

In this he was giving voice to what, musically, he offered in 'New Skin For The Old Ceremony'. He has responded to his necessities – painful as they were – allowed them to be heard, and followed them, not into silence but into the full glare of a public career, which now provided the opportunity for a double promotion. For, following hard on the new album's release came the release of his film *Bird On The Wire*, which was premièred in London at the Rainbow Theatre. It had cost him $120,000; the original version (produced by Tony Palmer) had failed to please him. As with other things – his first book of poetry, his first album – control was crucial, so he set his hand to edit it himself during a six-month stay in London, steering it away from what he termed Palmer's 'visual clichés' to demonstrate the deeper realities of his music; showing the conditions under which it was produced, how he interacted with his audiences; the emotions he evoked and channelled; and altering the film from its original 'artiness' to a documentary of the sound, the voice, within the music.

It was a good way to embark on his third European tour, his largest to date, which took him from Brussels to Eastbourne (the centre, that year, of the two day CBS sales convention), on to Paris, Edinburgh, Glasgow, Manchester, Newcastle, Liverpool, Bristol, Brighton, Sheffield, Birmingham, Brighton (again), London,

Copenhagen, Berlin, Dusseldorf, Hamburg, Munich, Cologne (for two consecutive nights), Rotterdam, Amsterdam, Heidelberg (also two nights), Frankfurt and Vienna. They played two nights at Barcelona where he dedicated the concerts to the memory of Federico Garcia Lorca and his 25-year influence on his life, and at Madrid, the intellectual home of Lorca, though unhappily this concluded with a disagreement between him and Spanish television, which wanted to record him singing 'The Partisan', imposing female voices Leonard found unacceptable; then back to Paris for two further nights. So great was the acclaim he secured in Spain that arrangements were immediately undertaken to translate his works into Spanish, which commenced a tie which has only been strengthened through the years. In all, 33 concerts in 50 days, from September 1 to October 19.

With him toured John Lissaeur, Jeff Layton, Johnny Miller, Erin Dickens and Emily Bindiger, all of whom had participated in the recording of the album. It was a punishing schedule, not least due to Leonard's policy of giving generous value for money, on which basis his sets now frequently offered between 26 and 31 songs, plus various improvisations – for example, 'The Shelter Of The Darkness', and 'Strangers In Town'. At Olympia, Paris, the second concert commenced at one am! At this Graeme Allwright offered his own improvisation – 'Mr Cohen must be going' – which involvement deepened Allwright's popular covering of many of Leonard's songs in French, begun in 1968.

Steve Turner reported on the London concert (which was rounded off by no less than six encores, though one reporter made it 10!), saying that the new songs 'provided light in a collection of songs which can amount to continuous shade.' It was always an overstatement – 'Suzanne', 'Sisters Of Mercy', 'Bird On The Wire', 'Tonight Will Be Fine', 'Famous Blue Raincoat' all condemn such negativism. But the differences he felt in Leonard's performance, he noted, in terms of his having 'discovered rhythm and broken away from the formula that created his first four albums,' emphasise that real artistic maturation was well under way. The word was getting through, not least by arresting chords and emphatic harmonies – his words thereby being charmed into the souls of his listeners: lip to lip and heart to heart, meditatively and otherwise.

Perhaps it is unfair to criticise a journalist for his stereotypes, but when Turner refers to 'his two-year lay-off' (by which he meant that Leonard had been out of *his* line of vision for two years!) one can see how easy they are to pass on – a few moments' idle scribbling – and how damaging they may be to an artist's reputation and career. Almost every interview from this time led with a comment about the depressive quality of his songs, his voice, his music, often sarcastically; that he was about to retire again, or how near he was to suicide. And the journalists who scoffed at this – and continue to do so today – fail to understand his closeness to real tragedy – such as the deaths by suicide of Tim Buckley and later Phil Ochs, former luminaries both, and now dead friends, in the most depressing of circumstances.

Some years later, his song 'First We Take Manhattan' refers to such myopia in its first line: 'They sentenced me to 20 years of *boredom*/ for trying to change the system from within.' Leonard was not a pot-boiler, nor was he ever willing to take the quick and easy route to success: he grinds his flour slowly, from his own corn, and simply refused – to his great cost – to operate slickly or superficially. It came from deep within, this art, and was carefully constructed to preserve its proper accuracy, a reflection of the real world which is often pained and strung-out.

Between the London and Copenhagen concerts he celebrated his 40th birthday – understanding now to the fore, and becoming profounder all the time, justifying the decision of the Royal Albert Hall to allow him to perform there, when 99 per cent of other 'popular' musicians were refused. On his return to America he was invited to join an Earle Scruggs' session, alongside such worthies as Scruggs himself (an idol of the fifties and sixties, famous for his 'hillbilly' rhythms), his brothers Gary and Randy, Roger McGuinn (of The Byrds), Reggie Young, Billy Joel (whose career was to boom in the next few years) and Willie Hall. The vocalists were no less eminent: Joan Baez, Buffy Sainte-Marie, Ramblin' Jack Elliot, and The Pointer Sisters. One of the numbers covered was 'Passin' Thru', to which Leonard's name was now firmly attached.

Following this he took his group on a tour of North America and Canada, commencing in New York on November 29 at the Bottom Line and finally closing on March 4 at Phoenix. (It was not only his 'neurotic affiliations' that he renewed on these returns to his homeland. As he had said a few months earlier to Grace Lichtenstein of *The New York Times* – where the point had particular application! – "I love Trudeau, I love Rene Levesque, I love the *fleur de lys*, I love the maple leaf, I love the idea of an independent Quebec, I love the idea of a Canada from ocean to ocean." The Statue of Liberty was observed smiling a little self-consciously at the time. Connections abounding!)

Once again their routine was demanding, averaging 26 songs per concert, and covering the much greater distances between New York (six concerts), Los Angeles (six concerts), Hamilton and London, Toronto, Passaic, Boston, Philadelphia, New York (again) and Montreal (which was the last time he performed there for 10 years.) After the concert he had one of his relapses into anguish over his deteriorating domestic condition, and so wrote: 'Across the street from her. Snow between us . . . You forgot your noble birth. And now she begins to remind you . . .' then on to Minneapolis, Berkeley and Phoenix, the latter place occasioning another song, as we shall see.

Not surprisingly, a good rest followed – not the 'lay-off' referred to by Turner – but the chance to reconnect with his family, to seek that reconciliation his individuality and destiny forbade, and to recharge his mental and spiritual batteries. His house on Hydra was the most apposite place to do this, well away from easy visiting, without a telephone, and hidden on the henspecked hillside above the harbour. So complete was his withdrawal that, in releasing his spectacular new album 'Desire' in 1975, Bob Dylan dedicated it to him: "This is for Leonard," he commented dryly, "if he's still here!" Dylan himself was wont to have 'lay-offs' from time to time, sometimes voluntary, sometimes enforced – as when he fell off his motorcycle – this 'Peter Pan of the throttle bums . . . something is happening and it ain't the ordinary kind of sound . . . and carrrrashhh and technicolor passion of berserk and Napoleonic and suicide . . . and the redblooded boy oozing all over . . . the defunct rockabilly . . .' The 'silence' created by these absences gave rise to other comments about Leonard, one of which John Bauldie wrote in a piece on Dylan's song – 'Dirge' in *The Telegraph:*

'No wonder then, that he's glad the curtain fell. It fell on a slave who had been beaten till he's tame. Where's the Lenny of yesteryear? The angry young ironist? And what was it all for? All for a moment's glory . . .'

Even in his successes the curtain fell for Leonard (of which he wrote in *The Energy Of Slaves:* 'you can call me Lenny now'), but in a different way; and he was not so much tamed as disillusioned (the word is Leonard's own) by his successes. Unlike many poets, particularly in the academic circles he decried, where poetry was written and admired for poetry's sake – to Leonard's way of thinking the quietus of art, which he believed must be functional: *doing* something, *saying* something (in Hebrew thought 'saying' is much more dynamic, words *do* things, achieve goals – not least in the service of the divine: 'he spake and it was done'). They were not merely decorative or ornamental.

His viewpoint differed from that of Seneca, who saw art as 'the imitation of nature' (except and insofar as it shared some reality with nature). His own view was much more operational: offering a broad discrimination between Hebrew and Greek modes of understanding as well as living: the Jew will sit under his fig-tree, and study; the Greek will sit under his fig-tree, and sit! And Leonard knew that the glory – so very different from that to which Dylan referred here – was indeed momentary. But in his very escape from 'the foolish game' of the pop world, when 'the side-shows' tended 'to take over' and envelop their victims, the depressing difference between dream and reality, daily-life and destiny would pierce through. He describes it in 'I Knelt Beside A Stream' (in *Death Of A Lady's Man*) in which he contrasted his former 'thin' state with the present, which was dated 'spring or summer of 1975,' in which an unsettling silence had been forced on him:

> '*Now I lie in a pool of fat, ashamed before the daisies to be what I am. Eight years ago, and then the obscure silence of my career, while the butchers climbed . . . and hacked . . . I was divided into three parts. One part was given to a wife, one part was given to money, one part was given to the daisies . . . Distant battle you may say, but God, how ugly your stripes are . . . And you are the winners!*'

The mood is continued in the blue-striped Italian Notebook, also from the summer of 1975 whose 'schizoid' state is precipitated by his double vision (which contrasts with the 'dimmed' vision in 'Dress Rehearsal Rag'), in which 'boredom' festers, in both professional and domestic spheres:

> '*Just now I actually saw two doves come down toward me in the style of the Holy Spirit descending . . . I have been sitting in a café for 25 years waiting for this vision. I surrender to the iron laws of the moral universe, which make a boredom out of everything desired. I will go back to my dark companion. I don't think I will . . .*'

His revolt against domesticity, or at least the limiting sort in which he felt enslaved, which had not only fragmented his conception of the Dove but alienated even the Baal Shem, finds despondent expression in this piece (from 'The Rebellion'):

> '*I rebelled against Domestic Conversation. All is calm now. I chained myself to the stone floor for an hour-and-a-half. No butterflies, not that I care . . . I am grumpy because I cannot indicate the vastness of my heart . . . I took a ghost to bed . . . I tried to crush her into some confession I cannot imagine, an unconditional apology . . . This damn case fits right over me, this iron spirit maiden.*'

He had reflected on his journey to Israel, '. . . and the priesthood forced me to resume/my old domestic conversations.' He got over his rebelliousness. He 'cleared the garden, perfumed his anger, established her sexual beauty and raised the graven image of a spiritual worker among the daisies, and began to worship it.' But to no lasting avail. The voice that he heard in such moods was his own, the voice of lost opportunities, recrimination, of conscience. As the Stratford Bard perceived:

'. . . Conscience doth make cowards of us all.
And thus the native hue of resolution
Is sickled o'er with the pale cast of thought.'

His worst reflections centred on the paling of his thought, his imagination: 'The Lord is faster than you/this is the working of sloth.' 'Why do you halt (limp along) between two opinions?' one had asked long ago. Leonard was now caught in that debilitating condition, sure of the irreconcilability of their relationship, and made desperate by a deeper principle to achieve it. As he said to Alberto Manzano, showing the precise orientation of his concern:

"I believe that a society cannot exist without (the) basic family unit (*unidad basica a la familia*). It is the only way to educate (the) children . . . Its destruction can put at risk the whole of society . . . I believe that it is the only form in which man and woman can live together."

Pressed by Manzano, Leonard was more than shaken, more than apprehensive. The experience, and the threat to those he loved most, was proving highly risky – not to say destructive.

The discipline of 'three pages a day' never left him, and even if he was not 'blackening pages' he would be reflecting – often with 'twisted feet' in the lotus position of his Zen Buddhism – endlessly meditating on life and love, male and female, soul and body: his landscape, at once traditionalist and surrealist, rarely serene; contrarieties abounding, connections scarce. As the proverb has it: 'the heart of man and the bottom of the sea are unfathomable.'

A 'pot-boiler' was produced by CBS at this time: 'The Best Of Leonard Cohen' (in Britain it was called 'Leonard Cohen's Greatest Hits'). The songs, culled in the usual way from previous albums, were: 'Suzanne', 'Sisters Of Mercy', 'So Long, Marianne', 'Bird On The Wire', 'Lady Midnight', 'The Partisan', 'Hey, That's No Way To Say Goodbye', 'Famous Blue Raincoat', 'Last Year's Man', 'Chelsea Hotel No 2', 'Who By Fire', 'Take This Longing'. It pleased the fans but, not unexpectedly, did not please the critics. The cult of novelty was now firmly entrenched; sated appetites required titillation, stale minds needed *divertissement*, jaded feelings craved for stimulation – more and more, newer and newer. One who did achieve some credit for newness was Judy Collins who, in one of her rare public performances from this time, offered another selection of Leonard's songs. Said *Billboard*, 'She seems most at home on Leonard Cohen tunes and reads new meaning into each one . . . unlike many performers. Ms Collins displays a human side that few others show. She is one of the last of the folk breed.'

Happily, Leonard fared better with CBS Disques France, in whose lists he was named as one of their top selling artists alongside

Simon And Garfunkel and David Essex. (CBS Switzerland likewise were doing well with him, and published a 'thank you' for it, at the time of an otherwise undisclosed visit. As did CBS Israel.) *Concert Canadien*, a 10-part documentary on Canadian artists (which ignored the disillusionment of punk) included Buffy Sainte-Marie, Ian and Sylvia and Leonard, among others. Talking to Jack McDonough of San Francisco, Leonard made his own observation:

"Nothing at all succeeded the hippies. That's what's beautiful about it. There are no definitions possible now. It's a condition I find easier to operate in. When people don't know who they are, they start getting in contact with more elements of their nature and are easier to approach."

Creedless and conceptless as ever; and ever himself, and becoming more so!

His fourth European tour – called by Karl Dallas his 'prolific phase' – again broke records for places visited and concerts performed – 55 in 78 days through late April, May, June and early July. They commenced in Berlin, then to Hamburg, Frankfurt, Ludwigshafen, Munster, Dusseldorf, Cologne, Saarbrucken, Mainz, Stuttgart and Munich then across to Dublin, and over the Irish Sea to Oxford, Leicester, Sheffield, Glasgow, Edinburgh, Newcastle, Southport, Manchester, Birmingham, Plymouth, Portsmouth, Bristol and London, from which – with but a four-day gap – he went on to Oslo, Gothenburg; then Amsterdam and Copenhagen; down to Paris (for four days of concerts, again at Olympia) and on to Rheims, Brussels, Vienna, Graz, Linz, Nurnburg, Karlsruhe, Zurich, Strasburg, Nancy, Montreux (where he played at the famous Casino), Besançon, Dijon, Lyon, back to Vienna, and then back to London for two concluding concerts at the New Victoria Theatre.

Once again the sets were large, frequently offering over 30 songs as his repertoire increased, some of which have still to be issued: 'Everybody's Child', '*Die Gedanken Sind Frei*' (a German folk-song from the 18th century), 'Do I Have To Dance All Night', and 'Store Room'. For the Dubliners he re-introduced his habit of combining poetry-reading with his songs ('I Did Not Know'; 'Come Down To My Room'; 'A Person Who Eats Meat'; 'The 15-Year-Old Girls'; 'It's Good To Sit With People'; 'Under Ben Bulben, Part V' – as he did riskily for the more sedate folk of Southport and those at Gothenburg (where he also offered 'The Music Crept By Us') and at the later of his Paris concerts.

Frequently his concerts were broadcast on local radio, or excerpted for television, though he also made special recordings for them. The level of interviewing had risen considerably, too, by which his life was endlessly examined, relived, analysed and displayed. Such repeated exposure increased his tendency to hoodwink those members of the press who came armed with misinformation previously fed into their files, which elongated, truncated and refabricated his career, according to whim and journalistic motive. Surprise was often registered at his charm, his politeness, his wide-ranging knowledge, his 'literaryness' (as Michael Watts called it on one occasion); the scorn of previous hacks was both demolished and reinforced, as was his standing as a writer, a musician, a singer. He had learned the art of enduring in the heat of the kitchen – to use Nixon's phrase – but its boredom was a diet that he found indigestible.

The musicians presently on tour were Sid McGuinness (guitar), Luther Rix (drums), Fred Thaylor (keyboards), and vocalists Cheryl Barner and Laura Brannigan – the latter was shortly to have distinguished success as a solo artist. Despite the pressures, they appreciated his songs and made good music with him: 'The whole mood among the Cohen entourage,' commented Karl Dallas in *Melody Maker* 'which has often been so heavy on past tours was so up, and especially his band . . .' And Michael Kidy reported for *Melody Maker* that Leonard is 'a changed man these days – gone is the doom and gloom . . . a man at his funkiest and wittiest . . . . a positively riveting performance. The difference is quite startling.'

On stage, before his eager followers and listeners, Leonard continued to excel – the word, the sound, the vision, was breaking through. There, almost alone in his 'meditations', each song was recreated afresh, each experience accurately transcribed – lip to lip, heart to heart. But the one who had never failed to refer to being 'wiped out', broken-down, finished, was in fact going into one of his most painful crises.

By this time Lorca had been born, a sister for his toddler son, Adam; but Leonard knew that his present relationship was doomed. Try as he might to stabilise it, to safeguard his lover's and his children's happiness, the mismatch gnawed at his soul; the vision threatened to dim yet more. His ethics exacerbated the situation for, love her as he did, he was torn apart by the stronger realisation of their essential incompatibility, and Jewish law forbids cohabitation if the woman knows that the man purposes to leave her. It made intensely solemn the puckish humour of the rabbis, 'a second wife is like a wooden leg,' and intimidating their sage warning, 'the first wife pulls the wagon; the second wife rides on the seat.'

So to Los Angeles he returned, where he bought a second house with some fellow-students close to his Zen master, Roshi, where he could find that solitude for which he yearned. His fourth 'novel', though dead, was now put together in a less hurtful manner, as he saw it, breaking up the sequences, making general the earlier statements of their life together. He sought to highlight her beauty, emphasise her charms, and stress the pleasant side of their life and love, but somehow it came out differently; the antagonisms burst through, the bitterness erupted, the disappointments and frustrations cascaded from the pages. It was, of course, the *death* of a lady's man of which he wrote, a living death.

The book, in some ways like his album, is a surging, kaleidoscopic *dénouement* of the inner man. It pulses with the energy of a man in crisis, fighting for his life, his integrity, breathless in the fear of losing it all; ultimate *angst*. From this erupts imagery of tremendous range and vitality; the book bristles with descriptive comment coursing from Eden's garden to Armageddon, from the initial alpha of their experience to the omega of its failed realisation. It surges between past and present, traverses his duties, his calling; it overleaps his life in Montreal, Hydra, New York, Franklin and Los Angeles; it sweeps across his thoughts and convictions. A mood of grim reality predominates, and its colour is black; black as the night, black as the stormiest day, black as the most cynical, piercing humour.

But, unlike the album, it is never reckless, even when it drops its guard. It was dedicated to his mother! This was not the first of his works so to be dedicated, she who had worried and cajoled him, loved and admired him, throughout his turbulent, changing career. The first was in *The Favourite Game*, but only in the British/Canadian edition. The American edition (whose cover picture has a startling likeness to Suzanne) was produced by offset-litho procedures from the British paperback edition which was dedicated to '------, as promised': the new lady in his life?

What his mother made of it we do not know, this elegant, wise lady from the East, half-Westernised, and deeply Jewish in the Hasidic sense of following the Baal Shem Tov, who opposed the formalised and casuistic learning of the western rabbis, extolling a simple faith in, and a joyous response to, everyday life and pleasure; a spontaneous, vivacious Judaism – of dancing and clapping and singing; one full of anecdotes and epigrams, to whom the fates had not been over-kind. She could recognise the pain and the honesty of its pages, be a little relieved perhaps at the partial return of the prodigal, cheered by the reminiscences he evoked of their former, united family life, when his father was alive.

Even if she understood it no better than Leonard, she agreed that 'all that happens is divine,' to use the Catholic novelist Leon Bloy's caricature of providence, which was a support when the storms blew. Her own homespun philosophy to him, through thick and thin (or should we say, fat and thin?) was, 'Follow your little heart' – the foundations had been laid; she could trust them to safeguard the edifice.

She agreed, too, with her compatriot Nicholos Berdyaev: 'God has laid upon man the duty of being free, of safeguarding freedom of spirit, no matter how difficult that may be, or how much sacrifice and suffering it may require.' She had so lived herself, and this book was a tribute to that youthful, courageous, mystical spirit which continually challenged and beckoned Leonard.

But it was the 'sacrifice and the suffering' that most worried him as he wrote first *A Woman Being Born*, then *My Life In Art*, then its several recensions. Not that which he caused himself – such was positive suffering: 'clean tears', holy-work, for which he was determined to continue. No, the sacrifice and the suffering he drew back from was that which he was bound to cause others – his 'second family' in particular. But the pact that he had made to himself when commencing *Beautiful Losers*, 10 years or so previously, was still in force. He could not welsh on his commitments to his art: the truth, accuracy, must predominate.

The resulting book is therefore much more a journey of renewal, following the path to forgiveness (of which we shall see much more) than merely 'the death of a lady's man.' It is that – as much as it could be to one of his nature – but much more. It reveals him 'divided' as never before; a schizoid state of loving and despising, of hoping and rejecting, of intense familial concern and desperate self-expression. As he said in one recension, 'I broke under the sentence of loneliness, and the wound of my beautiful twin.' Not so much divided as paraphrenic in his ambiguity.

The book resonates with this quest for oneness, for acceptance, this hunger for spiritual reawakening, as well as the sadder reiterations of their life and struggles. Indeed, the bold – though often disguised – cataloguing of them, is itself a path to forgiveness (the doctrine of 'complaint', which is the psychological counterpart to what the scientists term 'the suicide connection,' in which large electric motors running at full speed are thrown into reverse to neutralise stored energy, thus 'killing' its own magnetic field and renewing its potential for fuller running) as he embraced 'a position of uncompromising unforgiveness' in order to claim the 'surprises and rewards that follow in the wake of the undiluted expression of one's hateful seizures.' And they were hateful, for which he hated himself; and unforgivable, for which he could not forgive himself; even when he was himself very wounded through them (a wounding that would issue in his determination "not to be shattered again by love," as he said to Herve Muller of *Rock And Folk*).

The book, in prose and poetry, in narrative and diary form, with Coleridgean-type commentary, describes that death – and the life beckoning beyond it. Said Stephen Spender of the poetic enterprise:

'what matters is exploring one's soul, not putting oneself on show and in competition.' So here, *but* – and even more so – not aimed at putting those he loved 'on show': a caring, accurate, exploration; from which a true word issued.

Leonard explained that he felt duty-bound 'to protect the orphan and the widow' in New York, where he had met 'Alexandra' (the conqueror? or shades of Henry Miller?). Whatever, he later changes her name to Chandra: if he cannot have her, at least he can exercise the male 'prerogative' of renaming her! Despite her great beauty, her perfect body and athletic distinction (she was a dancer), she had 'a hand of chrome' which led him, he confessed in 1975, into '10 years of obscene silence' in his career. He remembers that he had made a treaty with those who *saw* (remember 'Do Not Pass Me By'?), but he broke it 'under torture' – the torture of the mismatched man. The problem was that his lover was 'bound to the world' – by babies and incessant baby-talk, a wordless gargle; moreover, he hated the remembrance of her 'swooning' in Poet's Corner, overwhelmed by his genius. She disliked his drug-taking, the particular orientation of his work, his lifestyle.

He failed in his attempts at reconciliation – he 'scattered his heart and made everyone uncomfortable'; he blamed God for 'entering him into a quarrel with a woman' and taking away his music: 'You were so beautiful as a song. You are so ugly as a god.' Like Job of old, he complains that God 'has hedged him in'; he renounces his work, his vision, his life – 'a worthless piece of junk.' The voice of conscience pricks deeply at his lechery, but he is concerned at 'disturbing another's heart' – surely fleeting encounters are better than that pain? He is pained by his frivolity, his inaction in the face of need and opportunity; by the lies in his life – or, at least, his 'stinginess to the truth.' He condemns the 'thuggery' of his criticising her, of rejecting her, of failing to give her his blessings.

He never knew her. She never revealed who she was. She passively left him to love her alone – there was no real depth to their lives together. Its shallowness tore him apart, as did his conflicting allegiances within it. Like concentric circles, their lives overlapped. He craved unity: the One Heart is 'the engine of energy' he said (an incidental fusion of the two great intimacies which were now so painfully disparate); there should only be one heart between them, their separate lives exposed the falsity of their 'armoured spirits'. Her beauty was insubstantial, it touched the periphery of his life and feelings but quenched the deeper longings. He could no longer listen to Lilith; he could no longer endure the bickerings; the disorder – seen as laziness and filth! – of their lives; he could not support the denial – worse, the scorning – of his traditions. He was all but buried in this 'cemetery of love.'

If only she would care for music! His work was alive; he had resurgent feelings of mercy; he felt allowed 'to come near' (like the temple-priests of old); words could flow again; a room waited for him; he could relearn – earn his solitude; hear again 'the still, small voice'; reopen his book. This fulfilment would enable him to render into common usage the high commands of pure energy (whose destruction was the nerve-centre of his complaint). But the price had to be paid by both of them: 'this is the house that you must leave to be free.' Spring came – the covenant of renewal, new life, new hope; when the Name made itself felt in more creative, life-giving ways. 'How does the humiliated spirit find its way out of the dead Kabala?' he asked. His heart 'longed to be a chamber for the Name.' 'Fill me with the Name, O Most High,' he prayed. 'I swim in your love, but I drown in loneliness.' 'Allow me the Name!' he implored. 'Without the Name I am a funeral in the garden . . . without the Name I am ashamed. Without the Name, I bear false witness to the glory . . . Let me continue!' His life, his existence, trembled on the edge of non-being.

Whispers from the past came through, of former loves, previous unity, fulfilling unions. His mind was seized by the discordance between darkness and light – between ignorance and comprehension, 'between blurred vision and clarity.' ("In my second relationship," he admitted to us, "there was a sense of alienation, a betrayal of vision." But worse, it dried up his inspiration; the muse withdrew; the destiny distanced itself yet more. In the year in which Dylan's divorce was granted, Leonard's own painful break-up from Suzanne appeared to be permanent.) She could not measure up to the standard his vision imposed –'You would have to be blonde for that,' he significantly comments. The accusations, the charges, turn into a song: 'Death Of A Ladies' Man':

> 'She took his much admired
> oriental frame of mind
> and the heart of darkness alibi
> his money hides behind
> She took his blonde madonna
> and his monastery wine –
> 'This mental space is occupied
> and everything is mine.'
>
> 'She took his tavern parliament,
> his cap, his cocky dance,
> she mocked his female fashions
> and his working-class moustache . . .'

The resultant realities of this vanity-fair experience were sheer pain and nauseating emptiness:

'So the Great Affair is over
but whoever would have guessed
it would leave us all so vacant
and so deeply unimpressed . . .'

Vacuity is but a step from futility, and both are well-served by frivolity. If the anguish he registered throughout this book is the price they both paid for their misjudgments, the unreason (ever the other side of the coin of frivolity) wrought emotional trauma of the deepest kind. There was unreason – flaring anger, vindictiveness, hurtful comment and pointless acts of folly and passion, such as all suffer from who give themselves to impercipience and superficiality. In this, as in other aspects of life, one sows the wind and reaps the whirlwind. Thus he yearned for an Egyptian bullet to quell the pain; but, alas! 'there is the bullet, but there is no death'! The self-recrimination (of his promiscuities, falsehoods, unfaithfulnesses) frequently turns into wider complaint – against his lover, his society, history itself. But, the more he sees and castigates, the more 'the working of Mercy breaks through'; the greater the pangs over his futilities, the higher soars the hope of restoration; the further the inroads into mindless acts, the brighter glows the oncoming vision: the lady's man might be dying but – through that death, as through a bitter Canadian winter – the oftener impinge the stabs of new life.

Of a piece with this travailing experience is the sixth album, 'Death Of A Ladies' Man', which actually preceded it. The plural is important. Angry and humiliated as he was, mercy had begun to break through. And in a true sense it was a necessary plural – he mourned the multiplicity of his liaisons, not least his two great loves, Marianne and Suzanne, even as he regretted the 'obscene silence' into which he had been plunged. (Suzanne appears on the cover of this album with her friend Ava Gordon, taken at the Kontiki restaurant.)

It was Leonard's lawyer, Marty Machat, who introduced him to the paranoiac Phil Spector – he acted for both of them. And Leonard welcomed the opportunity to have dinner with this legend of a man, even then only 36-years-old. He, too, had lost his father early in life – 'To know him is to love him' (itself a biblical collation: 'knowing' and 'loving') was inscribed on Spector Snr's tombstone, from which his son at only 18-years-of-age composed and arranged a song that made the top of the charts by the end of 1958. (Leonard was then working in his uncle's factory in Montreal, and recalls being charmed by the sound as well, no doubt, as by the deep sentiment conveyed.)

Leonard's fans tend to overlook his part in the arrangements – as if he were unaware of Spector's use of sound (the famous 'wall of sound' technique) and his use of echo with which Ellie Greenwich accused him of going 'crazy'. But Leonard did know, and looked forward to their collaboration as a step forward for his own music. As Stephen Scobie opined, this album 'is the record that Cohen always wanted to make . . . who better than Phil Spector to realise Cohen's ideals of pop music?' The internal bedlam out of which he was emerging invited such thoughts, no doubt. But the results were far from acceptable, to Leonard not least, and came out of a year's collaboration no less. In the process he not only 'lost control of the music' – as if, with Spector he may ever have had it (!) but also lost full claim to his words – all the songs are claimed as a Spector-Cohen collaboration: in that order! Even those which had previously been published under Leonard's sole name. And one of them – the scabrous 'Don't Go Home With Your Hard-On' – had actually been performed publicly by him at Bryn Mawr in 1975.

What was some sort of ego-trip for Spector became a spectral-haunt for Leonard, whose turbulent relationships were thereby trans-formed into another nightmare. The relationship was not helped by his finding Spector's house 'dark and cold' – the very antithesis of his own home, where light and warmth predominate, of the internal as well as the decorative sort. As Leonard has commented, he hoped to find Spector in his Debussy period, but had to deal with him in a Wagnerian mood instead.

The hope had grown out of what he perceived to be the failure of 'New Skin For The Old Ceremony'. The delicate arrangements of John Lissaeur found there had not completely worked for Leonard; "my heart was not in it," he admitted. And so to the Debussy – or Chopin – that he heard in Spector he went, hopefully as ever. Manzano says that they wrote 15 songs together, in three weeks, but the process was not as simple as that. They were, essentially, Leonard's own words; "Some of the most autobiographical texts I've ever written," he stated. *Billboard* called it, 'a noteworthy collaboration,' calling attention to Leonard's 'vivid images, in proper syntax, that separates them from the conven-tional word-groupings of standard artists.' It went on to highlight Spector revealing 'a new side to Cohen that older fans may seem confused by . . . he has gone rock and roll.' And it judged his motivations as 'a sell-out to the rewards of commercialism'!

Of the eight songs recorded on the album, only one – 'Memories' – was offered to the public in subsequent years. ('Iodine' had a very occasional airing – at three concerts only, in fact). This is a pity, for there is some very fine poetry as well as song on the album – and credit should be given to Spector for the melodious arrangements of 'True Love Leaves No Traces' (no trace of a scar here!), 'I Left A Woman Waiting' and the title track 'Death Of A Ladies' Man'. Indeed, had not

the music been engulfed by sound, the sensibilities by sheer technological brutality, it may well have been placed among Leonard's finest, if his
earthiest.

'As The Mist Leaves No Scar', Leonard's poem from his early
period on Hydra in quatrain form of three stanzas (or was it from an
earlier love, courtesy of the Canadian Arts Council?) is here attached to
a bitter-sweet recollection of unrequited love and familial concerns:
'the children come and the children go . . ./like shackles made of snow.'
The love is not so much unrequited as unfulfilled: 'True love leaves no
traces/If you and I are one': their tragedy was that it was not 'lost in our
embraces,' but emblazoned across their memories – not in any 'shield of
Abraham' way but in the pierced defences of injured pride and self-
respect. The union for which he yearned, of body and soul, was
disfigured and discarded; scars here remained, and hurt – long after the
anger had died away. That sharpness of affront and injury was
described in 'Iodine', where his needs and his risks were shared. He
loved her – 'till he was a failure,' he 'failed at love,' but was nevertheless
made 'to serve out his time.' She was compassion, she was pity – but
with 'the sting of iodine.'

In 'Paper-Thin Hotel' his sorrows are mitigated somewhat;
jealousy no longer consumes him (did it ever? The comment contrasts
sharply with his different kind of loving in 'Sisters Of Mercy' as if to
say this was meant for real). No, in hearing of her unfaithfulness, 'a
burden . . . a heavy burden lifted from my soul.' The last verse of 'I
Left A Woman Waiting' (from *The Energy Of Slaves*) is completely
different from that of the poem. In the earlier (pre-1972) form he tells
his 'faithless wife' to go to sleep, admitting the cruelty of the jibe. In the
song their essential disharmony is papered over by physical love, but
'truly dead were we/And free as running water.' The deadness of his
eyes and the death of her 'beauty' from the earlier song are now raised as
the poignant signposts to the *sterile* freedom of which he often wrote
(in 'The Kite'; 'Bird On The Wire', etc), a freedom which is but dire
servitude – *à la* Sartre's *nausée:* 'The way' he says in bitter farewell, 'it's
got to be, lover!' Browning might cry, 'Take my love, and our earth is a
tomb'; Leonard was here speaking of that more fearful 'love' in which
minds and souls are entombed, not merely bodies.

'Don't Go Home With Your Hard-On', a crude cast-back to
Beautiful Losers without the virtue of the *koan*, had an especially
distinguished cast: both Bob Dylan and Allen Ginsberg participated in it
'in deep background.' The latter poet was to speak of the experience,
somewhat indifferently, to Michael Krogsgaard of *The Telegraph* a
few years later:

". . .We (Dylan and Ginsberg) went out one night with Ronee
Blakely to Cantor's Delicatessen, which is on Fairfax. And we didn't

have anything to do and he said that Cohen was recording with Phil Spector . . . So we went over there, and Spector was taking a lot of cocaine and was in a kind of hysterical frenzy: totally Hitlerian and dictatorial and sort of crazed. He started pushing us all around, saying, 'Get in there! Get on the microphone!' The whole thing was total chaos.

"Cohen was in despair. Spector went in and started twiddling the dials and mixed it all, and it sounded perfect. It was amazing."

Amazing or not, he is probably alone in believing it to be 'perfect'. The raucous sound certainly fits the vulgarity of the words, but the sly seductiveness of the poetry – 'I've looked behind all of the faces/That smile you down to your knees/And the lips that say,/Come on, taste us/And when you try to,/they make you say, "Please",' – is completely drowned in the cacophony, here, as nearly everywhere else on the album; as is the teasing, frustrating torment of the lover. But it is not the cynicism of love only of which Leonard was singing, but also that of the superficiality of the age, its judgments, its styles, the shallowness of life:

> 'So I work in that same beauty salon
> I'm chained to the old masquerade
> The lipstick, the shadow, the silicone –
> I follow my father's trade.'
> (Copyright © 1977. Stranger Music Inc, New York.
> Used by Permission. All Rights Reserved.)

The difference between covering a dumpy matron's faults in quality cloth or cosmetics mattered little: he hungered for reality, fulfilment; his was an existential awareness, it demanded a fuller decision.

'Fingerprints', similarly, deals with identity – true or false; except that in this song (formerly a series of simple quatrains in *Parasites Of Heaven*) it was the poet himself who was offering the false image: 'My fingerprints were missing . . .' True, he castigates his lover for not caring for what she loses, for her flippancy and her very different 'style'. It is because of that, particularly, that he 'cannot face the dawn/ with any girl who knew me/When my fingerprints were on.' The seriousness behind his name prohibited the rashness – except in song and late-night revelry!

And so the climax is reached: 'Death Of A Ladies' Man' ('Cohen's latest masterpiece' according to Ed Harrison of *Billboard*), the longest and strongest song on the album, which Spector happily allowed to assert its own (slow) tempo, its own foreclosure. It was actually recorded at 2.30 am, in a mood of utter weariness.

It is a tale of appropriation, of use and abuse. Not of male dominance, but female chauvinism. She found him in distress – when he was 'hanging by a thread,' when 'his muscles . . . were numbered/

and his style was obsolete' – a reference to the sterility of the mid-sixties period, rather than that earlier one of transition; a time when all his virtues were burning 'in the smoky Halocost' (sic) – when preaching to one of St Francis' sparrows! (He had been invited to write the score for a film about St Francis which Zefferelli was contemplating, but the negotiations broke down when Leonard suggested that it would be more in keeping with the saint if they all worked for free!) She took him, and used him, won him and lost him – then slyly refused him; and so he was transformed, from the male chauvinist-cum-womaniser to the apprentice-woman: unmanned and emasculated: 'but he's not a woman, yet.'

It is, as we saw earlier, a song appertaining to the whole of his career as a ladies' man, one which consumed 'everything her lover lost,' who deluded 'the sentry of his high religious mood,' who took his identity, his safeguards, his past – even his most persistent and personal self-hood, 'his longing'; who crowned her sly possessiveness by giving 'her soul an empty room' – self-delusion complete; the album ends in a series of echoing repetitions as the sense of lostness disappears as it were into space, an endless death.

For many years surrealism had attracted Leonard, perhaps he found thereby a means of escape from his own nausea and painful solitudes. But in this album-making, life itself had become larger and rougher and crueller than he could ever have imagined. Quite apart from the agony of the break-up of his romance, the pain he felt in its breach for his children as well as his lover – and that at times was very destructive – he also had to put up with Spector's 'craziness', to use Ginsberg's word. Leonard recalls one occasion when he was trying to leave Spector's house where they had been working for nearly three weeks – when Spector drew a revolver on him, loaded, and held it to his head! There was probably never any danger, and certainly the producer's paranoia never resorted to that sort of violence, but it was threatening of composure, if not of life itself.

Sadly, nearly 4000 miles away, a real life was under final threat – that of his mother, who had been hospitalised for some time, but whose leukaemic condition was now worsening to the point that Leonard was obliged to make regular trips to Montreal, ensuring that her final moments were ones taken up with his caring and his presence.

the sound of
a mother

An anonymous Jewish proverb says 'God could not be everywhere, and therefore he made mothers'; the *Zohar* enjoins, 'Honour your father and your mother, even as you honour God, for all three were partners in your creation.' The health of his mother was such that Leonard moved his family back from Los Angeles to Montreal, to be near her. (His sister lived in New York and so was able to do the much shorter distance more conveniently.) But it was an uneasy time, with her in her final illness (from cancer), and Leonard in the death-throes of his relationship. At the end he visited her every day, often finding her in astonishingly good form; full of humour, vivacious, and a source of cheer – in anecdote and song! – to those who visited her. Sometimes Rosengarten accompanied him, when they would smuggle a bottle of gin into the ward, by the end of which all three were ready to ford the final river and back again, if need be.

But they were not all good times, however; many were the occasions when he hand-fed her himself, from a small spoon, filial piety consummated in tender caring, as we would expect from him. On one occasion, at a time of great weakness, when she needed to convey something to him but could not find the words, he was called to her side where she signalled for paper and pen. They were provided, and for a few minutes she worked busily at the page. On taking it from her, Leonard found nothing but scribble in front of him, not even malformed letters. But none were needed. He knew as clearly as ever he could have done that it was a demonstration of her pleasure in his work and successes; her encouragement to go on. Even as he, aged nine, had been compelled to communicate with his dead father, so now she in similar circumstances felt compelled to speak to him. Just before she died their home at Westmount was burgled. Nothing was taken, save his father's revolver which she had kept in a bedside drawer for over 45 years. Leonard was not slow to see the symbolism of the action. It was no longer needed; she was at peace, with herself and the world.

They were times of painful thought and decision. Jewish law forbids the needless continuation of life by chemotherapy. It respects the body's and the mind's indications that their life has been completed (which is not to be confused with any form of euthanasia). And Leonard now felt that the doctors were trying too hard, continuing a well-spent life beyond its allotted time. It was a point of very great delicacy and anguish, when – not for the first time – his ambiguities collided sharply.

When she died, full of years and faith, she left a gap which was larger than life and twice as impelling. She had been his teacher, his distant pillar of strength; she was his vital link with the past, his dearest traditions. It is via the mother that a Jewish boy obtains his lineage, is rooted to the Name and the nation, and thus – in a double sense – he owes his life to her. Almost a treble sense, in fact, for the early loss of his father created bonds of great affection and intensity which her sometime eccentricities and his continuous wanderings (not unconnected) could not weaken. He was most fortunate in having such a mother, who brought the eastern spice of life to his being, continually reminded him of it, and was ever there as a friend, a source of strength, a goad to his life and conscience.

He gave full credit to her in an interview with Chris Bohn of *Melody Maker* in early 1980: "She used to sing Russian songs around the house," he said. "She was a wonderful singer, a great deep voice . . . A week before she died I played her the Spector record . . . She sort of listened patiently to it, and said, 'People can dance to it!' And then, later, she said, 'Why don't you write songs like the ones we used to sing, you know, with the violin?' My mother produced this record." (She did more than sing at home. On several occasions before she was hospitalised, he and Rosengarten took her to a favourite Greek restaurant where, following their meal together, she would regale them – and the other diners! – with her singing, which was always well received, her melodious voice and 'foreign' songs adding richly to the occasion.)

He now faced the future alone. Bereft of both father and mother, deserted by his lover and at odds with himself – 'as tired of his longing as her absence/and so are we.' From now on, he said, he started 'to make friends with (himself).' He did it by renewing those dynamic affiliations which had pulsed through his mother, and his father's influence preserved by his mother; those intense and characteristic Cohen-like impulses which had so long buffeted him; by giving heed to the third person of his creation who alone was now left to him. He could never be forgotten, even as his parents' influence could not be ignored, even as his experience with his former lover became a new voice, a new awakening in his psyche:

> *'This is the land of work. I sit apart*
> *from you and long for you with all my heart.'*

He was indeed forced to recollect – not only as an act of confession, by which 'surprises and rewards' would materialise – but in order to regain the vision. But Scobie is wrong when he criticises this latest book for lacking 'specific reference.' 'Mercy' required such consideration; even as criticism requires insight. His shattered life is imprinted on every page; the book is replete with references to subject and source; the context has been written boldly and honestly – but also guardedly and pointedly – written sympathetically: opposites connecting! As he reflected in it, 'Destroy particular self and absolute appears,' which has Zen-like overtones, as his work of recent date now frequently displayed. 'Particular self' was too honest or, at least, honest in the wrong sort of way. To be useful it had to be general, 'absolute'. Bernard Barton described its process, if not its reality:

> *'As I walk'd by myself, I talk'd to myself,*
> *And myself replied to me;*
> *And the questions myself then put to myself,*
> *With their answers, I give to thee.'*

The process was furthered by time spent with Roshi. By now Leonard had been raised to a status of more than a student. He and Roshi had become firm friends – beyond their mutual interests in Zen, Japanese poetry and aesthetics. Significantly, in talking to Manzano of their relationship, Leonard had compared it to that which existed between him and Irving Layton and, not least, Roshi's 'off-beat character' (*'un ser extrano, como Irving Layton lo es para mi . . .'*). Important here was the Zen master's belief that the zendo training was not an end in itself, but a preparation for the work beyond it. (Shades here of Rinzai Girgen's triple formula of training, wandering, teaching.) Roshi, like the older Canadian poet, could let go; Leonard's freedom was secure.

He undertook much of the administrative work – Roshi's poor grasp of English rendered that imperative – and they enjoyed a relationship of friendship rather than one of master-and-student; their contacts were more social than meditative, not least centring on a mutual taste for good brandy! In his spare time Leonard worked at his weight-training at the local YMCA, increasing his muscle-power in order better to confront his reflections. Body and soul were once more coming together, making deeper connections of general usefulness.

His next album, 'Recent Songs', was the outcome of this renewed man, this new thinking; in part a reaction from (as well as a refined continuation of) 'Death Of A Ladies' Man', in part the charting of a new course on the basis of the old traditions having been reworked. For that reason he could say that its real producer was Masha Cohen. It was *her* sounds that came through – through his history, his consciousness, his words and, above all, his expertise. Leonard himself was the producer of the album with Henry Lewey. John Lissauer – who had very largely arranged for him to this point – was no longer the chief influence; that came from deep within Leonard, his early and late years, his need to return, alongside the sound of Henry Lewey who had been co-producer with Joni Mitchell for much of her career. He returned to another set of roots altogether in dedicating it to his old poet-friend, Irving Layton: 'My friend and inspiration, the incomparable expert of interior language.'

And the critics saw it! It combines 'the atmosphere of the early records with an unexpected musical sophistication,' commented Elizabeth Thomson in *Woman's Journal;* 'Cohen's biggest LP, sure to go silver, if not gold . . . his brilliance and vision shine through, as does his uncelebrated wit,' said Larry Sloman in *High Times;* 'the work's romanticism is tempered by a tough strain of realism in the narratives,' added Chris Bohn in *Melody Maker.* To him, Leonard was very open, describing disarmingly his motives and intentions, as Bohn raised a veiled criticism at the kitsch-like dangers of swans and roses etc (which were by no means new to Leonard's poetry) for today's market. He wrote, somewhat defensively:

"I felt for some odd reason like rescuing such imagery from the backs of Christmas cards; and returning those symbols, those images, to a place of honour – if they ever had one. Also to use the shabbiness and irony of those images to really get something from (them), as an ironic device; to rescue their real passionate romance. If they're successful they do create resonance and harmonies in the hearts of the listeners, and a landscape that (people) recognise as true: it's grotesque; it's shabby; it's beautiful! But beyond all that you're willing to forgive those conceits if you recognise them as true . . . I think the songs are guarded by those kinds of devices . . . I think everybody knows what's going on.

"(For) people who want to hear the song, who've got that kind of appetite . . . the songs penetrate directly and immediately . . . I don't want you to think (that) I sit around thinking about how I get a certain effect – that's like starting at the end. You feel a certain reality, a struggle to articulate it. It's more like a scavenger who, rather than sitting at a great luxurious table choosing one delicacy, then another, takes what there is; what suggests itself. To me, the only things I had to work with at the time (were) those clichés. I could not enter that experience through any other gateway . . ."

'Recent Songs' was recorded at the A & M Studios, Los Angeles, with a much wider use of musicians than Leonard was wont to use – strains, no doubt, of the potential he recognised in the Spector album. But he was not making an album 'for people to dance to'; he was out to create *resonance and harmonies in the hearts* of his listeners; he was writing and singing – as he had ever tried to do – for people with 'a particular kind of appetite'; songs which would 'penetrate directly and imme- diately.' As he replied to our questionings so much later, falling back on the stress of self-discovery, "I really had to rediscover some sort of basis; something I knew about. It was a coming home . . . a very rich period." He had never spoken more plainly of his work, never offered such detailed explanation; never been more the visionary; the prophet of the heart. The corner had been turned; the past was the past; the mantle was taken up, donned, exploited – and fully justified.

His selection of musicians, at least the ones essential to this particular work, was done with great care. John Lissauer was still there, at the piano; a devoted, sensitive and hearing man. As was the Russian – his mother's sound must out! – Raffi Hakopian, whose expertise was to inveigh the songs with great sentience and highly suggestible melody – 'a sobbing violin-sound' commented Bohn, for once being trapped in stereotype. It did not 'sob', this call of the past, this evocation of mystery and stillness; it invited, tenderly; it described, plaintively; it warned, lovingly; it nurtured the soul – devotedly; it sanctified the whole, bringing near those with ears to hear. Alongside these played Mitch Watkins on electric guitar; Roscoe Beck on bass (with Abraham Laboriel and Johnny Miller – the latter having distinguished himself on 'New Skin For The Old Ceremony' and the recent tour of Europe and North America); Steve Meador was on drums, Bill Ginn on piano, Randy Waldman on the organ (plus Garth Hudson, of The Band, also on the organ and the accordion); John Bilezikjian brought more eastern strains, and Paul Ostermayer played saxophone. In addition to these, for 'Humbled In Love', 'Our Lady Of Solitude' and 'The Smoky Life', Passenger, a Texas-based fusion-rock group played, enlarging the range and penetration. The finest instrument present, albeit a human one, was Jennifer Warnes, whose mellifluous tones added an overall elegance and melody. Leonard, too, was in very good voice – at times wistful, at times mysterious, at times assertive, at times regretful. In a sense his music had finally come of age: a true voice reinforced by highly agreeable sound.

It was a large selection, with 10 songs on it (only 'New Skin For The Old Ceremony' has more, with 11; though the pot-boiler – 'The Best Of Leonard Cohen' – has 12; 'Death Of A Ladies' Man', 'Live

Songs' and 'Songs Of Love And Hate' each have eight). It nearly had 11, but 'Misty Blue', which was only performed here and once in London remains to be issued: one of several still simmering on the back-burner of his mind. And the imagery used is equally large and ranging; not just with the swans and roses of Bohn's question, but culling – scavenging, indeed! – from Leonard's whole 'landscape' every image and symbol, every metaphor and simile, even every parable and allegory he can put together to articulate that 'certain reality' he needed to project. And it was very largely religious; the most 'religious' of all his works to date; a religion without holds, open in its sympathies, loyal in its affinities, non-credal, yet with a driving, compelling energy; Jewish and Christian and Buddhist.

We should note at this point that Leonard – unlike many Jews who found refuge in Buddhism (e.g. Allen Ginsberg) – never lost his monotheistic convictions; indeed, they appear to have become stronger over the years, not by any Dylanesque or Muggeridgean new birth, but by 'natural', i.e. organic growth – from fledgling believer to man of faith.

His attitude contrasts very sharply with the on/off experiences of Dylan or the reactionary Buddhism of Ginsberg, who commented thus on the poet's 'Christian' phase: '(Dylan) has a fixed notion and divinity, and I think that that's a mistake – as a non-theist Buddhist; that any solidification (sic) of the ideal God like the ancient Jews warned against naming the name of God – is a mistake. It's a psychological error on a simple point.'

Such language obscures the profundity of the matter. It exchanged the historical dimension for personal idiosyncrasy discon-nected from the external world – of time and history. Ginsberg's dependencies were more often than not drug-induced and escapist. Suffice it here to note that Leonard did not force monotheistic (i.e. one-god) doctrines; he did not command theistic (i.e. personal-god) beliefs; nevertheless, those with ears to hear – and many without – could not fail to catch the point, 'directly and immediately'; not out of contrivance or slick devising, but honestly – so that 'everybody knows what's going on.' It was only through that 'gateway' that he could enter, and emerge: with a meaningful word.

The songs are 'mystical'; parabolic in their ability to say things at different levels: the sacred and the secular, the human and the divine; projecting the heavenly by means of promoting the earthly; 'passionate romance' and spiritual truth: an alpha and an omega – 'understanding' now at its peak. And if some listeners (and commentators!) found parts difficult, Leonard himself could not always interpret them to his own satisfaction. All poets encounter this difficulty. We saw earlier Browning's view of the matter; it was not very different with Yeats:

'You must not give me as an authority,' he said of his own work. 'If an author interprets a poem of his own, he limits its suggestibility.' It is not otherwise with the poetry-of-song.

The album commences at that precise level, with 'The Guests', which is a song of the rich textures of life in an abundant world, and the final summing-up that all face; a song about the haves and the have-nots, the lucky and the unfortunate – the 'open hearted many' and 'the broken-hearted few,' though Leonard was not in his mathematical phase, to use a Dylanism, when he wrote it! A song about the dancers and the weepers who stumble and stride through life in singular independency, despite their corporate existence; all of them, individu-ally, questing and seeking: 'Do reveal yourself!' or 'Why hast thou forsaken me?' though many do not know 'where the night is going' or 'Why the wine is flowing.'

To answer such profundities, perfect love is required – the 'need' of the ages, of all men. The *denouement* comes – as Dylan said it would (compare Ginsberg's adverse comment in *The Telegraph*, 'this judgmen-tal Jehovaic theism in (Dylan's) recent works') – in an instant: 'The torches flare, the inner-door flies open.' The Voice is emphatic in its twice-repeated 'Welcome! welcome!' and they enter, their individu-alities never more obvious: 'in every style of passion.' It is the final messianic banquet, (though Manzano produced from Leonard, a memory of his early readings in Sufi mysticism, Attar and Rumi not least – Ishmael connecting! – which, he says, lay behind *Let Us Compare Mythologies* and later works; so the 'sweet repast' culminating every-thing: house and grounds dissolve – as the prophets had foretold they would; and 'one by one' the guests – they have no ownership, no claims of their own to make – are dealt with. And some dance on; and others weep – those 'who earnestly are lost/are lost and lost again . . .' It is the most solemn, the most captivating, the most foreboding of his creations to date; out of his own inner holocaust, a true and accurate word; mesmeric poetry and melody combined.

Interestingly, and at the same connection, the revised selected poems – to be called *New Selected Poems* includes The Feast passage from *Beautiful Losers* – Section 42 – which significantly follows the books definition of a saint. That definition describes a saint as 'someone who has achieved a remote human possibility . . . It has something to do with the energy of love. Contact with this energy results in the exercise of a kind of balance in the chaos of existence.' In the ensuing celebratory feast, Catherine symbolically spills her wine, its stain engulfs the world – a veiled reference to the messianic banquet which presages the Final Judgment. It was previously intimated in his poem 'Order' in *Flowers For Hitler:* 'The old sorceress, the spilled wine,/the black cards convince me: the timeless laws must not be broken.' There was no other way to start such an album as this – which could well have done with a more descriptive title. It is the *mise en scéne* for his return, by which he spotlighted the essence of his cosmic vision: a higher power; human freedom; man's trustee-relationship with the world and its potential; his deepest needs; ultimate realities – and accountings.

There follow two songs which detail how he came to such awareness, the path and the pain to his own revelations: 'Humbled In Love' and 'The Window'. Their shared qualities are extensive: his hopes and pledges with his lover; their failures in them; the regret that they cannot be renewed, by positive or negative action (repentance or revenge); their distress in the bad experiences; the knowledge that their love still remains, albeit thwarted and distant; the dangers that lurk for the ones who do not find a way out of the bitterness of their loss; the religious ideas that can help them through it.

To this community of ideas in the songs should be added things exclusive to the one or the other: where humiliation dominates in 'Humbled . . .' 'a sickness/That loosens the high silver nerve' is offered in 'The window'; whereas 'passionate' considerations operate in the former, 'beauty and pride' appear in the latter; emotional 'mud' grounds the injured of the first, a thorn – or spear-injured side occurs in the second; and the sharp, additional pain of their children 'ferrying' the pledges in 'Humbled In Love' may be set alongside the lack of comforters or observers of 'The Window'.

The first closes with a sideways look at 'the virgin' and the soldier – a Joan of Arc allusion; the second refers directly to 'the cloud of unknowing . . . the new Jerusalem'; above all, the former ends with a compromise: she can have both – her vision and her desire; he has never been so open nor so intimate as he now feels. To this he offers the Job's comfort of ultimate dedication: her 'rose' should be put on the altar-fire and given to the sun, which in turn will offer it to the splendour (read Shekinah) of 'The High, Holy One' – the completion of that cycle of incarnation, by which the creative word is returned through its 'continuous stutter' to its originator in the form of a letter – and the death of a letter.

By this last point he signals the movement from low to high, from earth to heaven, from woman to God (or, at least, from human love to the divine). As Leonard explained to Manzano, "The song is a sort of oration which allows both parts of the soul (sic) to unite, as in joining your hands in prayer." Its problem and agony is encapsulated in the refrain to 'The Window' in which the disparates are held aloft – and their contrariness poignantly emphasised:

> '*O chosen love! O frozen love!*
> *O tangle of matter and ghost!*

O darling of angels, demons and saints,
And the whole broken-hearted host:
Gentle this soul.'

What could be more complex than chosen-and-frozen love? What more difficult of resolution than a tangle of matter and spirit? What more endearing than the darling of all – heavenly, earthly and subterranean beings? And what more clear, or more conciliatory, than an appeal for gentleness? If 'The guests' is the peak of his world view, this surely must be that of the man-woman relationship, in which the divine receives its most precise expression to date.

The next two songs: 'Came So Far For Beauty' and '*Un Canadien Errant*' ('A Lost Canadian') also form a doublet, with some important differences. The subject is lost identity and the grief that it embodies. Surely, the least remote of human possibilities, and the most unbalancing. The first difference is in authorship, '*Un Canadien Errant*' having been written not by Leonard but by M.A. Gerin-Lajoie, and translated (badly!) by Edith Fulton Fowke, from her *Chansons de Quebec*. The second lies in focus, for in 'Came So Far For Beauty' it is Leonard and his destiny which is described, while in '*Un Canadien Errant*' it is an unnamed man who has been banished from his homeland as a result of the internal feuding (almost tantamount to civil war) that took place in the first half of last century, which was put down by force of arms. The third is that the exile cannot return home; he can only send messages of friendship to his former hometown and friends (*pays* serves for both country and hometown here); and only regret at irreversible loss.

Such was not Leonard's experience, still less his conviction. He could, as others did, have spent his days in self-pity and remorse – or anger; he chose not to do so – the upward path. Leonard's confession, for that is what this song and much of the album is, has to do with the 'trade' (to use his word from 'Humbled In Love') that he effected for his vocation – for 'beauty', 'reward', and 'the flesh'. It had to do with women, rather than a particular woman, for whom he neglected so much: his 'patience', his 'family', his 'masterpiece'. (Echoes in this latter reference to Pope's 'Nature's chief masterpiece is writing well.') It demanded effort and dedication, did this renunciation – it was 'a lonely choice,' made in 'a very hopeless voice.' He had to practise on his sainthood; he gave much away – 'to one and all'; he changed his style (from gold) to silver; he changed his clothes (from famous blue) to black; moreover, he changed his nature – from obedience ('surrender') to aggressive denial ('attack'). He positively 'stormed the old casino'; *he* decided what was good; forcing men to his will, breaking bones over his new vision. But all such efforts break up on the rocks of their own conceits (his word, to Bohn): the rumours of him touched her 'not at all'; he failed 'to touch her'; her 'star' was 'beyond his order' (recalling the Jewish toast, '*Maz'l tov!*', meaning: 'May your star be good: Good luck!'). She remained untouchable: 'her nakedness unmanned.' He repeats the first verse, by way of grieved recollection:

> '*I came so far for beauty,*
> *I left so much behind:*
> *My patience, and my family,*
> *My masterpiece unsigned.*'

If there is a glimpse of the one woman, not the many, in the previous paragraph, it comes into the open in 'The Traitor', which is a song of his life and career, one which also deals with his 'betrayed' destiny. But this one, like the following 'Our Lady Of Solitude', also has another dimension: In the same way that '*Un Canadien Errant*' reflects on the loss of homeland, (there was bold irony there, too: 'an English (sic) Canadian, singing a *Quebecois* song, accompanied by Mexican musicians from Los Angeles' to quote Manzano again) so these songs also refer to his international wanderings – this proud Canadian, who in *Beautiful Losers* had argued for his country's independence, who had warned – prophet-like – against American dominance. Even he had been tempted – by the swan of the English river; by the loveliness of her dressed in 'blue and silver,' the national colours of Greece; perhaps at times by the 'mythology' of the Virgin in Catholicism. (Compare his poem 'I Have Not Lingered In European Monasteries'.)

But this dimension merely highlights his greater 'treachery', his bad-faith, to love itself. For while he was enjoying the nocturnal delights of his 'sun-tanned woman . . ./The Judges watched from the other side.' Once again, as in 'The Guest' etc, ultimate reality obtrudes itself. In a rare reference to his mother, itself significant of the intensity of their relationship, he mentions *en passant* his caring for her feelings: suggesting she should half-blame (at least) 'the atmosphere', i.e. not herself. But his love sickened! and despite mutual delights she was to hold him to blame. Judgment resulted: he had missed the mark, just; and was enjoined to defend his position – the poets-and-such (i.e. Dreamers) against the activists, who would have fallen back. But, alas! he stayed with her too long, his thirst – like his 'hunger' was too great. He was immobilised by longing, inaccuracy and falsity. And so he failed his men, not least the younger ones, thus qualifying him to be 'listed with the enemies of love.' And she left, too. Left with a contemptuous offer and, while he takes it up, people call him Traitor to his face.

Those same actualities echo through 'Our Lady Of Solitude', for their love unfolded deliciously, all through the summer, elegantly and expertly. In her light and grace, with her poise and dexterity, she 'touched me'; and all summer long 'I knew her, I knew here face to face.' (Contrast a similar phrase used in an opposite sense in *Death Of A Lady's Man:* 'My wife and I made love this afternoon. We hid together from the light of our desire, forehead to forehead.'). He did not appear to learn much from this one of 'few and small' words, this 'vessel of the whole wide world,' this 'Mistress of us all.' But he had learned to cope; he had found in her very silence – the silence of 'the Queen of Solitude' no less – the message, the words he needed. A trait which Manzano thought evoked the innocence and romance of 'The Sisters Of Mercy', on which Leonard commented wistfully: "It took a long time to return to where I had left." Traitor he might be, but a traitor with open ears and open heart, by which he was qualified to hear and speak for others. But his ability to respond emphasises the inabilities of others, one in particular, so to do – which he now gently and deftly describes.

'The Gypsy Wife' pinpoints his feelings when left bereft; recalls 'the wild reports' that he could not believe, which echoes, if it does not rely on, the *Blood-Wedding* of Lorca, no less. (By now Suzanne had left North America for Aix-en-Provence.) But he is also left with a question as to whose head it is that she – Salome-like – dances with 'on the threshing floor,' whose darkness it is that 'deepens in her arms'? The scene changes to 'the tired old café, where the ghost of his wife (which is highly reminiscent of 'Is This What You Wanted?', now absent) 'climbs on the table.' As with the Queen of Solitude, 'her body is the light . . . the way' against which 'I raise my arm . . . I catch the bride's bouquet,' in deferred hope. But like all such emotions, his heart is sick: sick with the realisation that the timing is wrong, that reality is now something different. For in the days of judgment 'no man or woman/ Can be touched.' Nevertheless the judgment is severest to those who interfere, the meddlers and the pedlars:

> *'But you who come between them
> Will be judged.'*

*(Copyright © 1979. Stranger Music Inc, New York.
Used by Permission. All Rights Reserved.)*

'Where is my Gypsy-wife?' fades out the song, questioningly.

These proffered conciliations are furthered in 'The Smoky Life', in which her loving nature is portrayed, as well as his sound suggestion to allow to 'let go' their relationship. The spirit of the song echoes that of 'So Long, Marianne' of 1966, where he entreated his

former lover 'To laugh and cry, and cry, and laugh about it all again.'
He reminds her that he had held and supported and counselled her – but
'there's no one waving!' Reality requires soberness of mind, not the
anticipation of adulation. He bids her set 'your restless heart at ease' –
this one who earlier had prayed for 'a calm spirit'; to take a lesson from
nature which simply gets on with the job in hand. He suggests that
arguments are merely delaying, futile tactics; 'it's light enough/To let it
go,' which ends with the final invitation:

> 'Come on back if the moment lends;
> You can look up all my closest friends.'
>
> (Copyright © 1979. Stranger Music Inc, New York.
> Used by Permission. All Rights Reserved.)

The former questioning has turned into a positive, welcoming
response.

The album ends with a request, 'a prayer for the cowboy,' which
has strong overtones of his chasing Kid Marley's (lame) horse around
the pasturelands in Franklin, Tennessee, though actually the sound is
Mexican rather than Texan; strong and anguished! Despite the humour
(and that is rarely absent, though usually in ironic form, always
intelligent and deft), it is an allegory of his broken romance. His lost
love, 'his darling, his stray,' having 'run away,' 'gone like the summer
. . . like the snow,' has caused his world – like his day – to 'cave in';
everything goes wrong 'in the panic of loss': the river, the roads, the
bridges, even the crickets – ever the evocation of song and freedom –
conspire against him, 'breaking his heart with their song.'

And so it continues, through pain and loss, false vision and erring
hope; he, ever-searching, hoping; she moving further and further away
from him. He is aware of deeper things: 'his injury here – her
punishment there.' Summer comes, and lo! she is once more in front of
him, at least in silhouette, in the warmth of the summer sun 'where the
light and the darkness divide.' She comes to his hand! though not really
tame – but only to dash away again, till he once more catches her,
subdues her, binds her – by which he, too, is subdued and bound; unreal
in its staying-power, mocking in its insubstantiality – like a tune, like
smoke, like a song – like a man's life . . . (like Breavman's?)

radical revaluation, and peace

The outline of Leonard's life to date – as with so many men of passion and vision – may be seen to be falling across the years Diogenes-like: 'I am seeking a man!' lantern in hand, shoulders hunched, brow enquiring. His life was lived in the cold grip of *angst*. There never was a point, not at least since the death of his father, when he failed to feel the pang of existence: that bitter-sweet, unreal-disappointingly-real feeling that catches one in the stomach, Sartre's *le néant*, or nausea – which Anthony Quinton defined as 'what anxiety that isn't about anything is about'; Heidegger's *Das Nichts:* nothingness; or Camus' 'the absurd'. It is the senselessly negative feeling that hounds reflective man, all of it going back in one way or another to Soren Kierkegaard's manic-depressiveness. Behind him lies the figure of Qoheleth – the Preacher (or Great Orator), son of King David of Jerusalem, whose life was given to the reflection of life and meaning, man's place in the world, which resulted in his classic judgment: 'Vanity of vanities, all is vanity . . . all is vanity and a striving after wind.'

Leonard felt this deeply. In *Flowers For Hitler* – the *néant* was never closer than in the light of the diabolical holocaust – he commented, 'At my stomach gnawed/the divine emptiness' (on 'The death of an uncharted planet'); in *Death Of A Lady's Man* he expressed it so:

> 'Other angels tend me
> Nausea and fear
> No one can defend me
> From your judgment here'

It is surely significant that here – as elsewhere, but not exclusively – he attaches his sense of *angst* to a divine judgment, or at least gives it a theological dimension. It reminds one of Augustine's, 'O Lord, our hearts know no rest till they find their rest in thee.' Or Paul's, 'O wretched man that I am,' or Jeremiah's, or Isaiah's, or Moses' similar responses. Leonard flew from it into sensuality (as did Augustine – Paul merely trembled under its assaults) in his younger years, by which its perpetual ache was temporarily silenced; or by writing sharp words about it, by which he upset his friends and mentors – Dudek's 'obscure cosmological imagery of total negation of Leonard Cohen's and Daryl Hines' poetry at its best.'

It is fantastic to suggest (especially then, i.e. the late fifties; but also now) that such writing comes from 'social critics without a cause' as Dudek put it. The 'emptiness', 'aimlessness' or 'demoralisation' which he attributed to Leonard have deep roots, genuine connections, and heavy penalties for the victim. Leonard struggled to make his escape – the process took 30 years – by retracing his truer connections; redefining his name; following that 50-fold path which leads to life and liberty. As he said 'you have sealed every gate but this one.' He had centred himself on his appreciation of women and love, and the love-relationship (long and short), extracting from it an 'ethic' of general application, seeking to make of it an allegory of life and loving. But it cost him dearly, this 'escape'. Through it he chanced on many deceivers, personal and impersonal; went up many *cul-de-sacs;* followed many routes to false conclusions – from all of which he had to extricate himself, reassert his identity, redefine his direction and destiny, accept the humiliations and defeats:

> '*They on the heights are not the souls*
> *Who never erred nor went astray;*
> *Who trod, unswerving, towards their goals,*
> *Along a smooth, rose-bordered way.*
> *No! Those who stand, when first comes dawn,*
> *Are those who stumbled, but went on.'*
>
> (John Oxenham)

It was ever thus for this authentic seeker, who authenticated his own life by making those hard decisions – late, perhaps, eventually, maybe; but always manfully.

Following the release of 'Recent Songs' he again went on tour throughout Europe (but not Spain); rehearsing in Britain first. It was at this time that Lord Carrington is alleged to have said, 'The Queen is at Ascot, the Conservatives are in Downing Street, all is well with the world.' His many British admirers would doubtless have added, 'and Leonard is back at the Albert Hall'!; then to Sweden, Norway, France, Belgium, Germany, Switzerland, and back through England and

Scotland, across to Dublin and back again to England for a finale at the Dome Theatre in Brighton.

A Canadian television-unit accompanied him much of the way, which was made into yet another film, produced by Harry Rasky, and released in 1980 as *The Songs Of Leonard Cohen*. They covered 53 concerts in 44 cities over 69 days! The tour musicians were culled from the album group: Watkins, Beck, Meador, Ginn, Hakopian, Bilezikjian and Ostermayer, with Jennifer Warnes and Sharon Robinson as vocalists. They started out in early October and did not stop until mid-December; by which time – thanks to the two dozen songs-a-set rhythm, which gradually increased as they went along! – they were all exhausted. Commented Leonard to *Melody Maker:*

"Everybody on tour has had a tiny nervous breakdown at one point or the other. I don't know if it's the weather, or the tour's intensity, or the music, or the combination of the people. But everyone has had to go through a radical revaluation of their condition on the road. We're enjoying it now because we've surrendered to it. They just carry our bodies from hotel room to airport bus, and the music manifests itself each night!"

The weather was not good that winter. Not so much cold as wet and miserable, but the tour's 'intensity' certainly exacerbated matters, and such intense closeness as they had to endure made life nerve-wracking. Leonard was particularly busy, naturally, dealing at all hours with the press, making himself available for extra one-off shows *en route* (on French and German television, for example), and generally acting as pacemaker, arbiter and father-confessor! Raffi Hakopian, the Russian violinist, endured particular emotions as they skirted his homeland's borders, knowing that his wife and family were still 'imprisoned' there, denied the exit-visas they so much craved, which added pathos to the music, but great heartache to a fine and sensitive artist.

There were more sinister emotions emerging at times, the worst occurring at the Berlin Sports' Palace, where the crowd – ever-demanding, with a sophisticated taste for good music, sought to impose its clamorous will on the concert, stimulated by the failure of the tour equipment. For once Leonard lost his cool, as well as his discretion, and shouted – on the very spot where Goebbels had asked his historic question, and using the Nazi's own words: '*Wollt Ihr den totalen Krieg?*' ('Do you want total war'?) which was perceived as an affront; their demands turned to hostility, and a very ugly scene was barely averted – by sweet music, to be sure.

By this time a dozen years – and eight albums – had passed. Stars and groups had come and gone, tastes had changed, as had moods and hopes. The high octane of the sixties had been diluted by oligarchic interests and posturing Reaganomics and Thatcherism were now setting the pace, scything away aspirations, jobs and the last vestiges of broad and youthful schemes in the name of monetarism: the cowboys were truly taking over. When the morality was Victorian, which achieved its peak in the smug individuality and doomed jingoism of Rudyard Kipling, once more crowned, which worked *financially* i.e. cap-italistically, but still has to be paid for in human social unrest. Leonard's followers, very numerous, still very enthusiastic – despite the climate – had changed, too. As Elizabeth Thomson reported in *Melody Maker*, 'People of every age and from every walk of life stood to show their appreciation.' The 'Cohen-cult' had not only become established, and mushroomed, but was now spreading through all levels of society – among all of those people with 'a particular appetite.' Thomson raised the hoary question of his depressive image, to which Leonard replied:

"The confusion of seriousness with gloominess is an inaccurate understanding. We have an appetite for seriousness, and we can be destroyed as easily by mindless frivolity as we can by obsessive depression . . . Somewhere in between there's a condition that is quite peaceful. It's called 'seriousness', and it's an appropriate response to a number of things that happen to be going on at the crust of this star . . . Growing up involves forgiveness, not using relationships as an alibi."

An interesting collocation of the antonyms 'seriousness' and 'frivolity' occurs, in slightly different language, in 'Jazz Police' which was presently being processed through his and his band's mind: 'Jesus taken serious (not seriously!) by many; Jesus taken joyous by a few.' It shows a healthy regard for the founder of Christianity – thus finally undermining, as he had earlier – Vassal's comment that 'he abandons the theme of Christ for a theory of sainthood.' As the present interviewer saw, 'He made a whole generation of listeners search for some *real* meaning in songs.' (Her italics.) And he described, in this connection of meaning-for-life, his view of art itself: "(It is) the only kind of expression that can heal; the real and authentic expressions of a man's loyalty to his experience, however he sees (them)."

It is one of the ironies of his story that he came to the fore in the wake of the pop-music explosion. By 1967 the big names had all played their best, and the major festivals – 1969 was actually their high point – had become lively memories in the minds of those who were now settling down to the mundane duties of raising families. Moreover, some of them had produced very destructive backlashes by their empty-headedness: John Lennon had described The Beatles as 'more popular than Jesus Christ,' later retracted – but too late; the hippie-cult merely became a distraction – like faded wallpaper – and then a monstrosity, following the Charles Manson murders which were curiously, but unjustly, linked to The Beatles' song 'Helter Skelter' on their 'White

Album'; the star-backed protests against the escalating Vietnam War and the draft in particular created yet another backlash; police brutality against the flower-people was merely one expression of the use of violence to stem the student revolt which spread, like Catherine's spilled wine, across America, Europe, the world itself; the increasing wildness of some rockers such as Jimi Hendrix and Jim Morrison, not to mention the antics of The Rolling Stones and Janis Joplin, aided this reaction.

Decadence was in, and becoming popular. Moreover, the dangers of drugs began to be critically felt. What had been a mildly dangerous enjoyment was now recognised as a deformer, a killer; and the reaction to it by the authorities and by the public at large became increasingly hysterical, 'drug-busts' a way of life. What had started out as youth finding itself – in exuberance, and in self-fulfilment of all sorts – not least in music – now became a frustration, unmeaning: the necklace of unity burst cascading its bright reflections in all directions; *angst* took over; heavy-metal, then punk was born, the *néant* reigned. Leonard, who had formerly been fascinated by violence, now witnessed it at close quarters. He understood it. He kept up his friendships, he deepened his explorations (especially in music) which was to have interesting repercussions on his own musical developments, not least in jazz and its significant discordances.

Leonard had come to join the party, and found himself at a wake; of which he sang with defiant truthfulness. Bob Dylan characterised the prevailing atmosphere in his 'Ballad Of A Thin Man': 'There's something here but you don't know what it is, do you, Mr Jones?' Mr Jones, one of the press' less seeing members, did not; and years later, in proudly identifying himself as the star of the song, still appeared not to do so. As he remarked of it, he was 'flattered by attention and defensively dumbstruck (sic) . . . I had missed the point totally' – as did many.

Leonard was now working in an area of increasingly faster changing styles and moods, where to be a month late was to be *démodé*, still more so to be a season, a year. It was only as he truly found himself, his particular style, his historic self, that he really made his mark. He had been a leader of his generation – from behind; now he was to be a real pathfinder – by going further back, in which he rediscovered the message, the word, the vision for today. A peaceable condition. In so doing he became – as he had ever been – though more so – a song-writer's song-writer. Men of the calibre of Bob Dylan, Kris Kristofferson, Neil Diamond (to say nothing of women of such star quality as Judy Collins, Joni Mitchell, Jennifer Warnes) now expressed a willingness to line up, and listen. The artist had become an artist's artist, a leader of fashion – as the Suzanne Vegas, Tracy Chapmans, Tanita Tikarams and their ilk demonstrate today.

Astonishingly, his Spanish friend and biographer, Manzano, missed the point. He describes Leonard's life as a series of experiments: poetry, fiction, song-writing, singer, exponent of mystico-religious awareness; experimenter in sex, drugs, women, alcohol, the religious kick. As such it is a complete travesty. Leonard did all those things, but not piecemeal, departmentalised. His life is a tapestry, not a strip-cartoon. He has not lived 'from frame to frame,' but by following threads – at times of wondrously fine texture and composition – but following them, nevertheless; even when they appeared to be 'of endless length . . . the same colour as the night' – and by so doing he started, *petit à petit*, 'to sew the world together . . . a comforting message, a beautiful knowledge of unity.'

The sheer artistry of his work, doubted by some – Dudek, Birney, even Mandel, and rejected by others – the Woodcocks and the Waymans – was recognised in various quarters where artistic excellence had broader meaning. For example, *Two Views And Seven Poems* was commissioned by his publishers and appeared in 1980, alongside the drawings of 'G.F.' (Gigino Falconi). In some respects it antedates *Various Positions* in its dioramic attitudes. It comprises seven of Leonard's poems, alongside which are placed illustrative lithographs in the following sequence:

Cohen	G.F.
'My Lady Can Sleep'	*'L'urlo'*
'This Morning I Was'	*'Atmosfera'*
'Dressed By The Wind'	
'Slowly I Married Her'	*'Nudonella stanza'*
'The Absence Of Monica'	*'Pensiera verso id vuoto'*
'Snow Is Falling'	*'L'animale'*
'Traditional Training And Service'	*'Un gesto verso il rosa'*
'Another Man's Woman'	*'Meditazioni'*

They had all appeared in print before this special edition. 'My Lady . . .' in *The Spice-Box Of Earth;* 'This Morning . . .' and 'Snow . . .' in *Parasites Of Heaven;* the others in *Death Of A Lady's Man.* All of them capture Leonard's poetic instinct; they quiver on the page like song-birds – this one high, this one low; this one excited, this one meditative. All of them speak of love, of his observances of his beloved – no crass Wayman-like 'holes' here; no scornful chauvinism – just tenderness, and a certain wonderment at her form and features and beauty. Only in 'Slowly I Married Her' does a harsher note obtrude – not so much the crow cawing from its disdainful heights, as the robin casting about for its mate. It is a species of frustrated love, of unfulfilled hopes; all the more plaintive, time – lots of time: the 'slowly' of the title – was taken to woo; but only woe resulted. As it began, so it ended: 'Years in the coming/and years in retreat.'

The essence of its woe is expressed in the admission (it forms the basis of the self-accusation) that their union was 'sanctioned by none/ with nobody's blessings (and certainly not those of the Kohanim)/in nobody's name.' Moreover, it had taken place 'amid general warnings/ amid general scorn.' A note of apology resonates through 'Traditional Training And Service': 'I am sorry I asked you to live with me in the snow,' which is transformed into a sort of self-inflicted apprenticeship in the final piece, in which the beloved 'entangles' him with another, an unapproachable person (or Person?) 'in order that you may refine your love for me.' 'Look at beauty (such an important Cohen-word) *now*,' she challenges, closing the 'views' and thereby 'silencing' his arguments. It was issued in a folio-sized boxed set, beautifully produced by McClelland and Stewart Ltd, of Toronto, as a limited edition of 100 and 55, signed by both author and illustrator, a fine tribute to the enduring qualities of Leonard's work and vision.

What this work recognised on the small scale, Australia now recognised more largely, continentally in fact. (It is a curious fact that Australia has always led Canada culturally, as the late Professor Earle Birney points out in relation to poetry, in his delightful memoir *Spreading Time*.) Ever since his friendship with George Johnston and Charmaine Cliff, Leonard had cherished the hope to go there. It was now realised magnificently, and the Australians reacted very favourably indeed, thanks not least to the careful pre-tour work done by his host, the Paul Dainty Corporation. His new promotion agency also prepared the way well, issuing a series of memoranda to him as consecutive updates to the growing Australian response were received, and fed into his ever-changing itinerary.

Leonard, too, had prepared himself carefully for the tour, spending a fortnight in retreat at his Buddhist monastery then on Mount Baldy, just outside Los Angeles. Here the essential 'meditative' techniques of the concerts were quietly produced, raising the dimension of the songs' meaning to their supra-mundane level, honing the verbal instruments to their sharpest, conditioning mind and soul so as to avoid the 'tiny nervous breakdowns' of the last tour. As did his musicians – the same as for the last tour – which earned them the highest accolades. Commented John Monks of *The Australian*:

"There's this little man named Cohen on stage under an unflattering lime green spotlight pouring out his soul in a voice that ranges from reedy Dylan to mid-range Kristofferson. Add to that what must be *the best backing group ever to tour Australia* and you have the show-biz magic that is Leonard Cohen . . . destined to be the cult-figure *extraordinaire* of the eighties . . . the Cohen concert is the performance Australians will be talking about for months to come . . ."

Not so little, at five-foot eight-inches, and looking – as *The Daily Telegraph* reported – 'a good seven or eight years younger than his 45 years,' (46 going on 47, actually!). They played in Melbourne, Adelaide and Sydney, to packed houses – and ecstatic responses. Monks speaks of 'three frenetic hours which encompassed five encores, countless standing ovations and the heartfelt chant of 'more, more, more!' probably never before heard at Melbourne's stately old Comedy Theatre.' He listed 'with awe' the repertoire offered – complex, moody melodies, new and old songs, country music and Jewish music, Russian, rock, folk and spiritual music . . . 'Not for years have I been able to enjoy a performance in which every softly sung word could be heard and understood . . . and wonderful backing . . .'

He went on (and on!) to describe the group 'each of them, I would guess, capable of filling any hall in Australia at which they chose to give a solo performance.' To cap it all, Leonard threw in a new – and so far unissued – song, 'a rollicking Cohen spiritual about the hot gospeller Billy Sunday who tried unsuccessfully to shut down Chicago's sin and sex centres,' capping his own report by the claim that Leonard's renown had been 'acclaimed by the Sinatras, Streisands and Diamonds of this world.' He also sang 'Thirsty For The Kiss', an early version of 'Heart With No Companion' which had its first presentation at the Hammersmith Odeon the previous December.

It was no passing moment of glory. Throughout his tour he and his team earned glowing tributes for their hard and thoughtful work, of which Steve Hunter of the *Adelaide Advertiser* wrote, 'He was having a ball . . . (with) his marvellous colleagues'; and the *Sydney Mirror* referred to 'Leonard Cohen . . . the music renaissance man' (dropping the comment *en passant* that his books had now been translated into 'more than 20 languages.') *The Sydney Morning Herald* called him 'the darling of the thinking flower-children,' and another paper referred to him as 'Legendary Leonard.' To one journalist Leonard described his 'razor-blade philosophy' (the *Advertiser*'s description, not the singer's):

"I believe there is a lot of goodwill in society and in man . . . You can in some way place yourself at the disposal of the goodwill that does exist, or you can say that there is no goodwill in society and what we must do is destroy the whole thing. I believe that in the most corrupt and reactionary circles there is goodwill. I believe that men are mutable and that things can change. It's a matter of how we want things to change."

'Razor-blade philosophy' or political truth, it owed more to Hasidic doctrine than suicidal despair or Stuart Mill reasoning; still less Ockhanite logic: the word-beyond-the words was getting through, on the other side of the world. He had said similar things to the *Sun And*

Herald by telephone, prior to his arrival (such was his present buoyancy): "I have a feeling that something's coming, a new kind of music for me. I don't know how to describe it. It's just a feeling that something is about to end and a new beginning will make itself felt," – which earned him the *sobriquet* 'the most enduring and emotionally honest poet . . . on the fringes of rock and roll.' To this *The Flinders News* issued a single judgment: 'spellbinding'. John Hiscock interviewed him before he left, also for the *Australian*, to whom Leonard explained the personal aspect of his work more fully, and more frankly:

"I can't get beyond that. I don't have the confidence, the nerve or the insight to write about the vast movements of mankind – if there are such things. I never got out of my personal life."

It is quite different from artistic or poetic conceits; more profound than merely 'the first-person singular' reflex of his early years; it is a serious response to man's existence, as one among many and – by extension – one on behalf of many. It is a species of that 'oneness' which ever plagued, and eluded, him; of which Janis Joplin (who was far better read and more profound a thinker than her show-biz persona demonstrated) reported, when she said to her biographer Myra Friedman: "I'm into me, plus they're into me, and everything comes together." And, picking up the threads of the Thomson interview, Leonard commented (to Pat Bourring, of *The Sun*), "People who laugh and smile all the time can drive you to a nervous breakdown. Being serious is a pleasant condition!" Karen Hughes dared to suggest that he was more Buddhist than Jewish, which was bluntly denied by Leonard: "I am not a Buddhist, but a Jew."

His ability to appreciate truth behind teaching or symbols of any description had been part of his mental furniture from his teens, part of his unsatisfied quest for ultimate truth. But he would not renounce his Judaism. He was in fact moving towards it more conservatively now, towards even the Orthodox position. But that did not quench his thirst for knowledge – never better epitomised than when he escorted Roshi to Thomas Merton's former Gethsemane Monastery in Kentucky, for talks with its Abbot. They were invited to attend Mass, which they did, Leonard finding the occasion very moving – especially the bell-ringing at the elevation of the host.

The Australian experience was crowned by CBS issuing a statement that his album had gone gold – after all those years with feet of clay! – and issuing a boxed set of four of his albums as a special momento of the tour. In leaving Australia, Leonard had confided to the *Sydney Sun And Herald* that he was planning to "go off somewhere quiet for a couple of years." But it did not quite turn out that way, for the newspaper also reported his being involved in a sort of *Kramer*

Versus Kramer situation, which was, as Professor Andrew Greeley has pointed out, not just about the tug-of-war child but about personal and sexual fulfilment in a relationship that has matured sourly. The upshot was that he spent his summer months with Adam and Lorca, now eight and six-years-old respectively, thoroughly enjoying their company in Montreal and on Hydra.

In Montreal Leonard's 25th anniversary in art was celebrated in a special show co-written by David Blue (an old friend of Bob Dylan's from the 'Kettle Of Fish' days), Barrie Lee Wexler and Catherine Latraverse. It gathered material from his novels and songs, and projected this 'with enormous respect' in biographical terms. Leonard, who dislikes this form of publicity, expressed his regret that he was unable to be present, due to being on retreat (or in retreat?) in New York. He found time to revisit his monastery, and rebuild his spent forces with Roshi, before appearing at Berkeley's 'Bread And Roses' Festival, in the Greek Theatre – connections abundant! One of the highlights of this was 'a stunning performance' he and Jennifer Warnes gave of 'Memories', from the Spector album. After which there was more time 'twisting his feet' – and facing the ambiguous dilemma expressed in George Wither's 'Mistress Of Philarete':

> *'Thoughts too deep to be expressed*
> *And too strong to be suppressed'*

He may never 'have got out of (his) personal life,' but from within it he was discovering truths and messages that connected all round the world – heart to heart, and lip to lip . . .

His mind and energies were well occupied with domestic matters during the summer of 1980, but by late October they were once again on tour – his sixth of Europe, to which some concerts in Israel were added. Once again, they played to packed houses, Leonard and his 'marvellous musicians', offering his 'new kind of music.' Such were the pressures that they only found time for a single day's rehearsal, at Besançon, following which they were off via Geneva and Zurich to Lille, Brussels, Amsterdam, Vienna, Munich, Dortmund, Bonn, Eppelheim, Frankfurt; returning via Nancy, Strasbourg, Mulhouse, St Etienne, Lyon, Clermont-Ferrand, San Sebastian, Barcelona, Toulouse; then back into Germany again – by now one of Leonard's largest centres of following and interest – to Berlin, Hamburg and Freiburg, from which they took their leave for Tel Aviv.

'They change their clime, not their disposition,' said Horace, 'who run beyond the sea.' And it is so with those who soar beyond the clouds, too. Though still buffeted by domestic and emotional discharges, still given to sharp pangs of guilt, he was in fact beyond his Rubicon. He could sense – and write – 'the new music' precisely because 'the war' was over; only the mopping-up operations remained, which he undertook in terms of 'blackening pages,' twisting his feet at home in Montreal and California, and in the greater solitude of Hydra. Lewis Furey accompanied him.

Leonard was now studying Spenserian stanzas, ("I get engrossed in form every few years," he commented), which gave birth to the idea of a song-cycle, the story of a rock-star who got 'burned out'. He found he was able to write the songs 'very quickly,' Lewis liked them, and they eventually developed into *Night Magic*, as we shall see. It was at this time that Manzano stayed on Hydra, researching for his biography. The children were with him, and Leonard was clearly enjoying immensely his role as *père de famille*. One of the interview-sessions was interrupted by Lorca bringing flowers to her father (who was actually in bed with 'flu); Manzano noticed that the food he prepared for them was Jewish, as well as noticing that the album 'Hymns Of The Temple' was one of three records in the house. (The others were by Bach and Keith Jarret, the latter an old friend from Leonard's Newport days.)

It was not only a time for Leonard to make his own reassessments, but for the academic world to make theirs' too. Books and theses at all levels had been gathering in Canada and other places, analysing, construing, proposing and disposing of his talents – or alleged lack of them – according to their writers' position or stance. Jacques Vassal had published his *Leonard Cohen* (in collaboration with Jean-Dominique Brierre, who wrote on *Beautiful Losers*) in Paris as far back as 1974, in a *livre de poche* format, essentially an uncritical overview of his work. And Stephen Scobie had published his *Leonard Cohen* in the *Studies In Canadian Literature* series of Douglas And McIntyre Ltd, in 1978, a much more rigorous assessment of his work to that date (which included a preview of the withdrawn manuscript *My Life In Art* – later released, though much changed, as *Death Of A Lady's Man;* and a reference to *The Woman Being Born* which has never appeared, though it lent its name at one stage to a recension of *My Life In Art*).

It is characteristic of Scobie's assessment (as became a study in 'Canadian Literature') that the poetry is covered in 64 pages; the novels in 53; and the songs in a mere 38 pages – i.e. his written work (covering 13 years offers 117 pages, or 60 per cent of the whole) in which Leonard's 'finest achievement' was said to be *Beautiful Losers;* and the songs, although 'written', only claiming 20 per cent of the available space for 12 years in which Scobie says that it is typical of Leonard to risk all, which he is believed to have done in this type of work!

Yet it is at least arguable that Leonard took far greater pains, and influenced far more people, with his songs. The songs are treated but superficially by Scobie; they are not connected with the life (he admits to having never met him and astonishingly disowns the need). And so, while interesting and often informative, the viewpoint is shallow, if not paltry. It reminds one of the foolish saying of Beaumarchais, quoted earlier: 'That which is not worth saying is sung' – which ignores the immense influences of war-songs and national anthems, psalmic and hymnic traditions, the early bards and troubadours and so on, most of whose songs – and much more has regrettably been lost – flourished in a pre-writing (or, at least, pre-printing) day. It is another demonstration of the scholar being overawed by his own *métier* (if not his own words) and of failing to understand the sheer importance of 'non-literary' modes (though Leonard's peers in the music industry, and not a few outside it, emphasised the immense contribution he was making to song by his own literary standards). Said Anatole France, setting truer standards, 'The good critic is he who narrates the adventure of his soul among the masterpieces'; and Pope warned: 'Tis hard to say if greater want of skill/Appears in writing or in judging ill.' It is the wise critic who follows their lead.

One who did follow that lead was Gene Ornelas who commented, at the time of launching the musical *Bird On The Wire*, an off-Broadway production, which had its première at the American Arts Festival, 'His stuff (sic) is timeless. I mean he writes about love, war and suicide; and no matter where you are, what era you're from, it hits home.'

The director of the show, Stefan Rudnicki, said of his production: "(It is) a fast-paced and passionate musical that examines the integrity of the individual in contemporary society." In addition to 'Bird On The Wire', Rudnicki used 17 other songs and poems of Leonard's, as well as dance-routines. (Shades here of his mother's criticism, perhaps; but an important foretaste of his development into dance, as we shall shortly see.) The director stressed that his aim was, "to bring the audience to a point of rapport with the actors; create a spatial and emotional relationship that will encourage them to come to grips *with the question of personal freedom as opposed to involvement in social and political issues.*" (Our italics.) Said Leonard, who had flown back from Greece to see the dress rehearsal on hearing of this 'second-generation' interest in his work, and was clearly pleased at their perceptions: "It was designed to last. It is carefully constructed to be ageless . . ."

Leonard, meanwhile, was moving towards his most important work to date – if one takes seriously his 30-year struggle with his self-identity, his destiny, which found its high plateau in the new songs of this period and reached its *apogee* in his *Book Of Mercy*. A piece of work that kept him out of the public eye, shuttling between Montreal, New York, Hydra and Los Angeles, one which required the concentration of 'heart and soul and might.'

'an unstrain'd
quality of mercy'

When Leonard published *Book Of Mercy* he faltered. And from time to time he has faltered over it since. He knew how dangerous it was to release it, what comments it would invoke in the half-seeing, the little minds dedicated to self-interested comment and criticism. It could be called the most courageous act of his life, not least because, having decided to do it, he had to commit himself publicly. He had to go all the way. But we should not underrate or minimise its importance to him. Through his experiences he had been inwardly *broken;* his 'silence' was of the ultimate sort – the cessation of his work, the death of his hopes, the destruction of his destiny. But such finality in the religious life never takes place with those who still have faith, be it ever so small. 'Where there is life, there is hope' is true primarily of the inner life. The spark having been rekindled, Leonard had no choice but to fan it, and persevere. It was that, or inner extinction.

The book's cover-design uses a logo drawn by Leonard himself, which could have killed the book! A star of David – the sacred *mogen David* – set up in the form of intertwined hearts. The snideness of some critics apart, it is a brilliant projection of the hexagram, and of the truth in the statement, to quote the rabbis again, that 'The heart sees better than the eye.' But it is part of Leonard's 'wider ecumenism', too. He has 'taken the corners' off the hexagram, he explained, to lessen its angularity; he was not willing – despite his pride in his Tradition – to be isolated by it. He was aware that 'no one will love me for it,' for trying to hold the Tradition 'in a common place,' amid tension 'between those who will dissolve the edges and those who hold them.' He knew what he was about, this 'prophet of the heart': not mere romanticism; not mere emotion; not mere sensation; certainly not sentimentality – not even sentiment: but that 'quality of mercy' which is one of the profoundest ethics in religious awareness.

This mercy needs to be commensurate with 'the quality of the experience' that precipitated it. 'Mercy' is one of the most important words in Judaism; indeed, it is its fulcrum. Its English equivalent is best understood as 'loving-kindness' but there are strong overtones of forgiveness and reconciliation within it. The ethical demand can, in fact, only be fulfilled out of the reconciliation that is offered by it. It is a true counterpart to the divine nature itself. Despite the myopia of some critics, it has been a constant in Leonard's work from the start. Gillian Harding Russell may speak of, 'Cohen's new reverence for things of the spirit,' and Peter Goddard may draw our attention to 'new life on the road,' but that is merely to fail to see the continuous outline of the upward path; what is new is the *experience* of the quality of mercy, not the developing concept itself.

In his books of poetry, we find it, for example, in *The Spice-Box Of Earth* (1961) in 'If It Were Spring'; in *Flowers For Hitler* (1964) in 'The Project' and 'I Had It For A Moment'; in *The Energy Of Slaves* (1972) in 'I Am No Longer At My Best'; in *Death Of A Lady's Man* (1977) in no less than six references: 'The News You Really Hate', 'The Beetle', 'A Working Man', 'The Window', 'Sacrifice' and 'Now I Come Before You'.

In his songs, it found secular expression as far back as 1966, when the 'Sisters Of Mercy' had comforted him in his icy loneliness in Canada, far from home and at odds with himself. It reappeared on his second album (1969), in 'The Story Of Isaac', when he appeals – against the genocide of Vietnam and other wickedness – to have 'mercy on our uniform/Man of peace and man of war/The peacock spreads his (deadly) fan.' It had a strong contention in 1974, in *New Skin For The Old Ceremony*, when, in 'A Singer Must Die For The Lie In His Voice' (i.e. for the lack of accuracy) he agrees to ask for 'the mercy that you (the false judges) love to decline.'

And the album he was presently working on, at the time when he was putting the final touches to this book, has four references to it: first, in 'The Law', in which he says his faults have been such that he cannot honour them even with the concept of guilt – 'I'm not asking for mercy/Not from the man'; still less so in the early proceedings – 'You just don't ask for mercy/While still on the stand.' It occurs in 'The Captain' in which he calls on Christ to have mercy on the captain's soul for 'making such a joke' of the holocaust and the crucifixion: 'the captain who was dying/though the captain was not hurt.' And it reaches its most pregnant expression to date in 'If It Be Your Will' in the prayer-song – 'If it be your will . . ./Let your mercy spill/On all these burning hearts in hell . . .' (The Shavian attitude, it will be recalled, was 'to build a Heaven in Hell's despair.')

Through these usages he has very skilfully brought the matter from the earthly – our human, passionate experience – to the heavenly – our knowledge of and need for mercy in the highest 'court' of all, the divine presence. It is very significant that in every reference prior to 1974 there is a *secular* orientation: the quality of mercy is human, neighbourly (itself a key Jewish concept); in the mid-seventies, in the throes of his great trauma, which threatened to still his voice for ever, he discovered – or rather, appropriated personally – its fuller dimension. It is similar with his books: only in 1977 (in *Death Of A Lady's Man*) does he break through the secular connotation of the word, and even then only in the last two references given above though if 'The Woman Being Born' refers not to Leonard himself but mercy, as a female attribute, then that would mark the significant beginnings of the development.

The first, in 'Sacrifice', a poem in the form of a series of open couplets, a beautiful prayer – equal to anything he ever wrote – which Leonard describes as 'the working of Mercy.' It might be termed 'The song of the converting sensualist,' for its whole thrust lies in self-conscious shame that he only has his lower nature to offer, which is positively Augustinian in tone – or even Paulian. In 'Now I Come Before You' we have a series of quatrains which are full of poetic aspiration and prayerful penitence:

> '*Grave decision to be holy*
> *Rebel cry to storm the sky*
> *Boring tracks of reason's folly*
> *Stumbling back to wonder, why?*'

It concludes, as all genuine spirituality does, with a prayer for others:

> '*Mercy, mercy on your creatures*
> *Judge the world from every heart*
> *Bless us with your gentler measures*
> *Keep our lives and deaths apart.*'

And that is precisely where it all started, 3,500 years ago, on Sinai, where Moses's call was – via Aaron, the first *Kohen*, to make known the divine mind, which was 'to will mercy' on his people, and through them, the world. It is so important a concept – here Ginsberg's 'naming' comment could not be more ignorant – that the divinity is called 'the god of mercy and compassion.' So powerful is the concept that it now acts as the fulcrum for Judaism, Christianity and Islam – to say nothing of worldwide influences beyond them over 4000 years and more.

Book Of Mercy is therefore a confession, a prayer, an *apologia*, a psalm of praise. Indeed, it was very nearly termed 'A Book Of Psalms' – the name of the manuscript first taken to his long-time publisher and friend, Jack McClelland (he still refers to it as such today, the word meaning 'praise' more than our 'psalm'). In doing so Leonard was not driving a completely new course, nor plotting a new way forward, as some reviewers have suggested. We have seen that the tapestry of his life is gold-threaded with such awareness. True, he may at times – like Augustine of old – have prayed 'Lord, make me pure; but not yet!' But it was always there.

Now if the age of 40 is 'for understanding,' that of 50 – which Leonard was now approaching – 'is for counsel,' according to Talmudic wisdom. He had earned his position of authority not by inheritance or good breeding (both of which he could claim), but by hard learning – in the school of life; by experience, and the revealed wisdom that flows through it. He had learned to 'follow his little heart'; suffered in its cause; and so could now step forward with an unfolding of that wisdom 'from heart to heart, lip to lip'; the voice had never been more specific nor clearer.

There are two points prefatory to this concept that are essential if the book is to be understood and if its structure is to be meaningful: The first is that the acts of mercy or kindness (which we saw in another context above) are technically known in Judaism as 'the sanctifying of the Name' (*Kiddush ha-Shem*): God is made holy by their performance. So great was the sense of awe and respect at the word 'God' that they refused to spell it out, and so would write it as G-d, or even as 'the Name' (*ha-Shem*), which Leonard was now tending to do.

The second point refers to the process by which one who has been away from God, ignored his precepts, could return. It lay in reciting the psalms which 'is a specific practice that has the power to bring a person back to God,' as Nachman of Bratislava commented. He explains – and the point is by no means easy – that there are 50 'gates of return' – 49 of which are in man's power, the 50th is within God's alone. The 49 gates are symbolically paralleled to the letters of the names of the 12 Tribes of Israel, in Hebrew. Each 'gate' is identified with one of those letters. The practice rests on the fact that the Israelites wandered for 49 days in the wilderness between Egypt and Sinai; so each letter is reminiscent of a day's travel in their path back to the Promised Land; each letter is a gate of return. On the 50th day, in Sinai, they received the divine revelation, not least the word of mercy to forgive and restore. The *Book Of Exodus* recounts that story, and the very first line in it says '*These are the names of Israel's sons who came* out of Egypt.' The final letter in Hebrew of each of these italicised words, when put together forms the word *tehillim* – that is the Hebrew word for 'Psalms'. Hence the reading and recitation of psalms is construed as a way back to God. Any man can find it by so doing. King David was the 'sweet psalmist of Israel,' hence his importance for the Tradition.

Moreover, in *II Samuel* 23:1, which records poetically 'the last words of David,' the king is described as the one 'who raised the yoke' ('raised on high' in the English versions) which the Talmud interprets as, 'the yoke of repentance and return to God.' His sin with Bathsheba – which progressed from covetousness to adultery, to attempted deception, to murder, and then to perjury – his subsequent penitence, and his honourable actions – not least vis à vis Bathsheba, despite it all, was regarded as *the* paradigm for the repentant man. *Psalm 51* is the expression of that experience, which starts the second cycle of readings. An even more circuitous contact between David and Egypt is found in the Hebrew word for Egypt: *Mitzraim* comes from the word *metzar*, i.e. 'throat'. It is said that this connects with the 'highest' type of repentance: a low confessional groan which is made by narrowing the throat, as if in pain. David is understood to have made that confession in *Psalm 51*.

Leonard himself made a further, and unique, point to Tony Paris, when he referred to the characteristically 'Lorcan' aspect of *duenta*, (compare *duende!*) as "deep throat, so to speak . . . that feeling, that emotion, that comes from the singer." The etymology may not be exact, but the perception is – more disparates connecting! Be that as it may, the spiritual equation reads: honest self-awareness + repentance = psalm-reading = restoration = public usefulness (i.e. acts of kindness).

Leonard, for his 50th birthday, signified his own 'return' not only by treading the recognised path of formal repentance (friends at this time commented on the regularity of his synagogue attendance – frequently a daily observance), but by penning his own 'psalms' – 50 in all, which are representative of his own wanderings from enslavement, (*The Energy Of Slaves* is a true harbinger of *Death Of A Ladies' Man*, and of this book). For obvious reasons – not least with its gold Star of David emblazoned on the cover – there was anxiety, not posing, behind the release of the book. And it was justified!

The times were not, at least on the surface, propitious for such a book. Too many convenient 'rebirths' had occurred, quite apart from a prevailing disinterest in religion. Further, he knew that with his reputation old scores could be settled; manipulation and misrepresentation were more than possible. The purblind scanner of the *Montreal Gazette* called it atheistic, which merely demonstrated a fine ignorance of language. Such are the acids of inanity! Moreover, to say that *Book Of Mercy* 'attempts to be nothing less than a modern counterpart to the biblical psalms,' as Mark Abley did, is to claim too much. Such misconceptions were by no means few. But one point was well made: that the book 'provides resplendent evidence of an arduous spiritual journey,' which places it in the much more sensible line of such works as Augustine's *Confessions*, Bunyan's *Pilgrim's Progress*, or Newman's *Apologia Pro Vita Sua*, if on a lower scale. Howard Schwartz – an expert in Jewish poetry – wrote more perceptively when he spoke of Leonard as 'one of the leading Jewish poets of his generation,' who 'took the risky step of writing a book of modern psalms, many of which unabashedly address issues of spiritual and religious belief. Remarkably, the book succeeds . . .'

To *Now*'s reporter he revealed that he had not set out to write a book at all (still less 'a modern counterpart to the book of psalms'): "I wrote it out of the deepest kind of urgency . . . I was lucky (that) I could find the language of prayer that ended my silence. In a sense it's a formal piece – they are psalms; it is prayerful expression . . ." In an interview with Peter Goddard of the *Toronto Star* Leonard commented:

"There are times when you feel yourself stopped and silenced, and you have to penetrate that source of mercy, that source of forgiveness in your own life. That's what these psalms are about – trying to locate that source of mercy that enables you to re-enter the world."

And to Beverley Slopen he described it more concisely: "It's a little book of prayers," adding that he had put it together "about a-year-and-a-half ago . . . the result, I guess, of looking into these matters for three or four years." This shows that his path of return commenced in early 1979 – in the wake of *Death Of A Lady's Man*, though there are indications in that book (e.g. 'I have begun to turn against this man and against this book') which show in which direction his mind had been moving. Similarly, in *The Energy Of Slaves* which prepared the way for *Death Of A Lady's Man*, he had indicated a like response: 'the poems don't love us any more.' It is a very great mistake to say that he was quitting poetry with this latter book. His expectations of it, his style in it changed, but his poetry became much more the language of the heart – the prophetic mode – in writing or in song. His path of return was thus over many years, a genuine, upward path.

Of the guilt that lay behind the experience, he made a point of critical importance for the understanding of his mind:

"People should not be afraid of feeling guilt; it's the only way they know if they are on the wrong track. Sin is equitable with that sense of alienation, isolation, of profound loneliness that is the result of ourselves distancing ourselves from this world which we are meant to inhabit."

This is a much more positive response to guilt than that which is encapsulated in his description of Breavman: 'One day what he did to her, to the child (a new note this), would enter his understanding with such a smash of guilt that he would sit motionless for days until others carried him and medical machines brought him back to speech.' The essence of 'mercy' is new hope, new life, new language.

Despite the book's detractors, it was good enough to win the 1985 Canadian Authors Association Literary Award for Poetry – connecting anew in his homeland, but for many more around the world with a particular appetite, with ears to hear.

The title of our chapter is actually from Shakespeare's *The Merchant Of Venice*, but the phrase runs back through literature, not least to the *Zohar* itself. Gershorn Scholem has summarised part of its doctrine thus:

'The totality of Divine powers forms an harmonious whole . . . The wrath of God is symbolised by His left hand, while the quality of mercy and love, with which it is intimately bound up, is called His right hand . . . Thus the quality of stern judgment . . . is always tempered by His mercy . . .'

Once again we have opposites, contradictions, a paradox; once again we have oneness, connections; beauty and unmeaning. In the light of which discovery and strength Leonard was returned to work, and that in the wake of his broken romance and its effects on him, not least in the wake of his two more negative reactions – in *Death Of A Lady's Man*, the book, and 'Death Of A Ladies' Man', the record. He had to consolidate the truer voice of 'Recent Songs'. He could only do that effectively by prayer; he knew only too well the rabbinic *caveat:* 'Better pray for yourself than curse another.' "*Book Of Mercy* is literally an act of prayer," he remarked to Michael Mirolla of *The Gazette*. "It is not a luxury or a choice . . . the writing of it, in some ways, was the answer to the prayer . . . The book is the result of my devotion to my God and to a religious tradition. It came about out of what I had been doing; out of a need within me." He went on to explain, as he had done many times before, in defending the personal details and experiences of his life being made into poetry and fiction, in books and songs by saying:

"It is true (that) these are the intimate conversations between my heart and the source of mercy. But my feeling is that if the thing becomes intimate enough and personal enough and true enough, then it will speak for everybody . . . This is the condition for universality, this absolute intimacy."

The poet of the two great intimacies thereby unveils his *apologia*. As Joseph Kertes commented in *Books Canadian*, '*Book Of Mercy* will stand as one of the most honest and courageous attempts in Canadian writing to grapple with ultimate truth.' But it does not do so easily. Like

Job of old, like the psalmists themselves, they had to lay their plaints before God. That was the confession; that was the way back, the word was never more scarring.

The book is dedicated 'for my teacher' i.e. his Zen-Buddhist master, Roshi – a title curiously close to the Hebrew *rosh* meaning head or chief, which produced several Rashis. (Yet more connections!) Now an old man of 75 but still full of vigour and profound wisdom, it was a fitting tribute to his almost 20 years of tuition and counsel, but most of all friendship, from which Leonard had benefited. "I am enamoured of this old Japanese," commented Leonard candidly.

Some find in this relationship yet another contradiction, this reliance on non-Jewish succour, but really it is simply another thread – perhaps of shorter duration than others – by which Leonard's multi-faceted world is sewn together. Similarly, he could use Catholic ideas and terminology, even finding space in this book for the startling expression 'Our Lady of the Torah' – as audacious an epithet as one could conceive; virginal, no doubt! Perhaps, more surprisingly, is the reference to the eternal enemies of the Jews in the 14th piece: 'Blessed Are You . . .', by which a prayer of blessing is offered for 'the sons of Ishmael,' the Arabs. And that despite the recent wars, in one of which Leonard himself had served. Although it is a remonstrance, too: 'Blessed be Ishmael for all time, who covered his face with the wilderness, and came to you in darkness' . . .

But Roshi was not the sole teacher of this heart. The 21st piece carries a diatribe against his false teacher, who appears to be some dried-out, would-be guru who knew all the names, controlled all the arguments, directed by too much counsel – of the wrong sort, in the wrong way, and untimely to boot: 'My teacher gave me what I do not need, told me what I need not know . . . He referred me to the crickets when I had to sing, and when I tried to be alone he fastened me to a congregation. He curled his fist and pounded me toward my proper shape . . .' Whether it was Roshi – his friend and wise counsellor – acting as devil's advocate; or whether it was an actual 'guru', or type of guru, is not important. He deals here with the typical reaction from the fundamentalist who, knowing too much, reveals that he knows very little – if anything at all.

It ends on a note of bitter irony, of Savonarolan intensity and disgust: 'When he was certain that I was incapable of self-reform, he flung me across the fence of the Torah.' Now 'Torah' not only means 'law', 'teaching' or 'doctrine' (notably the Mosaic law and doctrine), but also Judaism itself; to live or live by, or practise Torah, means to be a Jew, to have that sort of commitment, espouse its beliefs, philosophy and values. To 'fence the Torah' is to protect it – even as Moses had to fence-off Sinai, i.e. keep its sanctity intact.

There are not a few references in Leonard's work to his being persecuted, labelled 'a traitor'. None is more direct than that in 'Recent Songs', in which – in 'The Traitor' (never performed publicly, so far as we can trace, so scalding are its words) his leaving his mother and all that she signified, by whom his Jewishness was realised – he is censored in grim judgment. It was not merely the judgment of those Judges 'from the other side,' who pronounced against him, but his contemporaries; who saw him risking his destiny for love, ruining his love in order to seek his destiny, yet missing ('by a fraction') his destiny because of his rejection of his love, and failing in his ultimate role as defender of what his destiny stood for through his belated actions and persistent loving: a Catch-22 situation. Such 'people' rise up and 'call me Traitor to my face.'

But years before this he had written similarly, in 'The Old Revolution' wherein he highlights his predicament: 'Lately you've started to stutter/As though you had nothing to say,' upon whom he turns in brass-necked annoyance (no signs of repentance then, in 1969, for that true quality of mercy had not been learned, nor was it really sought): 'To all my architects, let me be traitor . . .' He was even willing, then, to don the mantle of the *bogade*, the renegade-traitor in Judaism, whose judgment was to be 'flung . . . across the fence of the Torah.' An episode of harsh judgment which deeply wounded his family – not least his mother and her family's exalted rabbinic traditions. As is so often the case in religious returning, one's confession involves others – not infrequently to their cost, too.

The book is in two parts, a technique he used in his novels. The first 26 pieces occupy the first part, the remaining 24 pieces the second; an arrangement that cleverly breaks the 49 letters of the names of the 12 tribes at that of the Tribe of Levi, whence sprang Moses and Aaron, Leonard's own 'tribe'. Given some latitude the book breaks in a different way: the first part is personal, anguished, confessional; the second is national, even super-national, hopeful and decisive in its rededication. The first part is inward-looking, the second extroverted. The first indulges in self-abasement; the second rejoices in heavenly favours. What is barely anticipated in the first, finds exuberant declaration in the second. But with this limitation; that the book is a carefully wrought whole; its break is organic, not artificial; new life comes out of the old; it is not a new man that the second portrays, but a man renewed – and renewed according to his former longings, his highest aspirations. To the desperate plea, 'O shield of Abraham, affirm my hopefulness,' is rejoined the act of faith: 'But you are here. You have always been here . . . your name unifies the heart.' Oneness will out! The Great Potter has not discarded the old clay, he has remodelled it; the old hexagram is still there – if slightly redrawn; the brightness is still David's – a star of hope and wholeness (the double triangle represents that, as it does the Davidic peace itself) for the world: a quality and a magnitude of extraordinary dimensions, 'a necklace of incomparable beauty,' and very great meaning – for those who will 'connect'.

As we have learned to expect in Leonard's work, the book is a very rich depository for those prepared to ponder and meditate. It is not possible to touch on more than a small fraction of his insights, and in any case this biography is not the place to do it. (See our forthcoming 'commentary' on his songs, *Leonard Cohen: Troubadour Of Truth*, in which fuller information is offered.) But we should at least note the prophetic resonance of his voice in the opening section of Part Two:

> *'Israel, and you who call yourself Israel, the Church that calls itself Israel, and the revolt that calls itself Israel, and every nation chosen to be a nation – none of these lands is yours, all of you are thieves of holiness, all of you at war with Mercy.'*

Breavman may distance himself from Isaiah; in this passage Leonard is truly – and trenchantly – Isaianic. He goes on to harangue the nations – America, France, Russia, Poland are listed; even 'Ishmael' is called to account: 'The Covenant is broken, the condition dishonoured, have you not noticed that the world has been taken away?' The greatest of all the differences between the two parts – for those that have ears to hear, and not merely hang their jewellery on – is not between the personal and the supra-personal, not between the pain and the joy, nor even between the anticipation and the reality; but in the man himself: *he has confirmed his role.* The priest has become a prophet, indeed.

On such a basis, one question only can be asked, whose parts are: For whom does this man speak? Of whom does he speak? What is the source of his vision, his authority, his 'mercy'? That is perhaps the most triumphant point of the book. Out of his condition of being 'stopped and silenced'; from deep within his high sense of guilt and his low sense of self, he has emerged enlightened, even inspired. He has found the Name. He has 'penetrated' to the Source of mercy; he has 'located' it. Out of 'the deepest kind of urgency' he found 'the language' which ended his 'silence'. It was found to be 'not a luxury or a choice'; he admitted that he faltered in offering it for publication, but his courage won through: 'the intimate conversations between (his) heart and the source of mercy' found due expression.

The word is out: with those with ears to hear . . .

word as healing

'Great men are usually first understood when framed by the perspective of years. Something to give them perspective is necessary. The world is far-sighted and always confused by what takes place under its nose.'

ROBERT W. CHAMBERS

'Pay homage to the physician before you need him.'

JEWISH PROVERB

'You let me sing, you lifted me up, you gave my soul a beam to travel on. You drew tears back to my eyes. You hid me in the mountain of your word. You gave the injury a tongue to heal itself.'

LEONARD COHEN

varying positions

Psalms were not meant to be read. They were meant to be sung or recited, with instrumentation, backing vocalists, antiphonal balancings, and the fullest range of melodious accompaniment possible. Psalm 150 shows the way: calling for the use of horn, psaltery, harp, timbrel and dance, for stringed instruments and pipe, loud-sounding cymbals and clanging cymbals, 'and everything that has breath!' Leonard first had to learn the language – hear the voice, excise the unmeaning, plumb the depths before he could 'speak'; not out of his own silence, still less with his own words – and in marked contrast to mere verbal or musical dexterity. The journey took 30 years – the age when a prophet was permitted to speak in old Israel. It began with *Let Us Compare Mythologies;* it nearly died with *Death Of A Ladies' Man* – what a spectre! It found its comprehensive expression in 'Recent Songs', and achieved full expression in *Book Of Mercy* and then in 'Various Positions', his ninth album.

With it went various commitments and entertainments and, perhaps curiously, an increased willingness to talk to the press. He had never refused to speak to them in the past – to his cost; his candour not infrequently being misunderstood for naïvety. But now he sought to elicit intelligent questionings; to which he offered disarmingly frank replies (except about his family life); and even when the more mindless stereotypes were regurgitated he rerouted the questioner into real issues instead of playing verbal games with them. He who had confessed in *Book Of Mercy* that he had 'torn my soul on 20 monstrous altars, offering all things but myself' – a savage denouncing of his work, or at least of himself in the hands of his critics – now found new vistas opening up, new opportunities of work (and commentary) presenting themselves to him; the tide which occurs in the affairs of men he was taking at the flood – and speaking as never before.

In the Spring of 1983 he conceived the idea of making a film *I Am A Hotel* (shades of *I Am A Camera* perhaps?), which he wrote with fellow-Canadian Mark Shekter; Ann Ditchburn provided the choreography, and Allan Nichols (an associate of Robert Altman) was the producer. It incorporated five of his most provocatively imaged songs: 'The Guests', 'Memories', 'The Gypsy Wife', 'Chelsea Hotel, No 2', and 'Suzanne'. ('The Guests' was included twice in fact.) It was described by one reviewer as 'an off-beat musical drama,' but it was more of a species of resurrected (and filmed) *theatre naturelle;* the idea behind it being the personalised reminiscences of a hotel which reflects on its own history, recalling its past and the people who have used it, a not unsurprising development for he who had recently described himself as 'the kilt of Mount Royal.'

Leonard himself features largely in it, though not as one of the characters in the five scenarios which project the links – ephemeral and otherwise – between the residents of the hotel, but as the catalyst between them all, pensively puffing at a cigarette, a Hitchcock-styled presence who said little but inveighed the whole with a stream-of-consciousness meaning, not without autobiographical shadow.

To accomplish it he set up another company – his third – called the Blue Memorial Video Ltd of which Leonard was chairman (Moses Znaimer was president, and Barrie Wexler was vice-president. They called themselves 'the Montreal mafia'!). It was filmed at the prestigious King Edward Hotel, Toronto, and so delighted some previewers that it was entered for the 'Golden Rose' international television awards which take place at Montreux, in Switzerland where Leonard first played in 1976. It won First Prize, and got such excellent ratings that it was telecast at prime-viewing time both in North America and Europe. The poet-cum-novelist-cum-singer-songwriter-cum-priestly-prophet had become a producer of no uncertain mark. (The excellent responses to it fathered the idea of *The Favourite Game* being made into film, a much more ambitious scheme, which we may yet see.) In many and various ways the word was getting out – even if this one 'extended' the original meanings of the songs somewhat. A point Leonard was anxious to stress when interviewed by Daniel Gewertz of *The Boston Herald:*

"There's so much superficial information bombarding us, but entertainment can be more than distraction. This is a serious affair, this existence of ours. It's important that the real feelings in society and the life of the heart be affirmed."

As the Talmud expressed it, 'God wants the heart.' And Leonard was far too experienced a traveller, had lived in far too many hotels, not to realise the rich tapestry of humanity which could be found there.

I Am A Hotel, with its particular choice of songs, is his view of life – not least his own life – from that perspective.

He wrote with another Canadian, Lewis Furey, who had played the violin in 'New Skin For The Old Ceremony', a pop opera called the *Merry-Go Man* (also called *Night Magic* at its Cannes début, known elsewhere as *The Hall* or *Angel Eyes* – such was their uncertainty as to how to project it). Leonard penned the words on Hydra as we saw, and Furey wrote the music and directed the cast. To Michael Zwerin, of *International Herald Tribune*, Leonard confessed his relief at not having to sing: "I wrote the lines quickly because the story was outlined already . . . what a pleasure not to have to struggle with original meaning," he added, significantly.

It is an important cameo-view of his involvement with words, meaning and significance; showing that he could 'write to order' when required, as so many of his *confrères* did. But the real work, the one which conveyed the real word, 'the serious affair' came (as he so often said) 'a word at a time . . . line by line.' He was completely unwilling to be found judged 'for the lie in his voice' when himself responsible for conveying the message.

Night Magic was actually more ambitious than *I Am A Hotel*. Furey, a former sidesman-musician-singer, had now moved from musician to writer to film director (Leonard actually saw it as a ballet, he said, not a film), and seems to have relied more on stagecraft than plot; the result being a somewhat drawn-out and sketchy *pastiche*. 'Edna', of *Variety*, found it merely 'a series of songs and reflections about the clash between art and life, and the dedication of the creative spirit to his creation, to the exclusion of everything else,' which would have been an important portrayal had it come off. Perhaps it demonstrates the sagacious proverb '*chacun à son métier.*'

Leonard had left his real job for this, consented to do a pot-boiler (for all its sumptuous production, its technical competence and use of top actors such as Nick Mancuso, or top dancers such as Frank Augustyn and Anik Bissonette). The voice failed to appear. He had overlooked the old advice of Sir Thomas Browne: 'Though the world be Histrionical, and most men live Ironically, yet be thou what thou singly art, and personate only thy self. Swim smoothly in the stream of thy Nature, and live but one man.'

Both of the foregoing facilitated Leonard's 'return' though both were somewhat out of the public eye, which brought his almost five-year span of silence (from 1979 to 1984) to an end. Much of it was taken up with his self-assessments, self-abasements and writing, being a father to his children, which he was devotedly, and not least 'twisting his feet' with Roshi in the Californian monastery, where he had even agreed to raise money for the monastery, help build it physically, as well as ponder the perplexities of his life and lifestyle.

Out of that crucible pure silver issued, first tried in the Quadrasonic Sound Studios, New York; then released as 'Various Positions' on Jem Records' Passport Label. It immediately achieved Top 10 status in Spain, Portugal and Scandinavia, but only moderate success elsewhere; in America (where CBS had refused to handle it!) it had a disappointing response. As he explained to Paul King of *The Toronto Star* (with regard to his book, but its actuality was realised in the album), "I just wanted to sing and dance before the Lord." In that he was being true to his nature, swimming smoothly in its stream, and surmounting from time to time (like a glorious Canadian salmon!) each waterfall and impediment with dexterity.

Once again Leonard was the main producer, aided by John Lissauer, John Crowder on bass, Richard Crooks on drums, guitarist Sid McGuinness who had accompanied him on his European tour of 1976, Kenneth Kosek on fiddle and Ron Getman on harmonica. The most interesting vocal development was Leonard himself, whose voice – now a little deeper (thanks, he said, to heavy cigarette smoking) – had found its true level, well modulated, a soft baritone of extraordinary sympathy; with good breathing, pitch and projection, as good as anything in the past and very much better than most. The sound discovered earlier was now raised to something beyond mere sound – a melodious and mellifluous issuing of great spiritual intensity, a poem-in-song, a hymn, a psalm, a chant – and all of these things in very stylish harmony, even without the magic of Raffi Hakopian and John Bilezikjian.

And it was not merely religious; not overtly spiritual. He still managed to offer highly sensual feeling, demonstrate the beauties of physical love and longing; still offer, even to those without 'particular appetite', a feast of music and song. The songs on this album were 'Dance Me To The End Of Love', 'Coming Back To You', 'The Law', 'The Night Comes On', 'Hallelujah', 'The Captain', 'The Hunter's Lullaby'; 'The Heart With No Companion', and, 'If It Be Your Will'. Nine songs which offer not so much a panorama of viewing, but a diorama of experience, of 'various positions' from which one may perceive reality, according to need and taste.

As he said to Zwerin, "I think of myself as a reporter looking at a landscape. I try not to complain too much. I try to be objective. I don't think you can maintain that self-respect unless there's an element of objectivity." The reporter had difficulty (not for the first time!) with the word 'objective', failing to realise that the 'landscape' to which Leonard referred was the interior one. He missed the point of Leonard's 'objectivity' (better, accuracy) so the point was further explained in which Leonard sought to show how his own experiences could have meaning for others (the personal/intimate – general/universal axis), now a firm principle. As he further remarked: "The lines are free to assume various positions . . . but anybody who lifts their voice in song has to be hopeful." It reflects the truth behind his retort on the *Saturday Night* programme about being able to pour 'any emotion' into them; not because they are literally 'empty' – as if devoid of meaning – but as with a mould – which can transmit 'the mix' from one shape to another only by itself being in the condition conducive to the process.

In putting the songs together thus, he was not 'melding . . . romance and religion, sex and epiphany,' as Goddard stated. As Leonard himself confessed with more than a hint of humour (ever present in his work), "I've probably achieved the ultimate confusion of woman and God (his two great intimacies again) with this album. But, you know, sometimes when you meet a person who is really touched by the spirit, it looks like (he's) in love. (But) you can't tell in love with what."

'He is still in touch with 'ultimate truth',' to quote Joseph Kertes, despite the earthiness of his songs, a point the less seeing reviewers, such as Trevor Dann (in the *Sunday Telegraph*) could not grasp. 'The most thoroughly miserable performer since Robb Wilton,' he moaned; attempting to liven his whinging by quoting Atkin and James' parody of 'Bird On The Wire': 'Like a cat on a rail, like the next note up the scale, count to 10, pause and them, down again.' But the squib failed: reporting at its feeblest. The simple fact is that his high points of romantic love are expressed in a supra-physical consummation. Indeed, such is his reverence for the created order – our bodies not least, the ordained vehicle for that 'image of God' – that he can gladly highlight its importance, emphasise its meaning, exult in the joy of spirit that it gives alongside that proper joy of body and senses.

As we saw in *Beautiful Losers*, sainthood – the expression of the energy of love – adheres to this world and its 'chaos'; to men and women, good or bad; matter matters. Experience had reinforced, not weakened, the characteristically Jewish approbation of physical love which is considered as a holy urge, a sacred duty, even a divine joy. As Jacob Epstein expressed it: 'The sex organ should be considered no different from the hand, the foot or the nose. The hand is noble when it writes a Torah . . . the sex organ is noble when it expresses purity and love . . .' The *Shulchan Aruch* (the part of the Talmud dealing with marital and sexual relationships) even details the occurrence and regularity of intercourse: 'Men of strong constitution should perform their marriage duty nightly; labourers . . . twice a week; merchants . . . once a week; travellers to distant places . . . once in thirty days; learned men from Sabbath Eve to Sabbath Eve.' There is serious intent in the suggestion that 'learned men' – i.e. the rabbis – should be involved continuously in love-making. It was understood – and therefore strongly emphasised – that in so doing they were better fitted to serve God.

Jewish writings call on all men to behave so – to talk tenderly to, and be gentle with, their wives in order to appreciate the divine gifts, of which human love, fully consummated, is the finest and most complete expression, even as Paul and John would do in Christianity. Even the Catholic Church has started to believe in this fuller meaning, the deep 'oneness' that comes of male/female intimacy; as Greeley its sociologist-priest comments in *Confession*, 'Sex is edifying and religious and important.' The message of *Beautiful Losers* is getting through! Matter is now seen to be holy; magic is alive!

One of the problems with establishing a reputation for free loving, despite his learning (the problems are many, and painful, whether earned or not), is that people thereafter tend to view one through that prism, journalists not least. So it was not surprising to find some questioning him about 'Various Positions' as if he had written a postscript to the *Kama Sutra*. They had failed to hear him when he spoke in *Book Of Mercy*, failed to understand the 'major transformation in his outlook,' as Mark Paytress accurately perceived in *Record Collector* – not in repudiating sexuality, still less in espousing any form of celibacy – a denial of biblical doctrine, but in moving towards a much more orthodox commitment. As he said to Paul King: "I was brought up Conservative, but am veering more towards the Orthodox (position)."

Leonard had said that the book was his 'final statement' on religious awareness, which is important to note. He who had found himself by discovering mercy, and thereby confirmed his true *métier*, could now give himself to its perfecting and its proper accomplishments. But it was not to be his last – merely his latest. And not by any means his least important, for at least two of the 'positions' he was to take up in the new album were stoutly religious; indeed, they can be said to be the most important, and provide a *raison d'être* of the album – the *raison d'être* of Leonard himself, for in them the two great intimacies of the heart seriously understood – receive glorious expression. The 'brightness' of St Francis – the *Shekhinah* itself – was breaking through.

The 'positions' offered in song are almost as numerous as the metaphors he uses, and they may be detailed according to their position on the album as well as the mood and attitude they generate individually. But two things need to be said first: One, that the panorama offered – the landscape of his interior life – moves from the past through to the future; a full circle of experience encompassing the horrors behind 'Death Of A Ladies' Man' and the similarly titled book, through the period of pain and searching, hope and finding, to a position of peaceful resignation. The method and madness of *Beautiful Losers* has been sloughed off, the Danish Vibrator has given way to a more overt, if not more substantial DV (deo *volunte*): a triumphant yet humble surrender. He had learned the wisdom that 'he who tries to resist the wave is swept away, but he who bends before it abides.'

The second thing is that *Various Positions* can claim to be the most personal, the most honest of all his work yet. But with this distinction: that in the highly intimate unveilings of the past there has frequently been a note of anger, at times of bitterness, sometimes of frenzied denunciation. This one has none of that. It has candour, and honesty – and compassion. The mercy that had restored his equilibrium, remade his life and redirected his energies (not least the creative ones) is now offered to all who will listen, and think. He does not fudge the realities. He remains true to the principle of accuracy – not least in manifesting an honesty of tone, a breadth of understanding, of love and forgiveness, which places it head and shoulders above even 'Recent Songs'. That 'position' is the most important of all: 'to err is human,' as Pope saw long ago, 'to forgive, divine.' We have in this album, therefore, not only a kaleidoscopic viewpoint of earthly things, but also more than a gleam of the heavenly: a grand tour almost!

A third point, already made several times, is that with such a thinker as Leonard, who includes or implies, 'a blaze of light' in virtually every word he writes, no more than a fraction of his meanings, least of all his crypto-amnesia – selected to support and elucidate the life – can be given here. Our forthcoming commentary will naturally take this further. Stephen Holden described his general position on the album in the *New York Times* as demonstrating, 'the dialectical implication of vocal interplay of plus and minus, i.e. male and female; and the new album's most ambitious songs have the power of Old Testament fables secularised as troubadour song-poetry . . . The Jewish Blues are really a combination of C&W music and synagogue liturgy.' 'More pointedly allegorical,' quipped another reviewer, with discrimination.

Havelock Ellis commented in *The Dance Of Life*, that 'Dancing is the loftiest, the most moving, the most beautiful of the arts, because it is no mere translation or abstraction from life; it is life itself.' It is a recurrent theme in Leonard's writings – in his poems, novels and songs – whether it be the teenage Bunny Hop of Breavman; the 'frantic jitterbug or the slow foxtrot' of the Palais d'Or; 'those Roman girls/ who danced around a shaft of stone' in 'Celebration'; or even his and Layton's 'Hasidic dances to upset the Gentiles'!; or their dancing the *freilach*. Even as music, singing and dancing have always been a strong feature of synagogue activity, so life itself was indeed a dance to Leonard, despite the opposite image given by some members of the press and, whether engulfed in beauty or in panic, his hope – as with his first song here – was to be danced to the end of love: 'to sing and dance before the Lord.'

And it is human love of which he sings, which has always been a sacrament of the divine, in Judaism and in Christianity, and that suitably projected by invoking the *sirtaki* rhythms of Greece. Behind it, however, was a song of profound influence, one hummed by the Jews on their way to the ovens. As one of the riddles (read *koans*) of the Hebrew scriptures state: 'Out of the eater came forth food/And out of the strong came forth sweetness.' The Philistines, needless to say, could not understand it.

But this is not to 'confuse woman and God,' as he informed Goddard. It is to be able to signal the one by the other. Much of the imagery of this song is drawn from a religious, i.e. biblical, database: the dance itself – a *very* Davidic concept, beauty not least 'the beauty of the word' – olive branches, the dove, Babylon, and the tent of shelter. It is – his first main position – a position of joy and hope. It is a song of hopeful love, a prayer conveying trust. It was released as a single, and then further extended (ostensibly as a promotional video) by Dominique Isserman's brilliant photography in 'Dance Me To The End Of Love'. Significantly, it was made in black and white – so much of Leonard's work exists in 'monochrome' – not out of any 'depressive' sense however, but because ultimate reality is thereby best conveyed. Said Leonard to Manzano, "We all move between beauty and death. Eros and death are the two decisive poles between which our life is made (*que originan nuestra vida*)."

To the hope of this opening song is attached the desolation that he had encountered so often in the past – another position. In a condition of 'still hurting', he announces that she knows that he still loves her, even though he cannot speak; he looks for her anxiously 'in everyone'; even though he lives alone, he was still 'coming back' to her. But he knows that it is a futile hope: 'all the senses rise against this/Coming back to you'; hence, more silence is demanded – 'another mile' of it, in fact – while he's coming back to her, ever hopefully. He knows there are many others now in her life; that he has to deal with the 'envy' resulting from that. So he resigns himself to the reality: he'll 'never get it right' – and thus all that he has said in this song was mere vocal effusion: 'was just instead of/Coming back to you' – like Job's 'words without knowledge,' which merely 'darken counsel'.

If desolated hope was the stance of 'Coming Back To You' – an impossible return – then the guilt resulting from its cause is the position he takes up in 'The Law' (which was placed on the B-side of the single mentioned above). Pierced as he was by those 'sharp qualities of the law' of which Shakespeare wrote, but even sharper and deadlier when penetrating one's soul as well as one's conscience, he here develops the effects that one's actions have on the whole of life. 'Mercy' may be available, but we still have to live with the consequences of our folly, he warns.

Again the dialogue is with his former lover, asking how many times she called him, thus not accepting all the guilt himself, understanding that there is a principle of recompense at work: 'There's a Law, there's an Arm, there's a Hand,' the capitals suggesting the suprahuman quality of the process at work. His heart is grieved 'like a blister/ From doing what I do'; he is going 'to miss you forever/Though it's not what I planned.' The arrangement was fouled from the start – 'since dirty began'; he cannot ask for mercy, this one who has just discovered it: justice must be done; moreover, he does not 'claim to be guilty/ Guilty's too grand.' He *fell!* and with him fell his (guardian) angel – despite the Hasidic principle that angels can neither deteriorate nor improve. It was 'Down the chain of command that he fell'; he diminished himself in falling – his failure demanded this silence.

In 'Night Comes On' a very different position is taken up. The loving has been described, examined, costed; the dance of life has turned into a desolate shuffle of lonely servitude; the silent hurt continues. In such a condition a man naturally returns to the good times, the happy memories, his childhood, if fortunate – and Leonard was in many respects a fortunate man. And so, amid 'the thunder and the lightning,' he found his way to that solemn yet beautiful hillside called Mont Royale, sanctified by the cemetery wherein lay his father and mother, as ever, waiting for him. Cohens are forbidden to enter cemeteries, which cause (ceremonial) uncleanness, hence the graves of their dead are always at the entrance. Such is his need, his deprivation, that he risks all to attend her who 'lay waiting' for him.

He talks to her of his fears, of the blackness of the night which is worsening; how he simply cannot go on. Conflict is the position he describes – within himself, and against the world. A conflict from which he would feign escape. She sends him back! Assuring him of her continued presence, of her shawl about him, of her hand upon his head. 'Go back to the World,' she commands; the fighting is not over. He has a job to do. It raises the memory of the fighting in Egypt, in which he sees his father being fatally injured. But he commanded him to try to go on – with his books and his gun! But to remember, always, 'how they lied.'

Another scene confronts his memory: the kitchen fights of recent domestic agitation, from which he fled into religion. He needed, then, his solitude; she did not understand, and remained; he wondered how long she would stay. But family responsibilities – children's games – thrust themselves upon him; there was no escaping his conflicts (and as far as his children went, there was no wish to escape them). He was lost

– 'lost in this calling/. . . tied to the threads of some prayer.' And his former lover can but mock him in his need, saying, 'I'll be yours, yours for a song!' So in the midst of his night he takes to drink, he toasts the health of those (the few) who 'forgive what you do/And the fewer who don't even care.' The war of which he had so often sung before – 'the tumult and the shouting' – continues; and his mother's voice resounds: 'Go back!' It is the most comprehensive, all-round expression in his work of his parents' caring, the fraught condition of domestic dispeace, the wounding pain of the loss of his children, his grave loss of calling and destiny, the lengths to which its torture drives him – and the insistent, ennobling, command: 'Go back!'

From which position a different vista opens up: one with a broader backcloth, a profounder meaning, because it is now touched with faith. From conflict, and the courage required to face it, sweet psalmody arises in the form of a 'Hallelujah' (meaning 'Praise be to Jah' – i.e. God). It was the high point of his new vision of life; the secret of refound strength – David's 'secret chord which pleased the Lord.' David, we saw, is the paradigm for repentance; but more positively he is 'the sweet psalmist of Israel' – in Leonard's phrase 'the master-musician in our culture.' It was 'the figure' of the man David, however, that touched him: 'The figure – the man.' He is by no means alone in this, the Jewish scriptures themselves project him as a 'front-man' in the Tradition. Moses, for example, the great founder of the nation, occurs just over 700 times; David over 1100. Abraham, the father of the people, has under 200. Not surprisingly, 'David' means 'beloved'. The position of this song, which took him (he told Bob Dylan) a year-and-a-half to write, is again one of conflict in dialogue, the cause of his pain through which he found himself.

Again and again the description of the hallelujah is interrupted by the domestic quarrel: 'You don't really care for music, do you?' he states. Whatever he did, or did not do, in the past; whatever he said, or meant, was all now transformed by the new position. It centred on the Tradition – 'the baffled king composing . . .'; even his fall through seeing Bathsheba 'bathing on the roof' who 'broke your throne and cut your hair' – by which comment Leonard offers a side-view of the prophet Samson as well as King David's fall. The Hebrews never spared their heroes' feelings!

In the line 'Your faith was strong, but you needed proof,' Leonard indicates a view of man's proneness to temptation as being a beneficial aspect of providence, for by it strength can arise – a very Hasidic opinion. Alas! It can also lead men astray, as it did with David: 'her beauty and the moonlight overthrew you,' forcing the king from his calling into 'domestic' quarrels. But even there the Hallelujah was 'forced' from his lips.

It was no different with Leonard, though an accusation that 'I took the Name in vain' is hurled against him. This quarrel is not divulged for the sake of whim or personal vindication, but because Jewish law required confession of sins affecting men to be confessed to men (as opposed to those against God being directed to God alone). He retorts, 'I didn't even know the Name/But if I did, well really, what's it to *you*.'

(In the former phrase, 'I didn't even know the Name' a *double entendre* is present: the present quarrel is uppermost, but there is also a deliberate dissociation from 'the priestly wisdom' of manipulating the letters. "I am saying that I am not one of those masters," Leonard emphasised.)

His attitude to her requires their mutual consideration, that affecting God is none of her business! But he does know something: 'There's a blaze of light in every word,' (i.e. in every letter, name or description of God, whether Jah or whatever) and 'It does not matter which you heard: the holy, or the broken Hallelujah.' (The point that it is not being, *not* our knowledge of the Name, or dexterity with it, but the totally safe and dependable fact of being 'embraced by the Name.' The 'broken Hallelujah' recalling Bacon's 'a knowledge broken'; from which point he can make the very fine admission – in *Book Of Mercy* – 'All my life is broken unto you . . . Let me raise the brokenness to you, *to the world where the breaking is for love.*' (Our italics.)

He has done his best: 'it wasn't much'; he has 'told the truth' and so – triumphantly, through deceived hope, a desolate heart, a guilty mind and great personal conflict, he avows: 'I'll stand before the Lord of Song (surely, the best of all names for this wandering, singing poet)/ with nothing on my tongue but Hallelujah.' Like Job of old, amid his own tragedies and griefs, he has learned the greatest lesson of all, 'though he slay me, yet will I trust him.' It is the counterpart to that raised in 'Bird On The Wire' where – in similar circumstances – he avows 'But I swear by this song/And by all that I have done wrong/I will make it all up to thee.'

'The Captain' (which took 'months of intense work') takes up yet another position, and advances it through exclamation and dis-avowal to positive action. It was written as a series of simple quatrains (13 in all) and gave him much pleasure. "I love rhyme,' he remarked, "rhyme is balance. It provides you with surprises; invites you to consider new ideas, submit to new meanings . . . Words create; we create by words."

Commenting thus led him into a reflection on the *logos* idea in Judaism, notably in Philo (who was also a Cohen). Once again the dialogue form is prominent, as the young soldier (called a corporal in the original version) is given command of the shattered and scattered army by the disillusioned captain ('the captain, he was dying/But the captain wasn't hurt'). It is a story adumbrated at the end of *The Favourite Game* in which two soldiers face each other on the battlefield 'ordained for glory,' but having forgotten 'why they stumbled there.' Despite his cynicism, despite the lost cause, despite the call of a distant wife and an even more distant baby, and against his better judgment, he pins the silver bars of rank and authority to his shirt; a position of courageous acceptance has been reached; the fight *is* on.

In 'The Hunter's Lullaby' a very different vista is opened up in which he, uniquely, speaks from his lover's viewpoint – that of the mother of his children. It is a song in explanation to the child of its absent father who has gone 'hunting', 'through the silver and the glass,' i.e. the baubles of stardom and fame, yet got lost in the process. It is ironical that much of this took place in the vicinity of Hollywood/Los Angeles, for light in Southern California is at its near-perfect colour temperature there, hence the film industry making it its centre; alas, the adulatory glare of the public has often eclipsed the truer light of balance and reason.

It is too rough and dangerous a trail for accompaniment by his family, even though his wife knows the way. He is lost! Moreover, he has lost his lucky charm, and his guardian heart (i.e. angel). He has gone; and no one should stop him, nor even try to do so. From that position of lostness, the 'Heart with no companion' has its own, very different, position – one 'from the other side/Of sorrow and despair'; therefore a position of able hopefulness.

It is the first time that he has ever spoken 'from the other side' – which comes with his greeting. He has broken through the silence and the suffering to a position of deep understanding, of outgoing thoughtfulness – as becomes one who had fathomed the depths and the heights of true love, and can now speak from that pinnacle of virtue's profoundest reality. He has found the condition of love, albeit 'shattered' and so 'vast' that it can 'reach you everywhere.' And so he offers it to the shipless captain, the childless mother, the lonely hearts, the solitary souls and the inept ballerina 'who cannot dance to anything.' A promise, he warns himself, is a promise: it has to be kept, whatever the cost, whatever the condition, even in 'days of shame' or 'nights of wild distress.' It is a position of high principle and undaunting dedication; he is willing to underwrite the agreement, even though it 'counts for nothing' with her.

The positions have been proposed and examined. The whole of life is there from the cradle to the grave, from early history to the present and even into the future, for men and women, parents and children, in dancing and in shame, in love and in rejection, in hope and in defeat, in work and at leisure, as believer and as agnostic. Through it all a strong view of man's potential – as lover, friend, parent, and very much more is offered. Yet life's brutality is also there – in the kitchen and on the battlefield, in the depths of one's individuality and in society, inviting, calling, mocking and judging our best – and our worst – efforts. The world of bitter-sweet experiences is sewn together, which offer incomparable beauty, for mercy has eliminated unmeaning.

The only safe place, the only certain position to take in all this, he says in his last song – which is more a prayer than a song (rather, a psalm) – is in resignation to God: 'If it be your will.' Not that he is preaching, this prophet of the heart. He is but praying – on a world stage! – and believing that 'the intimacy of the conversation' will have some use for the generality of people beyond, of whatever race or creed, in whatever position they may find themselves.

It is a prayer of total resignation: to speak or to be still; to act or to abide; to sing or to praise. In it hope has become faith; despair has turned to optimism; shame replaced by dignity. Personal envy and other considerations have been replaced by a cosmic vision – 'Let the rivers fill/Let the hills rejoice!' And the end? Nothing less than Mercy, for one and all: 'Let your mercy spill . . . If it be your will/To make us well.'

Also rising from this vast, if shattered love, comes a prayer for conciliation and unity: 'And draw us near/And bind us tight/All your children here/In their rags of light.' The thought, the life, has turned full circle. It began with a call to compare mythologies; it ends with 'a vision of unity' – but always predicated on a spiritual condition, a position of positive surrender:

> 'And end this night.
> If it be your will.'

'an inspired
prophet'

"Nothing is more mysterious than song," we heard Leonard remark to the reporter from *Le Figaro* during the tour following the release of 'Various Positions'; and in replying to his subsequent question, *"Quels sont vos projets?'* ("What are your aims?") Leonard answered: "To be even more attentive to things and to people." He who had discovered 'mercy' was now living mercifully – his whole life consumed by the need to be attentive to the things that matter, and the people about him.

Those immediately about him then were his musicians and vocalists: Mitch Watkins, Ron Getman, John Crowder, Richard Crooks and Anjani Thomas, the first female keyboard player to accompany him. She also sang back-up, as did Watkins, Getman and Crowder. They spent two days rehearsing in the Stadthalle at Speyer, and then commenced (on January 31) the 52-day tour which took them across Germany (Munster, Wiesbaden, Berlin and Hamburg), to Oslo in Norway, then to Finland, Sweden and Denmark playing in Helsinki, Stockholm and Copenhagen; from which they flew to Holland for a concert at Rotterdam; then on to Strasbourg, Lausanne, Bilbao, Madrid, Cascais; turning northwards to Paris for three concerts, London for two, then Manchester, Birmingham and Dublin, also for two concerts, then back on to the mainland of Europe, to Brussels, Basle, Vienna for two, Linz, Munich, Boblingen, Cologne, Hanover and Essen; back into Sweden, for concerts at Gothenberg and Stockholm and – a new experience – behind the Iron Curtain, into Poland. There they played at Poznan, Wroclaw, Katowice and Warsaw, where Leonard was 'complimented' by the state radio network, which called his music 'decadent'. "I was thrilled!" he said later. He was even more thrilled to get a personal invitation from Lech Walesa, but he and his musicians were unable to follow it up – undue shades of political wariness perhaps. He did, however, when playing in Boston later, dedicate 'The Partisan' to Solidarity, as a mark of his respect for the workers' courage and tenacity. The tour was rounded off by a return to Italy, where they played two concerts at the Teatro Orfeo in Milan.

Altogether, they played 42 concerts of the usual two dozen-plus songs at each – sounding out, again and again, and meditatively, the things that matter to those who came; caring, loyal 'service of the heart.' As Aurelien Ferenzzi of *Quotidien de Paris* remarked, 'He is more than a singer: (he is) a writer, an inspired poet, most of all a man of great intelligence and great finesse,' – a *finesse* of the spirit, to be sure. Interestingly, he was not only aware of his Jewish roots, and witnessing constantly to the mercy he found there, but now spoke freely of other important influences on him: of Albert Camus' 'simplicity'; James Joyce's particular form of consciousness – an 'interior monologue' which Leonard found highly congenial – not least as it bore close resemblance to Judaic habits of prayer and meditation; Henry James, whose style he wrote tempered his passion; T.S. Eliot whose distinctions between 'appearance and reality' (*à la* Bradley) is so often obscured – though not for this poet-singer, whose finesse laboured at the distinctions, ever seeking to understand that reality which tricked and titillated his mind and soul; and Ezra Pound – ill reputed for treachery and anti-Semitism, but still, to Leonard, who was of too large a heart merely to accuse, but sought above everything else to understand, a great poet: connections abounding, connections contradicting.

And it was from this time that he began to talk openly of '*la stance Spencerienne*,' the Spenserian stanzas of the *Faerie Queene*, (i.e. eight five-foot iambic lines, followed by an iambic line of six feet, rhyming ababbcbcc), on which he is presently doing serious work. No doubt aware that he shared himself a background of tailoring with the Elizabethan, as well as a fine ability to dress and adorn language.

Claude Silberger (for *Le Quotiden de Medecin*) pointed out that Leonard's concerts were always 'an event,' not least because he situated himself 'outside the fashions' – not of clothing, but of the ever-faster changing fads and fallacies of 'pop' music. A just remark, which highlights his position as a singular thinker whose message, though new, was yet very old: as old as his Tradition, as the heart of man itself. As the rabbis said, 'The heart is small, yet it embraces the world.' And this embrace – it was that, an expression of the love he found in the mercy – embraced *the world*: east and west, north and south, French delicacy and Teutonic perfection, Italian effusiveness and Spanish surrealism, Scandinavian vivacity and British phlegm, Polish obduracy and Dutch courage. A world, a universe of experiences and positions, which he sought to understand – and sew together; in a service of the heart.

And the word was getting out! Not merely in his 40-odd concerts across Europe, extended a thousand times by means of radio and television, newspaper and magazine items, but in that lip-to-lip, heart-to-heart passage of daily life. It is one thing to sing, 'She loves me, yeah, yeah, yeah' (which the Israeli troops were singing among their own Israeli folk and Jewish songs at the outbreak of the June 1967 War, according to Yael Dayan) – no small thing, if 'accurate'; but a vastly different thing to speak of the why's and the wherefore's of it, the complexities of its breakdowns, the challenges of its attempted reconciliations – still more of that higher love, which truly 'sews the world together,' of which the earthly is but a shadow, which drives forward with an irresistible force, universal in scope, cosmic in dimension and eternal in degree. Thus spoke Leonard Cohen: and thus he was heard; by those with ears to hear.

Stephanie de Mareuil (for *Elle*) was stunned by the sheer beauty of his word: '*C'est le premier video-clip triste de l'histoire,*' she exclaimed of 'Dance Me To The End Of Love'. ('It's the first sad video in history!') But she got the word wrong. Significantly, the word 'sad' occurs only once in his poetic work and only once in all his songs. He was for ever resisting the epithet of melancholy which reporters pinned on him – and that word is completely absent from his work. She was moved not so much by 'sadness' as by 'ultimate truth', which can be – very often is – 'moving' – as all real art must be, whose ability to seize us where we are, exactly as it finds us, has resonated through history, through those of fine appetites.

It is precisely what Leonard's great friend and teacher, Roshi, meant when he said (Leonard recounts it in *Death Of A Lady's Man*), 'Yah, Kone, you should write more sad.' They had been listening to the crickets, drinking brandy together (after which, given the right quantities, and they were on their second bottle, even crickets sound like Ferrier, or Callas – or both together, for that matter). Leonard had already written 'a cricket poem,' and said so to Roshi. But the undaunted Japanese proposed one, then another, then another. Leonard only liked the first, and said so. Roshi gave up. He knew he could not excite the muse artificially and that in any case was not his line. There is a time, even for a Zen master, when one has to listen to the expert: 'Write more sad,' he simply exhorted. You have the crickets! King David had them, too, as well as the sadness. Hence the popularity of the psalms. But we should not forget that after he had 'danced before the Lord,' Michal his wife 'despised him in her heart.' The name 'Michal' means 'Who is like the Lord,' but her behaviour suggests that she, as with so many, could never have even started to answer that question. She was both antagonised and disgusted by David's spontaneity, a final condition of deep sadness; the dancing is misunderstood.

But not all misunderstood it. *Rock* called him 'an inspired prophet,' not least because of the present emphasis on the words 'serious' and 'seriousness'. Said Leonard to Jeff McLaughlin of *The Boston Globe*, "I'm a serious writer. I believe in the value of high seriousness, especially in a public culture which is devoted to frivolity and distraction. We do live in a moral universe. There is a judgment. We all live the life of the heart; people do take their lives seriously."

'Heart', it should be noted, in Hebrew thought, means more than 'the seat of the emotions'; it also stands for the mind, the thinking-centre of man – as in 'the imagination of men's hearts,' etc. "The life of the heart is," as Leonard often repeated, "the nature of the heart." The 'heart' occurs no less than 18 times in his songs to date; 'mind' but eight. And his poetry is strewn with references to it. He had always known the truth of the rabbis' comments, 'The heart is half-prophet.' He knew that when his late mother said, 'Follow your little heart'; she meant 'be true to yourself,' 'trust your own judgment.' He had long learned to do so, and in so learning found that he could fulfil his destiny in ways undreamed of hitherto, on a wider platform. 'Seriousness' was being fulfilled. (He referred to a different form of seriousness when, to a reporter from *USA Today* about this time, he confessed that it had taken him "10 years to recover from the serious use of LSD." He no longer needed such stimulants to mind-expansion; there was too much to feel and understand without them.)

McLaughlin knew his stuff. He found it 'not surprising' that Leonard was appealing hugely to 'the post punk singers who were mining contemporary feelings of alienation,' e.g. Ian McCulloch, Nick Cave, Morrissey, and Andrew Eldritch – to name but a few. In 'alienated' Poland there was even an annual Leonard Cohen Festival at Krakow which Leonard came upon by accident, and much to his surprise, discovering in that lovely, if scarred, land not only traces of his own ancestry, but also a high involvement with 'seriousness' the things of the heart as his songs were translated into Polish. Great-grandfather Lazarus Cohen and grandfather Klinitsky-Klein would have been delighted – another wheel turned full circle; yet more connections!

To Daniel Pantchenko of *L'Humanité – Dimanche* Leonard expressed his problems of communication, of style. He felt, he said, like the member of a government in exile. He declared that he did not have a country of his own, merely 'constituents in each of the countries' he visited. But – and this is no new note – "What is certain is that the various aspects (read 'positions') are not outside politics. The single thing towards which I am moving," he maintained, "is the truth, even if it is uncomfortable."

He had long ago reached the point Maimonides achieved when he declared, 'When I see no way of teaching a truth except by pleasing one intelligent man and offending 10,000 fools, I address myself to the one, and ignore the censure of the multitudes.' Hence the *'rigueur du langage'* (the phrase was from *Le Monde*'s Claude Fleoter) which he expressed; through which the word was being heard. Richard Williams, of *The Times*, could not understand it. He found it 'striking' that so many 'younger people' could attend a Cohen concert; one in particular, 'a very fashionable young man' had caught his attention, who 'probably connected his romantic pessimism with the tradition running from The Velvet Underground through Joy Division to The Smiths, who are today's heroes in that line.' Probably. But we should not be either surprised or mesmerised by a such a response any more than the yippies of yesteryear. For, as Mick Brown reported for *The Guardian*, his performances were now characterised by 'taste and discretion' – the purist's 'politics of the heart,' a connection of the fragile threads of existence which has very particular echoes, for those with a particular kind of appetite.

What is astonishing is the sheer weight of serious comment Leonard now attracted. There was still the occasional Woodcock-like eruption – from a gross appetite here, a jaded appetite there. But on the whole (and the clippings fill boxes) people were *listening;* perhaps not following, but at least hearing the sound – music and words; and the commentary, too. They were learning the comment of the old Jewish cynics, too: 'The moment you ask a rabbi a simple question, he starts to give you a complicated answer.' It was not so very different with prophets – even prophets of the heart. They awakened the consciousness, then offered a challenging prospect.

Leonard and his group had no sooner returned from Italy than they were off again, the same team of tour managers and musicians, this time on a tour of North America, Canada and Australia, returning via America and Europe to Israel, and then back into Europe for extra concerts. On the first leg they played in Philadelphia, then Boston and New York – 10 years after his last performance there. Following the concert, *Rolling Stone* described them as 'the best group of musicians he has ever assembled,' adding that his version of Pee Wee King's 'Tennessee Waltz' – for which Leonard had written a new verse – was 'beautiful'.

The concert took place on the 10th anniversary of the ending of the Vietnam war. Leonard therefore recited 'The Captain' as his own tribute to its victims and protesters. Following this they went north-west to Ottawa, then Montreal, Toronto, Winnipeg and Vancouver, from which city (in mid-May) they flew to Brisbane, then to Sydney, Melbourne, Adelaide and Perth. From Perth they flew on to San

Francisco (where Anjani Thomson's singing and keyboard expertise was described as 'stunning') then to Los Angeles, where both Bob Dylan and Joni Mitchell caught the show. It was at this performance that Mikal Gilmore of the *Los Angeles Herald And Examiner* described 'The Story Of Isaac' as 'the best anti-war song of the past 30 years.' They then returned to Helsinki, Roskilde, Helsingborg and Oslo. And then to Jerusalem and Caesarea.

It may well be that Leonard was more than disappointed in the response to this return to the land of every Jew's prayer. David Horovitz, of the *Jerusalem Post*, found his performance 'insincere' – perhaps the most destructive of all the epithets that could be levelled at him, to Leonard's way of thinking: truth, and accuracy undermined, no less. Leonard and his group were described as 'relaxed and having fun.' The truth was that he was tired yet over-exhilarated by the occasion, and took more risks with those he thought would understand, forgetting that 'They are not all Israel that are of Israel.' His asides were resented, even if the music was 'magnificent' and 'exquisite'. The two most appropriate songs – 'Who By Fire?' and 'Hallelujah' – were severely criticised: the first for being over-earthly, the second for being 'one of his weakest, corniest songs' even if 'the crowd loved it' (sic).

Such comments merely indicate that his music, to be understood, must go 'from heart to heart'; that even the songs modelled on the sacred *piyutim* (the liturgical poems, which augment the prayer service of synagogues, and are based mainly on scriptural quotations or allusions) can fail to convey meaning to those 'unconnected' with the underlying realities – and not, as the reporter surmised, that Leonard had 'grown out of his songs,' and no longer 'felt their relevance.' At any rate it was a sober Leonard that made his way back into Europe: to Vienna, Graz, Montreux, San Sebastian, Zaragoza, Guehenno, Borgholm, Nice, Rome and Saint-Jean-de-Luz, where their travels (provisionally, at any rate) came to a halt, on July 21, and over 60,000 miles after starting out, 'a path of unending length' maybe, but most of the disparates connecting – 'things and their images' – on their way.

For all the talk and all the travelling, 'Various Positions' was not a great commercial success. Only in Scandanavia, Spain and Portugal did it get top ratings. American CBS's refusal to release it, did not help matters either. The president of his record company told Leonard, "We know you're great, Leonard, but we don't know if you're any good!" A Thackerayan compliment: 'How very weak the very wise/How very small the very great are.' *The Toronto Star* merely said that the album 'failed to impress anyone but the faithful.' And Leonard was not surprised to find this additional truth to the dictum that 'a prophet is not without honour, save in his own country,' when reviewed by the ever-disdainful *Gazette* of Montreal, which described his performances as having 'all the charisma of a small-town undertaker'; that despite the concerts being sell-outs. *Plus ça change . . .*

Prior to the tours Leonard had been living in a hotel in 'an anonymous neighbourhood on 44th Street, New York,' at the back of Times Square. The reason for this was to be near to his children, Adam and Lorca, now aged 12 and 10, respectively. To this 'anonymity' he now returned – save for a visit or two to Roshi, to his home-town of Montreal and to even less occasional 'events' to express the word. One of these, at New York's 'Carnival Of The Spoken Word' underlined the seriousness in which he was held, by some at least. In over two months of prose and poetry readings, from March to May, he secured top ratings on three consecutive days (which was unique throughout the carnival), even Ginsberg only got one day, such was Leonard's ongoing appeal.

He got another vote of confidence, initially more personal but soon to have even greater public acclaim, when Jennifer Warnes invited him to help record her own album of his songs which was issued as 'Famous Blue Raincoat'. (At one stage it was proposed as 'Jenny Sings Lenny'!). It came out later that year, to great acclaim, justifying Ms Warnes' faith in his songs, as well as demonstrating her own 'particular appetite,' even if the tempo was upbeat, and the sense of some of his meanings obscured, (e.g. in 'Bird On The Wire' where the line 'I will make it all up to *thee*,' changed to 'you').

One of the main causes for the upbeat tempo was the presence of Stevie Ray Vaughan, whose virtuosity on the guitar Leonard high-lighted by wearing a very fetching promotional baseball cap when being interviewed! There was, after all, a limit to 'seriousness' which she and her colleagues well understood. Even with this success the *Gazette*'s reporter had to emit gaseous fumes, describing him as 'the man who writes tunes to die for!' As Leonard's ancestors might have said of such petty reporting, 'He acts rich, he owns a whole head of cabbage!' But such negativism in the wake of his personal breakthrough was having an effect, and Leonard was beginning to talk of doubting his future as a song-writer, despite *Goldmine Review* calling the latest album 'a pop landmark,' and *Stereo Review* citing it as 'one of the year's most stirring recordings.' The great success of Warnes' album – it reached the eighth spot in the American charts, was listed for seven weeks in the UK, and went gold in Canada – plus the considerably favourable reactions to his work on Lorca, happily reinspired Leonard in his own creative work.

His activities during this 'anonymous' period were largely limited to interviews and involvements in other people's projects – such as Terry Gross' 'Fresh Air' broadcast in early May, and David Tarno's 'The John Hammond Years' later on.

In September he participated in an event of very special interest for him, the *Poetas en Nueva York* which was recorded at Studio Montmartre in Paris, in celebration of the 50th anniversary of Federico Garcia Lorca's death. The following month, in Granada, he was filmed at the full-scale celebration of the poet. Leonard's voice was recorded alongside such stars as Scotland's Donovan, France's Georges Moustaki, Greece's Mikis Theodorakis, Brazil's Raimundo Fagner and Chico Buarqul, as well as Spain's Paco de Lucia.

Leonard had discovered Lorca, as we saw earlier, 13 years after the poet's death, and had been continuously inspired by his style and imagery. For this auspicious celebration he decided to offer a version of the Spaniard's 'Little Viennese Waltz', only to find that all the translations into English fell far below what he knew to be the standards set by Lorca. So Leonard set about doing his own (helped, he said, by a Puerto Rican girlfriend). He spent 150 hours on the poem, and produced a masterpiece. Fans of Lorca exulted in the translation; critics of Leonard merely sulked. But honour it certainly was – 50 years late, and from the 'new world' the poet so much admired – before his own disillusionment set in: a heartfelt word of poetic solidarity.

your man

Following several months at the meditation centre with Roshi, Leonard settled down to write again. In June he reappeared to attend the Medicine Show's production of *Sincerely, L. Cohen,* called by the publicity people 'A fully-staged trip through the songs and writings of cult-figure Leonard Cohen.' It was a Broadway production, produced by Barbara Vann, which lasted for 75 minutes and developed out of a similar series of readings that took place in 1986. It aimed to chart 'in a non-realistic fashion an emotional and imagistic journey.' It plays with the meaning and meaninglessness of symbolic life. 'Like all living things, it is best not dissected.' 'Come back, F,' one is inclined to say, 'all is forgiven!'

But whether it was related to such an inaccurate rendition of his meanings (not 'meaninglessness' and 'plays' particularly) or not, Leonard was again struggling – in the throes of a 'nervous breakdown', *The Toronto Star* stated: 'And the night went on,' indeed . . . "What I mean by 'breaking-down'," Leonard told the umpteenth reporter that morning, "is that you can't get out of bed, you can't move." And to the *Chicago Tribune* he explained, "They didn't have to take me away or anything. I'm pretty cool. But you know when you're broke, and it gets harder and harder to lie . . ." And using another image to the interviewer from *Musician* he said, "It's taken me a long time to come out of the shipwreck of 10 or 15 years ago, of broken families and hotel rooms . . ."

But it was not a 'you can call me Lenny now,' situation. He who had heard the voice commanding, 'Go back to the world,' was not about to give up the fight. Doubt, he might; fret, he was wont to do; but retire? Never! He had seen the beauty of the word, he had heard the sound, he had recognised the voice. He could only go on, and fight. And that in song: 'I'm Your Man' was the brilliant result; the more he appeared to suffer, the better he became!

By this time he had moved back to Los Angeles where he had stayed earlier for four months, helping Jennifer Warnes complete her album, not least in re-writing some of the songs for her. Once again the key-note was the simplicity of 'the room' that he chose with such care, his blue electric guitar in a corner, alongside some experimental reels of his latest poem-songs which were maturing quietly, like good wine; a small bookcase with a few selected volumes. One, *The Positive Value Of Depression*, indicates one of the issues which had long absorbed him. As he said of his hero, Nachman of Bratislava, "He treated depression as a holy condition, a mechanism. He saw it (as he saw many things, even evil itself) as a necessity. It is a great blessing to cry out, and if it is from the heart it has an immediate, and healing response."

When *Pulse* magazine inquired as to Leonard's 'Desert Island Discs' selection, he replied: "It depends on what desert island." He is after all, the 'elegiac connoisseur of islands!' He listed the usual selection of 10: Rodrigo's 'Guitar Concerto' (preferably John Bilezekjian's version); Edith Piaf's 'Greatest Hits'; Banner Records 'Voices Of The Temple' ("One of the greatest cantorial records"); Ray Charles' 'Greatest Hits'; Bob Dylan's 'fictional' 'Greatest Hits' (but preferably "some of his latest work"); one of Bach's 'passions'; some Flamenco singing; a blues record, one of Robert Johnson's ("who wrote only 27 songs") whom Dylan "worshipped . . . a ghost who haunted the darker side of his street"); an album by George Jones; and Hank Williams' 'Greatest Hits'.

The new album came together over a period of time – in Los Angeles, Paris and in Montreal – with several colleagues working with him: Jeff Fisher, Roscoe Beck (who played bass on 'Recent Songs', travelled throughout Europe, Israel and Australia with him, and played a major role in 'Famous Blue Raincoat'), Michel Robidoux and Jean-Philippe Rykiel (who was on the synthesiser for the 'Poetas en Nueva York' album). They did work with him – or, rather, he with them! – on a new phase of his work, a new style was appearing: the zestful collaborative artist.

And this collaboration with his colleagues was matched – despite the varied background of the individual songs – by a much more holistic conceptualisation than hitherto. "It is unified," said Leonard contentedly, "and (that) has been given aesthetic consideration. It had to be finished from A to Z to live in terms of its own creation." An aesthetic that he deliberately linked with 'the state of grace' – equilibrium – centred thinking which 'had always had its place.' As with the Warnes' album, on which they discussed and argued, reasoned and wrangled the varying possibilities until a consensus was reached, so here with this new work. Even some of the words were generously credited to others – Sharon Robinson (of the 1979 and 1980 tours), to Jeff Fisher, and – most precious of all collaborations! – to Federico Garcia Lorca.

The production, likewise, was a coordinated effort: mainly from Leonard and Roscoe Beck, but also with Michel Robidoux and Jean-Michel Rousser. For vocalists Leonard enjoyed the company of Jennifer Warnes ('ad libbing' *and* 'directed'!), 'Anjani' (Thomson – of 'Various Positions' and the subsequent tours); plus Jude Johnstone, Evelyine Hebey, Mayel Assouly and Elizabeth Valleti; while his musicians were Raffi Hakopian (on violin), and John Bilezikjian (on oud), Jeff Fisher (on keyboards); Richard Baudet (on saxophone); Vinnie Colniuta, Michel Roubidoux and Tom Brechtlein (on drums); Peter Kisilenko (on bass); Bob Stanley (on guitar); Sneaky Pete Kleinow (on steel guitar); Lenny Castro (on percussion); and – rescuing his schooldays' talent for piano and keyboards – Leonard himself, with Michel Robidoux and Larry Cohen.

The title chosen for the album takes us back beyond the 'position-centred' thinking of his album. 'I'm Your Man' posits what he intends the album to be, a manifestation of himself, not some platform or pulpit for his views, however grasped. Like Amos of old, the prophet had returned to his own fig tree – not, certainly, to sit and sit, but to ponder and declare, not in the full thrust of spiritual experience but certainly still holding the two great intimacies in tandem.

The album was released in Great Britain for St Valentine's Day. Behind that (admittedly legendary saint – or saints, as two seem to claim the honour) lies the very ancient festival of Lupercalia, a Spring fertility rite celebrated in the slaying of a goat (a symbol of sexuality), rather than the 'wolf' implied in the name: connections (not to say mythologies) running back to the first and deepest observation on human nature: 'It is not good for man to be alone.'

The sound is still there! The music is dominant, and rising. It has become more 'mainstream' than anything of Leonard's work to date, more secular even, yet protecting the voice, accurately projecting the man. And the public loved it; the critics, too. It was nominated for 'best album of the year' on both sides of the Atlantic; and won for its creator the coveted Crystal Globe that Columbia Records reserves for its Top People. (Only 22 have won it in its 60-year history; it is geared chiefly to the overseas reputation its recipients win and rests on their having sold five million albums.)

In Norway and Spain it immediately secured the number one slot in the charts, but everywhere there was jubilation. The market had changed. If anything, in recoil from decadence and punk; heavy metal, and flimsy plastic not to speak of ephemeral gloss, it had now moved nearer to Leonard's natural style; it had become more verbal, less unwitting – perhaps even more 'religious' in a hazy-lazy sort of way. Fundamentalism in political and religious creeds was rising, as were 'hung parliaments', consensus. The voice of the people was slowly – so very slowly – making a comeback. As Vin Scelsa remarked in *Sounds*, "I'm Your Man' is so good it might even turn out to be the one that speaks for the whole damn decade.'

And at 50-plus, having said all that he wanted to about returning, about mercy, about his religious roots; Leonard, too, was making a comeback – by ignoring the public projection of his views and concentrating on his 'art', which had not died, which had returned him to himself, his life in art. To Pia Southam, of *Vancouver Magazine*, he recalled Irving Layton's comment (one does not forget old friends as the years roll by), "This is the end of a lot of archetypes. Such as the poet-archetype! He always said Leonard, we're the last ones. Don't look for new ones! The priest is gone. The warrior is gone. Those ideas have gone. They threw away the mould. They are not going to be remaking these men any more; so forget it." And Leonard repeated a similar thing, albeit more personalised, to Kerry Doole of *Musical Express:* "When I look for nostalgia in my character, I find amnesia . . . I can't forget; I can't forget. But I don't remember what's recurring!"

He did remember some things, his lost love, his great hopes of reconciliation (which he knew to be unrealistic), his *métier* as a man; the ongoing belief that love can outlast, and overcome everything else; that 'one heart sympathises with another'; that the plight of the jilted or cuckolded man is of immense attraction and strength to others; that even distance – in time or place – cannot quell the ache of the true lover; that flight is no answer – all such manly themes vibrantly alive in this new album. 'Bleakness' there may be in it; bitterness, a little; irony, to be sure; humour – black and white certainly; but it was the mix that counted, the emphasis made more powerful in this 20th year of his recording career.

Steve Morris of *Vinyl* found it . . . 'His most radical departure since Phil Spector's the 'Ladies' Man' LP (sic) a decade or so ago.' There were only two; and Morris ignores his books! But radicality *was* there – literally so: a returning to his roots in art, to love and passion, frustration and fear, loneliness and alienation, disharmony and anxiety, disconnections, woundings, scars even (for the word is certainly there), nakedness, feelings, longings – and ever-persistent hope.

The *New York Times* commented of it laconically, 'pure – and by no means simple,' calling it *en passant* 'a masterpiece,' alongside of which 'Famous Blue Raincoat', for all its commercial success, is 'hopelessly bland.' Divina Infusione, for the *San Diego Union* also made the point, albeit backhandedly: 'When you're feeling real bad, there's nothing quite so good as Leonard Cohen, even in '88!' Ken Tucker was more precise in the *Philadelphia Inquirer* when he remarked: 'If you want Cohen as music, buy Jennifer Warnes magnificent 'Famous Blue Raincoat'; if you want Cohen as unique experience, buy 'I'm Your Man'.'

'It is easier to know 10 countries than one man,' says the old Jewish proverb, and in this album we are given the mature, yet unfathomable sense of a man, a man of large measure. A man of multifarious features, at once youthful and middle-aged, combining both east and the west, spiritual and earthy, fulfilled and restless, suave and formal, impulsive and irrepressible. We have seen him at home, at school, at university, in company and in solitude, playing rough with the boys and charming the girls, blackening his pages and composing his music; screwing his eyebrows together in agony, and keeping the world at bay with his 'stony semitic stare,' drinking and eating, laughing and joking, philosophising and praying; and that across the world, in the east and in the west, from Los Angeles to Helsinki, from Edinburgh to Adelaide – and yet we do not really know this man!

The first song on the new album, which *Newsday* described as his 'most *coherent* effort since 1969's 'Songs From A Room',' is both retrospective and prospective. He recounts his '20 years of boredom' – surely a cut at the moguls of CBS, in whose power his art was incarcerated for 'trying to change the system from within.' But the worm has turned! The time of just deserts is at hand: he is about to reward them, himself.

His programme starts in Manhattan – home of the mighty broadcasting and record empire, and the nerve-centre of American business life and activity, which the author of *Beautiful Losers* found so discomforting and dangerous to Canada's own. Then on to Berlin, which was, Leonard told Andrew Tyler nearly 17 years earlier, the toughest city in the world to play: "They are very critical, until you demonstrate a certain kind of power that they admire," (in *Beautiful Losers* Leonard listed Berlin as a recurrent disaster in news broadcasts of the day!). Ironic, therefore, that Stephen Williams found Leonard 'closer to Berlin or Zurich . . . than SoHo . . .!'

In the same way that he had felt disarmed and deflated in meeting the power-barons of the recording industry (which nearly broke him), the former capital of world Jewry, so he could look eastwards to that other (also former) capital, where the infamous *Wollt Ihr totalen Krieg* had reverberated through Europe, through history – where the atomic bomb was plotted and planned, though the Americans got in first with their own 'Project Manhattan'. The rewards would be sweet as he had warned in his poem of St Francis, 'beware of what comes out of Montreal, especially during the winter. It is a force corrosive to all human institutions.' To achieve this he is guided 'by a signal in the heavens . . . this (Jewish) birthmark on my skin . . .' and 'the beauty of our weapons.' Well, they may both fear: the word is mightier than the sword.

The sudden change from a world stage, from an historical dimension, to a private life, is characteristic of this new man: He really wants to live with her; he loves her body, her spirit and her clothes. But has she seen him poised for action, already in the ticket queue? 'I told you, I told you, I was one of those.' He reminds her of her former attitude towards him – as a loser. Now she is worried because he is on the attack, and she does not have what it takes – the discipline – to stop him. It's all happening! 'How many nights I prayed for this: to let my work begin.' It reminds him of his hatred of their most characteristic aspects. In Manhattan, the fast-changing fashions, their flashy styles, the drugs, the effects on his family. And the insulting behaviour in Berlin as they jeered at his words and music, and contemptuously sent him a monkey and a plywood violin to play with! But he is about to repay them: he practised every night; now he is ready, to take them both – Manhattan and Berlin! But he cannot forget the matters of the heart. Does she remember him, who used to live for music? Who brought the groceries in? And the bitterest memory of all? 'It's Father's Day, and everybody's wounded' – himself, at the unforgettable loss of his father; at not being with his children; them, for being 'fatherless'; she for the hurt it triggers in her mind. Manhattan and Berlin will pay for all this – first!

The tale of broken love is continued in 'Ain't No Cure For Love' which, he told one journalist . . . "Started from the heart of man and (proceeded) to the heart of God, but the ladder's been removed. And there ain't no band-aid big enough to cover up this wound," which in one sense is the story of his life, his entire repertoire. He was even more explicit in introducing the song publicly, e.g. at the Royal Albert Hall, where he spoke of the song as "a vision experienced by Christ on the cross." 'A stab in the heart leaves a hole,' the rabbis said – whether it be of earth or of heaven, initiated by someone close or by events beyond one's control. He had sung of it often enough, but in this song he wants to make a single point: he will never stop loving her. He has loved her 'for a long, long time'; it's real; it all went wrong, but that does not matter – it does not change how he feels; time cannot heal *this* wound; there's no cure for such love.

Merely to remind himself of her is to realise how much he loves her: he aches for her, he cannot pretend otherwise; he needs to see her as she is (in body and mind; in the previous song he loved her body, her spirit and her clothes, i.e. style); he has her 'like a habit,' and he cannot get enough of her. No cure for that! So his mind wanders off surreally, envisioning the mad scramble of the explorers, the mystical searchers, the doctors, all 'working day and night' for a cure; there is none – in drink or drugs, nothing 'pure enough' to be a cure for such love. He sees her on the bus, lying alongside him, waking up; he sees her hand, her hair, her bracelets, her brush. He calls, but hears no reply. He does not call 'soft enough'! He is too querulous, too demanding, too urgently and loudly seeking her. No cure for such love as this!

And, unlike his experience in 'Night Comes On', when he felt 'lost in this calling,' he walked into an empty church, with nowhere else to go; he heard 'the sweetest voice' imaginable, which touched his very soul. It was not of his calling this time that the all-penetrating voice spoke, nor of his need for forgiveness. It was written in sacred tomes, written in blood; even the angels declared it from above: 'There ain't no cure for love.' He has underlined the high importance of human love – there's 'no ladder' to take it higher than that now; solemn calling and destiny has given way to the delights and restraints, the provocations and even the humour of love, incurable love, sufficient in itself.

When faith and vision dies, bitterness and cynicism ride high. And so, on that wave praising earthly love – and with 'nowhere else to go,' he touches rock-bottom; yet without losing his humour, his cool. It is a new man that so speaks. A man who knows that everybody knows that 'the dice are loaded,' that life's a game of dice; that the war – of which he has so often sung (not least 'between the man and the woman,' but also 'between the left and right . . . between the black and white . . . between the odd and the even') – and that 'the good guys lost': 'the fight was fixed: the poor stay poor, the rich get rich . . . that's how it goes.'

He piles metaphor on metaphor to emphasise the inequalities, the unfairness of it all: a leaking boat, a lying captain (not for the first time), 'this broken feeling that their father or their dog just died'; that everyone's out for themselves, their own desires, be it chocolates or roses. As the reviewer in the *New York Times* called it, 'a procession of nihilistic verses!' But Leonard comments, 'all the archetypes we have – of lover, husband, politician, warrior, priest, man, woman and lover (twice) – are dissolving right before our eyes.'

He turns on his lover, who is not guiltless – but who does (he feels) need to be forgiven. Everybody knows she loves him, and has been 'faithful' to him, more or less; her 'discretion' is equally well-known, as were the many she had to meet – naked. And so the chips are down: it is now or never; it is me or you. Everyone knows that the writer 'lives forever.' But the deal is rotten; the blacks are still poor. Everybody knows, too, that the plague is coming, fast; that honesty (i.e. 'nakedness') is merely a leftover from past unreality. 'The scene is dead'; and her bed will be 'metered' for the day of reckoning. She is in trouble! Everybody knows the enormity of her problems, the sheer historical and geographical extent – which reached even to the

millionaire's playground. It's about to happen: a reckoning; 'the Sacred
Heart' itself will be destroyed. Everybody knows. Sympathy has gone;
confession – once reduced to an art-form by him, is no longer available;
bitterness reigns; cynicism explodes in self-righteous anger. But
everyone knows that!

If the ultimate in failed love, in hurt love, was reached in the
preceding song, its agonised appeal is made in the album's title-track
which comes next. In it he sings of, extols and exemplifies, the
unlimited nature of true love. Put simply, there is nothing that he will
not do, or be, in order to regain her affections; he will love her in any
way, by any means, to please her. If the screech-owl was heard in an
earlier piece – Lilith, who preceded Eve (in the tradition) as Adam's
wife, the epitome of lust, temptation and illicit sex (an ironical
connotation, for Adam's name for 'Eve' was *havah* – 'the mother of all
living,' which is very close to *ha-ra* – 'evil' etymologically!) – so now
'Zeus' – who subdued and deflowered the Greek counterpart to Lilith,
Lamia by name, is now heard – equally loudly, if only in a posture of
importunate supplication. He will disguise his looks, he will be an equal
(i.e. 'partner'), he will be a foil for her anger; a boxer, a doctor, a driver
– or even a fool. 'I'm your man!' he reiterates over and over again. The
reason for his importuning is his longing: thus he complains about the
moon, the chains, the beast. He reminds himself of past promises made
to her, which he never kept; he realises that a man never got his woman
back by begging, but he would crawl and fall, howl and claw, and tear,
for her – 'please, please: I'm your man!' He will sleep for her, disappear
for her, be a father to her child for her – or merely walk her across the
sand (of time?) but: I'm your man! It fades out, this refrain, even as his
plea sounds on across the air-waves: 'I'm Your Man!'

In 'Take This Waltz' we enter a less real world than the one of his
disappointed, if undying, love; the broken-hearted experience of his
stony-hearted lover, who deceived and rejected him; who appears deaf
to his pleas. 'Less real' because based on the super-real poetry of
Federico Garcia Lorca, who inspired Leonard's love of poetry, who
showed him his real – or supra-real – landscape and world. As Leonard
said on the 50th anniversary, "I read him like a brother, and in a way he
led me into the racket (sic) of poetry. He educated me."

Little wonder that this album made number one in Spain! He
explained further that, "The song fits right in with the record because in
the poem Lorca was discussing old romantic ideas that even in the 1930s
were rotten and overripe and had no currency." The waltz itself had, of
course, been dying for years; not the least of those 'old romantic ideas'
he now addressed. He expanded the point by commenting that Lorca
(and flamenco) "do something to the dignity of human experience in the
face of adversity," – no small compliment from a Jew who said – it is

the only other reference to the word as used by him – that he started to be 'educated' when he saw the first pictures of the concentration-camps in 1945, as he said to us in pained and wistful conversation, "We Jews are the professionals in suffering." And that is what the song is all about: 'the dignity of human experience in the face of adversity' – the dance of life, which ends in death. But the 'dance of life' is punctuated by high moments and developments, when a man knows himself, and rises above himself. It starts in longing; it ends in ecstasy. The 'great death' even if preceded by many small deaths (*petits morts*), with its 'broken waist': life is as serious as that, ultimately.

And so from the ultimate fact of human experience, through the ultimate experience of human life, *qua* human, he reverts to his own addition: the Viennese concert hall (where Leonard never played), where the reviews were sensational, but where the real music has been stopped 'by the blues.' In it someone 'climbs to your picture, with a garland of freshly cut tears.' Longing takes over, an attic scene – 'the mist of some sweet afternoon'; the 'dance' is dying; but she will never be forgotten. And he *will* dance with her in Vienna, suitably clad, his 'soul' buried in a scrapbook (of reviews?), alongside the photographs, and the moss! And he will yield to her, and be carried by her, and be mesmerised by her, and transformed and exhilarated by her, which gives way to an impassioned plea, therefore:

> 'O my love! O my love!
> Take this waltz, take this waltz
> It's yours now. It's all that there is.'

> (*Copyright © 1988. Stranger Music Inc, New York.*
> *Used by Permission. All Rights Reserved.*)

There is not much left to say, after such an ecstatic unveiling of his soul. He has offered his all: his very life. But there is always something more in the fertile, fruitful imagination of Leonard Cohen – not least when it is stimulated by Lorca. 'Jazz Police' surprised and disappointed, and even annoyed, some of his followers. It is very different from his normal musical style – even though his first public performance – in Dunn's Jazz Parlour, in Montreal – was the recitation of his poem 'Gift' to jazz-backing so many years ago. But Jazz became a cult entity, unpopular to many (but not to Leonard, who always enjoyed it for a certain mood), and in this song we have the mature blossoming of a plant that had been quietly growing over 30 years.

It commenced, he told Mark Rowland of *Musician*, out of his concert-work with the fusion group Passenger (who played on 'Recent Songs'). They had an 'understanding' that if Leonard caught them playing augmented fifths or even sevenths he would 'call them' on it, because he had always felt tempted 'to a certain sound.' He was himself the Jazz Police! But he did confess to bewilderment as to what the lyrics really signified now. The idea was to take the premise and let it run on, either into a full expression or its own absurdity. It thus caught the mood in which he found himself, following his 'nervous breakdown', of 'fragmented absurdity.' So he let it stay: the Hound of Heaven perhaps pursuing him still. His whispered voice, in sharp contrast to the backing descant, highlighting the mood of furtive – if not disreputable exploration, into which he fell at times. And the words are sensational! Clever, and pithy, sardonic and deft, surreal – yet with an intensely important message which has close connections with both the first and the last tracks of the album.

The bells, the bells! sound out in warning; yet nothing has ever happened – he has been sitting there since Wednesday morning, so should know. The Jazz Police are on the prowl: looking through his papers, talking to his family, issuing their orders. Disarm yourselves! Jesus – whether popular or not; Paul Getty or Paul Getty II – are all behind them: power and money talk. As he remarked at the New Music Seminar in New York on whose panel he served, there is 'an unholy marriage – or a marriage of convenience – between music and money.' But care! For 'He hears them calling, he thinks he is falling for them!' Despite his wildness, he applauds their Chief. But are they after *him*. They will never understand what it's all about, this culture of his, this Tradition; even though they are working for his mother. His 'blood' will protect him. Once again, he wants to change, change his nature, change his job. His tastes have already become exotic, untraditional, not least musically!

Yet, despite that, he cannot forget his past – even if he does not remember what it was – the refrain for his next song 'I Can't Forget'. The song starts off with an unbelievable struggle – unbelievable to him, that is – with himself one morning. He got ready for that 'struggle' that we saw him sinking into, in the wake of his 60,000-mile tour through Europe, North America, the Holy Land, Australia and Europe again.

Having 'tightened up my gut,' he gets on with it – taking off for Phoenix, through which he passes on his way from Nashville and New York to Los Angeles and Roshi. There were two of them, and so he was making for an old friend's place 'high and fine and *free*.' But he could not forget, could not forget – but what? He will arrive with 'a big bouquet of cactus' – no roses or lilies there – the vehicle 'runs on memory'; they will never be caught, but if they are – simply say it was him. And then the final statement: 'I loved you all my life, and that's how I want to end it'; a prayer and a confession – in reverse order. 'The summer's almost gone. The winter's tuning up,' it's getting late (shades of the warning of 'Everybody Knows') but even with the summer gone – 'a lot goes on forever.' And he can't forget, he can't forget – but what?

Roots will out; 'radical' or not, they will find him yet. Amnesia will yet give way to knowledge, if not more revelations.

'Tower Of Song', the last on this album, 'was written, produced, arranged and played by Leonard Cohen,' according to the sleeve. Only Jennifer Warnes participated with him on it, and that in an unemphatic way. It is his counterpart to Sinatra's ebullient song 'I did it *my* way.' He started with a veiled reference to his recording company; he now concludes with one – more explicit, more affirmative, and decidedly more risky. They may think he is 'great'; they may doubt whether he is 'good' – but he will show them! A final throw of the dice: win or lose all. –

It starts with his paralleling his love-life with his life in art, the two have been inextricably mixed from the start in any case. Despite his ageing – or because of it? – he is still 'crazy for love, but not coming on'; he is merely, 'paying my rent every day in the Tower of Song.' What he was wont to call the CBS building on 6th Avenue, New York, 'the tomb to the unknown record' – he now takes up here, in lonely entombment, albeit it with the dead great: Hank Williams, whom he hears 'coughing all night long, a hundred floors above me . . .' (Williams was, after all, one of his greatest heroes.)

He recounts how 'destiny' – that strong code-word, implicit here – invaded his life: he was 'born like this. I had no choice I was born with the gift of a golden voice'; and '27 angels from the Great Beyond' tied him to his table – in the Tower of Song. The angels – the word means 'messenger' in Hebrew – were probably there as the 'ministering angels of God' – not the destructive sort (among which Lilith is named). Why 27 is known only to Leonard – or God – but the number does have a certain significance in the scriptures: e.g. it was on the 27th day after the Flood that the earth was found to be dry, and so it betokens a certain deliverance, a signal of confidence for the future (shades of Noah's dove again). More importantly, perhaps, it was in the 27th year of Ezekiel's prophetic outpourings that judgment was laid on Egypt, Israel's old enemy, thus 'reversing' the wounds and traumas of the past.

Whatever the meaning, what is certain is that he is free from hurt, from voodooism – or any other sort of superstition – be her desire to 'get him' ever so great: 'They don't let a woman kill you, not in the Tower of Song,' he cries triumphantly. He agrees that a charge of bitterness may be laid against him. But the fact is 'the deal is rotten' – the poor are handicapped (despite his disavowal of social concerns, they ever obtrude!) – and 'a mighty judgment' is coming against them for it, *perhaps:* 'He can hear their funny voices in the Tower of Song.' All this reminds him of her place in his life. He can still see her, but he cannot get to her; nor does he know how the distance – 'the river' – got so wide between them. He really loved her 'way back when.' But the bridges across are burning; he feels 'so close to everything that we lost.' But it's gone for good: 'We'll never have to lose it again.' So, regrettably, he bids her farewell. There is no saying when he will be back: they are moving him to another 'Tower' now (in Nashville? Los Angeles?). But she *will* hear from him – long after he has gone – 'speaking to you sweetly from a window in the Tower of Song!'

So he draws to a close the present relationship – and this phase in his career, to tumultuous success.

'a cathedral
in his throat'!

'Words that come from the heart enter the heart,' said Moses ibn Ezra authoritatively. He should know, for he also was a melancholy poet, a linguist of philosophical bent, and an authority on Hebrew poetry. The people who now listened to Leonard – even at CBS – knew it, too. It was not only his album that 'took off', its sound resonating through America, Europe, the Middle and the Far East, but also his personal appearances and, most of all, his concerts.

So he set off on his most extensive tour to date, an eventful series of 65 concerts, which commenced in Frankfurt, Germany and moved in an awesome ark via Stuttgart, Munich, Berlin, Cologne, Mannheim, Hannover, Hamburg, into Belgium, where he played at Antwerp, before going on to Holland for Amsterdam, then into Scandinavia, playing in Gothenburg, Copenhagen, Lund, Stockholm, Helsinki, back to Stockholm and then into Norway – for Oslo, Bergen, Stavanger, Oslo again, across Europe to Madrid, then back into Germany for Nuremberg; down to Vienna, Zurich, Milan, Bilbao, Mallorca, Seville, Barcelona; then north to Paris, across to London where his concert bookings were extended, and then across the Irish Sea to Dublin, concluding the 61 days of touring, on June 4, in the capital's famous Stadium.

With him was now a tour company of over 20 people, including six musicians – Bob Furgo on keyboards and violin, Bob Metzger on guitar and pedal steel guitar, Steve Meador on drums, Stephen Zirkel on keyboards; two brilliant vocalists – Julie Chrisensen and Perla Batalla; his musical director – the multi-talented, ever-loyal Roscoe Beck; a tour manager – Geoff Clennell; and his road crew on montitoring; sound and lighting engineers; line-riggers and backline technicians; truck and coach drivers; and his personal merchandisers for Leonard was now a star! In addition to these were travel agents and their companies, trucking and transport companies, lighting and publicity companies, programme-makers and designers, photographers and so on – a modern-day Noah's Ark, the tide and the word being taken at the flood.

It was now possible to buy pendants, T-shirts and sweatshirts, superbly designed programmes, even a limited edition of Leonard's own water colour paintings. Amid all the brouhaha, was the man himself, a little inscrutable, perhaps the suggestion of a smile playing at the corner of his mouth, surrounded by the usual bevy of acolytes, press, and the ubiquitous hangers-on. But essentially unchanged, too old at the game to be overcome by the adulation, too disciplined to be caught by the pressures. Settling into his own mould, setting his own pace (which younger men found to be exhausting); being himself – from whence his art issued, more melodious than ever, the voice deeper, unquestionably more musical, more overtly secular, more simple, but nevertheless, an artist's artist, of high spiritual tone.

The peacefulness that now haloed his life was a sign of the deep inner happiness he had secured for himself after so much anguish – domestic and professional, but not least personal – that which drives a man on, restlessly; the force for self-knowledge, self-fulfilment – Thoreau's 'Great God, I ask thee for no meaner pelf/Than that I may not disappoint myself.' His word, finally secured, had sounded out in poetry and prose, in fiction and in direct statement, in music and song and on film; he could 'claim to be happy for the first time in his life,' as the *Los Angeles Weekly* reported towards the end of the tour.

Still an early riser – despite being, perforce, a 'late retirer' – his day is comprised of up to three hours of meditation, blackening pages, working at his music – in continuous experiment and rehearsal, meeting the press (controlled at 39-minute intervals – sometimes as many as 10 per day on tour, once 14), discussing artistic and business matters with his managers, often at long-distance; rehearsing with his group and vocalists, in an 'Orbisonian' manner. (He and his group had a sort of joke which centred on the phrase, 'May the Roy be with you!' by which that characteristic sound – as projected, for example, in 'Mystery Girl' – was conveyed, behind which lay a very serious musical intent for which they developed their own verb, 'orbisize': 'Orbisize this song' Leonard would say to his group), listening to and discussing the possibilities with them, undergoing soundchecks and – the consummation of it all – live in concert.

It was for this that everything else existed, and he never failed his audiences. For this reason the two hours or so before a concert were sacrosanct: regaining the mood, adjusting the inner voice and equilibrium, clearing the channels. And, once on stage, it was all systems go: a nervous wave to the audience in response to their clapping, whistling and other noisy greetings, a half-smile to his group and vocalists – and then the opening chords, which produces total silence in the large auditoria. The lights dim, the spot-lights pick him out, his legs slightly apart, left hand over his heart, clutching his microphone cable, the right clutching – slightly too hard, if anything – the microphone itself, eyes closed, head back; an average-sized man, of black hair tinged with grey, in a designer suit, also dark. And that sound of music: the rhythms of eternity, the beat of the cosmos, an ageless melody; the sound of a voice: like dense dark chocolate, at once sympathetic and penetrating, at once caring and authoritative; and the backing singers: now rising above his baritone modulations, now descending in an alto support of heart-rending melody. This is not a performance, it is a sacrament – of song; these are not glee-singers or serenaders, but high priests and priestesses of the inner-life; this is not a group at work, earning bread, but temple musicians offering sacrifice, burning incense, conveying grace and truth – to those with ears.

To study the audience is an experience in itself. It comprises a complete cross-section of modern-day life: business and academic types, casual and free-roamers, sophisticated and otherwise; young, middle-aged and old; as many men despite one of the corniest stereotypes of all – the ebullient and the introverted singles and families. All eyes are focused on the stage, the man and his music. Few stir, only an occasional laugh or murmur can be heard, eyes are frequently wet, mouths slightly open, hands grasp the programmes or fold themselves neatly in laps; not a few grasp their lovers' hands in a position of mutual receiving. The auditorium is dark, the atmosphere is electric: the voice, the music, sound out: every word distinct, every chord important, every phrase a pleasure.

And where is Leonard in all this? On centre-stage physically, for sure; but where else? With whom? It is not a performance, a show, but a love-scene, a reconciliation, a meditation: as the Talmud says, 'prayer is the service of the heart.' The *San Francisco Chronicle* commented on 'the awed silence and religious reverence' that was felt on such occasions, adding that they made it 'clear they felt securely in the grips of High Art.' Further, the paper added, 'He is not a voice; he is a reverberation. The man has a cathedral in his throat.' Shades of the *metzar*, and the *duende*, no doubt!

They were not striving after mere effect, this man and his talented group, but seeking to enter into communion with those who came to hear them – effect a dialogue, to use that jaded word. As Jennifer Warnes explained the process in an abundance of mixed metaphors to the *Miami Herald*, "People want to climb into music and wear it themselves. If you make music with all the numbers filled in, it turns the listener into a voyeur; it assumes the audience doesn't have anything to say. Leonard Cohen taught me that. There has to be some communion." And Leonard himself set the scene by including at the front of his deluxe programme his much-hailed piece from *Death Of A Ladies' Man*, 'How To Speak Poetry':

> 'To use this word (butterfly) it is not necessary to make the voice weigh less than an ounce or equip it with small, dusty wings . . . Do not act out words. Never act out words. Never try to leave the floor when you talk about flying . . . What is the expression which the age demands? The age demands no expression whatever . . . You are playing to people who have experienced a catastrophe. This should make you very quiet. Speak the words, convey the data, step aside . . . There is no more stage. There are no more footlights. You are among the people. Then be modest. Speak the words, convey the data, step aside . . . This is an interior landscape . . . Respect the privacy of the material.'

What he exhorted in speaking poetry, he fulfilled in singing song: a service of the heart – natural, modest, respectful: pure dynamite in its quiet, mesmerising penetration. A sound that echoed around Europe, America, and far beyond; which echoes still. As he commented to *The Boston Globe*, "Nobody has mentioned the sacramental relationship between musicians and audience." Nobody but him, that is. And it could move both ways: from secular to sacred, and back again.

We noted above the movement 'away' from the very explicit religious tones of *Book Of Mercy* and 'Various Positions', to a more 'secular' one in 'I'm Your Man'. Such polarising – remembering his lifelong quest to bridge the polarities – is dangerous. Nevertheless, the point receives strong confirmation in 'Hallelujah' which, between the recording and the concerts, underwent a transformation. A transformation that has a profound religious and philosophical – i.e. anti-dualistic – basis: oneness must out!

We saw earlier that, in experiencing mercy, he was able to say 'Let me raise the brokenness to you, *to the world where the breaking is for love.*' (Our italics.) Even as it was not necessary for Moses to stay on top of Sinai (he died and was buried in secret); even as Isaiah did not need to stay in the temple where he had his vision (he, too, had an anonymous death and burial); so Leonard may go forth: he has confirmed his destiny, he has learned his message; 'the breaking' has been for that essence of 'sainthood' – to do with the energy of love, for the world: the 'two great *intimacies*' are now of universal purport! In it his practice of sliding a religious – or at least, a mystical – awareness under one of human loving is clearly demonstrated. Its parallel movement may be seen in substituting the history of the Jews by a personal *vignette*, such as we saw in 'I Can't Forget', of which Leonard said to Mark Rowland of

Musician: "The song started off as a song about the exodus of the Hebrew people from Egypt . . . But I *wasn't* born in chains, and I *wasn't* taken out of Egypt. I was on the edge of a very serious breakdown. So I *hadn't* had the burden lifted . . . the whole thing was a lie . . . wishful thinking." It was originally titled 'The Darkness Is Not Hidden', and began:

> '*I was tied with chains*
> *when I was taken out of Egypt*
> *I was broken by my burden*
> *When my burden was raised . . .*'

In 'Hallelujah' (which took him over 18 months to write) the movement is conclusive: from the *mise en scène* of David's 'secret chord', he substitutes, 'Baby, I've been here before/I know this room, I walk this floor . . .' The whole song has moved momentously from history to his-story; from the past to the present; from the tradition to the trauma, from sacred to secular (understanding those terms as opposite sides of the same coin, not dichotomising it).

Likewise the explicit 'row' between the lovers has been transmuted into a refined admission, 'I've seen your flag on the marble arch/ When love's not a victory march'; and the former optimism of 'The holy or the broken Hallelujah' has now become the 'cold and . . . broken Hallelujah.' Whereas the original had a specific scriptural landscape, the revised edition relies on imprecision, even ambiguity: he is not now told (by her? by Him?) 'What's really going on below' – still less shown it. But he does remember the highly erotic (in the *highest* sense of that word) 'I remember when I moved in you/Yes, and the holy dove, she was moving too/And, yes! every single breath that we took was 'Hallelujah'.' The condition is one of their love-making, the reference to 'the holy dove' recalling the Jewish belief that in making a child three are involved: its father, its mother – and God himself.

Accordingly – gladly recognising (if only implicitly) that he does know something of the Name – he avows 'there's a God above,' even though (transferring the setting back to the earthly, if not the earthy) 'all I ever learned from love/Is how to shoot at someone who out-drew you'; by which the (presumably wounded) man at least goes down fighting . . . It closes at a different angle, too: 'it's not a complaint that you hear tonight,' contrasts sharply with the self-justifying 'I did my best . . . I've told the truth' of the original. There the effect is defiant: 'Even though it all went wrong . . .' here it is regretful, forgiving, even conciliatory: 'It's a cold, and a very tender, broken Hallelujah.'

There is one further difference between the two versions: the earlier is considerably shorter, by one verse, but also shorter in line-length. It is not merely a case of accommodating to the secular outlook of his audience, his followers – or, rather, their preference for a secular expression of the underlying religious feeling; he accommodates, too, the impatience of the age, the insistence of the moguls that 'time is money,' the need to arrange artistic creations to fit the man-made patterns of the air-waves: the 90-second 'sin-drone'.

The album went gold in several countries, and platinum in Norway (where it was number one for no less than 17 weeks, displacing A-ha, their top pop group). In Spain, the ecstatic live responses he got from his concerts inspired several promotional programmes on radio and television, scores of mainly welcoming and adulatory press reviews and an increased particular appetite in his followers. In Iceland, he was the Guest of Honour at a party thrown by the mayor of Reykjavik, from which he went on to be received by the President himself (as he had in France, with President Giscard D'Estaing), being invited in addition to play at the Icelandic Arts Festival. He was also invited to perform at The Prince's Trust Concert in London, following which he was presented to H.R.H. Prince Charles who got his name wrong!

Columbia Records had released a single, 'Ain't No Cure For Love', to help the tour along in April in addition to the Crystal Globe party they gave him, and Leonard made his own point, too. On April 1 he sent out personal letters to all the company's field-staffers, asking them to make a few telephone calls on his behalf while he was in Europe. 'I've enclosed a couple of bucks to pay for the calls' he commented; and, sure enough, in each envelope were two *very* used dollar bills! Dates can be important, even for those trapped in a Tower of Song.

On his return, CBS Television promoted a special programme, *The Song Of Leonard Cohen*, as did the Canadian Broadcasting Corporation, when he was made the subject of a *Raskey's Gallery* programme, which included poets, painters, singers and saints, as did BBC Television in its *Leonard Cohen: Songs From A Life*. They were discovering how good he was; the weight of their cash-boxes proved it; no other proof was necessary.

Perhaps the best response of all came from his teenage son, Adam, at this time: "Dad, I've just been listening to 'Various Positions', and I want you to know that I really respect your writing." A man can go for many days on such fare as that. It is worth far more than all the awards and acclamations rolled into one: 'with honour; in his own country.' And he was delighted to find Lorca writing her own poetry, too.

Following his return to the quiet life – more blackening of pages, more twisting of his feet, and time for his children, himself; Leonard settled down to the now very gratifying rhythm of his life as an honoured artist – in Montreal, in New York, in Paris (where his children now live), in Los Angeles, on Hydra, ever "in and out of reality," as he commented to one reporter in Boston! The man of islands and cities and travel still needed them – not least his monastery and friend-cum-tutor of 20 years, Roshi Josua Sasaki. His quiet now interrupted by an invitation for a small film part here (e.g. *A Moving Picture, Miami Vice*), or a musical gig there (e.g. with Sonny Rollins, the New York-based jazzman). Sometimes his quiet would be spoiled with bad news – as when his lawyer friend of two decades died and left him with appalling administration headaches, or at the sad news of the sudden and unexpected death of his good friend Roy Orbison; or – with good news – such as the honouring of him – among 29 composers and 16 publishers – by the Performing Rights Organisation of Canada for the three songs performed by Jennifer Warnes, or being named one of Canada's 'Top 10 Sexiest Men'.

When in Montreal – his main centre, affiliations firmly secured – he is surrounded by a few good friends of the calibre of Morton Rosengarten, that 'organic gentleman' of over 40 years friendship. Leonard now a father-figure to the rising generation of artistes who appear to be gathering around him. Sometimes they turn up at his door for advice, encouragement, and at other times for different forms of support. His telephone rings endlessly, and he seems to have difficulty in trusting his answerphone service. He has often been seen around the poorer districts late at night, emptying his pockets in the direction of the deprived and jobless (one of whom actually froze to death on a park bench while we were there).

At one point, interrupting the *café au lait* which recalls him now to his responsibilities, he pointed to a sad-looking man, hunched over his own coffee. He excused himself, went across and spoke to him patting him on the shoulder. "He's just lost his father," Leonard explained sympathetically, "and is still going through hell." He knew the hell of that, alright. With all the success and trust now placed in him, he can afford to rest on his laurels, though he will not.

Billboard, which had not spared his blushes in the past, now calls him 'the most gifted writer of his musical era'; and Irving Layton, *poet extraordinaire*, now in his late seventies, describes him as 'one of the great lyricists of our time.' *The Toronto Star* may think that he is 'returning to secular interests,' but he is used to such myopia; chuckles (or sometimes writhes), and presses on.

The crassest, i.e. most 'inaccurate' comment came from *Melody Maker* which remarked, 'except in his first novel Cohen's Jewishness doesn't seem paramount in his work . . .' reminding one of the Yiddish proverb that 'you can educate a fool, but you can't make him think.' The London *Independent*, identifying one of Leonard's distant literary heroes, was even more quaint, 'he is funny the way Kafka is funny'; it equals the *San Francisco Chronicle*'s comment that he is 'an existential comedian!' The *Los Angeles Times* interpreted the tower as 'not a temple, not a rest home but an asylum, throwing a slightly different light on his religious vision,' and *Newsday*, in even sillier mood, spoke of 'Tower Of Song' as 'an ode to impotence!' *The Village Voice*, with greater discrimination, cited it as 'possibly the greatest song ever written about rock 'n' roll . . .' Opinions come, and opinions go – as do journalists and reviewers; Leonard soldiers on – now in his fourth decade of seeing.

There is still much work to be done; the interior landscape is never fully explored. Unlike those writers who have 'never had an unpublished thought,' Leonard's files and disks are full of material – manuscripts and snippets – as he mentioned to *Now* magazine recently. But he is under no compunction as to seeing it published. The life and the experiences have not changed, but the viewpoint is different. Gone are the days of an almost mesmerised self-indulgence when the mirror-imagery was of particular importance, when he sought to reconcile the essentially pagan adage that 'man is the measure of all things' with his own Tradition and commitments: 'all the disparates of the world, the different wings of the paradox, coin-faces of the problem, petal-pulling questions, scissors-shaped conscience, all the polarities, things and their images . . .' – a Pandora's Box of ambiguity and contradiction.

As he said to *Time Out* magazine, "The old records have a certain vulnerability in them, but I guess I've turned a corner in my recent life that's enabled me to develop a perspective that includes strength with the vulnerability . . . the true experiences of a 53-year-old with no subtractions." He cast a similar light on it in *The Vancouver Sun* when he quoted Roshi: "The older we get, the lonelier we become, and the deeper the love we need." And on more than one occasion he quoted Layton's line about 'the inescapable lousiness of growing old.'

Leonard was preparing to do so gracefully – and to the benefit of very many. But 'lousiness' was not what was evident when we met Irving Layton and his vivacious wife. Nearly eight hours were enthusiastically given to recollection and consideration of his friend of 30-plus years; robust cut and thrust! Vigorous statement and questioning! At almost eighty, a man still possessed of an astonishing zest for life and literature, pounding away yet at those 'petal-pulling questions,' honouring as ever the prophetic tradition which he has adorned for 50 years. As fond and as loyal as ever to Leonard; as perceptive of his work, and as appreciative of his skills as ever, too. A copy of one of his books of poetry was kindly offered on leaving, inscribed, 'to recall a marvellous afternoon (we concluded after 10 pm!) we both owe to a gifted poet . . .' It was never different, nor was it more sincere.

We left Leonard standing in his favourite café on Boulevard Saint Lawrence, very smartly dressed, talking to a young female novelist-poet who had been working there since our arrival. 'In the can' but still to be published, is an album of recitations drawn from *Book Of Mercy*, set to a string quartet conducted by Jeremy Lubbock. He is also involved with another album with Jennifer Warnes, which includes at least three of his songs, and is talking enthusiastically of a new edition of his selected poems: *New Selected Poems* (or *If The Moon Has A Sister!*) presently in production. This is to include some previously unpublished poetry, new and old, and some poetry which has not been available for a long time. It also includes several of his songs from recent albums, and some prose material.

Most interesting development of all is his motivation, of which two specific points were made by him: "This selection is important," he said. "I want the voice to come through." In tandem with that goes a rejection of four-letter words: "That period is over," he maintained. "Now it is necessary to remove them (by replacing the letters with hyphens). They've come out. They are powerful words (which I) always used as a literary device: demons of realism (with a) moral edge. They've come out. I doubt if I would use (them) today. I want to return them to the obscurity (they) once had, give (them) a veil."

In the course of a meal, when we talked about a venture we ourselves were planning on soul-mates, he produced from his inside pocket a scrap of paper on which was inscribed the first version of another new poem titled 'Soul Mates'. Connections abounding yet, even between Virgoans and Cancerians! We said our 'good-byes' to him and some of his good-hearted friends – Morton and Violet, his charming wife, Hazel and Maureen, Nancy Southam, Anne McLean, Elliott, Beograd. Morton told us that only that morning, he had heard Leonard's voice through the walls of his studio – full and hearty, easily rising above his powerful keyboard, experimenting, rehearsing, meditating.

There is now a new love in his life "more important to me than ever," he confessed to the *Globe And Mail* which, along with the Bible, the Jewish and Catholic liturgies, Zen meditation, and his new-found confidence and freedom, all fire and temper his reflective imagination. He is writing yet, composing, thinking and singing. And, as he himself believes, his best work is yet to be. The voice will go on – if we listen; the word is getting out – the scars are there to prove it. As Elbert Hubbard said in *Epigrams*, 'God will not look you over for medals, degrees or diplomas, but for scars'; therein is the evidence of a life, of a word understood.

'I want to sleep awhile,
a while, a minute, a century;
but all must know that I have not died;
that there is a stable of gold in my lips;
that I am the small friend of the West wind;
that I am the immense shadow of my tears.

'For I want to sleep the dream of the apples,
to learn a lament that will cleanse me of the earth;
for I want to live with that dark child
who wanted to cut his heart on the high seas.'

                                       FEDERICO GARCÍA LORCA

I. WORKS BY LEONARD COHEN

The following is as comprehensive as we could make it. Omissions will be rectified in future editions, and in our forthcoming *Leonard Cohen: Troubadour Of Truth*.

PRE-1954

Two unpublished pieces at least have survived: an essay on the death of a fellow Montrealian ([C] 1951;); and Leonard's Presidential Speech to the McGill Debating Society ([C] 1953/4;).

1954

'An Halloween Poem To Delight My Younger Friends' (*Òu Sont Les Jeunes?*) and '*Poème en Prose*' in *CIV/n*, Montreal, vol iv, pp 8,13 respectively. (The latter was renamed 'Friends' in *LUCM*, included with the former.)

'Folk Song', 'Les Vieux', 'Satan In Westmount' in *CIV/n*, vol v, pp 11. (The first and third were all published in *LUCM*, the second had a significant change in the last two lines of the second verse; the original read 'spitting blood in crumpled handkerchiefs/ twisting fingers against brittle years.')

'To Be Mentioned At Funerals', 'Just The Worse Time' in *Forge*, summer end., p 52 (which added 'He composes poetry to the guitar').

1955

'For Wilf And His House' in *Forge*, Spring edn., p 26

'Sparrows' in *VIC/n*, vol vii, p 14

'Two Sparrows: Thoughts Of A Landsman' was the title of his successful essay presented for the McNaughten Prize for Creative Writing, pp5. It is now housed in the Rare Books Collection of the MacLennen Library, McGill University. Five poems were offered: 'For Wilf And His House', 'Ste Catherine Street', 'Lord On Peel Street', 'The Story Of The Hellenist (to RK)', 'The Song Of The Hellenist to FK', 'Sparrows'. All but the third appeared in *LUCM*.

1956

Let Us Compare Mythologies, McGill Poetry Series Number One, Contact Press, Toronto (actually printed in Montreal privately by Leonard, but returning the courtesy extended to him), pp 80, with six line-drawings by Freda Guttman. Reprinted by McClelland And Stewart Ltd., Toronto, 1966.

'Had We Nothing To Prove', 'The Fly', in *Forge*, Spring edn., p 43 (which commented thereby that Leonard had won First Prize in the Daily Literary Contest).

1959

A Man Was Killed, a play in six acts, with Irving Layton; later published in *Canadian Theatre Review*, Spring 1977, pp 54-68. (They also wrote *Up With Nothing*, a play about 'hippiedom', and two or three other plays whose manuscripts are no longer in existence.)

1960

Beauty At Close Quarters, his first semi-autobiographical novel, rejected by his publishers. It reappeared as *The Favourite Game* in 1963, qv.

1961

The Spice-Box Of Earth, McClelland And Stewart Ltd., pp 128 Rp: Viking-Penguin, NY, 1965, Jonathan Cape Ltd., London, 1973

'My Mentors', 'For Marianne', 'Action', 'On The Sickness Of My Love', 'The First Vision' in *Poetry 62*, edited by Eli Mandel and Jean-Guy Pilon, Ryerson Press, Toronto, pp 91–94. The first two poems and fourth were published in *Flowers For Hitler* in 1964. (In 'My Mentors' the last two lines of the second verse were changed from 'They are inscribed with beautiful letters/ which nobody can understand,' to a more explicit Judaic reference. In 'The First Vision' the scenario of his mother entertaining to dinner her father and her first and second husbands is offered: 'anguished at their ingratitude,' recalling a similar incident in *The Favourite Game* between Breavman and his mother.)

1963

The Favourite Game, Secker And Warburg Ltd., London Rp: Jonathan Cape Ltd., pp 192, 1970, 1971, Avon Books, NY, 1965 (3rd edn 1969), McClelland And Stewart Ltd., 1970 (with an introduction by J. Rowland Smith), Panther Books, Granada Publishing Ltd., St Albans, pp 220, 1973

1964

Flowers For Hitler, McClelland And Stewart Ltd. Rp: Jonathan Cape Ltd., 1973, pp 156

1966

Beautiful Losers (formerly *Ballet Of Lepers*, n/d), McClelland And Stewart Ltd. Rp: Viking-Penguin, NY, 1966, Bantam Books, NY, 1967, Jonathan Cape Ltd., 1970, Panther Books, Granada Publishing Ltd., 1972, pp 240 (twice) Tr: *Les Perdant Magnifiques* (by Michel Doury), Christian Bourgois, Paris, 1972; rp as Livre de Poche, 1973

Parasites Of Heaven, McClelland And Stewart Ltd., Toronto and Montreal

'Les Vieux', 'Prayer For Sunset', 'The Bus' included in *Poetry Of Our Time*, ed by Louis Dudek, with a short introduction, MacMillan And Co Ltd of Canada, Toronto, pp xii plus 376

1967

'Out Of The Land Of Heaven. For Marc Chagall', 'The Genius', 'The Only Tourist In Havana Turns His Thoughts Homeward' in *Modern Canadian Verse In English And French*, ed by A.J.M. Smith, OUP, Toronto, pp xxvi plus 426.

1968

Selected Poems: 1956-1968, McClelland And Stewart Ltd., pp X plus 246. Rp: The Viking Press, 1968 (three times), 1969 (three times), 1970, 1972, 1976, 1977. Penguin Books Ltd., Harmondsworth and NY, Victoria, Ontario, Auckland, 1978, Jonathan Cape Ltd., 1969 (three times), 1970 (twice), 1971 (twice), 1973.
Tr: French: *Poems et Chansons*, adaptes par Anne Rivers, Allan Kosko, Jaques Vassal et Jean-Dominique Brierre; Union General d'Editions de Paris, 1972.

1969

Poems 1956-1968, an abridgement of *Selected Poems 1956-1968;* Jonathan Cape Ltd., pp 96. Rp: 1969, 1970 (four times), 1971 (three times), 1972

'Elegy', 'Story', 'I Have Not Lingered In European Monasteries', 'You Have The Lovers', 'Now Of Sleeping', 'As The Mist Leaves No Scar', 'The Genius', 'Style', 'For

EJP', 'The Music Crept By Us', 'Two Went To Sleep', 'Disguises' in G.Gedde's *20th Century Poets And Poetics*, pp 374-383. It was reprinted in 1985, adding 'The Bus'.

1975
New Skin For The Old Ceremony, Amsco Publishing Co., NY.

1978
Death Of A Lady's Man, McClelland And Stewart Ltd., pp 216. rp: Andre Deutsch Ltd., London, 1979. Viking Press, NY, 1979.

1980
Two Views, Seven Poems, with Gigino Falconi, McClelland And Stewart Ltd., Limited Edition (of 155 copies), signed by both poet and illustrator, cased set, pp 16. The poems included were 'My Lady Can Sleep', 'This Morning I Was Dressed By The Wind', 'Slowly I Married Her', 'The Absence Of Monica', 'Snow Is Falling', 'Traditional Training And Service', 'Another Man's Woman'.

1984
Book Of Mercy, McClelland And Stewart, pp 112 (the book is not actually page-numbered, but is composed of 50 'psalms' whose numbers constitute the reference requirements). Rp: Jonathan Cape Ltd. Villard Books, NY.

1990
New Selected Poems, a new edition of *Selected Poems 1956-1968* with some new poems and songs, offering a new perspective of Cohen's work, and particularly of his use of religious and profane language. It will present over 266 pieces in total from all Cohen's published work, including certain pieces not selected for earlier compilations.

UNDATED
Leonard Cohen Songbook, an apparently pirated work that was circulating in Holland in the late seventies; typed and duplicated, in a hand-bound cardboard cover. There is naturally no information as to publisher, origin, etc. It includes the words only from his first four albums (some of which are different, perhaps reflecting a live performance or faulty translation), pp 38.

II. SELECTED WORKS ABOUT LEONARD COHEN

Major biographies, reviews and critiques:

Chambers, D.D.C.: 'Leonard Cohen' in *Contemporary Poets Of The English Language*, Ed. Rosaline Murphy, St James Press, Chicago and London, 1970, pp 209ff.

Clifford, Jean-Marie: 'The Theme Of Suffering In The Novels Of Jack Kerouac, Leonard Cohen And William Burroughs.' MA Thesis, British Columbia University, 1970.

Davey, Frank: 'Leonard Cohen And Bob Dylan: Poetry And Popular Song', in *Alphabet*, Number 17, December 1970, 12-29

'Leonard Cohen', in *From Here To There*, Press Porcepic, Erin, 1974, 68-73; includes bibliography.

Djwa, Sandra: 'Leonard Cohen: Black Romantic', in *Canadian Literature*, 34, Autumn 1967, 32-42, (Rp in *Poets And Critics: Essays from Canadian Literature*, ed George Woodcock, OUP, Toronto, 1974; also in Gnarowski, qv.)

Dydk, Linda: *Faces Of Revolution In The English Quebec Novel* (includes a critique of *Beautiful Losers*) MA Thesis, 1981, 45-70

Elson, Nicholas William: 'Love In The Writings Of Leonard Cohen', MA Thesis, New Brunswick University, 1969, pp 150

Geddes, G: *Leonard Cohen*, Copp Clark Publishers, Toronto, no date.

Gnarowski, Michael (Ed): *Leonard Cohen: The Artist And His Critics*, McGraw-Hill Ryerson, Toronto and NY, 1976, pp 169; includes introduction and bibliography as well as a culling of some of the most useful articles on Cohen.

Hutcheon, Linda: 'Beautiful Losers: All The Polarities' in *Canadian Literature*, 59, Winter 1974, 42-56. Rp in *The Canadian Novel In The 20th Century*, McClelland And Stewart, 1975, 288-311

Jantzen, Dorothy Helen: 'The Poetry Of Leonard Cohen: His Perfect Body, MA Thesis, York University, 1971, pp 199

Johnson, Lewis Davis: 'Bird On The Wire: The Theme Of Freedom In The Works Of Leonard Cohen', MA Thesis, Dalhousie University, 1975

Kanary, Reynolds: 'Leonard Cohen: Sexuality And The Anal Vision In Beautiful Losers, MA Thesis, Ottawa University, 1974, pp112

Kerwin, Elizabeth Ann: 'Themes Of Leonard Cohen', BA Thesis, Acadia University, 1969.

Knelson, Richard John: 'Flesh And Spirit In The Writings Of Leonard Cohen: A Study Of His Poetry', MA Thesis, Manitoba University, 1969

'The Transformation Of Traditional Symbols In The Writings Of Leonard Cohen', BA Thesis, Manitoba University, 1968

Lee, Dennis: 'Savage Fields: An Essay In Literature And Cosmology', Anansi, Toronto, 1977, pp 125

Lyons, Roberta: 'Jewish Poets Of Montreal: Concepts Of History In The Poetry Of A.M. Klein, Irving Layton And Leonard Cohen', MA Thesis, Carlton University, 1966

Malus, Avrum: 'The Face Of Holiness In The Writings Of Leonard Cohen', PhD Thesis, Montreal University, 1975, pp 164

Mandel, Eli: 'Cohen's Life As A Slave', in *Another Time*, Press Porcepic, Erin, 1977, pp 124-136

Manzano, Alberto: *Canciones y neovos poemas, vols I and II*, Edicomunicacion SA, Barcelona, 1986, pp 160 and 117, illustrated

Matos, Manuel Cadafaz de: *Leonard Cohen: Redescoberta da Vida e una Alegoria a Eros*, Livres E (Co) logiar a Terra, Lisbon, 1975

Morley, Patricia A: *The Immortal Moralists: Hugh MacLennan And Leonard Cohen*, Charles Irwin, Toronto, 1972

Ondaatje, Michael: *Leonard Cohen*, McClelland And Stewart Ltd., 1970; includes an excellent bibliography

Pacey, Desmond: 'The Phenomenon Of Leonard Cohen', in *Canadian Literature*, 34, Autumn 1956, 5-23, reprinted in Gnarowski

Panter, Jack Bryan: 'Alienation And Aestheticism In The Art Of Leonard Cohen', MA Thesis, UBC, 1973

Scobie, Stephen: *Studies In Canadian Literature: Leonard Cohen*, Douglas And McIntyre, Vancouver, 1978, xii plus 194 pp; includes a very good bibliography.

Smith, Rowland J: 'Introduction' to *The Favourite Game*, in a new edition by McClelland And Stewart, Toronto 1970

Stearns, Linda J. Fong: 'The Saint Figure In Leonard Cohen And Robertson Davies', MA Thesis, Calgary University, 1975, pp 106

Vassal, Jacques, et Jean Dominique Brierre: *Leonard Cohen*, Albin Michel, Paris, 1974, pp 189; illustrated.

Whitman, Bruce: 'Leonard Cohen: An Annotated Biography', in *The Annotated Biography Of Canadian Major Authors*, ed Robert Lecker and Jacj David; Dowsview, Ontario, 1980, 56-95

Wilson, Paula Marie: 'In Search Of Magic: A Study Of The Creative Process In The Novels Of Leonard Cohen', MA Thesis, Queens University, 1972, pp 88

Woodcock, George: 'The Song Of The Sirens: Reflections On Leonard Cohen', in *Odysseus Ever Returning*, McClelland And Stewart Ltd., 1970, 92-110; rp in Gnarowski

Yeo, Margaret: 'Irony In Contemporary Poetry: A Study Of Irony In The Poems Of Margaret Atwood, Leonard Cohen, John Roberto Colombo, George Johnson, Alfred Purdy And Raymond Souster'; MA Thesis, Carlton University, 1968

SINGLES

Suzanne/So Long Marianne
CBS 3337 March 1968

Bird On The Wire/Seems So Long Ago, Nancy
CBS 4245 May 1969

Joan Of Arc/Diamonds In The Mine
CBS 7292 July 1971

Suzanne/Bird On The Wire
CBS 8353 March 1973

Bird On The Wire (live)/**Tonight Will Be Fine** (live)
CBS 2494 July 1974

Lover, Lover, Lover/Why By Fire?
CBS 2699 November 1974

Suzanne/Take This Longing
CBS 4306 May 1976

Memories/Don't Go Home With Your Hard-On
CBS 5882 November 1977

True Love Leaves No Traces/I Left A Woman Waiting
CBS 6095 March 1978

Dance Me To The End Of Love/The Law
CBS A6052 February 1985

First We Take Manhattan/Sisters Of Mercy
CBS 65 1352-7 January 1988

Ain't No Cure For Love/Jazz Police
CBS 63 1599-7 May 1988

EPs AND 12 - INCH SINGLES

McCabe And Mrs Miller
Sisters Of Mercy/Winter Lady/The Stranger Song
CBS 9162 July 1972

Bird On The Wire/Lady Midnight/Joan Of Arc/Suzanne/Hey! That's No Way To Say Goodbye/So Long Marianne/Paper-Thin Hotel
Picnick 75R 5022 (Scoop 33 Series) 1983

First We Take Manhattan/Sisters Of Mercy/Bird On The Wire/Suzanne
CBS 65 1352-6 (12-inch) January 1988

Ain't No Cure For Love/Jazz Police/Hey! That's No Way To Say Goodbye/So Long, Marianne
CBS 65 1599-7 (12-inch) May 1988

ALBUMS

Six Montreal Poets (eight poems)
Folkways FL 9805 (USA) 1957

Canadian Poets, I (seven poems)
CBC (Canada) 1966

Songs Of Leonard Cohen
Suzanne/Master Song/Winter Lady/The Stranger Song/Sisters Of Mercy/So Long,
Marianne/Hey! That's No Way To Say Goodbye/Stories Of The Street/Teachers/
One Of Us Cannot Be Wrong
CBS 63421 February 1968

Songs From A Room
Bird On The Wire/The Story Of Isaac/A Bunch Of Lonesome Heroes/The Partisan/
Seems So Long Ago, Nancy/The Old Revolution/The Butcher/You Know Who I Am/
Lady Midnight/ Tonight Will Be Fine
CBS 63587 April 1969
(reissued as CBS 32074, September 1982)

Isle of Wight/Atlanta '70
includes Tonight Will Be Fine
CBS 66311 1971

Songs Of Love And Hate
Avalanche/Last Year's Man/Dress Rehearsal Rag/Diamonds In The Mine/Love Calls
You By Name/Famous Blue Raincoat/Sing Another Song, Boys/Joan Of Arc
CBS 69004 March 1971
(Reissued as CBS 32219, September 1982)

Live Songs
Minute Prologue/Passin' Thru/You Know Who I Am/Bird On The Wire/Nancy/
Improvisation (of Nancy)/Story Of Isaac/Please Don't Pass Me By (A Disgrace)/
Tonight Will Be Fine/Queen Victoria
CBS 65224 April 1973
(Reissued as CBS 32272, March 1984)

New Skin For The Old Ceremony
Is This What You Wanted?/Chelsea Hotel No 2/Lover, Lover, Lover/Field
Commander/Why Don't You Try/There Is A War/A Singer Must Die/I Tried To
Leave You/Why By Fore?/Take This Longing/Leaving Greensleeves
CBS 69087 August 1974

Anniversary Special, Vol I
includes Passin' Thru
Columbia PC 33416 (USA) 1974

Greatest Hits (US: The Best Of Leonard Cohen)
Suzanne/Sisters Of Mercy/So Long, Marianne/Bird On The Wire/Lady Midnight/
The Partisan/Hey! That's No Way To Say Goodbye/Famous Blue Raincoat/
Last Year's Man/Chelsea Hotel No 2/Who By Fire?/Take This Longing
CBS 69161 November 1975
(Reissued as CBS 32644, April 1985)

Death Of A Ladies' Man
True Love Leaves No Traces/Iodine/Paper-Thin Hotel/Memories/I Left A Woman
Waiting/Don't Go Home With Your Hard-On/Fingerprinted/Death Of A Ladies' Man
CBS 86042 November 1977

Recent Songs
The Guests/Humbled In Love/The Window/Came So Far For Beauty/Un Canadian
Errant (The Lost Canadian)/The Traitor/Our Lady Of Solitude/The Gypsy's Wife/The
Smoky Life/Ballad Of The Absent Mare
CBS 86097 September 1979

Various Positions
Dance Me To The End Of Love/Coming Back To You/The Law/Night Comes On/
Hallelujah/The Captain/Hunter's Lullaby/Heart With No Companion/If It Be
Your Will
CBS 26222 February 1985

Cohen In Warsaw
Akamickie 03611-2 (twin cassette compilation), Poland, 1985

Poetas In Nueva York
(includes Take This Waltz)

I'm Your Man
First We Take Manhattan/Ain't No Cure For Love/Everybody Knows/I'm Your Man/
Take This Waltz/Jazz Police/I Can't Forget/Tower Of Song
CBS 460642-1 February 1988

COMPACT DISCS

First We Take Manhattan/Sisters Of Mercy/Bird On The Wire/Suzanne
CBS 651352-2 (single) January 1988

New Skin For The Old Ceremony
CBS CD CBS 69087 February 1988

Death Of A Ladies' Man
CBS CD CBS 86042 February 1988

Greatest Hits
CBS CD CBS 69161 February 1988

Various Positions
CBS CD CBS 26222 February 1988

Songs From A Room
CBS CD CBS 63587 February 1988

I'm Your Man
CBS 46042-2 February 1988

Recent Songs
CBS CD CBS 86097 May 1988

Live Songs
CBS CD CBS 65224 May 1988

**Ain't No Cure For Love/Jazz Police/Hey! That's No Way To Say Goodbye/
So Long, Marianne**
CBS 651599-6 (single)

SPECIAL APPEARANCE

Famous Blue Raincoat (Jennifer Warnes)
Joan Of Arc/Song Of Bernadette
RCA PL 90048 July 1987